FOREWORD

2019 was another record-breaking year of spectacular racing in the MotoGP™ World Championship; another season to write about in the history books. It was Marc Márquez who came out on top and made history as the Repsol Honda Team rider dominated the standings for his eighth World Championship – and Honda took the triple crown – but the season was full of some incredible battles to keep us entertained from the first lap to the last.

The man who finished runner up to Márquez was Andrea Dovizioso. Winner in Qatar and in Austria, the Italian beat the number 93 in two spectacular duels once again – both at the final corner. Maverick Viñales, meanwhile, put Monster Energy Yamaha MotoGP on the top step twice as well – winning the battle at the TT Circuit Assen and searing away to impress us once again at Sepang. He was third overall, with that decided in the season finale as he beat Team Suzuki Ecstar's Alex Rins.

Rins was another key figure in the season and joined the pantheon of premier class winners – twice. He, like Dovizioso, duelled the reigning Champion and came out on top, with Silverstone one of the races of the century. Thousandths separated the two, showcasing the very best of MotoGP™.

We saw new winners and new contenders in 2019, but we also saw new faces – one of which would go on to play a pivotal role in the story of the season. Fabio Quartararo's debut was a privilege to watch as the young Frenchman started breaking records and fighting for wins, becoming one of the most successful rookies we've seen in recent years. Podiums, pole positions and new lap records are what the 2019 Rookie of the Year and top Independent Team rider leaves in his wake, and we're excited to see where 2020 takes the number 20.

Moto2™, meanwhile, saw Álex Márquez become a two-time World Champion. The EG 0,0 Marc VDS rider was a dominant force for much of the season and took the crown with a race to spare – but by the time the flag fell for 2019, it was a close-run battle with Brad Binder. The South African went on an impressive winning run in the final three races to cut the gap, leaving Red Bull KTM Ajo with one more win before he moves up to MotoGP™. The two create another tantalising prospect for Rookie of the Year in 2020, as well as Iker Lecuona.

In Moto3™, it was another exciting season of close racing – and a record breaking one, with so many different winners. Leopard Racing's Lorenzo Dalla Porta became the first FIM CEV Repsol Moto3™ Junior World Champion to win the title in the lightweight class as he beat Aron Canet of Sterilgarda Max Racing Team, and we saw a host of new contenders hit their stride. Kaito Toba became the first Asia Talent Cup Champion to win a Grand Prix, Xavier Artigas impressed us all as he became the first European Talent Cup Champion to get a Grand Prix podium – and on the day Sergio Garcia became a rookie winner with Estrella Galicia 0,0. The Road to MotoGP™ continues finding and promoting important talents, and that makes us very proud.

2019 also saw the debut of an exciting new parallel path of racing: the FIM Enel MotoE™ World Cup. The first ever season of the electric-powered series was an amazing debut, and in the face of some real adversity. But after setbacks in pre-season, MotoE™ went racing and what a season of racing it was. Italian Matteo Ferrari was the inaugural Cup winner with Trentino Gresini MotoE, but we saw three more riders win races and some of the closest track action of the year.

That's true of all classes; I can't wait to see what 2020 brings. With Honda, Ducati, Yamaha, Suzuki, KTM and Aprilia making the show closer than ever this season, we already know that the premier class will continue to provide some of the best racing on Earth. And in Moto2™, Moto3™ and MotoE™, I'm sure the Champions of tomorrow will remind us once again why that future is even brighter than we could have imagined.

However, before we turn our glance towards next season, we must say goodbye to one of the true greats: Jorge Lorenzo. The five-time World Champion is one of the best riders our sport has ever seen, and I'm sure everyone will echo my sentiments when I say we will miss his presence on track and we thank him for everything he's given to the sport. Not only his racing, but also his voice and passion. I wish him all the best in his future endeavours and I will be very proud to induct him into the MotoGP™ Legends Hall of Fame in 2020.

CARMELO | **EZPELETA**

DORNA SPORTS CEO

NOVEMBER 2019

Published December 2019

A catalogue record for this book is available from the British Library

ISBN 978-1-5272-4319-4

PUBLISHED BY Motocom Limited, Liscombe Park, Liscombe East, Soulbury, Bucks, LU7 0JL, UK
www.motocom.co.uk

PRINTED & BOUND BY Gomer Press, Llandysul Enterprise Park, Llandysul, Ceredigion, SA44 4JL, UK

EDITOR & AUTHOR Mat Oxley

DESIGN & ARTWORK Peter Neal

SPECIAL SALES & ADVERTISING MANAGER David Dew
david@motocom.co.uk

PHOTOGRAPHY Dorna photographers (Diego Sperani, Luca Gambuti and Giorgio Neyroz), Alejandro Ceresuela Bermejo, Aprilia, Ducati, Honda, KTM, Michelin, Mat Oxley, Petronas SRT, Red Bull, Riders Club magazine, Suzuki and Yamaha

AUTHOR'S ACKNOWLEDGEMENTS Thanks to Lou Acedo, Thomas Alatalo, Romano Albesiano, Maider Barthe, Laura Beretta, Pol Bertran, Matt Birt, Alen Bollini, Peter Bom, Majo Botella, Gino Borsoi, Davide Brivio, Federico Cappelli, Toni Calvo, Lucio Cecchinello, Peter Clifford, Andrea Coleman, Barry Coleman, Simon Crafar, Gigi Dall'Igna, Steve Day, Matt Dunn, William Favero, Carlo Fiorani, Guido Giavazzi, Francesco Guidotti, Ken Kawauchi, Sebastian Kuhn, Tetsuhiro Kuwata, Isabelle Lariviere, Mats Larsson, Harry Lloyd, Hector Martin, Neil Morrison, Ken Nemoto, Simon Patterson, Elisa Pavan, Paolo Pezzini, Herve Poncharal, Mathilde Poncharal, Ali Rowland-Rowse, Ignacio Sagnier, Evangelia Sissis, Claire Sobas, Takahiro Sumi, Piero Taramasso, Julian Thomas, Federico Tondelli, Paul Trevathan, Irene Trimby, Mike Trimby, Kouichi Tsuji, Franco Uncini, Friné Velilla, Artur Vilalta, Tim Walpole, Mike Webb, Fran Wyld, Dr Michele Zasa, Andrea Zoccarato and all the riders, mechanics, Clinica Mobile staff, hospitality workers and everyone who keeps the MotoGP show on the road

In memory of Luca Semprini

MotoGP'S WHEELS KEEP ON TURNING...

Marc Márquez was king once again in 2019 but a new prince arrived in MotoGP, proving that the world's greatest race series never stands still.

Where do you go from perfection? The 2016, 2017 and 2018 seasons changed the face of MotoGP: new technical rules and new tyres created the most thrilling, most unpredictable racing seen for decades. The battles were so fierce that MotoGP attracted many new admirers, especially from the world of Formula 1 car racing, where drivers and engineers marvelled at the gladiatorial antics of the fastest riders.

The action during those three seasons drew comparisons with Grand Prix racing's last great age of heroes – during the late 1980s and early 1990s – when Kevin Schwantz, Wayne Rainey, Mick Doohan, Eddie Lawson and Wayne Gardner went into battle on their fearsome 500cc two-strokes.

An Italian boy grew up fascinated by those bikes and their riders. His name was Valentino Rossi. When he arrived in Grands Prix in 1996 he referred to his 500cc heroes as the "old dogs". In February 2019 the nine-time world champion celebrated his 40th birthday as he prepared for his 20th season in the premier class. Not an old dog, but certainly the veteran's veteran.

Rossi may not have been the championship force he had once been, but his continuing presence on the grid, alongside the youngsters who had grown up worshipping him, added a special dimension to the racing. Not many riders get to race with their childhood heroes, but most of the MotoGP grid does that nowadays. At Phillip Island Rossi celebrated his 400th Grand Prix, a mind-boggling statistic, because since the world championships started in June 1949 there have been about 940 GPs.

Many fans who consider it possible to name the greatest rider of all time believe that Rossi is that man. But during 2019 another name emerged in that debate. Now there is no doubt that Márquez is also one of the greatest of all time.

The young Spaniard's five MotoGP titles won between 2013 and 2018 had already granted him entry to the MotoGP pantheon, but during 2019 his riding was elevated to a higher plane. He is now in the VIP area of the pantheon, along with Rossi, Giacomo Agostini, Mike Hailwood, 'King' Kenny Roberts and a very few others. And at the end of 2019 he wasn't yet 27-years-old.

Motorcycle racing is all about racing through corners, leaning the bike to get it turned and balancing the centrifugal and centripetal forces. In other words, taking the forces of physics on a merry dance. No one has ever done that better than Márquez. At the Sachsenring he had his RC213V at 66 degrees from the vertical. At Phillip Island he reached 70 degrees during one of his Lazarus-style saves.

"It's not easy," said the world champion. "You cannot imagine how I play with my elbows all the time in mid-corner, how I play with my body, how I work at home on my physical condition."

When a sportsperson's rivals stand slack-jawed in admiration you know you are witnessing the rarest of talents. At Brno in August Márquez took pole position by 2.5 seconds, while using

MAIN | *As usual, European fans got their first chance to greet their heroes at Jerez*

CLOCKWISE, FROM TOP LEFT | *Quartararo's first MotoGP pole at Jerez was emotional; Lorenzo announced his retirement at the Valencia season finale; Márquez was mostly in a class of his own; Dovizioso was runner-up for the third consecutive year.*

slick tyres on a wet track. "I don't understand how the track was dry for Marc, but not for the rest of us," said Danilo Petrucci, voicing what the rest of the grid was no doubt thinking.

Márquez's sixth premier-class title in seven seasons was the greatest championship hit rate since the faraway days of Agostini, who won seven straight 500cc world titles between 1966 and 1972, mostly enjoying a significant technical advantage over the opposition aboard his MV Agustas, entered by Italian aristocrat Count Domenico Agusta.

Back in the 1970s some fans thought that Grand Prix racing would never be the same without MV and Ago. In the 1990s some believed GP racing would never be the same again without Rainey and Schwantz. Many think it will never be the same when Rossi finally retires. But the wheels always keep on turning. Márquez wasn't the only rider who dazzled during 2019. A rider seven years his junior came into the class of kings with no great expectations and stunned the paddock.

Fabio Quartararo's journey to the top was very different to Márquez's. While the Spaniard's progress was relentlessly upward: 125cc world champion in 2010, Moto2 world champion in 2012, then rookie MotoGP champion in 2013, the Frenchman's road was much rockier.

As a teenager Quartararo was so talented that the rules were changed to allow him to commence his world championship career at the age of 15, because he had already won back-to-back CEV Moto3 titles. But for various reasons he struggled when he graduated to Grands Prix.

"When you win the CEV title at 14 and people tell you that you are the new Márquez that doesn't usually help," commented Wilco Zeelenberg, team manager of the new Petronas Yamaha SRT squad that gave Quartararo his MotoGP break.

Quartararo didn't win a single Moto3 race in his first two seasons in world championship racing. In 2017 he graduated to Moto2 and again struggled. In 2018 he switched to the Speed Up Moto2 team and finally began to show his true potential, thanks largely to the family atmosphere within Luca Boscoscuro's outfit. He won his first Grand Prix at Barcelona in June 2018 and suddenly MotoGP teams took notice.

During 2019 the 20-year-old hardly stopped smiling. He obviously got a huge buzz from riding a MotoGP bike and he loved teetering on the very edge of control, his YZR-M1 kicking on the brakes and bucking on the throttle. "Every time he races, Fabio becomes stronger and stronger," observed Márquez. MotoGP's wheels keep on turning...

The Moto2 series burned with more young talent in 2019: Márquez's younger brother Alex, South African Brad Binder, Quartararo's former Moto3 team-mate Jorge Navarro, Augusto Fernandez, Rossi's half-brother Luca Marini, Lorenzo Baldassarri and Iker Lecuona, who was contesting only his third full season as a roadracer.

Márquez, Binder and Lecuona graduate to MotoGP in 2020, the title winner taking Jorge Lorenzo's Repsol Honda ride after the three-time MotoGP champion retired as a result of the fractured vertebrae he sustained at June's Dutch TT.

The wheels keep on turning, now powered by electricity as well as gasoline. The inaugural MotoE World Cup silenced the doubters by creating some thrilling racing. This was baby steps for MotoGP's first EV series but MotoE will only grow as battery power takes over the roads. The importance is "the elation of rapid motion through space", as James Joyce observed while watching one of the first motor races. In other words, it matters not if the power comes from electrochemical cells in a battery or from petroleum explosions.

The wheels keep turning bigger and bigger, too. In 2020 the MotoGP world championship expands to 20 rounds for the first time, with the return of the Finnish Grand Prix. And in 2021 the series grows yet further, with the return of the Indonesian GP, staged at a new kind of facility on the island of Lombok. The Mandalika venue will twist and turn between hotels and apartment blocks, a new kind of street circuit, with modern runoff.

Indonesia will become the third MotoGP round in South East Asia. Spain and Italy are still Grand Prix racing's heartlands, but South East Asia is fast becoming the most exciting place for motorcycling.

CLOCKWISE, FROM TOP LEFT | *Rossi was still fast enough for front rows and podiums; Márquez was all attack all of the time; Álex Rins became a winner in his third season; the old rivals hard at it; Maverick Viñales led a Yamaha renaissance; MotoGP's new horizons – plans for Indonesia's lavish MotoGP venue.*

THE SEASON IN FOCUS

From the factory stars to the wildcards and substitutes, the seasons of all 28 MotoGP riders analysed

MotoGP™ WORLD CHAMPIONSHIP STANDINGS

	RIDER	NAT	TEAM	PTS
1	Marc Márquez	SPA	Repsol Honda Team	420
2	Andrea Dovizioso	ITA	Ducati Team	269
3	Maverick Viñales	SPA	Monster Energy Yamaha MotoGP	211
4	Álex Rins	SPA	Team SUZUKI ECSTAR	205
5	Fabio Quartararo	FRA	Petronas Yamaha SRT	192
6	Danilo Petrucci	ITA	Ducati Team	176
7	Valentino Rossi	ITA	Monster Energy Yamaha MotoGP	174
8	Jack Miller	AUS	Pramac Racing	165
9	Cal Crutchlow	GBR	LCR Honda Castrol	133
10	Franco Morbidelli	ITA	Petronas Yamaha SRT	115
11	Pol Espargaró	SPA	Red Bull KTM Factory Racing	100
12	Joan Mir	SPA	Team SUZUKI ECSTAR	92
13	Takaaki Nakagami	JPN	LCR Honda IDEMITSU	74
14	Aleix Espargaró	SPA	Aprilia Racing Team Gresini	63
15	Francesco Bagnaia	ITA	Pramac Racing	54
16	Andrea Iannone	ITA	Aprilia Racing Team Gresini	43
17	Miguel Oliveira	POR	Red Bull KTM Tech 3	33
18	Johann Zarco	FRA	LCR Honda IDEMITSU	30
19	Jorge Lorenzo	SPA	Repsol Honda Team	28
20	Tito Rabat	SPA	Reale Avintia Racing	23
21	Stefan Bradl	GER	Team HRC	16
22	Michele Pirro	ITA	Ducati Team	9
23	Hafizh Syahrin	MAL	Red Bull KTM Tech 3	9
24	Karel Abraham	CZE	Reale Avintia Racing	9
25	Sylvain Guintoli	FRA	Team SUZUKI ECSTAR	7
26	Mika Kallio	FIN	Red Bull KTM Factory Racing	7
27	Bradley Smith	GBR	Aprilia Factory Racing	
28	Iker Lecuona	SPA	Red Bull KTM Tech 3	

When the premier-class is more closely fought than it's been in its seven decades of racing, but one man stands on another level to his rivals, it means something very special is happening. Márquez was better than ever in 2019 – faster, safer and cleverer. He seemed to make history at just about every race and he ended the year as Honda's most successful rider of all time and the third most successful Grand Prix rider of all time. Even his toughest rivals admit that he has it within him to become the greatest of all time.

NATIONALITY | *SPANISH*
DATE OF BIRTH | *17.02.93*
WEIGHT | *65 KG* ***HEIGHT*** | *169 CM*
2019 SEASON | *12 WINS, 18 PODIUMS, 10 POLE POSITIONS, 12 FASTEST LAPS*
TOTAL POINTS | *420*

Dovizioso is starting to make a habit of finishing second overall – it's simply his misfortune to be racing in the era of Marc Márquez. During 2019 he bothered the Honda star less than he had in 2017 and 2018 because Michelin's 2019 rear slicks lasted longer, which made his mastery of tyre life a less dangerous weapon for his opponents. But when Márquez overused his tyres – for example at Red Bull Ring – Dovizioso was able to pull off stunning victories. His main hope for 2020 is that Ducati finally fixes its turning issues.

NATIONALITY | *ITALIAN*
DATE OF BIRTH | *23.03.86*
WEIGHT | *67 KG* ***HEIGHT*** | *167 CM*
2019 SEASON | *2 WINS, 9 PODIUMS, 1 FASTEST LAP*
TOTAL POINTS | *269*

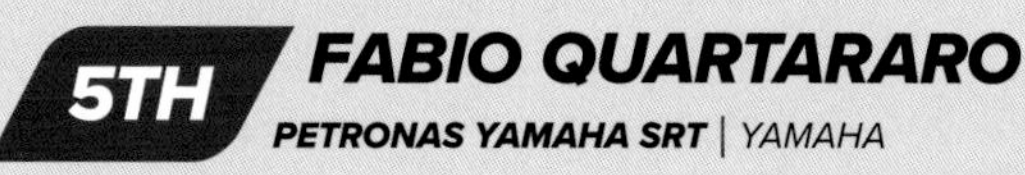

When the French rookie started the season-opening Qatar Grand Prix from pit lane and rode the fastest lap, many said he had only managed that because he had nothing to lose. Quartararo quickly disabused his doubters – at Jerez he took his first MotoGP pole position and chased Márquez in the race. Pretty soon everyone understood that the 20-year-old was the real deal: very brave, highly intelligent and hugely talented. If he can maintain his upward curve through the 2020 season he may give Márquez cause to worry.

NATIONALITY | *FRENCH*
DATE OF BIRTH | *20.04.99*
WEIGHT | *66 KG* ***HEIGHT*** | *177 CM*
2019 SEASON | *7 PODIUMS, 6 POLE POSITIONS, 2 FASTEST LAPS*
TOTAL POINTS | *192*

The burly Italian's entry into Ducati's factory team, seven years after his debut on a CRT bike powered by a street engine, promised a lot. Petrucci spent the winter training with team-mate Dovizioso – improving himself physically and mentally – and was soon at the front. His emotional first victory at Mugello was bracketed by third places at Le Mans and Barcelona. It seemed like he had made it. But a run of difficult races sowed the seeds of doubt and Petrucci struggled to find that speed he'd had in May and June.

NATIONALITY | *ITALIAN*
DATE OF BIRTH | *24/10/90*
WEIGHT | *78 KG* ***HEIGHT*** | *181 CM*
2019 SEASON | *1 WIN, 3 PODIUMS*
TOTAL POINTS | *176*

3RD MAVERICK VIÑALES

MONSTER ENERGY YAMAHA MotoGP | YAMAHA

Yamaha managed to turn things around for 2019 after one of its worst seasons in 2018, with a better engine and electronics. These were two factors in Viñales' return to the kind of form he had last shown when he joined Yamaha in 2017. At June's Barcelona tests he found a good base setting that allowed him to focus on his riding, rather than worrying about set-up. He even eschewed new chassis parts because he wanted the bike to stay the same, so he was totally familiar with its behaviour, which allowed him to push harder.

NATIONALITY | *SPANISH*

DATE OF BIRTH | *12.01.95*

WEIGHT | *64 KG* ***HEIGHT*** | *171 CM*

2019 SEASON | *2 WINS, 7 PODIUMS, 3 POLE POSITIONS, 1 FASTEST LAP*

TOTAL POINTS | *211*

4TH ÁLEX RINS

TEAM SUZUKI ECSTAR | SUZUKI

This was a mercurial season from Suzuki's most experienced rider. The 23-year-old achieved his first win at the third race at COTA, suggesting that Suzuki were in a position to fight for the championship after Ducati and Honda had won the first two races. However, Rins had one issue he struggled to overcome: he found it difficult to extract the maximum from the GSX-RR in qualifying, which invariably left him with too much work to do in the race. If Suzuki can fix this, Rins may have something for Márquez in 2020.

NATIONALITY | *SPANISH*

DATE OF BIRTH | *08.12.95*

WEIGHT | *68 KG* ***HEIGHT*** | *176 CM*

2019 SEASON | *2 WINS, 3 PODIUMS, 1 FASTEST LAP*

TOTAL POINTS | *205*

7TH VALENTINO ROSSI 46

MONSTER ENERGY YAMAHA MotoGP | YAMAHA

Two huge milestones for MotoGP's veteran superstar: his 20th premier-class season and 400th Grand Prix start. The fact that he is still racing is remarkable; the fact that he is still mostly competitive is astonishing. It's also unique: no other rider has raced at the top for so long. Rossi started strongly, with two podiums from the first three races, struggled through mid-season and regained some form after the summer break. At Silverstone he qualified on the front row and at Sepang he set a new lap record.

NATIONALITY | *ITALIAN*

DATE OF BIRTH | *16.02.79*

WEIGHT | *69 KG* ***HEIGHT*** | *181 CM*

2019 SEASON | *2 PODIUMS, 1 FASTEST LAP*

TOTAL POINTS | *174*

8TH JACK MILLER

PRAMAC RACING | DUCATI

This was the year the young Aussie came of age. Finally, for his fifth season in MotoGP, he was given a factory-spec motorcycle and he didn't waste it. His early speed (a third and two fourths from the first five races) convinced Ducati to take him even more seriously. Miller started taking himself more seriously too, tightening his focus on his job. His ability with the rear brake helped him squeeze the maximum from the hard-to-turn Desmosedici and as the year went on he got better at looking after his tyres.

NATIONALITY | *AUSTRALIAN*

DATE OF BIRTH | *18.01.95*

WEIGHT | *64 KG* ***HEIGHT*** | *173 CM*

2019 SEASON | *5 PODIUMS, 1 FASTEST LAP*

TOTAL POINTS | *165*

9TH CAL CRUTCHLOW

LCR HONDA CASTROL | *HONDA*

The Briton raced through 2019 with a lot of metal in his right ankle, the legacy of his huge crash at Phillip Island in 2018. Sometimes the metalwork caused him problems, other times it didn't. His motorcycle was somewhat the same. While Márquez made everyone look slow on his RC213V, Crutchlow found the 2019 bike a handful at some tracks, but not at others. He insisted his effort never wavered, so he got good results when the bike worked and he didn't when it didn't. Next season is likely to be Crutchlow's last.

NATIONALITY | *BRITISH*
DATE OF BIRTH | *29.10.85*
WEIGHT | *66 KG* ***HEIGHT*** | *170 CM*
2019 SEASON | *3 PODIUMS*
TOTAL POINTS | *133*

10TH FRANCO MORBIDELLI

PETRONAS YAMAHA SRT | *YAMAHA*

The 2017 Moto2 world champion switched from Honda to Yamaha and was expected to be the star of Yamaha's new Petronas-backed independent team. It came as a shock to him and to everyone else when he was eclipsed by his rookie team-mate. This definitely knocked Morbidelli's confidence, but he has always been a thinking rider who takes things one step at a time, so once he had got his head around the situation he started gaining speed. A regular top-four qualifier, the Italian will surely find better race pace in 2020.

NATIONALITY | *ITALIAN*
DATE OF BIRTH | *04.12.94*
WEIGHT | *64 KG* ***HEIGHT*** | *176 CM*
TOTAL POINTS | *115*

13TH TAKAAKI NAKAGAMI

LCR HONDA IDEMITSU | *HONDA*

Japan's best MotoGP rider since Daijiro Kato showed real class in his second premier-class season. The former Moto2 winner was equipped with Márquez's 2018 RC213V machines and immediately made pit lane take notice with a run of top-ten results against riders on later-spec bikes. The highlight was a fifth place at Mugello, five seconds behind the winner. His season went downhill at Assen, where he was taken out by Rossi. The shoulder injury he suffered in that crash forced him to end his season early for surgery.

NATIONALITY | *JAPANESE*
DATE OF BIRTH | *09.02.92*
WEIGHT | *70 KG* ***HEIGHT*** | *175 CM*
TOTAL POINTS | *74*

14TH ALEIX ESPARGARÓ

APRILIA RACING TEAM GRESINI | *APRILIA*

The Spaniard's third season as a factory Aprilia rider was the most frustrating of his career. The Italian factory took a wrong turning with its 2019 RS-GP, which left Espargaró often struggling to get into the points, let alone the top-ten. His main problem was getting on the throttle at high lean angles, because the RS-GP lacked effective anti-slide electronics. Once again he had by far his best race at Aragon, which is dominated by sweeping corner entries that help mask the RS-GP's straight-line braking difficulties.

NATIONALITY | *SPANISH*
DATE OF BIRTH | *30.07.89*
WEIGHT | *66 KG* ***HEIGHT*** | *180 CM*
TOTAL POINTS | *63*

11TH POL ESPARGARÓ

RED BULL KTM FACTORY RACING | *KTM*

Produced flashes of brilliance in KTM's third MotoGP season. The RC16 was not an easy motorcycle to ride and it took all of the Spaniard's rodeo-riding ability to get the best out of the bike. His standout performance was sixth place at Le Mans, just six seconds behind the winner. He impressed again at Misano, with seventh, despite greasy asphalt that the RC16 hates. His dedication and willingness to take risks were never in doubt. At Aragon he suffered a broken wrist and two weeks later scored points at Buriram.

NATIONALITY | *SPANISH*
DATE OF BIRTH | *10.06.91*
WEIGHT | *63 KG* **HEIGHT** | *171 CM*
TOTAL POINTS | *100*

12TH JOAN MIR

TEAM SUZUKI ECSTAR | *SUZUKI*

The former Moto3 world champion had a rookie MotoGP season of two halves. The highlight of the first half was a brilliant eighth in his debut at Losail, five seconds behind the winner. Steady progress followed, but it all went wrong during the post-Czech GP tests at Brno where he crashed at close to top speed. He was seriously hurt in the fall and missed two races. His return was impressive. He had lost none of his speed and in fact took great strides forward, taking a superb fifth-place finish at Phillip Island.

NATIONALITY | *SPANISH*
DATE OF BIRTH | *01.09.97*
WEIGHT | *68 KG* **HEIGHT** | *181 CM*
TOTAL POINTS | *92*

15TH FRANCESCO BAGNAIA 63

PRAMAC RACING | *DUCATI*

The 2018 Moto2 world champion was the star rookie of 2019's first pre-season test, so much was expected of him when the racing started. However, Bagnaia soon found out that stringing together 25 laps on a MotoGP bike is a very different proposition. He had a torrid run of four consecutive DNFs from Jerez that forced him and his team to change their approach. Bagnaia kept losing the front because he likes to use a lot of corner speed but the Ducati doesn't. A superb fourth at Phillip Island proved his potential.

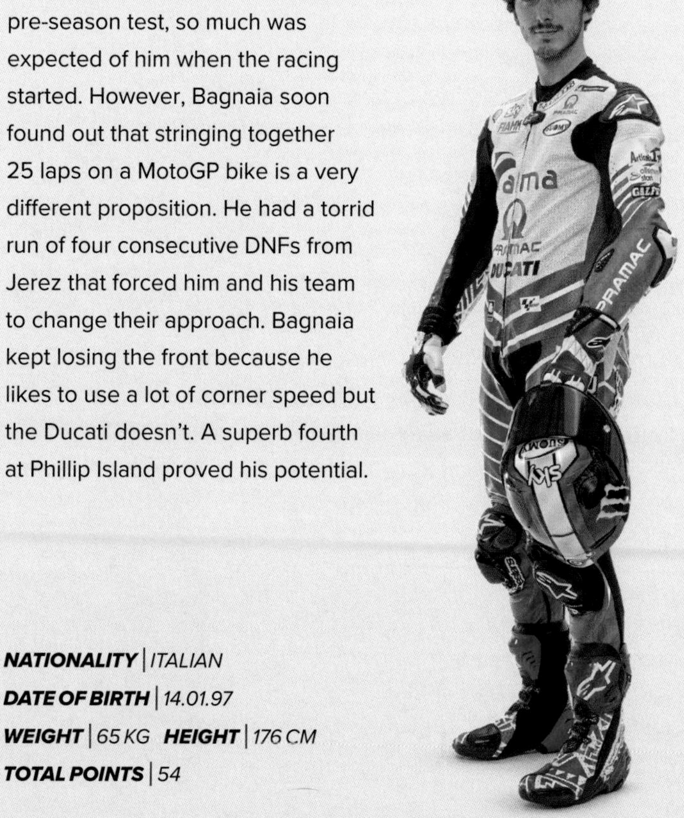

NATIONALITY | *ITALIAN*
DATE OF BIRTH | *14.01.97*
WEIGHT | *65 KG* **HEIGHT** | *176 CM*
TOTAL POINTS | *54*

16TH ANDREA IANNONE

APRILIA RACING TEAM GRESINI | *APRILIA*

From the factory Ducati team to the factory Suzuki team to the factory Aprilia team. Iannone has had a difficult time over the last few seasons, but there's still no doubt about his talent – his ability to overlay front brake and throttle is legendary – when he wants to use it. His biggest problem with the Aprilia was its electronics, which he rated as significantly behind his previous factory bikes. At least he made history at his beloved Phillip Island, where he became the first Aprilia rider to lead a MotoGP race.

NATIONALITY | *ITALIAN*
DATE OF BIRTH | *09.08.89*
WEIGHT | *74 KG* **HEIGHT** | *179 CM*
TOTAL POINTS | *43*

17TH MIGUEL OLIVEIRA

RED BULL KTM TECH 3 | *KTM*

There are few greater challenges in MotoGP than a rookie riding a bike that's still under development. Oliveira was also KTM's first MotoGP rider who hadn't climbed off a Yamaha, so his feedback was very useful to the Austrian factory. He showed his talent by beating factory KTM rider Johann Zarco on several occasions, but his year was undone when Zarco took him out at Silverstone, injuring his right shoulder. Another crash at Phillip Island forced him to end his season early, so he could have the shoulder fixed.

NATIONALITY | *PORTUGUESE*
DATE OF BIRTH | *04.01.95*
WEIGHT | *64 KG* **HEIGHT** | *170 CM*
TOTAL POINTS | *33*

18TH JOHANN ZARCO

RED BULL KTM FACTORY RACING | *KTM*

The twice Moto2 champ, who had dazzled aboard an independent Yamaha, signed for KTM aware that he was joining a development project. However, he never felt right on the RC16, always looking for the easy-riding feeling he had enjoyed on the M1. At the Austrian GP he told KTM he wanted to end his two-year contract a year early. Two races later KTM asked him to leave with immediate effect. His career was in limbo until LCR Honda gave him bikes for the last three races, when he reminded people how well he can ride.

NATIONALITY | *FRENCH*
DATE OF BIRTH | *16.07.90*
WEIGHT | *67 KG* **HEIGHT** | *171 CM*
TOTAL POINTS | *30*

21ST STEFAN BRADL

TEAM HRC | *HONDA*

HRC's MotoGP test rider did double duties during the 2019 world championship. Originally expected to contest two races in his primary role, the Spanish and Czech GPs, he was drafted in to replaced the injured Jorge Lorenzo at the German, Czech and Austrian GPs. He impressed on each occasion, scoring points at every outing, including top-ten finishes at Jerez and Sachsenring. His Jerez ride was special – equipped with HRC's experimental carbon-fibre-coated frame– he finished just 13 seconds behind winner Márquez.

NATIONALITY | *GERMAN*
DATE OF BIRTH | *29.11.89*
WEIGHT | *63 KG* **HEIGHT** | *170 CM*
TOTAL POINTS | *16*

22ND MICHELE PIRRO

DUCATI TEAM | *DUCATI*

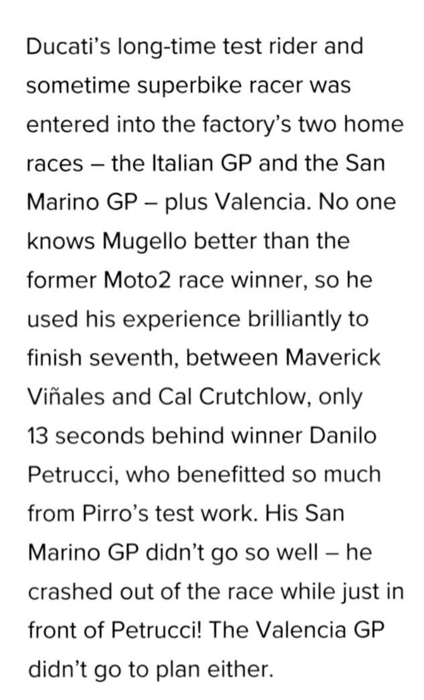

Ducati's long-time test rider and sometime superbike racer was entered into the factory's two home races – the Italian GP and the San Marino GP – plus Valencia. No one knows Mugello better than the former Moto2 race winner, so he used his experience brilliantly to finish seventh, between Maverick Viñales and Cal Crutchlow, only 13 seconds behind winner Danilo Petrucci, who benefitted so much from Pirro's test work. His San Marino GP didn't go so well – he crashed out of the race while just in front of Petrucci! The Valencia GP didn't go to plan either.

NATIONALITY | *ITALIAN*
DATE OF BIRTH | *05.07.86*
WEIGHT | *69 KG* **HEIGHT** | *177 CM*
TOTAL POINTS | *9*

19TH JORGE LORENZO

REPSOL HONDA TEAM | *HONDA*

The three-time MotoGP king had a turbulent 2019 which convinced him to quit. Great things were expected from him and Honda's RC213V, but he needed big changes to the bike to suit his style, just like he had needed at Ducati. His big concern was lack of front-end feeling. Two huge crashes in June left him with two fractured vertebrae that put him out of action for four races. When he returned to action he was often two seconds off the pace. At Valencia he announced he would retire from MotoGP – the Assen crash and back injuries had made him decide that enough was enough.

NATIONALITY | *SPANISH*
DATE OF BIRTH | *04.05.87*
WEIGHT | *65 KG* ***HEIGHT*** | *172 CM*
TOTAL POINTS | *28*

20TH TITO RABAT

REALE AVINTIA RACING | *DUCATI*

The 2015 Moto2 world champion very nearly ended his career when he crashed at high-speed during a Silverstone downpour in August 2018. Rabat was still limping heavily at the start of the 2019 season and he spent the year working constantly to rebuild strength in his broken right leg. He scored his first points since the accident at Jerez, a remarkable achievement. However, the leg was still far from perfect and, try as he might, he was unable to regain the impressive speed he had sometimes shown during 2018.

NATIONALITY | *SPANISH*
DATE OF BIRTH | *25.05.89*
WEIGHT | *67 KG* ***HEIGHT*** | *178 CM*
TOTAL POINTS | *23*

23RD HAFIZH SYAHRIN

RED BULL KTM TECH 3 | *KTM*

The Malaysian made the same journey as Johann Zarco in 2019 and struggled just as much. He stayed at Tech 3, but switched from a Yamaha M1 to a KTM RC16. During his rookie MotoGP season in 2018 Syahrin made it into the points at more than half the races, including several top-ten results. During 2019 he tried to adapt his riding style to work with a V4 instead of an inline-four, but he didn't find this an easy process. He scored points on only a handful of occasions and lost his ride, returning to Moto2 for the 2020 season.

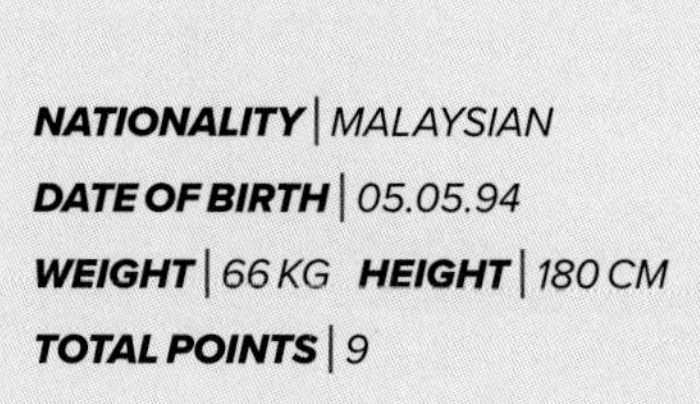

NATIONALITY | *MALAYSIAN*
DATE OF BIRTH | *05.05.94*
WEIGHT | *66 KG* ***HEIGHT*** | *180 CM*
TOTAL POINTS | *9*

24TH KAREL ABRAHAM

REALE AVINTIA RACING | *DUCATI*

Switched from the Ángel Nieto Team – which had its places on the grid taken over by the Petronas Yamaha SRT outfit – to the Reale Avintia squad for his eighth season in MotoGP and his fifth with Ducati. Was promoted to a GP18, on which the Czech rider immediately felt at home. However, the racing was more competitive than ever and Abraham had to work hard to get into the world championship points. Scored his first points of the year at Mugello and later agreed to stay with Reale Avintia into the 2020 season.

NATIONALITY | *CZECH*
DATE OF BIRTH | *02.01.90*
WEIGHT | *64 KG* ***HEIGHT*** | *180 CM*
TOTAL POINTS | *9*

25TH SYLVAIN GUINTOLI

TEAM SUZUKI ECSTAR | *SUZUKI*

The former World Superbike champion first tested for Suzuki's MotoGP team in 2017 and was the natural choice of rider when the factory established its full-time European test team in the early months of 2018. Guintoli put in many thousands of testing kilometres because Suzuki is obsessive about fully evaluating every new part and setting before transferring them to its full-time MotoGP riders. Rode the Catalan, Czech and Japanese GPs as test rider and substituted for the injured Joan Mir at the British GP.

NATIONALITY | *FRENCH*
DATE OF BIRTH | *24.06.82*
WEIGHT | *62 KG* ***HEIGHT*** | *179 CM*
TOTAL POINTS | *7*

26TH MIKA KALLIO

RED BULL KTM FACTORY RACING | *KTM*

A nasty knee injury while contesting the 2018 German GP as a wild card/ KTM tester threatened Kallio's career, but he worked hard to recover and was back on a bike in five months. KTM resolved to restrict him to testing duties in 2019 – they believe that racing can be a distraction – until they told Johann Zarco his services were no longer required after Misano. Kallio had his first race in more than a year at Aragon, steadily working his way up to speed until he scored his first points since Jerez 2018 at Motegi.

NATIONALITY | *FINNISH*
DATE OF BIRTH | *08.11.82*
WEIGHT | *58 KG* ***HEIGHT*** | *166 CM*
TOTAL POINTS | *7*

27TH BRADLEY SMITH

APRILIA RACING TEAM GRESINI | *APRILIA*

When KTM decided to replace Smith with Johann Zarco for 2019 the Briton found himself without a Grand Prix ride for the first time since 2006, when he raced for Alberto Puig's junior Honda 125cc GP squad. Aprilia gave him a lifeline as its first full-time test rider, with the opportunity to contest four world championship rounds. However, he crashed out of two of those four races – at Losail and Barcelona. His best result of the season came at Jerez, where he finished in 17th position, just ahead of Miguel Oliveira.

NATIONALITY | *BRITISH*
DATE OF BIRTH | *28.11.90*
WEIGHT | *68 KG* ***HEIGHT*** | *180 CM*
TOTAL POINTS | *0*

28TH IKER LECUONA

RED BULL KTM TECH 3 | *KTM*

The 19-year-old Spaniard was announced as Syahrin's Tech 3 replacement for 2020 and was then drafted in to replace Oliveira at Valencia: no pressure, just treat the weekend as a test session. Lecuona got the ride because KTM and Tech 3 owner Hervé Poncharal had watched him on his KTM Moto2 bike and studied his data. He rides aggressively, which suits the RC16, and has stunningly good front-tyre control. He impressed at Valencia, which completed the former Supermoto rider's third season as a roadracer!

NATIONALITY | *SPANISH*
DATE OF BIRTH | *06.01.00*
WEIGHT | *70 KG* ***HEIGHT*** | *180 CM*
TOTAL POINTS | *0*

MICHELIN
REPSOL
HONDA
One HEART.
RedBull

MICHELIN

THE ART AND SCIENCE OF MotoGP

Suzuki's GSX-RR is arguably the prettiest, best-handling bike on the MotoGP grid. This is the 2018 iteration, only really identifiable from the 2019 version by the lack of twin-pipe exhaust.

MotoGP mixes human talent (the art) and machine technology (the science). In 2019 the artistry of one man overcame all the machines.

The beauty of MotoGP is that sometimes it's not easy to see where the metal ends and the muscle begins. Like any motorsport, motorcycle racing is a combination of man and machine, both on the racetrack and in the garage, but in bike racing the lines are blurred more than anywhere else. Where does motorcycle technology end and human riding technique begin?

This is a question worth asking, because it's arguably the case that one rider's riding technique is currently worth more than the best motorcycle technology available on the MotoGP grid.

"The holy grail of motorcycle racing has always been to come up with a device that can save front-end slides," said one factory MotoGP engineer, preferring to remain anonymous. "And now Honda have one; he's called Marc Márquez."

The young Spaniard possesses a talent that has won him six MotoGP crowns in seven seasons. He has only lost the championship once since he graduated to MotoGP, when HRC went the wrong way with engine spec in 2015.

"Marc's riding style is quite unique," said Öhlins race engineer Thomas Alatalo who gets to inspect the data of all the top riders. "No one else can ride a front slide for so long. He has some kind of unreal feeling for how hard he can be on the brakes into the corner and in the trail-braking area. That's where he makes time.

"The way Marc rides, he is a master at balancing on the edge of the traction circle because he feels the limit better than everybody else: OK, now I'm outside the traction circle, I'm sliding the front and I'm going to crash if I don't do something about it. That reaction takes longer for other riders."

Michelin MotoGP chief Piero Taramasso has similar evidence of Márquez's advantage in riding technique.

"Last year at the Qatar pre-season tests he went out in the night with a hard front tyre, because he needed the harder tyre to support his style. No one else would go out with the hard front at night, when the track temperature is lower, but he told us, 'I want to try it'.

"So he went out and soon after that Jack Miller came back into his box. He told us that Marc had been in front of him and losing the front on purpose, trying to look for the limit. He said it was crazy because Marc was going to full lock. Jack went into Marc's garage and said, 'what were you doing in Turn Six [a low-speed left that claims many victims] – you were at 20 degrees of lean and turning the handlebars onto full lock?!' He said, 'oh, I was looking for the limit, because I want to know where's the limit and I want to feel the reaction'. No one else can do that."

During 2019 Cal Crutchlow rode the same spec RC213V as the world champion, so he knows better than anyone what Márquez can do on a motorcycle. Any motorcycle. "Marc would be on the podium with the Aprilia and he'd be on the podium with the KTM," said the Briton. "If people think otherwise they've no idea."

In other words, technique can overcome technology in MotoGP. Of course, that didn't stop the factories working harder than ever during 2019 – Honda trying to stretch their star rider's advantage, the others trying to close the gap.

MotoGP regulations cramp engine and electronics development, so chassis performance was once again the biggest area of work; or at least the most noticeable.

HRC worked to make the RC213V easier to ride and less easy to crash. Both Márquez and HRC knew this was vital after surgeons opened up his damaged left shoulder in December 2018 to discover that the joint was in such a bad way that it might threaten his career.

At May's Spanish GP HRC rolled out a carbon-fibre-coated frame. Suzuki started using similar technology the previous year, so composite carbon-fibre/aluminium frames could be a major avenue of development in MotoGP. All carbon-fibre frames have never succeeded in bike racing due to the reflex rate of carbon, which gives a harsh ride and can cause chatter. Legendary engineer John Britten fixed the front-end chatter on his amazing Britten V1000 by adding Kevlar to the bike's carbon-fibre forks.

Wayne Rainey's former crew chief and keen windsurfer Mike Sinclair tells the same story in windsurfing. Carbon-fibre surfboards give too harsh a ride, which can be improved by adding Kevlar and glass-fibre to the carbon.

This is what HRC are trying to achieve with their composite frames, getting the best of all worlds: strength, lightness and a perfect blend of rigidity and flex in various planes to make the motorcycle ride and turn better.

By 2019 most MotoGP factory teams were helping their corner-entry performance by monitoring Michelin's front tyre more closely than any Grand Prix tyre has been monitored.

The Michelin front slick offers delicate performance, largely dependent upon tyre temperature. Therefore, teams monitor front-tyre surface temperature, core temperature, air temperature and pressure, via infrared temperature sensors attached to the front mudguard and an internal device attached to the tyre valve.

This data is communicated to the rider's dashboard, because it has a crucial effect on the grip he has available. When tyre temperature increases the air expands, which increases air pressure, which changes the contact patch, which affects grip. If the tyre gets too hot, the pressure increases too much, the contact patch reduces and the rider has less grip. Some riders have simple green/red warning lights on the dash, others prefer exact temperature and pressure numbers.

Once the rider is into the corner his next concern is getting the bike turned as quickly as possible, so he can transfer load to the rear tyre and commence the all-important acceleration phase. Good mid-corner turning is achieved via the correct mix of geometry, centre of mass and chassis flex, hence all the effort on composite frames. Of course, the rider also plays a role, with body position and riding technique, crucially with his use of the rear brake.

This is why 2019 saw more riders adopt hand-operated rear brakes, while Brembo continued to work at improving this system. The riders who work the rear brake with their left hand are Karel Abraham, Pecco Bagnaia, Andrea Dovizioso, Jorge Lorenzo, Danilo Petrucci, Fabio Quartararo and Valentino Rossi.

The last named had previously tried a thumb-operated brake but gave up, because it's a huge ask to reprogram your brain to switch from right foot to left hand, especially when you're braking from over 340kmh/210mph. Márquez also tried a hand-operated rear brake a couple of years ago and gave up for the same reason.

Rossi's decision to try again may have been encouraged by Quartararo's results. The advantages of a hand-operated rear brake are clear: you can get to the lever better at full lean in right-handers and your hands have more finesse than your feet.

Brembo have done their bit to push the technology forward, creating a dual-line, four-piston rear caliper that allows riders to use hand and foot controls simultaneously, with the hand working two pistons and the foot the other two. During 2019

Abraham took the next step, using a scooter-style rear-brake lever, mounted below the clutch lever. Brembo are sure that more and more riders will switch to this scooter-style control.

MotoGP's biggest technical change for 2019 was the introduction of a unified IMU (inertial measurement unit) to complete the spec hardware and software package. There had been suggestions that some factories were bending the rules by getting clever with their own IMUs. Making everyone use the same IMU was the obvious way forward.

Of course, this just changes the game. Now electronics engineers must seek to find an nth of an advantage by getting clever with the spec IMU.

Dorna's unified software features a traction-control channel, which controls wheelspin, but doesn't include a slide channel, which most factories had during the days of tailormade factory software. Nowadays it is up to the rider to control slides, but if his electronics staff can find a way to help him in this vital area he will be able to open the throttle sooner, for more acceleration and top speed.

Some electronics engineers suggest this can be done by using the IMU's pitch axis – which measures fore-and-aft movement during acceleration to detect wheelies – to detect slides.

"I don't think anyone is cheating," said Aprilia's chief engineer Romano Albesiano. "When a car slides it's basically a yawing movement, but when a motorcycle slides it's more of a pitching movement, so maybe you can use the pitch axis of the IMU to detect the early signs of a slide. In this area you cannot rely on the traction control, because the spin value is very low. The bike is sliding, not spinning, so you cannot take the spin signal to detect the slide, or at least it's very difficult."

MotoGP's biggest technical change for 2020 will be Michelin's first new rear-slick construction since the start of the 2017 season. Riders tested the tyre on several occasions during 2019, all of them happy with its improved performance.

"The main difference is that the casing gives better grip, which helps everybody, but especially maybe Yamaha, because with more grip they can be faster," said Márquez. "But then maybe Ducati and Honda can use more torque with the extra grip. I think it will help everybody."

We can't wait to find out if he's right...

CLOCKWISE, FROM TOP LEFT | *HRC kept working to make the RC213V friendlier, by using a carbon-fibre-coated frame similar to the Suzuki's; Brembo did their bit for turning, with a four-piston rear caliper with separate lines to right-foot control and left-hand control, so riders could use both controls simultaneously; Andrea Dovizioso's crew chief Alberto Giribuola gives a pre-practice pep talk, but the Ducati still lagged behind in mid-corner; MotoGP's new-for-2019 control IMU gave the cleverest electronics engineers another challenge.*

THE 2019 BIKES

HONDA | RC213V

Honda's RC213V changed more than any other bike going into 2019 and the machine dominated the championship, thanks largely to the otherworldly talent of Marc Márquez.

One of the RC213V's biggest problems during previous seasons had been its lack of outright horsepower while battling with Ducati's Desmosedici. Until only recently, a small top-speed handicap hadn't been a great issue in MotoGP, but the closer the racing gets, the less room there is for any deficiency.

Hence HRC's major redesign at the front end, to coax more power and torque from the 90-degree V4. The boost came largely from improved intake efficiency: previous RC213V engines had air intakes curved around both sides of the frame, the incoming air entering the airbox through cut-outs in the frame. The 2019 iteration used a much more efficient tunnel through the steering column, allowing a much more direct route to the airbox.

Above the engine more room was made for the airbox and fuel injectors, by relocating electronics and switching to a rotary steering damper. The result of all this was a significant horsepower increase, so for the first time the RC213V could hold the Desmosedici's draft and very occasionally slingshot past, which required Márquez to take fewer risks on the brakes.

HRC's other concern was to make the RC213V more rider-friendly, specifically at the front end. The bike had been created in the Bridgestone era, to exploit the Japanese company's very stiff and very grippy front slick. Add Márquez's ultra-late-braking technique into the mix and no wonder the bike needed hard-compound front slicks. But harder tyres give less feel, which means less warning of slides and therefore more crashes. This is why Márquez and also Cal Crutchlow used to hit the ground so often.

The revised chassis obviously helped in this respect, because Márquez was able to race with medium-compound fronts. As a result his crash rate (and Crutchlow's) pretty much halved.

"We changed the balance of the bike, so now I can race with the medium front, which is good because the hard front can be too much risk," Márquez explained. "Also, we have more power, so now I can find the lap time in two or three different ways."

However, the revised chassis wasn't all good. Riders found the 2019 RC213V harder to turn, which required more physical effort and more lean angle. Márquez could handle this, new team-mate Jorge Lorenzo and Crutchlow less so. Hence HRC's experimental carbon-fibre-coated frame.

***1** | The carbon-fibre-coated frame which Márquez raced in Austria. Reduced lateral rigidity improved turning and increased rear grip*

***2** | Lorenzo's RC213V, with moulded fuel-tank flares and fairing knee supports to keep him more stable during heavy braking and turning*

***3** | HRC's aero update, new in Austria, made the bike less sensitive to turbulence and turn faster, without increasing drag*

***4** | When Márquez raced HRC's 'swinglet' he noticed increased rear downforce in braking, contradicting Ducati's claims about its item*

REPSOL
93
HRC
REPSOL
One HEART.
HONDA
Red Bull
GIVI
LAVOR
35

4
REPSOL
HRC
MICHELIN
YUTAKA
GOSHI
NGK
RK
ShinDengen
Snap-on
Red Bull

DUCATI | DESMOSEDICI GP19

Ducati went into the season as a growing force: two victories in 2016, six in 2017 and seven in 2018. It seemed reasonable to expect they would give Honda an even harder time in 2019.

But MotoGP is unpredictable, especially when the racing is so close, because the tiniest of changes can have a big effect on results.

Ducati's Desmosedici GP19 was a subtle upgrade from the GP18, so it was still a point-and-squirt bike, making its lap times into and out of corners, rather than through the corners, like the inline-fours. Ducati Corse kept working on the bike's major issue – mid-corner turning – by using two frame variations in 2019 with different rigidities.

"We are trying to fix the main problem, which is when the rider completely releases the brake and when he's waiting to open the gas," explained Ducati Corse general manager Gigi Dall'Igna. "You have to do your best to try to fix the problem the rider has, without losing anything in other areas. But for sure this is sometimes impossible, so you have to make a compromise between what you need and what you can have."

Indeed. Mid-corner turning remained the bike's biggest handicap, despite Ducati's labours, and by mid-season Andrea Dovizioso was vocal in his complaints, which is unlike him.

Dovizioso also talked a lot about tyres. Michelin changed its compound-mixing process for 2019 to create longer-lasting rear slicks, which worked against the Italian, whose mastery of tyre conservation had paid big dividends with MotoGP's 2017 and 2018 tyres.

"This year's tyres are a bit different, so the way you have to manage the tyres is different," said Dovizioso. "But they are the same for everybody, so it's not a complaint."

Ducati's other problem was also out of their hands: the Honda improved significantly and so did the Suzuki, so the competition was much tougher. More often than not Dovizioso was battling in the pack.

Meanwhile Dall'Igna continued looking for advantages wherever he could find them: the controversial 'swinglet' tyre cooler, front-and-rear wheel fairings and holeshot device, plus the parallelogram rear end and aero seat, which weren't raced. No doubt, Ducati engineers had read the MotoGP rulebook more closely than anyone else.

Although Honda's RC213V was occasionally quickest, Ducati mostly continued ruling the top-speed race, proving that the Desmosedici is the ultimate point-and-squirt machine. At Mugello the bike once again raised the all-time top-speed record to 356.7km/221.6mph.

1 | Ducati's carbon-fibre tyre-cooler was by far the biggest talking point of the season-opening Qatar Grand Prix

2 | Front-wheel fairings helped direct air to the 'swinglet'. Brake-cooling ducts were used at Red Bull Ring and other demanding tracks

3 | Yet more aero kit: the rear-wheel fairing arrived at Mugello, but can't be used in qualifying, because it complicates wheel changes

4 | Ducati first used its motocross-derived holeshot device (engaged by large wingnut on triple clamp) at the end of the 2018 season

Lenovo
AudiSport
MISSION WINNOW
NetApp
streparava
cefla
GIVI
PittaRosso
valsir
rielo
Audi Sport
Lenovo
MISSION WINNOW
alma
PRAMAC
Reflexallen
D.I.D
MICHELIN
brembo

FRECCIAROSSA
Reflexallen
4
ADVANCE
riello
DUCATI

YAMAHA | YZR-M1

There was no miracle turnaround for Yamaha during 2019. The factory continued working to master the combination of spec Magneti Marelli software and Michelin tyres but mostly only inched forward.

There were good days and bad days, because while Yamaha inched forwards their rivals did the same or better. For example, at several races the YZR-M1 was bettered on top speed by Suzuki's GSX-RR. New parts were slow to arrive, until later in the season.

Factory riders Maverick Viñales and Valentino Rossi had their moments, but often they were overshadowed by what some people suggested was Yamaha's most important 2019 power-up part – a 20-year-old rookie from Nice. The arrival of Fabio Quartararo shook up the factory riders even more than that of Johann Zarco in 2017.

"It's good to have someone like Fabio at Yamaha that can push more and help us understand which way to go with the bike," commented Rossi.

Whatever Viñales and Rossi did the M1's fundamental issues remained the same: lack of acceleration and poor tyre life. During 2019 the M1 continued to overuse the edge of its tyres, unlike Suzuki's inline four, which also uses the edge of its tyres to go fast. On his best days Quartararo found ways around that problem, partly through talent, partly through the fearlessness of youth.

Rossi often seemed more in trouble than Viñales and Quartararo, who are both smaller and lighter. "We suffer everywhere," he said at Mugello, where the M1 was the slowest bike on the grid.

Finally things did start to improve when Yamaha rolled out its 2020 prototype at August's Brno tests and at the subsequent Misano tests, during which the team also evaluated more immediate solutions.

A flurry of new parts were used at the San Marino GP, including a carbon-fibre swingarm, a Suzuki-style twin-pipe exhaust and a Ducati-style front-wheel fairing. A few days later came the news that Yamaha had hired one of Ducati's top electronics engineers – Marco Frigerio – for 2020.

"In reality, since 2016 we didn't test anything, or whatever we tested wasn't clearly better, until this year's tests at Brno and Misano," Rossi added. "Technically speaking that was a very difficult period and the gap to the other manufacturers increased. But since the beginning of this season something has changed – we have a lot of different people from Europe and especially from Japan. It looks like now we feel the effect."

It seemed like someone in Iwata had finally pressed the 'go' button again; in which case perhaps 2020 will be Yamaha's turnaround season.

1 | *Twin-pipe Akrapovič exhaust arrived at Misano. The system was pretty much identical to the exhaust used by Suzuki since Qatar*

2 | *Three infrared temperature sensors attached to the front mudguard monitor surface temperature at the centre, left and right of the tyre*

3 | *The factory team got its carbon-fibre swingarm at Misano. Rossi said the unit gave him a more precise feel for the rear tyre*

4 | *Intricately fabricated front-wheel fairing and brake cooling ducts were part of a flurry of new parts that arrived late in the season*

PETRONAS
PETRONAS
Visit Malaysia
YAMAHA
SEMAKIN DI DEPAN
ENEOS
46
MONSTER ENERGY
Revs Your Heart
YAMALUBE
A Liquid Engine Component
RCB
GILLES
AKRAPOVIC
D.I.D
MICHELIN
MONSTER ENERGY
YAMALUBE
BLUE CORE
ENEOS

4
RCB
D.I.D
GILLES
AKRAPOVIC
MICHELIN
MICHELIN
brembo
MICHELIN
46

SUZUKI | GSX-RR

During 2019 Suzuki had their best Grand Prix season in two decades, since Kenny Roberts Junior won four 500cc races with the RGV500 in 2000, the 500cc championship's penultimate year.

Step by careful step, Suzuki have tweaked the GSX-RR until finally it's a championship challenger. The bike's strongest point remained its chassis, recognised as the best handling and steering on the grid. The GSX-RR is particularly good in that crucial moment when the rider comes off the brakes and begins to turn the corner. Many other factories struggle in this area, but Suzuki have found a way to make it work. This gives riders Álex Rins and Joan Mir a real advantage.

Because the GSX-RR is so well balanced it's no surprise that Suzuki have the most conservative engineers on the grid. They rarely throw new parts at their bike like most other factories. Every part and every setting is tested at different tracks and in different conditions before it is deemed worth using at a Grand Prix.

Like Yamaha's YZR-M1, MotoGP's other inline-four, the GSX-RR's negative is peak horsepower, although during 2019 for the first time Suzuki sometimes sneaked ahead of Yamaha in the top-speed race and at Barcelona the GSX-RR was the quickest of all in the race! Again, this has been a step-by-step process. At Aragon in 2017 the GSX-RR was 10.4kmh/6.6mph slower than the fastest bike, in 2018 the difference was 5.4kmh/3.3mph and in 2019 the gap was reduced to 4kmh/2.5mph.

The 2019 engine boasted a horsepower increase of between just one and two percent, but more important was the engine's kindness to the tyres. Like the YZR-M1, the GSX-RR uses corner speed to make its lap times, but during 2019 it didn't burn the edge of its tyres like the M1. This was a consequence of that sweeter balance between engine, chassis and electronics.

"The overall balance of our bike is its strongest point; this helps a lot with tyre life," said technical manager Ken Kawauchi. "And we must say thank you to our riders."

Also important was Suzuki's introduction of a torductor, first brought into MotoGP by HRC, via Formula 1. This unit allows Suzuki's electronic engineers to create better maps for torque delivery, traction control and engine braking.

If imitation is the sincerest form of flattery then Suzuki engineers were flattered in 2019. HRC followed them by applying a carbon-fibre coating, used on the GSX-RR since mid-2018, to its RC213V; while Aprilia followed the GSX-RR by introducing engine mounts that allow rapid adjustments to frame rigidity.

1 | Suzuki's aero update arrived at the Austrian GP. It gave more top speed with no loss of downforce or side-to-side manoeuvrability

2 | The torductor – attached to the gearbox output sprocket – was new to the Suzuki and gave them a better handling on software mapping

3 | The twin-pipe Akrapovič was new at the start of 2019 and helped the GSX-RR's top-speed until it was sometimes faster than the Yamaha

4 | Rins' GSX-RR at Silverstone, where its superb handling, turning and tyre-conservation helped inflict defeat on Márquez and Honda

SUZUKI
ECSTAR
MOTUL
NGK
SPARK PLUGS
D.I.D
AKRAPOVIĆ
MICHELIN
brembo
@SUZUKIMOTOGP
42

4
NGK
SPARK PLUGS
AKRAPOVIĆ
D.I.D
MICHELIN
#GoPro GoPro #GoPro GoPro
SUZUKI
ECSTAR
MOTUL
Team
SUZUKI

KTM | RC16

KTM's third season in the premier class showed flashes of brilliance. Critics who thought the RC16 should've come further in 2019 should remember that most of KTM's rivals have been doing this for more than 40 years.

In racing, whether you are a rider or manufacturer, you usually build your outright speed first, so you learn how to throw everything you've got into one fast lap. Once you've done that you learn how to maintain that speed over a few laps and finally over full-race distance.

In fact KTM's first miracle of 2019 was Pol Espargaró's stunning sixth-place result at May's French Grand Prix, where he finished 5.9 seconds behind the winner, a deficit of just two tenths per lap. Espargaró needs lots of grip to go fast, so he loves Le Mans, which is why KTM's first dry-track front row, achieved by Espargaró at September's San Marino GP, was just as surprising, because Misano was treacherously slippery.

KTM and their backers Red Bull have impressive resources. Throughout the season a steady flow of new engine configurations and chassis parts kept the RC16 moving forward. A carbon-fibre swingarm, introduced at Le Mans increased grip and feel, for faster corner exits and better tyre life.

KTM motorsport director Pit Beirer explained how they climb the spiral. "We were good on brakes but turning was difficult, then the turning became better and we lost a bit of our advantage on the brakes, then we made the braking stronger again and made the turning better again. It's always a combination of chassis and engine. We have also changed things in the engine; making the power curve less aggressive to make the bike more rideable and to make the tyre last longer."

Dani Pedrosa's input was vital, once he had recovered from surgery to fix an old injury. The KTM is very similar to the Honda in overall configuration, so Pedrosa's 12 years of experience with Honda V4s is a huge win for the Austrian factory.

"Dani is focusing on the points which he thinks we need to work on to get the bike to do better things, so we're not having to shoot so much in the dark," said Espargaró's crew chief Paul Trevathan.

However, there was evidence that KTM were still climbing a steep learning curve. At Misano the RC16 appeared with its upper-rear engine bolts removed, to reduce lateral stiffness and regain some of that turning performance.

"We've changed a lot of things, just trying to get the bike to turn better, especially through long corners which has been one of our weaknesses," added Trevathan.

1 | *KTM's carbon-fibre swingarm arrived at Le Mans and made an immediate improvement to corner-exit traction and also tyre life*

2 | *Removing engine bolts to adjust frame rigidity isn't a new thing – KTM removed the RC16's upper-rear engine bolts at Misano*

3 | *KTM had the neatest answer to keeping the Magneti Marelli ECU cool in the garage. Keeping the rider cool was another matter*

4 | *KTM once again followed the RC213V's lead when they switched to a rotary steering damper at August's Austrian Grand Prix*

4

APRILIA | RS-GP

It's never easy being the smallest kid on the block and that is Aprilia's lot in MotoGP. The Italian brand may be owned by Piaggio, which produces half a million two wheelers per year, but Aprilia's MotoGP project has to get by on the smallest factory budget in the paddock.

After a grim 2018 season, when the RS-GP went backwards, there were high hopes for 2019, with a new bike that blended Aprilia's latest ideas with the best elements of the 2017 and 2018 machines.

Increased commitment from Aprilia and a team reorganisation that introduced ex-Ferrari man Massimo Rivola as project CEO, allowing Romano Albesiano to focus on engineering, also suggested good times ahead.

The 2019 RS-GP was better but not enough. Aleix Espargaró started his third season in Aprilia colours with a smile, which faded as the year went on.

"It's not that my bike isn't good," said the Spaniard. "The problem is that the others have improved more than us."

During 2019 Aprilia worked a lot on engine inertia and chassis stiffness. They even had a new frame, with adjustable stiffness, but the main issue seemed to be electronics, with below-par engine-braking, torque delivery and traction control affecting the bike's overall dynamics. Therefore Espargaró and new team-mate Andrea Iannone struggled to get the bike into and out of corners.

"Our traction is a disaster, so we have no acceleration at all," explained Espargaró. "This can be a combination of power delivery, chassis geometry, settings and electronics, but most of all I don't think our traction control is working very well."

Iannone suggested that Espargaró's lack of experience with cutting-edge electronics might explain Aprilia's lack of progress in this area.

"Aleix is a really good rider but he started in MotoGP with CRT and Open bikes, without proper electronics," said the Italian. "Then he was with Suzuki in their first year back in MotoGP, when they didn't have great electronics. When I first rode the RS-GP I was surprised: guys, this is not a MotoGP bike. A MotoGP bike is like this and this and this. Since then we have improved the electronics, but we need more time."

Albesiano agreed that finding the right route through the Magneti Marelli software was the key to getting the RS-GP out of corners faster.

"Our engine is very linear in torque and the restart of the combustion is very linear and very early, so the key point is how we deliver the torque," he said. "We have the torque we need, it's just the way we deliver it."

1 | Aprilia's 2019 frame featured removable engine plates to adjust rigidity. Mostly they just made engine removal quicker and easier

2 | An old trick employed at dusty COTA: grease smeared in the air intake helps catch dust and grit before it enters the engine

3 | Aprilia had also developed a 'swinglet' during winter 2018/2019, which they fitted to the RS-GP at the start of the European season

4 | The 2019 RS-GP promised much but Aprilia struggled to keep up with their richer rivals, especially on electronics development

Unibat
BOOST
aprilia
Gulf
MARSH
sky Q
TEAM GRESINI
UTILITY
DIADORA
MICHELIN
STAR
PIAGGIO GROUP
STM
41

4
STM
sky Q
aprilia
MICHELIN
TEAM GRESINI

25 LAPS TO GO
MotoGPTV

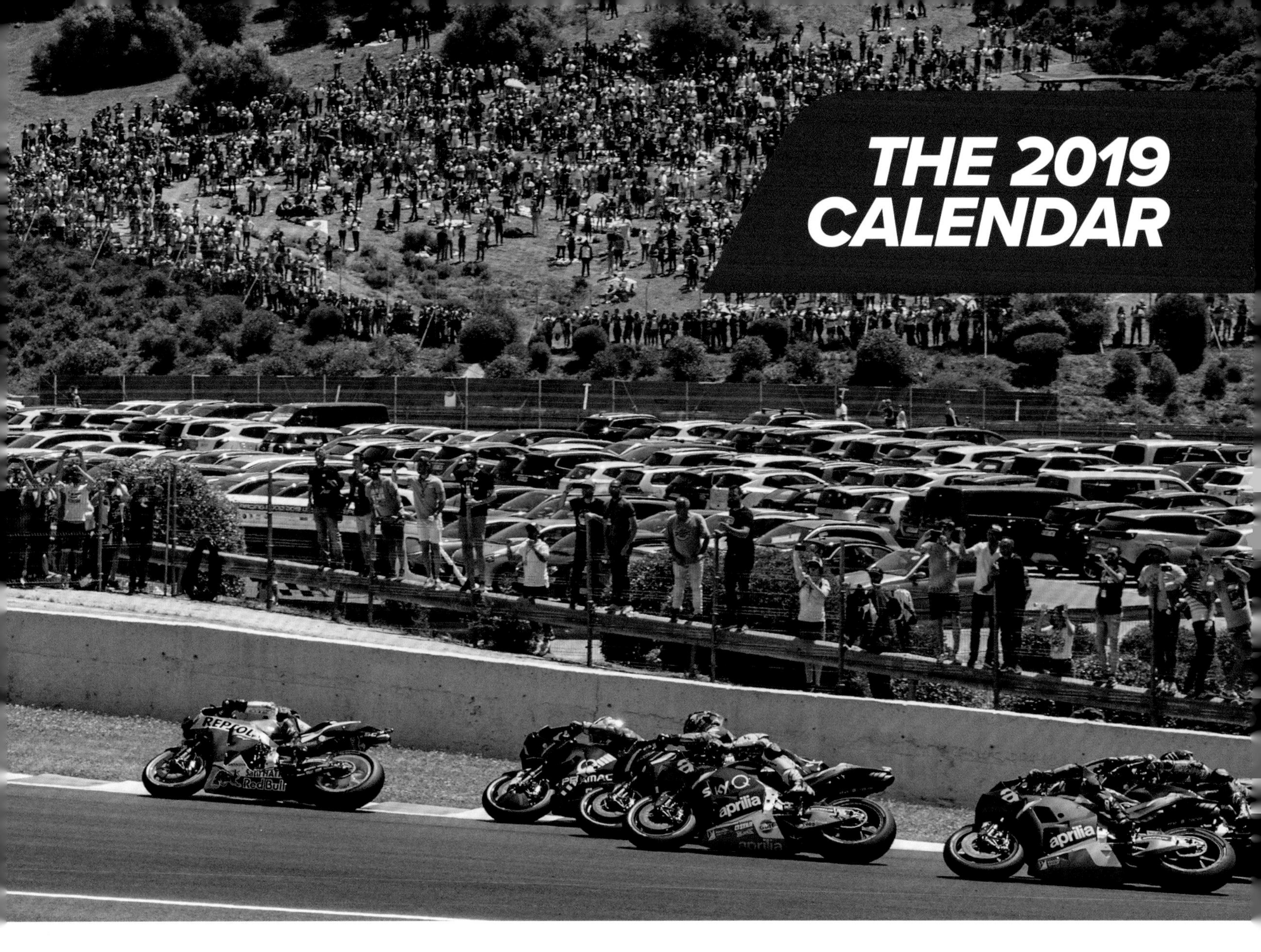

THE 2019 CALENDAR

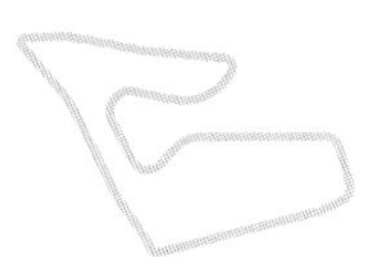

 11 | **AUSTRIA** | 118

myWORLD MOTORRAD GRAND PRIX VON ÖSTERREICH
RED BULL RING - SPIELBERG

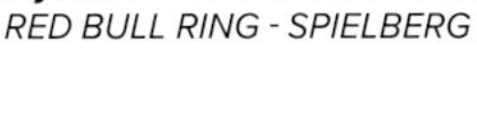

 12 | **GREAT BRITAIN** | 126

GoPro BRITISH GRAND PRIX
SILVERSTONE CIRCUIT

 13 | **SAN MARINO** | 134

GP OCTO DI SAN MARINO E DELLA RIVIERA DI RIMINI
MISANO WORLD CIRCUIT MARCO SIMONCELLI

 14 | **ARAGÓN** | 142

GRAN PREMIO MICHELIN® DE ARAGÓN
MOTORLAND ARAGÓN

 15 | **THAILAND** | 150

PTT THAILAND GRAND PRIX
CHANG INTERNATIONAL CIRCUIT

 16 | **JAPAN** | 158

MOTUL GRAND PRIX OF JAPAN
TWIN RING MOTEGI

17 | **AUSTRALIA** | 166

PRAMAC GENERAC AUSTRALIAN MOTORCYCLE GRAND PRIX
PHILLIP ISLAND

 18 | **MALAYSIA** | 174

SHELL MALAYSIA MOTORCYCLE GRAND PRIX
SEPANG INTERNATIONAL CIRCUIT

 19 | **VALENCIA** | 182

GRAN PREMIO MOTUL DE LA COMUNITAT VALENCIANA
CIRCUIT RICARDO TORMO

INTERNATIONAL CIRCUIT
46
DANNY
QATAR
REPSOL

The winning advantage was 0.023 seconds, four thousands closer than in 2018. Another hundred metres and Marquez could've drafted past.

VISITQATAR GRAND PRIX
LOSAIL INTERNATIONAL CIRCUIT
08/09/10 MARCH

DUCATI CONQUER QATAR AGAIN

Dovizioso's second consecutive Qatar victory headed the closest top-15 and created an inter-factory row

MotoGP's only night race is always a special challenge, for all sorts of reasons. This time it seemed like an even bigger challenge, following a chilly Saturday evening during which eight MotoGP riders fell in just one hour, all of them on left-handers and all but one at turn two, where the left side of the tyres get used for the first time in more than half a minute.

No wonder that teams were anxiously eyeing their temperature gauges and humidity meters on Sunday evening, as the 8pm start approached. Most riders chose the soft rear, while a few teams calculated that the combination of plummeting temperatures and rising humidity made the soft front the correct choice. Among them was Danilo Petrucci, the former Superstock rider preparing for his first race as a factory MotoGP rider.

"At 7.30pm the track temperature was dropping and at 7.45, when we chose my tyres, the temperature was still going down," said the Italian. "The problem for me was that after 7.45 the temperature stayed stable. It wasn't like Saturday night, when the temperature went down, down and down and the dew arrived. Tonight there was no dew."

Sunday night was three degrees warmer and ten percent less humid – enough to give much better grip during the race and enough for Petrucci's gamble to fail.

The race quickly turned into a rerun of the 2018 event, although this time there were more riders in the hunt. Andrea Dovizioso led most of the way, doing everything he could to slow the pace, so he could save his tyres for the final laps. That's one reason why the lead pack was so big and why the race delivered the closest top-15 in history.

Dovizioso is the king of tyre preservation, because he has developed a technique that neither overloads nor overheats his rear Michelin. He led into the first corner followed by Jack Miller, both of them having deployed the holeshot device on their GP19s. Miller's glory didn't last long. For all Gigi Dall'Igna's clever gizmos the Aussie was let down by a loose seat pad, which he jettisoned while in the middle of the lead group. That moment scattered those around him and let the three leaders – Dovizioso, Márquez and Cal Crutchlow – escape. For a moment, at least.

The men on the move were Álex Rins and his rookie team-mate Joan Mir. Rins had crashed twice the previous day but was far from gun-shy. In just two laps he picked off Crutchlow, Márquez and Dovizioso, then led for three laps before half-distance. He was riding beautifully, but the Suzuki had no answer to the straight-line speed of the GP19 and Honda's latest RC213V.

On lap 17 of 22 just 1.3 seconds covered the top eight: Dovizioso, Rins, Márquez, Crutchlow, Petrucci, Valentino Rossi, Mir and Maverick Viñales, who had gone backwards from pole position. This is when Dovizioso pulled the pin, confident he had enough rubber to make a fight of the last five laps. However, he wasn't the only one who had been saving his tyres. Márquez, Rins and Crutchlow went with him, while Rossi dug deeper to latch onto the back of the lead foursome.

On the penultimate lap Dovizioso's plan to control from the front nearly went to pieces. He got his bike unsettled into turn four, ran wide and immediately fell victim to Márquez. The pair were nearly off the track and in the pit wall as they swept past the start/finish to start the final lap, Dovizioso getting enough of a tow to draft back into the lead before hitting the brakes.

Would Márquez – whose left shoulder wasn't fully recovered from winter surgery – call it quits and settle for second? Of course not. He attacked at turn ten and briefly retook the lead, then nearly lost the front two corners later. Surely now he would accept second place? Nope. Just like 2018 he threw himself past Dovizioso into the last corner, but he was carrying too much speed and couldn't get turned in time. Dovizioso beat him to the flag by 0.023 seconds, Márquez right in his slipstream. In 2018 the gap was 0.027 seconds.

"It was a strange race," said Dovizioso. "I was managing the rear tyre, like everyone else. I'm especially happy because I didn't really follow anyone, so I didn't know my positive and negative points. I stopped Rins every time he got past, because his speed in the middle of the corners was amazing."

Márquez was possibly even happier, because the race had answered any doubts about his fitness. "I'm also happy because

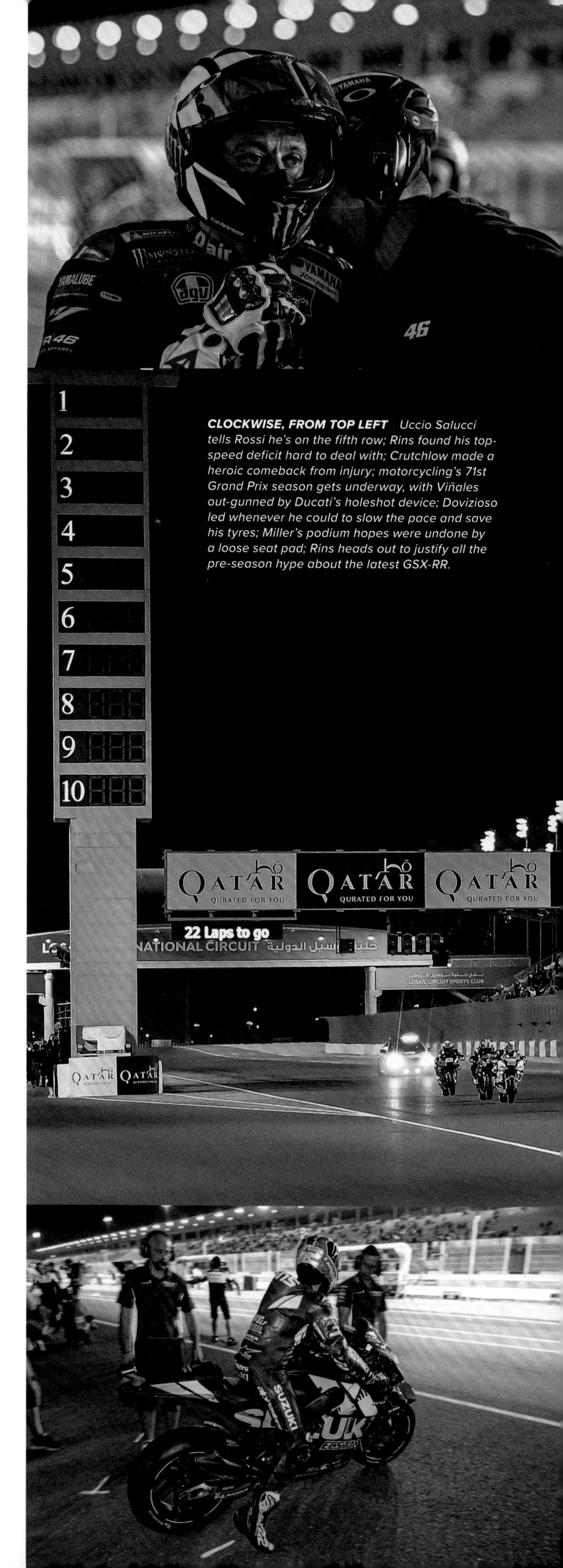

CLOCKWISE, FROM TOP LEFT | *Uccio Salucci tells Rossi he's on the fifth row; Rins found his top-speed deficit hard to deal with; Crutchlow made a heroic comeback from injury; motorcycling's 71st Grand Prix season gets underway, with Viñales out-gunned by Ducati's holeshot device; Dovizioso led whenever he could to slow the pace and save his tyres; Miller's podium hopes were undone by a loose seat pad; Rins heads out to justify all the pre-season hype about the latest GSX-RR.*

'IT WAS A STRANGE RACE – I WAS MANAGING THE REAR TYRE, LIKE EVERYONE ELSE.'

ANDREA DOVIZIOSO

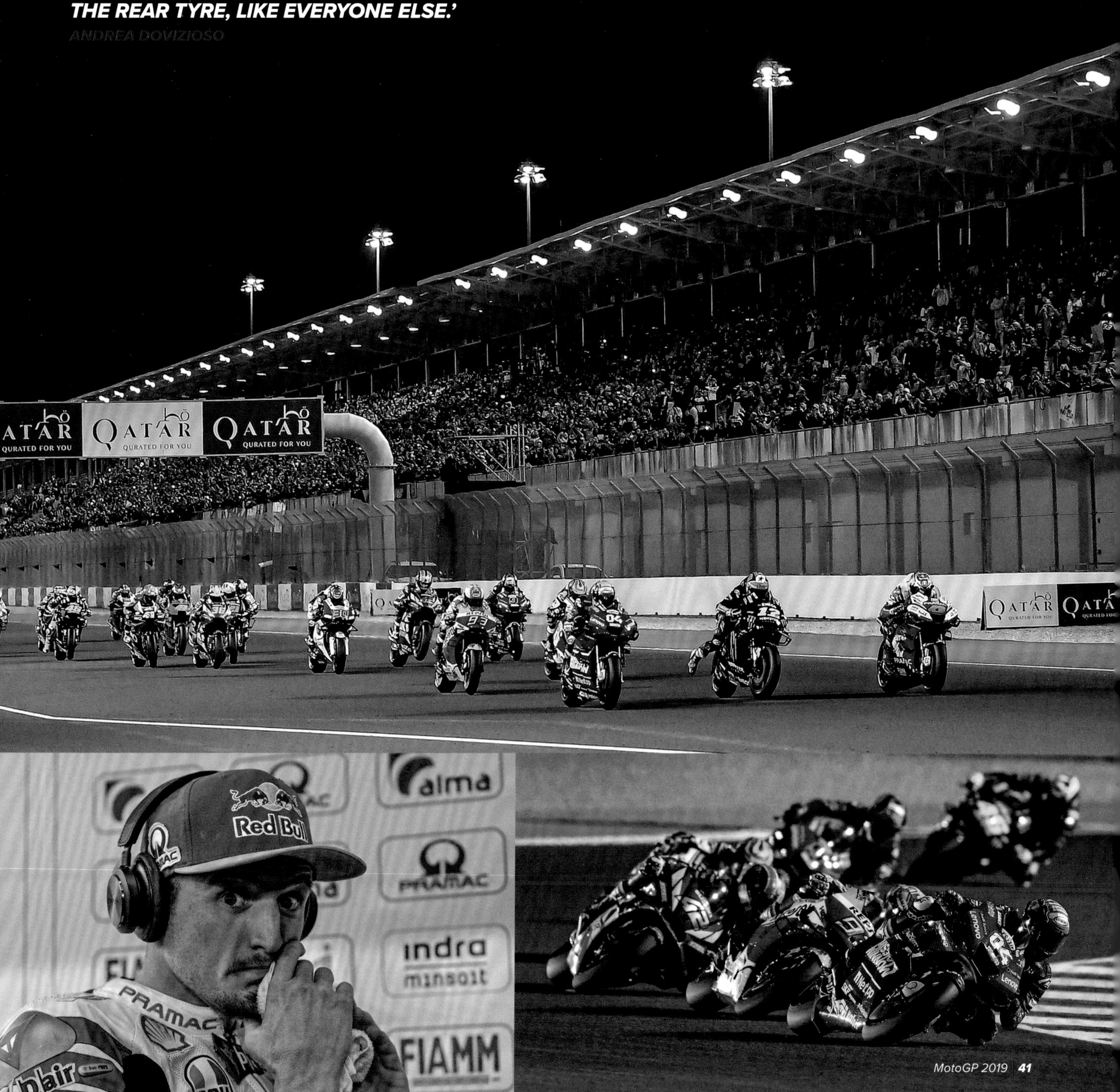

DUCATI'S SECOND WIN: AERO-GATE

Andrea Dovizioso's joy at his 13th MotoGP victory didn't last long. Soon after the race four rival manufacturers – Aprilia, Honda, KTM and Suzuki – lodged a protest against Ducati's latest widget, attached to the swingarms of the GP19s belonging to Dovizioso, Danilo Petrucci and Jack Miller. Only Yamaha deferred, because they use a not-dissimilar attachment to clear water from the rear tyre in the rain.

As usual, Gigi Dall'igna and Ducati's vehicles dynamics manager Riccardo Savin had been busy over the winter. Their latest attachment, used in conjunction with front-wheel fairings, was either designed to cool the rear tyre or create downforce. Or perhaps a bit of both. MotoGP's technical director Danny Aldridge decided there was nothing wrong with the device itself. The argument concerned its purpose: if it was a tyre cooler, that was fine, but if it was an aero device, that was not.

Ducati's rivals are certain the gizmo is an aero device that reduces wheelspin. This opinion is shared by Formula 1 aerodynamicist and bike racer Ali Rowland-Rouse. "It's a three-element, short-span wing device that gives a downforce gain," said Rowland-Rouse. "It reduces wheelspin by creating more load on the rear tyre, which helps avoid any spike in temperature from wheelspin, which is the worst for tyre degradation. What's really clever is that it's mounted on an unsprung part of the bike, so any force created goes straight into the tyre. That's the holy grail of downforce, because you get a greater effect on grip because it's not going through the suspension and you don't

we struggled a lot with the front tyre this weekend. It wasn't the best allocation for us, so I had to race the medium instead of the hard, so I couldn't push like normal at the brake points."

Crutchlow was definitely the hero. He had spent 111 days off bikes between his Australian GP crash and the start of pre-season testing. And his broken right ankle – reinforced with plenty of metal – still wasn't right. "I've got 70 percent movement, which isn't enough," he explained. "I use the rear brake a lot in the middle of corners, but I'm really struggling to get off the brake in right-handers."

Rins wasn't happy about getting mugged by the faster bikes on the straight, but at least he had proved that Suzuki's off-season labours had paid dividends.

Rossi's speed in the final quarter of the race was impressive but he wasn't happy. "The problem is that we are more or less like last year," he said. "In some areas we have improved but unfortunately we always struggle with rear grip. The Honda and Ducati can put more power on the track, so we lose in acceleration and top speed."

CLOCKWISE FROM TOP LEFT | *Márquez arrives at parc fermé a happy man, but not as happy as Crutchlow; F1 legend and MotoGP fan Lewis Hamilton was as impressed as always by his two-wheel counterparts; Viñales got pole, but it didn't mean much; Iannone leads Zarco, Oliveira, Quartararo and Lorenzo; Mir impressed mightily on his MotoGP debut; Dovizioso leads the Suzukis and Márquez, it was this close most of the way.*

have to compensate your suspension set-up."

Aprilia Racing's new CEO Massimo Rivola had earlier asked to use a similar device, to increase downforce, but had been told that wasn't admissible. Thus Aprilia and the three other manufacturers took their protest to MotoGP's Court of Appeal which a few days before the Argentine GP declared the device legal. During the appeal process Ducati engineers revealed data they claimed was proof that the device reduces tyre temperature by seven degrees and provides only 300g of downforce at 180kmh/112mph.

In Argentina HRC asked to use a similar spoiler, for aerodynamic use. The request was denied, but when they reapplied, claiming the fitment increased swingarm stiffness, the request was accepted.

1 | QATAR

VISITQATAR GRAND PRIX

LOSAIL INTERNATIONAL CIRCUIT
08/09/10 MARCH

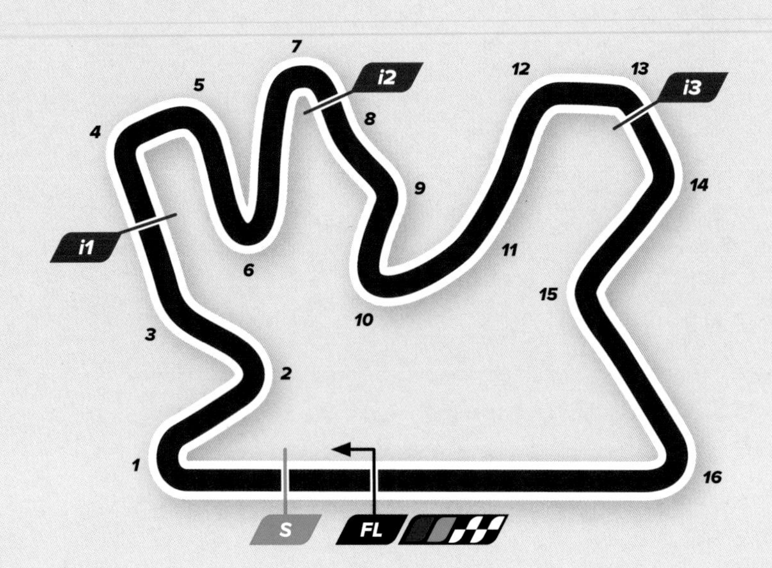

QUALIFYING RESULTS

	RIDER	NAT	TEAM	MACHINE	QP	TIME	GAP 1ST	PREV
1	Maverick Viñales	SPA	Monster Energy Yamaha MotoGP	YAMAHA	Q2	1'53.546		
2	Andrea Dovizioso	ITA	Mission Winnow Ducati	DUCATI	Q2	1'53.744	0.198	0.198
3	Marc Márquez	SPA	Repsol Honda Team	HONDA	Q2	1'53.745	0.199	0.001
4	Jack Miller	AUS	Pramac Racing	DUCATI	Q2	1'53.809	0.263	0.064
5	Fabio Quartararo	FRA	Petronas Yamaha SRT	YAMAHA	Q2	1'53.946	0.400	0.137
6	Cal Crutchlow**	GBR	LCR Honda CASTROL	HONDA	Q2	1'54.095	0.549	0.149
7	Danilo Petrucci	ITA	Mission Winnow Ducati	DUCATI	Q2	1'54.200	0.654	0.105
8	Franco Morbidelli	ITA	Petronas Yamaha SRT	YAMAHA	Q2	1'54.236	0.690	0.036
9	Takaaki Nakagami**	JPN	LCR Honda IDEMITSU	HONDA	Q2	1'54.239	0.693	0.003
10	Álex Rins	SPA	Team SUZUKI ECSTAR	SUZUKI	Q2	1'54.257	0.711	0.018
11	Joan Mir	SPA	Team SUZUKI ECSTAR	SUZUKI	Q2	1'54.390	0.844	0.133
12	Aleix Espargaró	SPA	Aprilia Racing Team Gresini	APRILIA	Q2	1'54.917	1.371	0.527
13	Francesco Bagnaia	ITA	Pramac Racing	DUCATI	Q1	1'54.472	*0.202	0.041
14	Valentino Rossi	ITA	Monster Energy Yamaha MotoGP	YAMAHA	Q1	1'54.537	*0.267	0.065
15	Jorge Lorenzo	SPA	Repsol Honda Team	HONDA	Q1	1'54.563	*0.293	0.026
16	Pol Espargaró	SPA	Red Bull KTM Factory Racing	KTM	Q1	1'54.740	*0.470	0.177
17	Miguel Oliveira	POR	Red Bull KTM Tech 3	KTM	Q1	1'55.122	*0.852	0.382
18	Tito Rabat	SPA	Reale Avintia Racing	DUCATI	Q1	1'55.428	*1.158	0.306
19	Andrea Iannone	ITA	Aprilia Racing Team Gresini	APRILIA	Q1	1'55.464	*1.194	0.036
20	Karel Abraham	CZE	Reale Avintia Racing	DUCATI	Q1	1'55.642	*1.372	0.178
21	Johann Zarco	FRA	Red Bull KTM Factory Racing	KTM	Q1	1'55.797	*1.527	0.155
22	Hafizh Syahrin	MAL	Red Bull KTM Tech 3	KTM	Q1	1'55.937	*1.667	0.140
23	Bradley Smith	GBR	Aprilia Factory Racing	APRILIA	Q1	1'56.036	*1.766	0.099

** Gap to the fastest rider in the Q1 session   ** Went forward from Q1 to Q2   Track severity = Wear + Temperature + Load*

GRAND PRIX INFORMATION

TRACK INFORMATION			
2019 WINNER	Andrea Dovizioso		
CIRCUIT LENGTH	5.4 km	3.34 miles	
LAPS	22		
RACE DISTANCE	118.4 KM	73.5 miles	
ALL TIME LAP RECORD	1'53.380	170.8 Km/h	Marc Márquez (2019)
BEST RACE LAP	1'54.927	168.5 Km/h	Jorge Lorenzo (2016)
RACE CONDITION	Dry		
AIR	18°C		
HUMIDITY	52%		
GROUND	19°C		

TYRE SELECTION

FRONT	
SOFT	WHITE
MEDIUM	GREY
HARD	YELLOW

REAR	
SOFT	WHITE
MEDIUM	GREY
HARD	YELLOW

L M R

< MILD — TRACK SEVERITY — SEVERE >

1 ANDREA DOVIZIOSO
The world number two had the race under control for most of the 22 laps, never allowing Márquez or anyone else to get ahead for longer than he wanted. He won the race with his usual blend of aggression and intelligence.

2 MARC MÁRQUEZ
Pre-season concerns that neither Márquez nor Honda's 2019 RC213V would be at full strength for the first race of the year were dispelled. The reigning MotoGP king was in the thick of the fight throughout, looking as strong as ever.

3 CAL CRUTCHLOW
Bounced back from a very difficult few months, weeks and days to score a podium that no one expected, least of all the man himself. Battled as hard as ever and used Honda's new speed to keep Rins' Suzuki behind him.

4 ÁLEX RINS
The young Spaniard confirmed all the pre-season hype by riding with the lead pack and showing race-winning pace throughout most of the 22 laps. In the end he lost a podium to the superior straight-line speed of his main rivals.

5 VALENTINO ROSSI
A bit like Márquez, great things weren't expected of the seven-time MotoGP champ. A gloomy few weeks of pre-season testing had drastically lowered expectations, but, as always, once the lights were out, he was back in the game.

6 DANILO PETRUCCI
Had hopes of celebrating his first race as a factory rider from the podium; but his hopes were spoiled by a tyre gamble that went wrong. Nonetheless he did briefly hold third and proved he had the speed to run at the pointy end.

7 MAVERICK VIÑALES
A wheelie at the start cost him time and places, which created a problem he hadn't previously considered. With other riders around he couldn't use the lines he had used to take pole position. Another lesson learned.

8 JOAN MIR
An impressive debut, which had the former Moto3 champ in the lead group for a while, so he could learn from the more experienced riders around him. On the other hand, Losail is less technical than many MotoGP tracks.

9 TAKAAKI NAKAGAMI
Nakagami's pace on his year-old RC213V underlined the massive step that HRC made from its 2017 bike (which Nakagami raced last year) to its 2018 model. Chose a soft rear, which allowed him to fight hard from the very beginning.

10 ALEIX ESPARGARÓ
Aprilia's first effort at forgetting the nightmare of 2018 was a good one, with Espargaró coming home nine seconds off the win, equalling his best ride of last season. Lost time in the early stages despite choosing a soft rear.

11 FRANCO MORBIDELLI
Dropped from eighth to 12th on lap one, then recovered superbly to latch onto the back of the lead group. However, he had chosen the soft rear and by half-distance was struggling with grip. Unable to resist Espargaró's last-lap attack.

12 POL ESPARGARÓ
Spent the first half as part of a KTM freight train with Oliveira and Zarco. Only got the better of the Portuguese rookie on lap 15. Finished 12 seconds behind the winner, compared to KTM's 31 and 33 second gaps in 2017 and 2018.

RACE LAP CHART

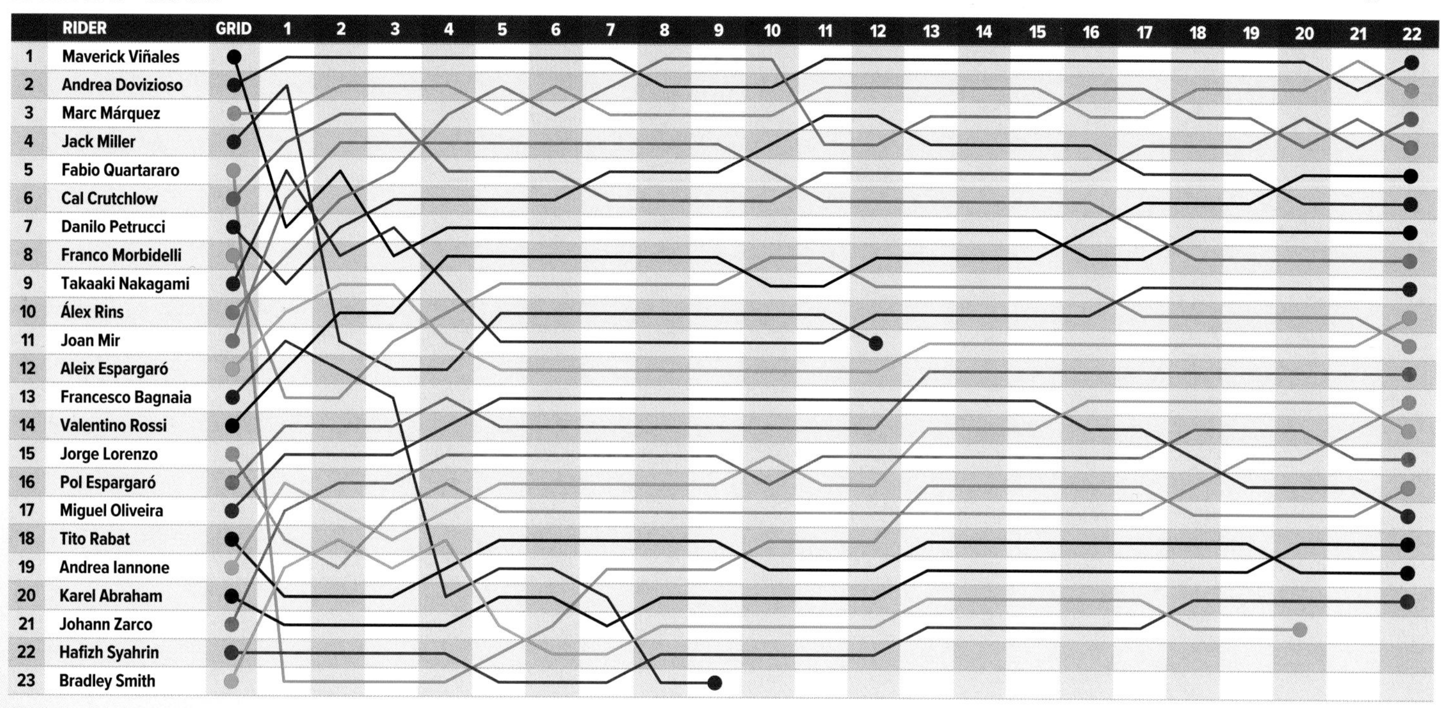

RACE RESULTS

	RIDER	NAT	TEAM	MACHINE	TIME	+GAP	TYRES
1	Andrea Dovizioso	ITA	Mission Winnow Ducati	DUCATI	42'36.902		M/M
2	Marc Márquez	SPA	Repsol Honda Team	HONDA	42'36.925	0.023	M/M
3	Cal Crutchlow	GBR	LCR Honda CASTROL	HONDA	42'37.222	0.320	M/M
4	Álex Rins	SPA	Team SUZUKI ECSTAR	SUZUKI	42'37.359	0.457	M/M
5	Valentino Rossi	ITA	Monster Energy Yamaha MotoGP	YAMAHA	42'37.502	0.600	M/M
6	Danilo Petrucci	ITA	Mission Winnow Ducati	DUCATI	42'39.222	2.320	S/S
7	Maverick Viñales	SPA	Monster Energy Yamaha MotoGP	YAMAHA	42'39.383	2.481	M/M
8	Joan Mir	SPA	Team SUZUKI ECSTAR	SUZUKI	42'41.990	5.088	M/S
9	Takaaki Nakagami	JPN	LCR Honda IDEMITSU	HONDA	42'44.308	7.406	M/S
10	Aleix Espargaró	SPA	Aprilia Racing Team Gresini	APRILIA	42'46.538	9.636	M/S
11	Franco Morbidelli	ITA	Petronas Yamaha SRT	YAMAHA	42'46.549	9.647	M/S
12	Pol Espargaró	SPA	Red Bull KTM Factory Racing	KTM	42'49.676	12.774	M/S
13	Jorge Lorenzo	SPA	Repsol Honda Team	HONDA	42'51.209	14.307	M/M
14	Andrea Iannone	ITA	Aprilia Racing Team Gresini	APRILIA	42'51.251	14.349	M/S
15	Johann Zarco	FRA	Red Bull KTM Factory Racing	KTM	42'51.995	15.093	M/M
16	Fabio Quartararo	FRA	Petronas Yamaha SRT	YAMAHA	42'52.807	15.905	M/S
17	Miguel Oliveira	POR	Red Bull KTM Tech 3	KTM	42'53.279	16.377	M/S
18	Karel Abraham	CZE	Reale Avintia Racing	DUCATI	42'59.874	22.972	M/S
19	Tito Rabat	SPA	Reale Avintia Racing	DUCATI	42'59.941	23.039	S/S
20	Hafizh Syahrin	MAL	Red Bull KTM Tech 3	KTM	43'20.144	43.242	M/S
NC	Bradley Smith	GBR	Aprilia Factory Racing	APRILIA	39'20.520	2 laps	S/S
NC	Jack Miller	AUS	Pramac Racing	DUCATI	23'23.795	10 laps	M/M
NC	Francesco Bagnaia	ITA	Pramac Racing	DUCATI	19'02.669	13 laps	M/S

CHAMPIONSHIP STANDINGS

	RIDER	NAT	TEAM	PTS
1	Andrea Dovizioso	ITA	Mission Winnow Ducati	25
2	Marc Márquez	SPA	Repsol Honda Team	20
3	Cal Crutchlow	GBR	LCR Honda CASTROL	16
4	Álex Rins	SPA	Team SUZUKI ECSTAR	13
5	Valentino Rossi	ITA	Monster Energy Yamaha MotoGP	11
6	Danilo Petrucci	ITA	Mission Winnow Ducati	10
7	Maverick Viñales	SPA	Monster Energy Yamaha MotoGP	9
8	Joan Mir	SPA	Team SUZUKI ECSTAR	8
9	Takaaki Nakagami	JPN	LCR Honda IDEMITSU	7
10	Aleix Espargaró	SPA	Aprilia Racing Team Gresini	6
11	Franco Morbidelli	ITA	Petronas Yamaha SRT	5
12	Pol Espargaró	SPA	Red Bull KTM Factory Racing	4
13	Jorge Lorenzo	SPA	Repsol Honda Team	3
14	Andrea Iannone	ITA	Aprilia Racing Team Gresini	2
15	Johann Zarco	FRA	Red Bull KTM Factory Racing	1
16	Fabio Quartararo	FRA	Petronas Yamaha SRT	
17	Miguel Oliveira	POR	Red Bull KTM Tech 3	
18	Karel Abraham	CZE	Reale Avintia Racing	
19	Tito Rabat	SPA	Reale Avintia Racing	
20	Hafizh Syahrin	MAL	Red Bull KTM Tech 3	
21	Bradley Smith	GBR	Aprilia Factory Racing	
22	Jack Miller	AUS	Pramac Racing	
23	Francesco Bagnaia	ITA	Pramac Racing	

13 JORGE LORENZO
His Honda debut wasn't what anyone had expected. An FP3 highside caused a broken rib (not confirmed until he got home), which left him sore and weak. In the race a slipping clutch dropped him down to 19th during the early laps.

14 ANDREA IANNONE
His struggles on Saturday evening put him on the seventh row, but convinced he would get better as the race wore on. He was correct, despite losing half of his RS-GP's aero at the first corner. Crashed on the slowdown lap.

15 JOHANN ZARCO
Two Saturday falls at the turn-two accident black spot left the Frenchman 21st on the grid and very much on the back foot. All things considered, 15th place, 15 seconds behind the winner, wasn't a bad first result on KTM's RC16.

16 FABIO QUARTARARO
Stalled his M1 on the warm-up lap, so had to start from pit lane, ruining the glow of his second-row start. With nothing to lose he rode a mighty race, setting the fastest lap, but by half-distance he was already running out of grip.

17 MIGUEL OLIVEIRA
Arguably, KTM's most impressive rider of the day. The MotoGP first-timer fought with fellow KRC16 rider Espargaró for more than half the race, only dropping his pace when his rear tyre lost grip and started chattering.

18 KAREL ABRAHAM
The Czech rider upgraded to a GP18 for the 2019 season and lined up on the grid between factory riders Iannone and Zarco. He completed the first lap in 21st position and made up places thanks to other people's problems.

19 TITO RABAT
Still limping heavily from his horrific Silverstone injury, the former Moto2 world champion had a difficult start to the 2019 season, losing so much grip from half-distance that his lap times dropped by a whole two seconds.

20 HAFIZH SYAHRIN
The Malaysian's first race on a KTM was in stark contrast to his first-ever MotoGP race the previous March, on an M1. He finished 43 seconds behind the winner compared to 23 seconds in 2018. Worst of all, he wasn't sure why.

NC BRADLEY SMITH
Didn't have the greatest of starts to his new job of Aprilia tester/racer. The former 125cc winner started from last place on the grid and spent much of the race with Syahrin, finally tumbling out of last position on the penultimate lap.

NC JACK MILLER
Had high hopes of a podium after missing the front row by less than a tenth and running second on the first lap. But then he lost time jettisoning his seat pad when it came loose. Eventually decided it was dangerous to continue.

NC FRANCESCO BAGNAIA
The Moto2 champion was confident of a great MotoGP debut, but his race went awry at the first corner where he made contact with another rider, losing his right aero set. He tried hard to keep going but it was impossible to continue.

MOTUL
DE LA REPÚBLICA
ARGENTINA
Termas de Río Hondo 2019
MOTUL
YAMAHA
REPSOL
MARQUEZ
PROSECCO DO

Smile for the mobile phone! Rossi, Marquez and Dovizioso line up for the obligatory podium 'selfie'

2 | ARGENTINA

GRAN PREMIO MOTUL DE LA REPÚBLICA ARGENTINA
TERMAS DE RÍO HONDO
29/30/31 MARCH

MÁRQUEZ ON A DIFFERENT PLANET

The world champion shared the podium with Rossi and Dovizioso, but he was on a different planet in the race

Three weeks after the closest top-15 in premier-class history Marc Márquez was so far ahead at Termas that his winning advantage would've covered the entire top-ten in Qatar.

This was the world champion on a mission. One year on from the chaotic 2018 Argentine GP, where he should have inflicted a similarly crushing defeat on his rivals, this was Márquez reminding everyone what he can do when everything goes to plan.

Márquez had a perfect weekend, with just one glitch, when the chain jumped off his RC213V's rear sprocket in FP4. A fault that would become a regular problem. He led all but one practice session and no one really expected to see which he way he went. His race pace – half a second a lap faster than the pursuing pack – was ominous. And even more concerning for his rivals was the way he raced away from them without the need to tread close to his limits.

"This is one of the most solid weekends of my MotoGP career," he said. "I understood the set-up and the tyres really well, I understood how to manage the race and I understood that the first laps were when I could make the biggest difference. At the end I wasn't pushing to my 100 percent, because I was trying to manage the risk."

CLOCKWISE, FROM TOP LEFT | *Dovizioso checks out Rossi during practice; Petrucci was smiling inside his helmet too, until he ran out of grip; Nakagami scored his best dry result on his 2018 RC213V; Dovizioso leads the charge through the rollercoaster turns 9/10 section, except Márquez is long gone; Crutchlow had another excellent weekend, ruined by the tiniest of errors; Gigi Dall'Igna and Paolo Ciabatti tell the media why Ducati's swingarm attachment is a tyre cooler, not a downforce device; Aleix Espargaró took his second consecutive top-ten – more importantly winning a duel with his younger brother.*

By the end of the first lap Márquez was already one second ahead. By lap five he was four seconds in front. By half-distance the TV cameras had given up trying to get him in the same shot as the pack battling to be first loser. No wonder that runner-up Rossi congratulated Márquez in the podium anteroom – the nine-time world champion fully understood the enormity of the Spaniard's 45th MotoGP victory, his biggest on a dry track.

"Marc won like this for many reasons," explained third-placed Andrea Dovizioso. "The low grip, the track layout, the Honda's style and his style allow him to do something very special here."

Honda's hard-won top-speed advantage didn't hurt either. For the second race in a row the RC213V was the fastest motorcycle. In 2018 the RC213V was fastest in just four races. In 2017 and 2016 the bike never topped the speed charts.

Rossi and Dovizioso had a thrilling last-lap shootout for second place, but they were so far behind the leader they were almost in another race. Shortly after half-distance Rossi's YZR-M1 seemed to have once again used up its tyres, which allowed Dovizioso past. Cleverly, Rossi stayed third, rather than counter-attacking, which allowed Dovizioso to set an interrupted pace that eventually drew the pair away from Jack Miller, Álex Rins, Danilo Petrucci, Maverick Viñales and Franco Morbidelli.

Thus Rossi had Dovizioso all to himself on the final lap. He used his M1's superior corner speed to ride round the outside of the Ducati through the long, sweeping turn six, which put him on the inside as the pair braked for the turn seven right-hander. It was a perfectly judged move and the perfect way to mark the 23rd anniversary of his first Grand Prix outing, the 125cc Malaysian GP at Shah Alam, on 31st March 1996.

"When I started it was like another era – it was black and white on the television!" laughed the 40-year-old after ending his longest absence from the podium since his Ducati days. "I have won a lot of races and a lot of championships. Then you come to a point when it's more difficult because younger and stronger opponents arrive. So at that moment you have to decide. Do you prefer to stay at home and look at your trophies and be happy about that? Or do you prefer to continue fighting because you enjoy it? I think this is my case."

Dovizioso wasn't happy about losing second place but he was otherwise delighted with his race. "Last year I was minimum one second per lap slower than today, so our improvement is huge," he said, attributing the improvement to the GP19's ability to change direction better, especially at high speed.

At the start of the final lap the five men disputing fourth place were separated by just one second. Rins had the best speed, having charged through from 16th on the grid to catch the group at two-thirds distance and get to the front with two laps left. But he didn't stay there for long because Miller quickly came back at him to secure fourth, while Petrucci slipped to sixth.

RULES AND RACING CAN BE CRUEL

Termas de Rio Hondo is Cal Crutchlow's best circuit. The Briton won the 2018 Argentina Grand Prix and finished on the podium in 2015 and 2017. And he should have stood on the podium once again in 2019.

Crutchlow's practice pace had him down as the only man capable of keeping Márquez in sight. Only in qualifying did he falter, when he lacked grip in his second run, which left him on the third row. He started well, moving up to sixth after the first lap, but two laps later his weekend was ruined when he got a "ride through" message on his dash. He had jumped the start.

Crutchlow didn't agree, but he took his punishment, re-joining the race dead last. With a clear road ahead he was the second fastest man on track and by the flag had worked his way up to 13th, 31 seconds behind Márquez. His penalty had cost him at least 26 seconds.

Chief steward Freddie Spencer took some flak from some people – including Crutchlow – for sanctioning what had been the slightest of movements before the lights went out. But the verdict and punishment were out of his hands, because the rules don't give the stewards the chance to use their judgement in such cases.

If Crutchlow had raced in a different era it might have been a different story, because the old rules allowed Race Direction to

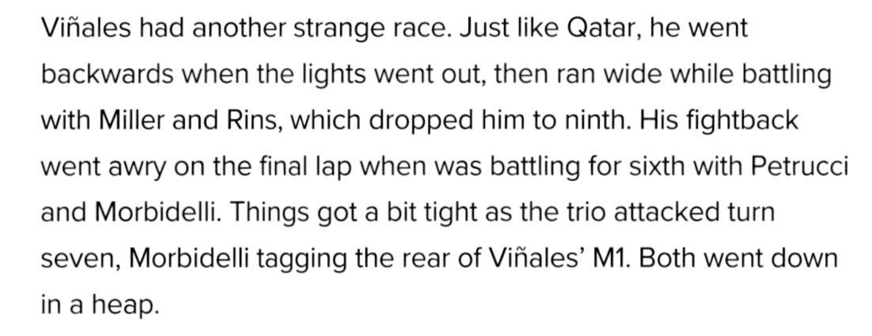

Viñales had another strange race. Just like Qatar, he went backwards when the lights went out, then ran wide while battling with Miller and Rins, which dropped him to ninth. His fightback went awry on the final lap when was battling for sixth with Petrucci and Morbidelli. Things got a bit tight as the trio attacked turn seven, Morbidelli tagging the rear of Viñales' M1. Both went down in a heap.

"I cannot understand how we lost so much grip going into the race," said Viñales, the only rider to run the soft front. "Honestly, it's been two and a half years that I've had this problem. Australia last year was the only time I've had grip. The feeling compared to morning warm-up was like I had really old tyres. I tried to change everything to be fast: I tried braking deep, braking early, opening the gas more smoothly, opening the gas more aggressively. And I tried all the switches, all the maps, but the result was the same."

Viñales wasn't the only one wondering what he needed to do to get better when he boarded the plane to Buenos Aires the next morning. The Circuit of Americas was next and how would anyone beat Márquez there?

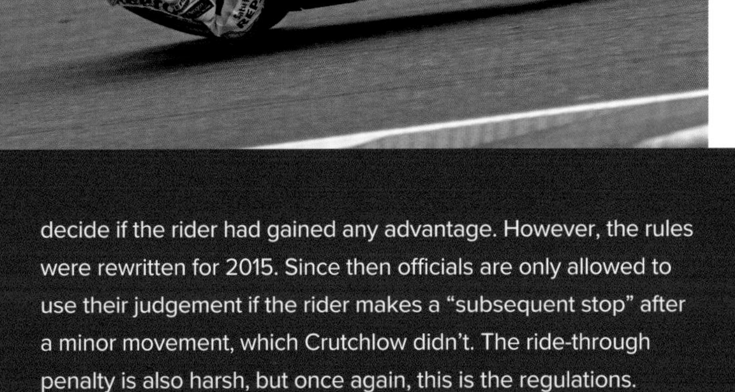

CLOCKWISE FROM TOP LEFT | *Márquez was overjoyed by his biggest dry win yet; old but gold, Rossi was just as happy with his perfectly judged last-lap lunge into second place; Miller was getting closer and closer to the podium; Márquez does a lot of stretching as part of his fitness and safety regime; Lorenzo activated his pit-lane speed-limiter at the start and suddenly found himself in last place; the Termas de Rio Hondo crowd is one of the rowdiest of the year and loved Rossi's first podium of his 20th season in the premier class.*

decide if the rider had gained any advantage. However, the rules were rewritten for 2015. Since then officials are only allowed to use their judgement if the rider makes a "subsequent stop" after a minor movement, which Crutchlow didn't. The ride-through penalty is also harsh, but once again, this is the regulations.

Despite his anger, Crutchlow didn't want the rules rewritten. "I don't want the rules changed now because riders who've done the same thing as me won't get punished!" he said two weeks later at COTA. "I'll just make sure it never happens again to me."

Crutchlow might have learned his lesson but Joan Mir and Maverick Viñales hadn't learned theirs. At COTA both jumped the start and both were given ride-through penalties.

2 | ARGENTINA

GRAN PREMIO MOTUL DE LA REPÚBLICA ARGENTINA

TERMAS DE RÍO HONDO
29/30/31 MARCH

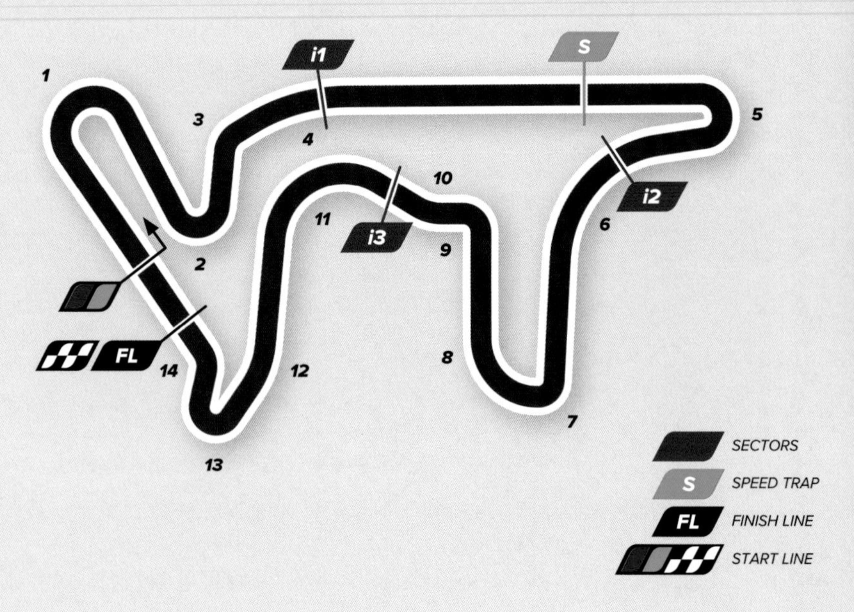

QUALIFYING RESULTS

	RIDER	NAT	TEAM	MACHINE	QP	TIME	GAP 1ST	PREV
1	Marc Márquez	SPA	Repsol Honda Team	HONDA	Q2	1'38.304		
2	Maverick Viñales	SPA	Monster Energy Yamaha MotoGP	YAMAHA	Q2	1'38.458	0.154	0.154
3	Andrea Dovizioso	ITA	Mission Winnow Ducati	DUCATI	Q2	1'38.468	0.164	0.010
4	Valentino Rossi	ITA	Monster Energy Yamaha MotoGP	YAMAHA	Q2	1'38.545	0.241	0.077
5	Jack Miller	AUS	Pramac Racing	DUCATI	Q2	1'38.548	0.244	0.003
6	Franco Morbidelli	ITA	Petronas Yamaha SRT	YAMAHA	Q2	1'38.886	0.582	0.338
7	Fabio Quartararo	FRA	Petronas Yamaha SRT	YAMAHA	Q2	1'38.897	0.593	0.011
8	Cal Crutchlow	GBR	LCR Honda CASTROL	HONDA	Q2	1'38.955	0.651	0.058
9	Takaaki Nakagami**	JPN	LCR Honda IDEMITSU	HONDA	Q2	1'39.038	0.734	0.083
10	Danilo Petrucci	ITA	Mission Winnow Ducati	DUCATI	Q2	1'39.093	0.789	0.055
11	Pol Espargaró**	SPA	Red Bull KTM Factory Racing	KTM	Q2	1'39.489	1.185	0.396
12	Jorge Lorenzo	SPA	Repsol Honda Team	HONDA	Q2	1'39.520	1.216	0.031
13	Aleix Espargaró	SPA	Aprilia Racing Team Gresini	APRILIA	Q1	1'39.288	*0.224	0.071
14	Miguel Oliveira	POR	Red Bull KTM Tech 3	KTM	Q1	1'39.298	*0.234	0.010
15	Karel Abraham	CZE	Reale Avintia Racing	DUCATI	Q1	1'39.331	*0.267	0.033
16	Álex Rins	SPA	Team SUZUKI ECSTAR	SUZUKI	Q1	1'39.384	*0.320	0.053
17	Francesco Bagnaia	ITA	Pramac Racing	DUCATI	Q1	1'39.387	*0.323	0.003
18	Johann Zarco	FRA	Red Bull KTM Factory Racing	KTM	Q1	1'39.571	*0.507	0.184
19	Joan Mir	SPA	Team SUZUKI ECSTAR	SUZUKI	Q1	1'39.605	*0.541	0.034
20	Tito Rabat	SPA	Reale Avintia Racing	DUCATI	Q1	1'39.978	*0.914	0.373
21	Hafizh Syahrin	MAL	Red Bull KTM Tech 3	KTM	Q1	1'40.053	*0.989	0.075
22	Andrea Iannone	ITA	Aprilia Racing Team Gresini	APRILIA	Q1	1'40.118	*1.054	0.065

** Gap to the fastest rider in the Q1 session* *** Went forward from Q1 to Q2* *Track severity = Wear + Temperature + Load*

GRAND PRIX INFORMATION

TRACK INFORMATION			
2019 WINNER	Marc Márquez		
CIRCUIT LENGTH	4.8 km	2.99 miles	
LAPS	25		
RACE DISTANCE	120.2 KM	74.8 miles	
ALL TIME LAP RECORD	1'37.683	177.1 Km/h	Marc Márquez (2014)
BEST RACE LAP	1'39.019	174.7 Km/h	Valentino Rossi (2015)
RACE CONDITION	Dry		
AIR	27°C		
HUMIDITY	75%		
GROUND	41°C		

TYRE SELECTION

FRONT	
SOFT	WHITE
MEDIUM	GREY
HARD	YELLOW

REAR	
SOFT	WHITE
MEDIUM	GREY
HARD	YELLOW

L M R

< MILD — TRACK SEVERITY — SEVERE >

1 MARC MÁRQUEZ
The world champion called this a perfect day and he wasn't wrong. He knew that if he got the holeshot he could lay down a pace that would leave his rivals floundering. When he feels that sweet with the bike no one else stands a chance.

2 VALENTINO ROSSI
Was as relieved as he was delighted to climb a podium for the first time since July 2018, especially after crashing out of top-three results at Sepang and Valencia. His braking was pure perfection, to within one centimetre.

3 ANDREA DOVIZIOSO
Termas has never been kind to the Ducati, so the Italian was happy to be in the podium fight and get 16 points. His main issue was higher-than-expected rear-tyre consumption, which left him unable to try shaking off Rossi.

4 JACK MILLER
This was effectively Miller's first race of the year, following his AWOL seat pad incident in Qatar, so he lacked experience fighting with his 2019 rivals and lost a lot of time with Petrucci and Morbidelli in the mid-stages of the race.

5 ÁLEX RINS
His race was compromised by a lowly grid position – he struggles to get the most out of new tyres in qualifying – which left him 12th on lap one. He fought back to join the lead pack, but lost out to Miller in the last two laps.

6 DANILO PETRUCCI
Mistakes in qualifying left him with a lot of work to do. Eighth after lap one he spent a lot of time with Miller and Morbidelli. He was fourth with two laps to go, but finally didn't have enough grip left to fend off Miller and Rins.

7 TAKAAKI NAKAGAMI
Honda's latest Japanese MotoGP star continued climbing his impressive learning curve to score his best dry-track result, albeit four seconds behind Petrucci. Gained two places on the final lap when Morbidelli and Viñales fell.

8 FABIO QUARTARARO
After balancing out the ignominy of his Qatar grid mishap by setting the fastest lap of the race he had his first normal MotoGP outing. He spent much of the 25 laps chasing Nakagami after getting the better of Aleix Espargaró.

9 ALEIX ESPARGARÓ
Made a last minute tyre change, from the medium rear to the soft. His planned attack on Quartararo came to nothing when the tyre lost grip and he ran into serious wheelspin problems. Nevertheless, was satisfied with ninth.

10 POL ESPARGARÓ
Spent the race chasing his brother, despite lacking grip. Got in front with a few laps to go, but Aleix successfully counter-attacked on the last lap. However, this was a good result at a track that had never been kind to KTM.

RACE LAP CHART

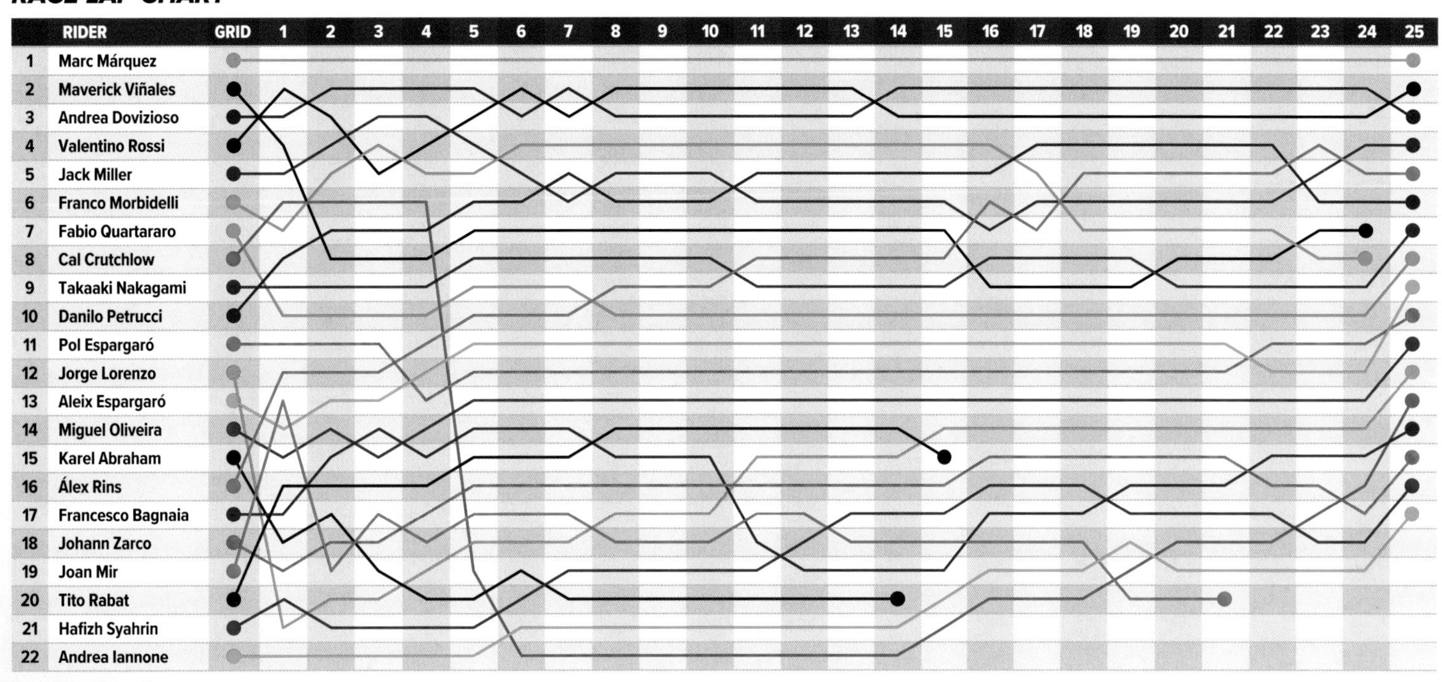

RACE RESULTS

	RIDER	NAT	TEAM	MACHINE	TIME	+ GAP	TYRES
1	Marc Márquez	SPA	Repsol Honda Team	HONDA	41'43.688		H/S
2	Valentino Rossi	ITA	Monster Energy Yamaha MotoGP	YAMAHA	41'53.504	9.816	H/M
3	Andrea Dovizioso	ITA	Mission Winnow Ducati	DUCATI	41'54.218	10.530	H/S
4	Jack Miller	AUS	Pramac Racing	DUCATI	41'55.828	12.140	M/S
5	Álex Rins	SPA	Team SUZUKI ECSTAR	SUZUKI	41'56.251	12.563	H/S
6	Danilo Petrucci	ITA	Mission Winnow Ducati	DUCATI	41'57.438	13.750	H/S
7	Takaaki Nakagami	JPN	LCR Honda IDEMITSU	HONDA	42'01.848	18.160	H/S
8	Fabio Quartararo	FRA	Petronas Yamaha SRT	YAMAHA	42'04.091	20.403	H/M
9	Aleix Espargaró	SPA	Aprilia Racing Team Gresini	APRILIA	42'08.980	25.292	H/S
10	Pol Espargaró	SPA	Red Bull KTM Factory Racing	KTM	42'09.367	25.679	H/M
11	Miguel Oliveira	POR	Red Bull KTM Tech 3	KTM	42'09.543	25.855	H/M
12	Jorge Lorenzo	SPA	Repsol Honda Team	HONDA	42'11.185	27.497	H/S
13	Cal Crutchlow+	GBR	LCR Honda CASTROL	HONDA	42'15.086	31.398	H/M
14	Francesco Bagnaia	ITA	Pramac Racing	DUCATI	42'16.581	32.893	H/S
15	Johann Zarco	FRA	Red Bull KTM Factory Racing	KTM	42'17.060	33.372	H/M
16	Hafizh Syahrin	MAL	Red Bull KTM Tech 3	KTM	42'19.233	35.545	H/M
17	Andrea Iannone	ITA	Aprilia Racing Team Gresini	APRILIA	42'21.926	38.238	H/S
NC	Maverick Viñales	SPA	Monster Energy Yamaha MotoGP	YAMAHA	40'16.294	1 lap	S/S
NC	Franco Morbidelli	ITA	Petronas Yamaha SRT	YAMAHA	40'16.485	1 lap	H/M
NC	Joan Mir	SPA	Team SUZUKI ECSTAR	SUZUKI	36'01.267	4 laps	H/S
NC	Tito Rabat	SPA	Reale Avintia Racing	UCATI	25'19.982	10 laps	H/S
NC	Karel Abraham	CZE	Reale Avintia Racing	DUCATI	23'43.512	11 laps	H/S

+ FIM MotoGP Stewards Race penalties - Cal Crutchlow : Jump start, ride-through penalty

CHAMPIONSHIP STANDINGS

	RIDER	NAT	TEAM	PTS
1	Marc Márquez	SPA	Repsol Honda Team	45
2	Andrea Dovizioso	ITA	Mission Winnow Ducati	41
3	Valentino Rossi	ITA	Monster Energy Yamaha MotoGP	31
4	Álex Rins	SPA	Team SUZUKI ECSTAR	24
5	Danilo Petrucci	ITA	Mission Winnow Ducati	20
6	Cal Crutchlow	GBR	LCR Honda CASTROL	19
7	Takaaki Nakagami	JPN	LCR Honda IDEMITSU	16
8	Jack Miller	AUS	Pramac Racing	13
9	Aleix Espargaró	SPA	Aprilia Racing Team Gresini	13
10	Pol Espargaró	SPA	Red Bull KTM Factory Racing	10
11	Maverick Viñales	SPA	Monster Energy Yamaha MotoGP	9
12	Fabio Quartararo	FRA	Petronas Yamaha SRT	8
13	Joan Mir	SPA	Team SUZUKI ECSTAR	8
14	Jorge Lorenzo	SPA	Repsol Honda Team	7
15	Miguel Oliveira	POR	Red Bull KTM Tech 3	5
16	Franco Morbidelli	ITA	Petronas Yamaha SRT	5
17	Andrea Iannone	ITA	Aprilia Racing Team Gresini	2
18	Francesco Bagnaia	ITA	Pramac Racing	2
19	Johann Zarco	FRA	Red Bull KTM Factory Racing	2
20	Hafizh Syahrin	MAL	Red Bull KTM Tech 3	
21	Karel Abraham	CZE	Reale Avintia Racing	
22	Tito Rabat	SPA	Reale Avintia Racing	
23	Bradley Smith	GBR	Aprilia Factory Racing	

11 MIGUEL OLIVEIRA
Undoubtedly one of the rides – if not the ride – of the race. In only his second MotoGP outing the Portuguese rider harried Espargaró throughout, crossing the finish line less than two tenths behind the factory KTM.

12 JORGE LORENZO
The black cloud of ill luck still hung over Lorenzo. He made it into Q2 for the first time with Honda, but struggled when the track lost grip. At the start of the race he engaged his pit-lane speed-limiter by mistake and was last away.

13 CAL CRUTCHLOW
There was no doubt Crutchlow had the pace to finish in second place. Like Márquez he can ride a racetrack very well when there's not much grip. However, bike racing is all about avoiding even the tiniest of mistakes.

14 FRANCESCO BAGNAIA
The Italian rookie's Qatar DNF made this his first full MotoGP race. Fought his way into the points at one-third distance, but then made a mistake that cost him several positions. After that it was a big battle to get back into the top-15.

15 JOHANN ZARCO
Nearly collided with the speed-limited Lorenzo at the start, which put him near the back. Made up some places but his RC16 was too physical to ride, so he ran out of energy and lost a duel with Bagnaia during the final few laps.

16 HAFIZH SYAHRIN
Finished 17 seconds closer to the podium than he had in his humbling first race on the KTM, so the Malaysian was at least starting to feel comfier on the hard-to-handle bike. Suffered rear-grip loss from three-quarters distance.

17 ANDREA IANNONE
Got confused in practice and took the wrong direction on set-up, which left him 22nd fastest and last on the grid. Bizarrely, he found his RS-GP's performance reduced as the grip increased. Finished a lonely last.

NC MAVERICK VIÑALES
Once again, his weekend went perfectly, until Sunday afternoon. He qualified second fastest and yet by lap two he had dropped to eighth, even though he had started with soft tyres. Got taken out by Morbidelli on the last lap.

NC FRANCO MORBIDELLI
Qualified on the second row and enjoyed riding with mentor Rossi, Dovizioso, Miller, Petrucci and others. On the final lap it got busy between the Italian, Petrucci and Viñales, whose rear tyre he tagged, bringing them both down.

NC JOAN MIR
Found Termas more difficult than Losail. Tried to go with Rins in the first laps but couldn't run that pace and soon encountered a major rear-tyre issue which forced him to withdraw from a race for the first time in his GP career.

NC TITO RABAT
Had a complicated weekend, but managed to get his GP18 sorted out in time for warm-up, which made him more optimistic for the race. Was just inside the points when he lost the front at turn one, while behind Lorenzo.

NC KAREL ABRAHAM
Qualified five places better than he had in Qatar, so had expectations of fighting for some world championship points. But it was not to be. He lost the front at turn one, the lap before his team-mate fell at the same place.

NYALAKAN NYALI
ECSTAR
MICHELIN
SUZUKI
AKRAPOVIC
MOTUL
motogp.com
official website

No surprise that the entire Suzuki squad was ecstatic with their victory; the factory's third in the MotoGP era.

3 | USA

RED BULL GRAND PRIX OF THE AMERICAS
CIRCUIT OF THE AMERICAS
12/13/14 APRIL

RINS WINS!

Márquez was expected to continue his unbeaten run at COTA. Instead Rins took his first MotoGP victory

Suzuki and Álex Rins had been ready to win a race in the latter half of 2018; it just never quite happened. Together they finished on the podium at three of the last four rounds, so it was only a matter of time before the ever-improving GSX-RR and the young Spaniard's burgeoning talent made it to the top step.

Perhaps Rins would've had to wait a while longer for his first premier-class success if Marc Márquez hadn't slid off, but there's no arguing with that old adage: to finish first, first you must finish.

Rins has always been a bit of a stealthy rider, who makes progress through the pack barely noticed, largely because he's so clean and smooth on the bike. Certainly by Sunday morning at COTA there was no sign that the 23-year-old would be a contender. He had ended Friday sixth quickest and qualified seventh quickest, at best half a second off the top. And yet the first two days had been confusing, with riders troubled by the bumpy COTA asphalt and the stormy Texas weather, with FP3 cancelled after warnings of lightning strikes.

Whatever the circumstances, another Márquez victory seemed inevitable. The reigning world champion had his first MotoGP success at the inaugural Americas GP in 2013 and had never been beaten there since. Indeed he hadn't been bettered on U.S. asphalt since his first visit on a Moto2 bike in 2011. Most American

CLOCKWISE, FROM TOP LEFT | *Dovizioso found the GP19 hard work through COTA's bumpy twists and turns; MSMA representative Takanao Tsubouchi with legends 'King' Kenny Roberts and 1969 250cc world champion Kel Carruthers; rookie Quartararo was getting faster and faster; it's only the first corner, but Márquez, Rossi, Rins, Miller and Crutchlow are already on the edge; Rossi celebrates with Kevin Schwantz, who helped design COTA; Petrucci mustered his usual aggression but missed the podium again; this time Márquez couldn't save it when he lost the front.*

'NOW WE HAVE A VERY BALANCED BIKE, SO WE CAN FIGHT AT MOST OF THE TRACKS'
ÁLEX RINS

tracks turn left, which delights Márquez, who spends a lot of time turning left around dirt-track ovals.

On Saturday afternoon he maintained his unbeaten qualifying record at COTA, taking pole by almost three tenths from Valentino Rossi, whose rejuvenation continued apace. Last man on the front row was Cal Crutchlow, keen for some kind of revenge for what had happened in Argentina. The Italian and Briton got better starts, but Márquez did them both on the brakes into turn one. And that was surely that.

By lap three he was 1.2 seconds ahead. By lap eight he was 3.7 seconds in front. And then it happened. Braking from over 340kmh/211mph to 67kmh/41mph for the turn 12 left-hander Márquez lost the front. And this time even he couldn't save it. To add insult to injury, he toppled over while trying to restart his RC213V. All this simply confirmed the even older adage that all good things come to an end.

"I didn't do anything stupid – I wasn't over my limit," he explained later. "I was riding very smoothly, trying to save the front tyre. But mistakes happen, we are human."

The huge roar from the crowd had less to do with Márquez's exit than with the fact that Rossi now led the race, with the chance of scoring his first dry-weather victory since Barcelona in 2016.

Earlier the veteran had been duelling for second with Crutchlow, who lost the front at turn 11 three laps before his fellow HRC rider went down. Crutchlow also admitted he had made a mistake, but added that he had been having problems. "Our bike is unstable in braking," he said. "It snaps around in the braking zone, then when it re-grips you can't keep control of the brake lever." Most likely this also contributed to Márquez's downfall. HRC's misery was complete when Jorge Lorenzo's RC213V stopped, with a suspected electronics glitch.

At the end of lap nine few people were bothered about the answer to questions regarding HRC's woes. Rossi was in front, a whole second ahead of Rins, who had got the better of Jack Miller moments before Márquez's howler. However, the unexpected prospect of a first victory stirred Rins to greater things. "When Álex saw Marc go down he clicked up a gear," said Miller.

Lap after lap Rins closed on Rossi, who try as he might could not muster the pace to resist the youngster's advance. With four laps to go the gap between hunter and hunted was down to two tenths. And then Rins was past, using the GSX-RR's stunning corner-entry performance to slice past the Yamaha through COTA's slalom section.

Rossi undertook one over-optimistic counter-attack later the same lap, which ran him so wide that he realised it was time to wave the white flag. "Alex rode very well," he said. "He had two or three places where he had very good lines to avoid the bumps and he was very strong in braking. The Suzuki is good now and he can take it to the limit. For sure he's a title opponent."

COTA'S RODEO ROLLERCOASTER

MotoGP tracks mostly get smoother and smoother, as the championship's venues undergo upgrading. This is good, although most people in the paddock agree that the end goal shouldn't be 19 billiard-table smooth racetracks. A few bumps and camber changes add to the challenge for both riders and engineers. After the COTA race Rossi commented that part of Rins' winning secret was his ability to find a smooth way between the bumps; that's a talent worth having.

The bumps were a particular challenge at COTA; because these weren't the usual ripples caused by Formula 1 downforce and general deterioration, but rolling undulations created by forces deep beneath the ground. And they were at their worst on the back straight.

Many riders had tank-slappers at high speed, including Jack Miller. "I got a huge headshake in morning warm-up; I thought it was game over. The bike started tank-slapping on me and I literally had no idea what was going on. My feet came off the 'pegs and when I got to the end of the straight the brakes were gone; I had to pull the lever six times."

The riders also used their talents to make the most of the bumpy corners, the worst of which was turn two.

"Going into turn two you roll off early, then get back on the gas and accelerate over the bumps to get the chain force back," added Miller. "Otherwise the bike gets all flopped out. But in

Rins started from row three, an improvement on his fourth- and sixth-row starts at the first two races, all due to his struggles to get the best from new tyres during qualifying.

"For sure we need to do better in qualifying," he beamed after taking Suzuki's third MotoGP victory, its second with the GSX-RR and its first since Maverick Viñales' Silverstone 2016 success. "Suzuki have made a big step since last year – the team gives me good vibrations and now we have a very balanced bike, so we can fight at most of the tracks."

Miller was delighted with his first dry-weather podium, just ahead of a hard-charging Dovizioso. "Since we glued the seat on properly after Qatar it's been roses," laughed the Aussie, despite suffering some discomfort after one of the most physically tough races of the season. "My groin is hanging off now! Trying to change direction through that first sector really gets you."

Dovizioso had been thwarted by Saturday's iffy weather and failed to make it into Q2 for the first time since Jerez 2017. He fought back from 13th to fourth; enough to fly home to Europe leading the world championship.

"We always struggle at COTA, but our situation is much better compared to last year," he said. "And when you take a good result from a bad situation it makes you confident. Also, Marc's crash shows he doesn't have everything under control."

CLOCKWISE FROM TOP LEFT | *Miller reflects on his hard-won and first dry-weather podium; the paddock turned out in strength to honour the late, great Nicky Hayden; Hayden's father Earl embraces Freddie Spencer, another American world champion; Lorenzo hobbles back to his garage after his RC213V quit during qualifying; Morbidelli scored his best MotoGP result yet; Rins chases Viñales and Bagnaia through COTA's coolest corner – the daunting, high-speed turn 11. As always, his corner speed was super quick.*

doing that you're going through the most crucial part of the corner with the gas on, which takes the load off the front. Towards the end of the race I nearly lost the front three or four times there; I was on my elbow big time."

The track also required suspension technicians to work their magic, but there wasn't much they could do, without losing performance in other areas.

"You can make the bike more compliant," said Öhlins racing manager Mats Larsson. "But when you run softer spring rates, a bit more preload and softer damping the bike becomes too much of a streetbike, so it's difficult to slide and eats the tyres. Really, it's down to the riders – they can't sit like couch potatoes, they have to stand on the 'pegs."

3 | USA

RED BULL GRAND PRIX OF THE AMERICAS

CIRCUIT OF THE AMERICAS

12/13/14 APRIL

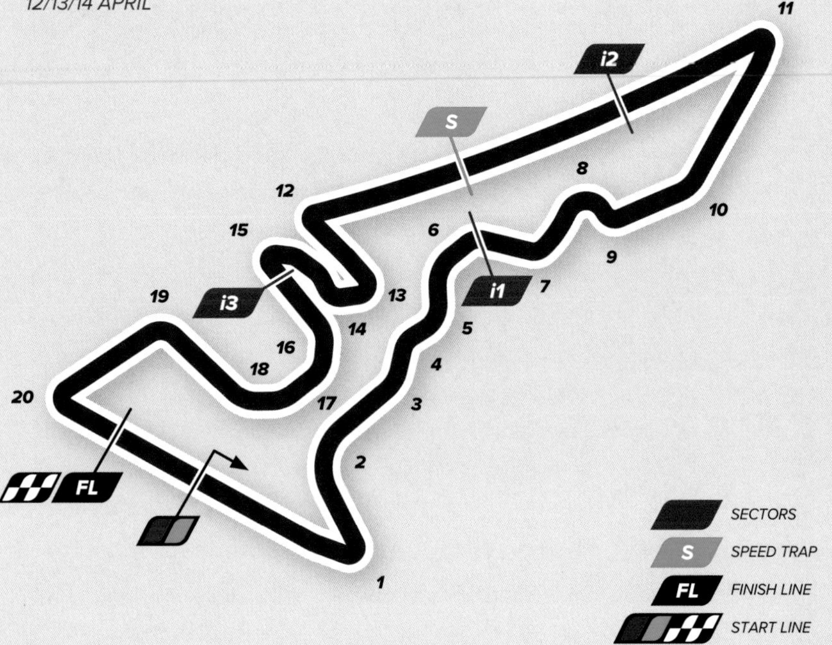

QUALIFYING RESULTS

	RIDER	NAT	TEAM	MACHINE	QP/TIME		GAP 1ST/PREV	
1	Marc Márquez	SPA	Repsol Honda Team	HONDA	Q2	2'03.787		
2	Valentino Rossi	ITA	Monster Energy Yamaha MotoGP	YAMAHA	Q2	2'04.060	0.273	0.273
3	Cal Crutchlow	GBR	LCR Honda CASTROL	HONDA	Q2	2'04.147	0.360	0.087
4	Jack Miller	AUS	Pramac Racing	DUCATI	Q2	2'04.416	0.629	0.269
5	Pol Espargaró	SPA	Red Bull KTM Factory Racing	KTM	Q2	2'04.472	0.685	0.056
6	Maverick Viñales	SPA	Monster Energy Yamaha MotoGP	YAMAHA	Q2	2'04.489	0.702	0.017
7	Álex Rins	SPA	Team SUZUKI ECSTAR	SUZUKI	Q2	2'04.534	0.747	0.045
8	Danilo Petrucci**	ITA	Mission Winnow Ducati	DUCATI	Q2	2'04.696	0.909	0.162
9	Fabio Quartararo	FRA	Petronas Yamaha SRT	YAMAHA	Q2	2'04.941	1.154	0.245
10	Franco Morbidelli	ITA	Petronas Yamaha SRT	YAMAHA	Q2	2'05.278	1.491	0.337
11	Jorge Lorenzo**	SPA	Repsol Honda Team	HONDA	Q2	2'05.383	1.596	0.105
12	Francesco Bagnaia	ITA	Pramac Racing	DUCATI	Q2	2'05.887	2.100	0.504
13	Andrea Dovizioso	ITA	Mission Winnow Ducati	DUCATI	Q1	2'05.907	*0.052	0.016
14	Joan Mir	SPA	Team SUZUKI ECSTAR	SUZUKI	Q1	2'06.147	*0.292	0.240
15	Takaaki Nakagami	JPN	LCR Honda IDEMITSU	HONDA	Q1	2'06.324	*0.469	0.177
16	Aleix Espargaró	SPA	Aprilia Racing Team Gresini	APRILIA	Q1	2'06.464	*0.609	0.140
17	Andrea Iannone	ITA	Aprilia Racing Team Gresini	APRILIA	Q1	2'06.527	*0.672	0.063
18	Miguel Oliveira	POR	Red Bull KTM Tech 3	KTM	Q1	2'06.543	*0.688	0.016
19	Johann Zarco	FRA	Red Bull KTM Factory Racing	KTM	Q1	2'06.824	*0.969	0.281
20	Karel Abraham	CZE	Reale Avintia Racing	DUCATI	Q1	2'07.129	*1.274	0.305
21	Hafizh Syahrin	MAL	Red Bull KTM Tech 3	KTM	Q1	2'07.308	*1.453	0.179
22	Tito Rabat	SPA	Reale Avintia Racing	DUCATI	Q1	2'07.417	*1.562	0.109

** Gap to the fastest rider in the Q1 session   ** Went forward from Q1 to Q2   Track severity = Wear + Temperature + Load*

GRAND PRIX INFORMATION

TRACK INFORMATION			
2019 WINNER	Álex Rins		
CIRCUIT LENGTH	5.5 km	3.43 miles	
LAPS	20		
RACE DISTANCE	110.3 KM	68.6 miles	
ALL TIME LAP RECORD	2'02.135	162.4 Km/h	Marc Márquez (2015)
BEST RACE LAP	2'03.575	160.6 Km/h	Marc Márquez (2014)
RACE CONDITION	Dry		
AIR	21°C		
HUMIDITY	32%		
GROUND	39°C		

TYRE SELECTION

FRONT	
SOFT	WHITE
MEDIUM	GREY
HARD	YELLOW

REAR	
SOFT	WHITE
MEDIUM	GREY
HARD	YELLOW

L M R

< MILD — TRACK SEVERITY — SEVERE >

1 ÁLEX RINS
Applied his personal turbocharger when Márquez went down and he realised that a first MotoGP victory was finally within his grasp. Despite the increased pressure he rode as smoothly and as cleanly as ever.

2 VALENTINO ROSSI
A second-consecutive podium suggested that Yamaha really were back in the game. He attributed the M1's new-found speed to detailed tweaks to engine-mapping, engine-braking, engine smoothness and overall bike balance.

3 JACK MILLER
Did what he'd been threatening for a while: climb the podium for the first time after a dry MotoGP race. Kept his 100 percent 2019 top-five grid record and finished top Ducati at a track that's not kind to the Desmosedici.

4 ANDREA DOVIZIOSO
A masterful afternoon of damage limitation. The world number two was helped in a big way by Ducati's holeshot device, which took him from 13th to seventh at the first corner. Kept his head and ended the race leading the points.

5 FRANCO MORBIDELLI
Scored his first top-five finish, bettering his eighth-place result at the 2018 Australian GP. Recovered well from his worst qualifying result of the year to get the better of Viñales and then keep Petrucci behind him.

6 DANILO PETRUCCI
In the final stages the Italian started bridging the gap to Morbidelli, but then had a couple of front-tyre lock-ups and decided discretion was the better part of valour. A lot of riders suffered the same front instability issues.

7 FABIO QUARTARARO
The rookie achieved his best result so far, albeit considerably further behind the winner than he had been at the first two races; this was to be expected at such a technical track. Learned a lot when he was riding with Petrucci.

8 POL ESPARGARÓ
Fiery riding in Q2 put him fifth on the grid – a best-ever for KTM – and he bettered his 2019 race time by 16 seconds, while the race itself was 6.5 seconds faster. Eased off on the final lap and was nearly caught by Bagnaia.

9 FRANCESCO BAGNAIA
The Italian won the 2018 Moto2 race at COTA, even though the track isn't one of his favourites. Riding a bike that also doesn't like the layout he acquitted himself well, recording his first top-ten finish in the premier class.

10 TAKAAKI NAKAGAMI
Rode to his fourth consecutive top-ten finish, despite struggling to find grip in the early laps. Once he had got into his groove he ran a decent pace and during the final laps began closing down Espargaró and Bagnaia.

RACE LAP CHART

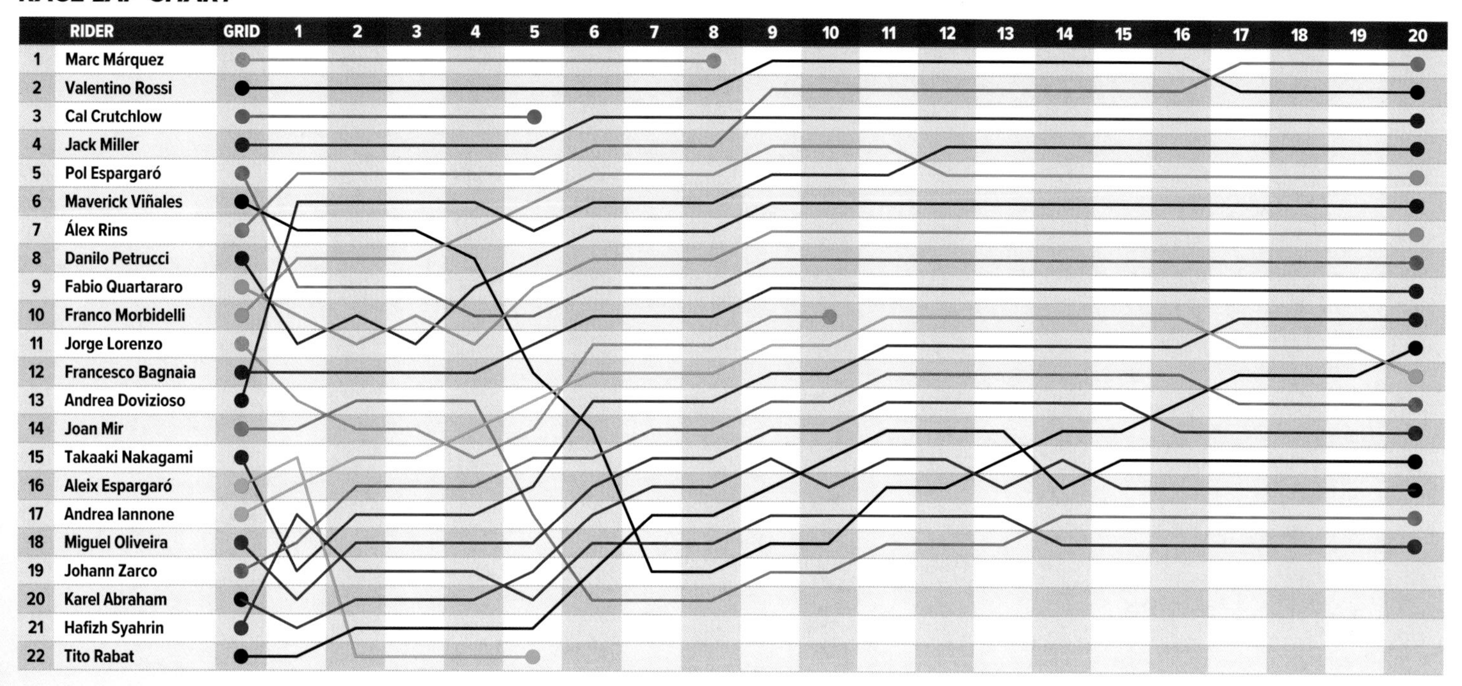

RACE RESULTS

	RIDER	NAT	TEAM	MACHINE	TIME	+GAP	TYRES
1	Álex Rins	SPA	Team SUZUKI ECSTAR	SUZUKI	41'45.499		M/M
2	Valentino Rossi	ITA	Monster Energy Yamaha MotoGP	YAMAHA	41'45.961	0.462	M/M
3	Jack Miller	AUS	Pramac Racing	DUCATI	41'53.953	8.454	S/S
4	Andrea Dovizioso	ITA	Mission Winnow Ducati	DUCATI	41'54.919	9.420	S/M
5	Franco Morbidelli	ITA	Petronas Yamaha SRT	YAMAHA	42'03.520	18.021	M/M
6	Danilo Petrucci	ITA	Mission Winnow Ducati	DUCATI	42'06.975	21.476	S/S
7	Fabio Quartararo	FRA	Petronas Yamaha SRT	YAMAHA	42'11.610	26.111	M/M
8	Pol Espargaró	SPA	Red Bull KTM Factory Racing	KTM	42'15.242	29.743	M/S
9	Francesco Bagnaia	ITA	Pramac Racing	DUCATI	42'16.107	30.608	M/S
10	Takaaki Nakagami	JPN	LCR Honda IDEMITSU	HONDA	42'16.510	31.011	M/M
11	Maverick Viñales	SPA	Monster Energy Yamaha MotoGP	YAMAHA	42'19.576	34.077	S/M
12	Andrea Iannone	ITA	Aprilia Racing Team Gresini	APRILIA	42'20.278	34.779	M/M
13	Johann Zarco	FRA	Red Bull KTM Factory Racing	KTM	42'27.957	42.458	M/S
14	Miguel Oliveira	POR	Red Bull KTM Tech 3	KTM	42'29.771	44.272	M/S
15	Tito Rabat	SPA	Reale Avintia Racing	DUCATI	42'30.122	44.623	M/S
16	Karel Abraham	CZE	Reale Avintia Racing	DUCATI	42'30.239	44.740	M/M
17	Joan Mir	SPA	Team SUZUKI ECSTAR	SUZUKI	42'33.562	48.063	M/M
18	Hafizh Syahrin	MAL	Red Bull KTM Tech 3	KTM	42'53.182	67.683	M/M
NC	Jorge Lorenzo	SPA	Repsol Honda Team	HONDA	21'09.050	10 laps	M/M
NC	Marc Márquez	SPA	Repsol Honda Team	HONDA	16'36.393	12 laps	M/M
NC	Cal Crutchlow	GBR	LCR Honda CASTROL	HONDA	10'25.480	15 laps	M/M
NC	Aleix Espargaró	SPA	Aprilia Racing Team Gresini	APRILIA	11'32.227	15 laps	M/M

CHAMPIONSHIP STANDINGS

	RIDER	NAT	TEAM	PTS
1	Andrea Dovizioso	ITA	Mission Winnow Ducati	54
2	Valentino Rossi	ITA	Monster Energy Yamaha MotoGP	51
3	Álex Rins	SPA	Team SUZUKI ECSTAR	49
4	Marc Márquez	SPA	Repsol Honda Team	45
5	Danilo Petrucci	ITA	Mission Winnow Ducati	30
6	Jack Miller	AUS	Pramac Racing	29
7	Takaaki Nakagami	JPN	LCR Honda IDEMITSU	22
8	Cal Crutchlow	GBR	LCR Honda CASTROL	19
9	Pol Espargaró	SPA	Red Bull KTM Factory Racing	18
10	Fabio Quartararo	FRA	Petronas Yamaha SRT	17
11	Franco Morbidelli	ITA	Petronas Yamaha SRT	16
12	Maverick Viñales	SPA	Monster Energy Yamaha MotoGP	14
13	Aleix Espargaró	SPA	Aprilia Racing Team Gresini	13
14	Francesco Bagnaia	ITA	Pramac Racing	9
15	Joan Mir	SPA	Team SUZUKI ECSTAR	8
16	Miguel Oliveira	POR	Red Bull KTM Tech 3	7
17	Jorge Lorenzo	SPA	Repsol Honda Team	7
18	Andrea Iannone	ITA	Aprilia Racing Team Gresini	6
19	Johann Zarco	FRA	Red Bull KTM Factory Racing	5
20	Tito Rabat	SPA	Reale Avintia Racing	1
21	Hafizh Syahrin	MAL	Red Bull KTM Tech 3	
22	Karel Abraham	CZE	Reale Avintia Racing	
23	Bradley Smith	GBR	Aprilia Factory Racing	

11 MAVERICK VIÑALES
Had another nightmare. Jumped the start by a fraction and misunderstood the penalty, so mistakenly rode a long-lap, then came in for the prescribed ride-through. Rode the sixth-best lap, three tenths slower than Márquez.

12 ANDREA IANNONE
Moved up from 16th to 12th in the first few laps and was promoted to tenth by the exit of both Repsol Hondas. But his RS-GP got twitchy and difficult to ride, so in the final laps he was unable to resist Nakagami and Viñales.

13 JOHANN ZARCO
Had a lot of work to do from 19th on the grid and soon found himself being chased by a non-factory KTM rider. Spent much of the 20 laps managing his energy better than he'd done at previous races to keep Oliveira behind him.

14 MIGUEL OLIVEIRA
The Portuguese rookie was unable to better his superb 11th-place finish in Argentina, but nonetheless impressed with his pace at a track that makes life especially difficult for MotoGP apprentices, matching Zarco lap after lap.

15 TITO RABAT
A great day for the former Moto2 champion – his first points since his horrific Silverstone accident, which broke his right femur into three pieces. His injuries made COTA a tougher challenge than ever. Finished right behind Oliveira.

16 KAREL ABRAHAM
Led Avintia team-mate Rabat for the first half of the race, but once the Spaniard got past the Czech rider didn't quite have enough to mount a proper counter attack, despite riding his fastest lap on the final lap.

17 JOAN MIR
Was too keen to get away from the fifth row and was hit with a jump-start penalty. The rookie's best race lap was faster than those of Quartararo, Petrucci and Pol Espargaró, underlining the performance of the GSX-RR.

18 HAFIZH SYAHRIN
Another morale-battering outing for the Malaysian, who was more than a minute behind Rins at the flag. Changed to a soft rear tyre before the race and complained of an early and significant drop in grip and performance.

NC JORGE LORENZO
The three-time MotoGP king's third race on an RC213V and his third dose of bad luck: a cracked rib and clutch slip at Losail, activating the pit-lane speed limiter at Termas and this time his bike quit when he was running tenth.

NC MARC MÁRQUEZ
Sometimes the impossible does happen. Márquez had owned COTA since 2013, taking the pole/victory double every year. But this time he lost the front while apparently cruising to what could have been another dominant win.

NC CAL CRUTCHLOW
Once again he had the pace for the podium and once again he paid a hefty price for a small mistake. Like many others, he was struggling with front-end lock-ups, then the rear snapped on him and down he went.

NC ALEIX ESPARGARÓ
Struggled with his traction control in morning warm-up, then had a nasty highside at turn 13 on lap two. Aprilia stayed at COTA for Monday tests, when they tried their rear-downforce swingarm attachment for the first time.

alpinestars
MARQUEZ

The legions of Márquez fans enjoyed his victory much more than his rivals

GRAN PREMIO RED BULL DE ESPAÑA
CIRCUITO DE JEREZ - ANGEL NIETO
03/04/05 MAY

ANOTHER MARC MASTERPIECE

Two weeks after his shock exit at COTA Marc Márquez wanted to send a message to his rivals at Jerez

Sometimes the races that look easy are anything but. The records show that Marc Márquez led the 2019 Jerez Grand Prix from the first corner to the finish, after beating the Petronas SRT M1s of pole-sitter Fabio Quartararo and Franco Morbidelli away from the grid.

His progress wasn't as electric as it had been in Argentina and the USA, but he made sure no one got close enough to attack and on the final lap he was able to ease off and enjoy the enthusiastic crowd's appreciation. In the final analysis, it was another demolition job.

But not easy at all. Crashing out of the lead at COTA – while under no pressure – put him under a lot of pressure for his home race. First, to win the race and regain the championship lead. Second, the even greater pressure of making sure he didn't crash again.

"After my crash at Austin many people said, ah, this is his weak point: he crashes too much, blah, blah, blah," said the 26-year-old after his 46th premier-class victory. "But we understood what had happened at Austin, so I had the confidence to be in front from the beginning to the end, to show the fans and especially my opponents that I'm the same Marc with the same confidence. I feel good this year."

During the two weeks since the US round HRC engineers had

CLOCKWISE, FROM TOP LEFT | *A Petronas SRT QP one-two: Quartararo and Morbidelli showed just how fast Yamahas can be; Mir had two crashes: the first scarier, the second costlier; Iannone was down and out after a nasty tumble in FP4; Márquez out-dragged the pack into turn one and that was that; Lorenzo still hadn't found what he was looking for; Bradl rode a great race with HRC's carbon-fibre-covered RC213V frame; Ducati celebrated Dovizioso's 200th MotoGP start with some local horsepower.*

'I WANTED TO SHOW THE FANS AND MY OPPONENTS THAT I'M THE SAME MARC WITH THE SAME CONFIDENCE'
MARC MÁRQUEZ

crunched the numbers in the RC213V's engine-braking software to give Márquez smoother deceleration. "I feel better because the engine is more predictable," he added. "This helps make me safer on the bike, because I was making some mistakes I didn't understand. We had the problem at the first three races; even in Argentina, where I was able to adjust, but at Austin I wasn't able to adjust. Now we are working in a better way."

Despite the champion's dominance there was a sensing of changing generations. Márquez was the oldest rider on both the front row and the podium. Pole position went to stellar rookie Fabio Quartararo, just weeks after he had turned 20-years-old, which bettered Marquez's youngest-ever pole record. Suddenly, Márquez was no longer the kid on the block.

Quartararo's qualifying speed was a joy to watch – perfectly smooth on the ragged edge – and he was every bit as impressive in the race. It took him 11 laps to get past team-mate Morbidelli, who had given the Petronas Sepang team a qualifying one-two, and then he raised his pace to set off in pursuit of the leader. Márquez responded and then Quartararo was out, his miracle ride ended by a broken gear-shifter.

For a few minutes the youngster was inconsolable in his garage, then he was over it. "It was amazing to ride with the top riders," he said. "I learned many things. I was riding the bike like I have more experience. I made some mapping changes and when I saw that the tyre pressure was high I managed to get it cooler. We will leave all the negatives here and take the positives home."

Quartararo's exit coincided exactly with Álex Rins overhauling Morbidelli. The COTA winner had once again flunked qualifying, ending up on the third row. He spent the first six laps trying to outfox Andrea Dovizioso, whose Ducati stopped better and accelerated faster than the Suzuki. Next he had to get past Maverick Viñales, who had finally found some speed for the early laps. By the time he got into second he had 12 laps to eat up Márquez's 3.7-second advantage. It was never going to happen. But what if Rins hadn't wasted the first half of the race compensating for his lowly grid slot?

"I would like to start better, but putting the bike on the limit for one lap is difficult, because trying to understand the bike when it's on the limit isn't easy," he explained. "Also, the front starts to move and the rear starts to move."

Viñales looked mightily relieved with his first top-three of 2019, at a track where he had never finished on a MotoGP podium. "We were there in the early laps, which was our first objective," he said. "I saved the tyres a bit in the early laps to be faster at the end, but we still need more grip in the traction area over race distance."

Dovizioso threw everything he had at Viñales during the final stages, when both rode their fastest laps. "I pushed really hard and took a lot of risks because I wanted the podium, but the negative points of our bike – our speed in fast corners – is too

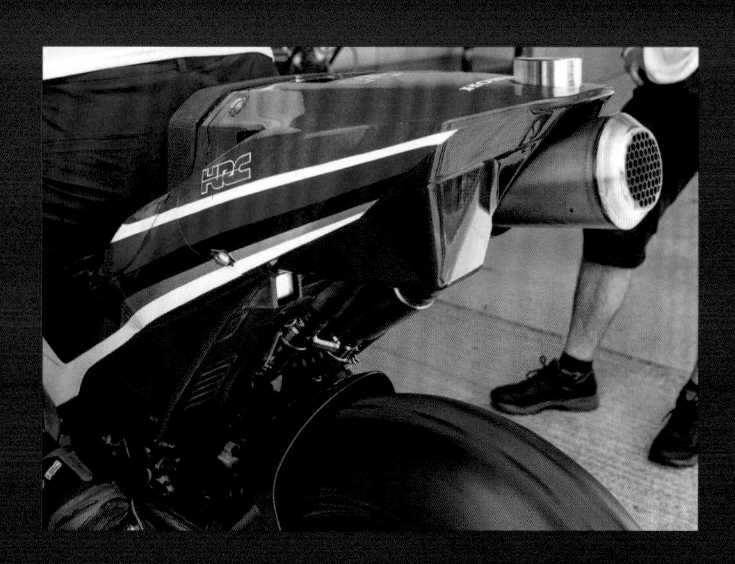

HONDA'S NEW CONCEPT RC213V

Honda raced a modified RC213V at Jerez, which was surely an important factor in HRC test rider Stefan Bradl's impressive ride to tenth place. Márquez tested the bike the day after the race.

Bradl's machine, which he evaluated back-to-back with a conventional 2019 RC213V, featured a frame covered with a carbon-fibre skin. The frame itself was also different, apparently designed to retain longitudinal stiffness while increasing lateral flex.

"Historically speaking, the Bridgestone tyres had a much harder construction, so everything was much harder: the triple clamps, the chassis and many other parts," said HRC technical manager Takeo Yokoyama. "Since Michelin tyres were introduced we are going

big," said the world number two, who seemed to doubt about his title challenge. "This season will be hard."

Danilo Petrucci spent much of the race breathing his team-mate's exhaust fumes but ran out of steam in the final few laps. The last man that Petrucci bettered was Morbidelli, who ran out of tyre sooner than most, steadily going backwards from second to seventh. His final laps were spent battling with his mentor Valentino Rossi and Cal Crutchlow. Rossi beat him, Crutchlow didn't.

Rossi had had a busy weekend with his VR46 Academy pupils. On Saturday Pecco Bagnaia had bumped the VR46 boss out of Q2, subjecting him to a fourth-row start, which had him 11th after the first lap.

Second at the two previous races, Rossi believed he would've had a chance at the podium if he had got away with the lead group. From there it was a long road to sixth place.

"We are stronger than last year, but the road is long and the challenge is very high," he said. "I'm not fully happy for sure, but we are working in a good direction and we can fight. The biggest problem is Márquez, because he is clearly the fastest, but we are there, we are only nine points behind and it looks like we can fight to try and get some more podiums and try to win some races."

CLOCKWISE FROM TOP LEFT | *Zarco's weekend turned blue, in all kinds of ways; Viñales was delighted with his first podium of 2019, Rins the same with his second; Petrucci leads Crutchlow and Miller, who was hanging off his GP19 more than ever; Márquez won his second consecutive Jerez MotoGP race; history-maker Quartararo leads Viñales soon after the start; Marquez all alone out front, chased only by his shadow.*

softer and softer, to get more feedback, to get more feeling and to make the bike turn better. We are still going in this direction."

The idea of the carbon-fibre skin is to alter the frame's flex character, because when aluminium flexes it tends to reflex (return to its original shape) too quickly, which gives a snappy feel. In other words, the skin doesn't so much soften the frame as soften the way it reacts. This is all part of HRC's efforts to create a more rider-friendly chassis.

The development RC213V also featured an underseat container, first seen at the Sepang tests. The container is similar to Ducati's so-called salad box and was nicknamed HRC's bento box. Most likely the container contains electronics. Placing weight far from the centre of mass can damp out chatter.

4 | SPAIN

GRAN PREMIO RED BULL DE ESPAÑA

CIRCUITO DE JEREZ - ANGEL NIETO

03/04/05 MAY

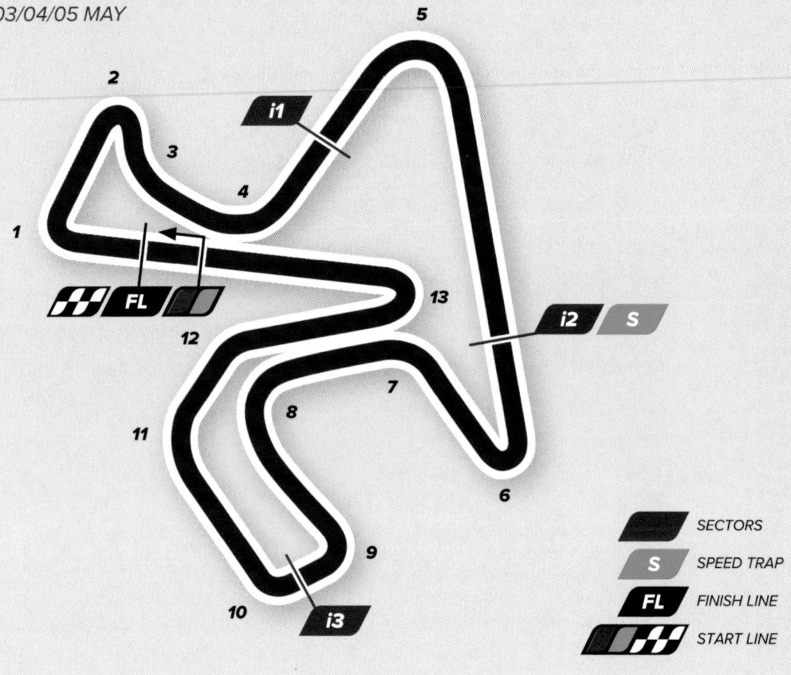

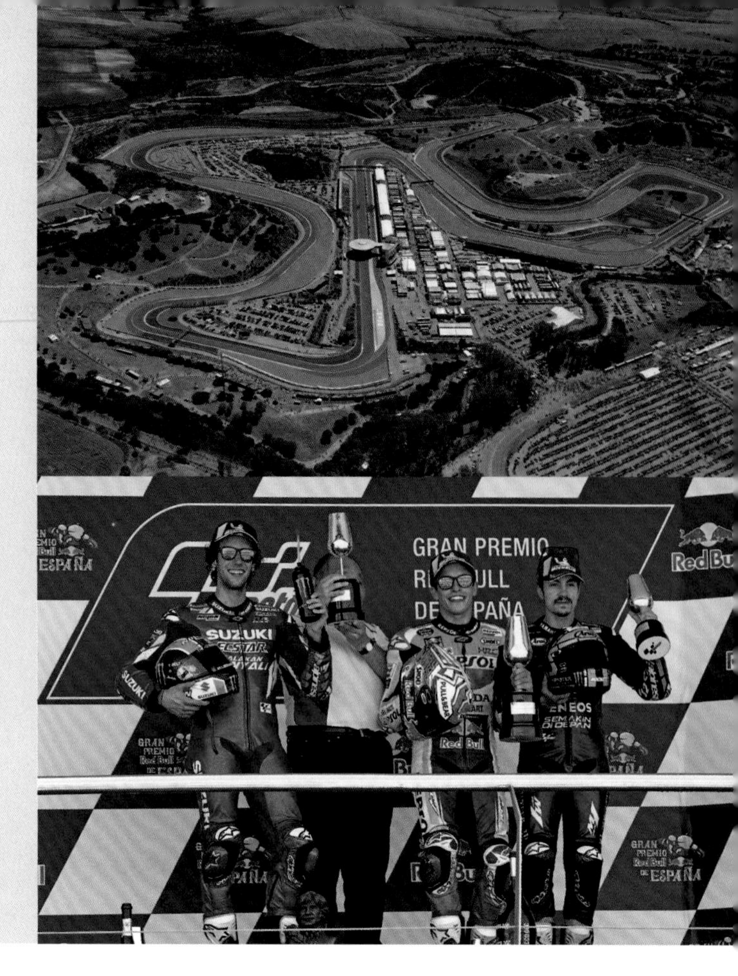

QUALIFYING RESULTS

	RIDER	NAT	TEAM	MACHINE	QP	TIME	GAP 1ST	PREV
1	Fabio Quartararo	FRA	Petronas Yamaha SRT	YAMAHA	Q2	1'36.880		
2	Franco Morbidelli	ITA	Petronas Yamaha SRT	YAMAHA	Q2	1'36.962	0.082	0.082
3	Marc Márquez	SPA	Repsol Honda Team	HONDA	Q2	1'36.970	0.090	0.008
4	Andrea Dovizioso	ITA	Mission Winnow Ducati	DUCATI	Q2	1'37.018	0.138	0.048
5	Maverick Viñales**	SPA	Monster Energy Yamaha MotoGP	YAMAHA	Q2	1'37.114	0.234	0.096
6	Cal Crutchlow	GBR	LCR Honda CASTROL	HONDA	Q2	1'37.175	0.295	0.061
7	Danilo Petrucci	ITA	Mission Winnow Ducati	DUCATI	Q2	1'37.209	0.329	0.034
8	Takaaki Nakagami	JPN	LCR Honda IDEMITSU	HONDA	Q2	1'37.332	0.452	0.123
9	Álex Rins	SPA	Team SUZUKI ECSTAR	SUZUKI	Q2	1'37.351	0.471	0.019
10	Francesco Bagnaia**	ITA	Pramac Racing	DUCATI	Q2	1'37.384	0.504	0.033
11	Jorge Lorenzo	SPA	Repsol Honda Team	HONDA	Q2	1'37.496	0.616	0.112
12	Joan Mir	SPA	Team SUZUKI ECSTAR	SUZUKI	Q2	1'37.514	0.634	0.018
13	Valentino Rossi	ITA	Monster Energy Yamaha MotoGP	YAMAHA	Q1	1'37.371	*0.207	0.072
14	Stefan Bradl	GER	Team HRC	HONDA	Q1	1'37.406	*0.242	0.035
15	Jack Miller	AUS	Pramac Racing	DUCATI	Q1	1'37.605	*0.441	0.199
16	Aleix Espargaró	SPA	Aprilia Racing Team Gresini	APRILIA	Q1	1'37.625	*0.461	0.020
17	Pol Espargaró	SPA	Red Bull KTM Factory Racing	KTM	Q1	1'37.798	*0.634	0.173
18	Johann Zarco	FRA	Red Bull KTM Factory Racing	KTM	Q1	1'37.820	*0.656	0.022
19	Bradley Smith	GBR	Aprilia Factory Racing	APRILIA	Q1	1'38.357	*1.193	0.537
20	Tito Rabat	SPA	Reale Avintia Racing	DUCATI	Q1	1'38.403	*1.239	0.046
21	Karel Abraham	CZE	Reale Avintia Racing	DUCATI	Q1	1'38.447	*1.283	0.044
22	Miguel Oliveira	POR	Red Bull KTM Tech 3	KTM	Q1	1'38.894	*1.730	0.447
23	Hafizh Syahrin	MAL	Red Bull KTM Tech 3	KTM	Q1	1'40.042	*2.878	1.148
24	Andrea Iannone	ITA	Aprilia Racing Team Gresini	APRILIA	FP3	1'38.327	1.370	

GRAND PRIX INFORMATION

TRACK INFORMATION			
2019 WINNER	Marc Márquez		
CIRCUIT LENGTH	4.4 km	2.75 miles	
LAPS	25		
RACE DISTANCE	110.6 KM	68.8 miles	
ALL TIME LAP RECORD	1'36.880	164.3 Km/h	Fabio Quartararo (2019)
BEST RACE LAP	1'38.051	162.3 Km/h	Marc Márquez (2019)
RACE CONDITION	Dry		
AIR	21°C		
HUMIDITY	61%		
GROUND	42°C		

TYRE SELECTION

FRONT	
SOFT	WHITE
MEDIUM	GREY
HARD	YELLOW

REAR	
SOFT	WHITE
MEDIUM	GREY
HARD	YELLOW

L M R

< MILD — TRACK SEVERITY — SEVERE >

1 MARC MÁRQUEZ
Another masterpiece. Under pressure as a result of his COTA crash he took a while to feel confident enough to push at 100 percent, but never even relinquished the lead while doing so. This was a big concern for his rivals.

2 ÁLEX RINS
Made a great job of recovering from a poor grid slot and left Jerez fully aware that he must find some extra speed in qualifying if he's to properly challenge Márquez. His race progress was as smooth and unruffled as ever.

3 MAVERICK VIÑALES
Rated his first podium of the year as good as a victory. A settings change allowed the Spaniard to be more precise in the early laps, so for once he didn't go backwards, while also saving his tyres for later in the race.

4 ANDREA DOVIZIOSO
Had everything he needed to get a podium at Jerez, except a motorcycle that turned well through the circuit's numerous fast sweepers. This was most obvious when Rins rode past him, as had Rossi in Argentina.

5 DANILO PETRUCCI
Chased his team-mate for much of the race, struggling with the same corner-speed issues. Ran out of tyres faster than Dovizioso, which wasn't a surprise, considering that he weighs 11 kilos more than his compatriot.

6 VALENTINO ROSSI
Couldn't make up his mind between the medium and hard rear, until he finally opted for the hard, which he later believed was a mistake. Didn't have the pace to overtake in the early stages, but was stronger in the later laps.

7 FRANCO MORBIDELLI
Rode a great race, heading the chasing pack in the first few laps, then managing the situation as he lost grip and positions. Kept his head throughout and finished top independent-team rider, a first for the Petronas team.

8 CAL CRUTCHLOW
Had a disappointing weekend, considering the podium pace he had at the previous two races. Made the opposite tyre choice to Rossi – the medium instead of the hard – and was also wrong. Took home his first points since Qatar.

9 TAKAAKI NAKAGAMI
Another very solid ride from the HRC rider who uses a 2018-spec RC213V. Was happy enough with his race pace but less happy with his first few laps, when he lost some positions because he wasn't quite aggressive enough.

10 STEFAN BRADL
An impressive ride from HRC's test rider, who hadn't raced since Valencia 2018, when he subbed for the injured Crutchlow. Raced Honda's new carbon-covered RC213V frame for the first time, designed to improve chassis friendliness.

11 ALEIX ESPARGARÓ
The Spaniard was as aggressive as ever in the early laps, which compensated for his sixth-row start. Was chasing Miller and Nakagami in the final laps when the Aprilia and Ducati collided, which allowed Bradl past and let Nakagami go.

12 JORGE LORENZO
Another tough one for the Honda newbie. Crashed in qualifying, which put him 11th on the grid, but he didn't have the pace in the race either. His main concerns were getting the bike stopped for the corners and hitting his apexes.

RACE LAP CHART

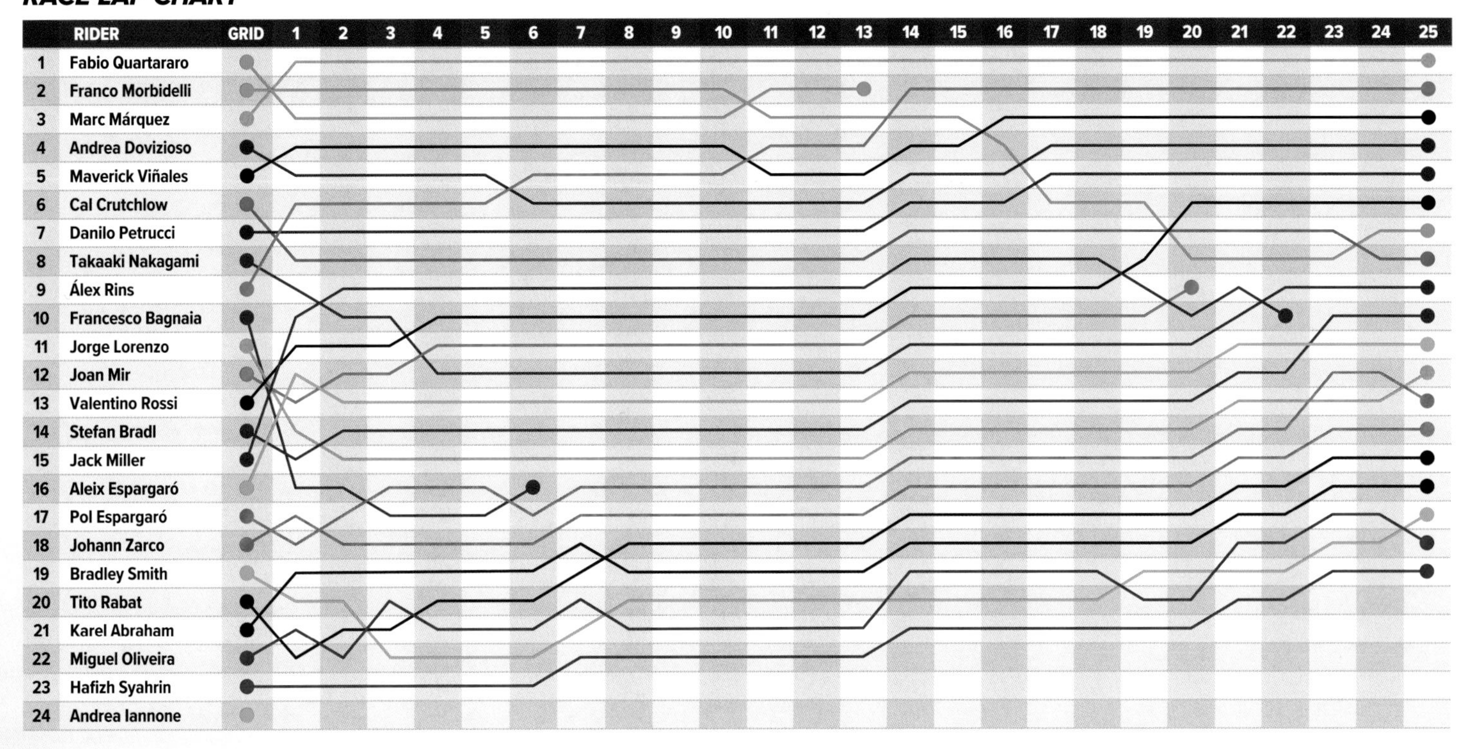

RACE RESULTS

	RIDER	NAT	TEAM	MACHINE	TIME	+ GAP	TYRES
1	Marc Márquez	SPA	Repsol Honda Team	HONDA	41'08.685		H/H
2	Álex Rins	SPA	Team SUZUKI ECSTAR	SUZUKI	41'10.339	1.654	M/H
3	Maverick Viñales	SPA	Monster Energy Yamaha MotoGP	YAMAHA	41'11.128	2.443	M/H
4	Andrea Dovizioso	ITA	Mission Winnow Ducati	DUCATI	41'11.489	2.804	H/H
5	Danilo Petrucci	ITA	Mission Winnow Ducati	DUCATI	41'13.433	4.748	H/H
6	Valentino Rossi	ITA	Monster Energy Yamaha MotoGP	YAMAHA	41'16.232	7.547	H/H
7	Franco Morbidelli	ITA	Petronas Yamaha SRT	YAMAHA	41'16.913	8.228	H/H
8	Cal Crutchlow	GBR	LCR Honda CASTROL	HONDA	41'18.737	10.052	H/M
9	Takaaki Nakagami	JPN	LCR Honda IDEMITSU	HONDA	41'18.959	10.274	H/H
10	Stefan Bradl	GER	Team HRC	HONDA	41'22.087	13.402	H/H
11	Aleix Espargaró	SPA	Aprilia Racing Team Gresini	APRILIA	41'24.116	15.431	H/H
12	Jorge Lorenzo	SPA	Repsol Honda Team	HONDA	41'27.158	18.473	H/M
13	Pol Espargaró	SPA	Red Bull KTM Factory Racing	KTM	41'28.841	20.156	H/H
14	Johann Zarco	FRA	Red Bull KTM Factory Racing	KTM	41'35.391	26.706	H/H
15	Tito Rabat	SPA	Reale Avintia Racing	DUCATI	41'37.198	28.513	H/H
16	Karel Abraham	CZE	Reale Avintia Racing	DUCATI	41'45.543	36.858	H/H
17	Bradley Smith	GBR	Aprilia Factory Racing	APRILIA	41'50.075	41.390	M/H
18	Miguel Oliveira	POR	Red Bull KTM Tech 3	KTM	41'50.255	41.570	H/H
19	Hafizh Syahrin	MAL	Red Bull KTM Tech 3	KTM	41'59.253	50.568	H/H
NC	Jack Miller	AUS	Pramac Racing	DUCATI	36'23.178	3 laps	H/H
NC	Joan Mir	SPA	Team SUZUKI ECSTAR	SUZUKI	33'03.645	5 laps	M/H
NC	Fabio Quartararo	FRA	Petronas Yamaha SRT	YAMAHA	21'27.688	12 laps	H/H
NC	Francesco Bagnaia	ITA	Pramac Racing	DUCATI	10'05.207	19 laps	H/H

CHAMPIONSHIP STANDINGS

	RIDER	NAT	TEAM	PTS
1	Marc Márquez	SPA	Repsol Honda Team	70
2	Álex Rins	SPA	Team SUZUKI ECSTAR	69
3	Andrea Dovizioso	ITA	Mission Winnow Ducati	67
4	Valentino Rossi	ITA	Monster Energy Yamaha MotoGP	61
5	Danilo Petrucci	ITA	Mission Winnow Ducati	41
6	Maverick Viñales	SPA	Monster Energy Yamaha MotoGP	30
7	Jack Miller	AUS	Pramac Racing	29
8	Takaaki Nakagami	JPN	LCR Honda IDEMITSU	29
9	Cal Crutchlow	GBR	LCR Honda CASTROL	27
10	Franco Morbidelli	ITA	Petronas Yamaha SRT	25
11	Pol Espargaró	SPA	Red Bull KTM Factory Racing	21
12	Aleix Espargaró	SPA	Aprilia Racing Team Gresini	18
13	Fabio Quartararo	FRA	Petronas Yamaha SRT	17
14	Jorge Lorenzo	SPA	Repsol Honda Team	11
15	Francesco Bagnaia	ITA	Pramac Racing	9
16	Joan Mir	SPA	Team SUZUKI ECSTAR	8
17	Miguel Oliveira	POR	Red Bull KTM Tech 3	7
18	Johann Zarco	FRA	Red Bull KTM Factory Racing	7
19	Stefan Bradl	GER	Team HRC	6
20	Andrea Iannone	ITA	Aprilia Racing Team Gresini	6
21	Tito Rabat	SPA	Reale Avintia Racing	2
22	Karel Abraham	CZE	Reale Avintia Racing	
23	Hafizh Syahrin	MAL	Red Bull KTM Tech 3	
24	Bradley Smith	GBR	Aprilia Factory Racing	

** Gap to the fastest rider in the Q1 session   ** Went forward from Q1 to Q2   Track severity = Wear + Temperature + Load*

13 POL ESPARGARÓ
Was mad with himself after the race because he misread his pit-board, sitting up at the end of the penultimate lap, thinking it was the last lap. Nevertheless, finished marginally closer to the race winner than he had at Jerez 2018.

14 JOHANN ZARCO
A torrid weekend made worse by a camera crew that caught him unleashing an expletive-filled rant in his garage. Crashed twice on Friday and didn't feel too confident in the race, so he focused on finishing and getting points.

15 TITO RABAT
Left his home race with the last world championship point. During the weekend he focused on finding better grip with his GP18. His next focus was making the bike more agile, to ease the pressure on his still-healing left leg.

16 KAREL ABRAHAM
Made a big mistake at the start – selected second gear instead of first gear before launching from the grid. Had a battle with his team-mate, which he finally lost after making a few mistakes during the closing laps.

17 BRADLEY SMITH
This was the Aprilia test rider's second race of the year, so he felt a bit rusty. Used the medium front, which caused him braking issues, because he hadn't had time to try the hard. Managed to get the better of Oliveira on the last lap.

18 MIGUEL OLIVEIRA
The rookie finished outside the championship points for the first time since his MotoGP debut in Qatar. Used new KTM chassis parts, but found that he didn't have enough set-up time to make him fully at ease with the new kit.

19 HAFIZH SYAHRIN
Made some last-minute changes in morning warm-up, but they didn't deliver the desired effect. Even so, he managed to ride his fastest laps of the weekend in the race, briefly catching Oliveira and Smith before running out of grip.

NC JACK MILLER
The COTA podium finisher started from 15th on the grid and rode an amazing first half, which had him in seventh just after half-distance. But then struggled with feeling and crashed after making contact with Espargaró's Aprilia.

NC JOAN MIR
Had a scary practice accident when he glanced at his lap-timer on the start/finish, looked up again and had to run straight at turn one. Had a good race, climbing into the top-ten. Crashed at the last corner with five laps to go.

NC FABIO QUARTARARO
What a weekend for the 20-year-old: made history in qualifying and was running second in the race when a minor mechanical put him out. Impressed the entire paddock and proved he has the speed and style to make it big.

NC FRANCESCO BAGNAIA
The first two days of the Spanish Grand Prix went very well for the VR46 rookie; the last day not so well. Lost six places on the first lap and in trying to fight back from that poor start he crashed at the final corner on lap seven.

NC ANDREA IANNONE
Crashed heavily at turn ten during FP4 and was so badly battered that the Clinica Mobile deemed him unfit to take part in the race. On the Monday the Italian tried to take part in the tests, but was still in too much pain.

SHOEI
PULL&BEAR
GIVES YOU WINGS
REPSOL
93
HRC
Red Bull
agv
PRAMAC
Lifter
indra
MICHELIN

Márquez quickly retook the lead from Miller – his front tyre needed cool air.

5 | FRANCE

SHARK HELMETS GRAND PRIX DE FRANCE
LE MANS
17/18/19 MAY

MÁRQUEZ GOES SOFT, STILL WINS

Márquez won an historic Grand Prix victory for Honda, leading most of the way to prevent his soft front tyre from overheating

Jack Miller didn't quite make the podium at Le Mans, but perhaps he should've been given a special trophy for being the first rider to actually overtake Marc Márquez since Andrea Dovizioso snuck past the reigning world champion at the final corner in Qatar. In other words, Márquez had gone ten weeks without anyone putting a move on him. True, he crashed out at COTA, but there's no doubt that he had found a genius groove, even by his standards.

Neither was Le Mans a straightforward weekend, with a rainy Saturday and cold track temperatures contributing to a total of 90 crashes. France's all-new home hero Fabio Quartararo led FP1, Maverick Viñales topped the next two sessions, but when it mattered Márquez was back on top, taking pole in front of three Ducatis: Danilo Petrucci, Miller and Andrea Dovizioso, who all used the GP19's acceleration and braking performance to the maximum around this tight, stop-and-go circuit.

Miller was the thriller of the race. He set off after Márquez like a man possessed: head under the bubble and sweeping past the champion at the start of lap five like he wasn't even there. Two laps later Márquez took his revenge at the same corner. Miller immediately counter-attacked but ran wide into La Chapelle and Márquez didn't need a written invitation to retake the lead.

MICHELIN
3
MICHELIN
2
DUCATI
UnipolSai
Lenovo
X-lite
NetApp
valsir
Audi Sport
Red Bull
GIVES YOU WINGS
SHOEI
PULL&BEAR
FIAMM
PRAMAC
43
REPSOL
ENEOS
MONSTER ENERGY
YAMAHA
46
12

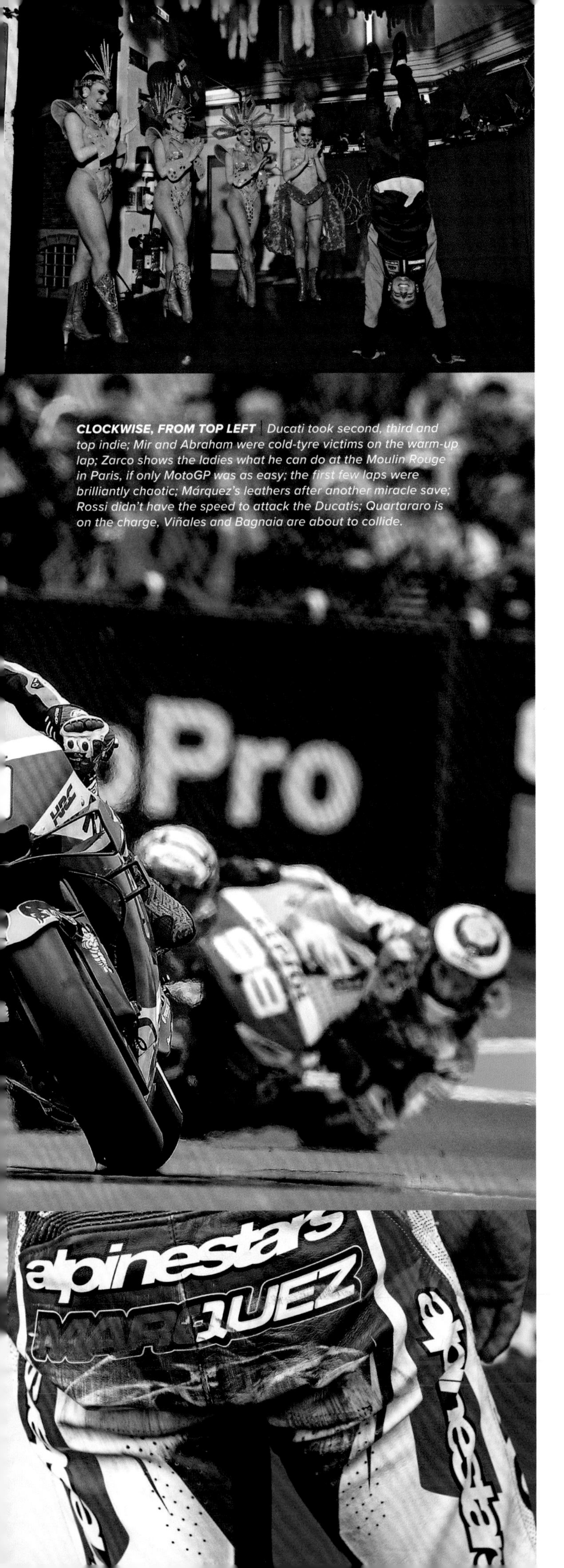

CLOCKWISE, FROM TOP LEFT | *Ducati took second, third and top indie; Mir and Abraham were cold-tyre victims on the warm-up lap; Zarco shows the ladies what he can do at the Moulin Rouge in Paris, if only MotoGP was as easy; the first few laps were brilliantly chaotic; Márquez's leathers after another miracle save; Rossi didn't have the speed to attack the Ducatis; Quartararo is on the charge, Viñales and Bagnaia are about to collide.*

The Spaniard didn't hang around to continue the duel. He rode his fastest laps of the race, because he needed to get out of the group. "I used the soft front tyre, so my strategy was to lead the race, because if you aren't in front you will overheat the tyre," he explained. "The good thing is that before this we weren't able to use the soft front, while Yamaha and Ducati could. Now we can, so the bike turns better."

After the race Miller was every bit as entertaining as he had been during the race. "At about halfway I was calling myself an idiot," he laughed. "I'd got carried away chasing down Marc and trying to show how great I was, which cooked the edge of the tyre. After that I reverted to what I should've been doing – waiting until I was off the edge of the tyre before I opened the gas."

While Márquez eked a small gap out front, Miller came under increasing pressure from his fellow GP19 riders. Dovizioso took him at two-thirds distance and Petrucci a few laps later. The Ducatis finished in that order, less than a second between them.

This was Dovizioso's first podium in three races, so he was happy, but not that happy, because his speed/tyre consumption mix wasn't good enough to stay with Márquez, let alone attack. "I couldn't push 100 percent and do something crazy to stay with Marc, which is what we need," he said. "Marc and Honda are doing something very special at the moment."

Petrucci wore a bigger grin. After all, this was his first podium of the year and therefore his first as a factory rider. It didn't come without a fight, because he made a mess of the first few laps, dropping to sixth behind Valentino Rossi and KTM's hard-charging Pol Espargaró.

"I told myself this is not right!" said Petrucci. "So from there I pushed very, very hard." In the second half of the race he closed down Dovizioso and actually nudged ahead a few times, but he lacked the acceleration to get the job finished.

Miller only just hung on to fourth, finishing a few metres ahead of Rossi, who had spent the last ten laps working hard to cut the gap to the Ducatis. He was top Yamaha for the fifth consecutive race, but the result gave him little joy.

"It looks like we suffer very much on the straights this year," he said. "This makes it difficult to manage overtakes. The problem is that this is the engine [all engines are sealed before the first race] – so I don't think we can improve a lot this year."

Fewer than three seconds behind Rossi and fewer than six behind the winner came an ecstatic Espargaró. KTM had achieved their best dry-weather result, instantly banishing the bad taste of Jerez, where things had gone badly wrong.

There were several reasons (there always are) for his new-found speed. Most important was KTM's first carbon-fibre swingarm that gives less lateral stiffness and more torsional stiffness to help the rear tyre find more grip, to look after the tyre and to

'IF I TRIED TO USE MORE CORNER SPEED I LOST THE FRONT'
ALEX RINS

THE STORY OF HONDA'S 300 WINS

Honda won its first premier-class victory on the afternoon of 22nd May 1966, when Rhodesian Jim Redman and the factory's brand-new RC181 500 beat Giacomo Agostini's MV Agusta by 26 seconds. Fifty three years later Marc Márquez won Honda's 300th premier-class race at Le Mans aboard HRC's RC213V, beating another Italian rider and another Italian motorcycle.

Soichiro Honda built his first Grand Prix bikes for the smaller classes, but his greatest racing ambition was always to win the 500cc riders title. The RC181 (pictured left) might have achieved that goal, but for rider injury in 1966 and a broken gearbox in 1967. However, the RC181 did win ten GPs during its two seasons and the 1966 constructors crown.

improve the rider's feel for the tyre.

"It gives a good feeling with used tyres, so even when the tyre is spinning I can do consistent lap times," said Espargaró. "And it stops the tyre spinning earlier, so when I pick up the bike out of the corner I'm going faster."

Espargaró's super-aggressive technique also suits Le Mans – he got his best result on the Tech 3 Yamaha at the track in 2014 – and so did the grippy dry asphalt.

The French crowd's hopes of witnessing Quartararo fighting at the front were not fulfilled. Qualifying was part wet, part dry, not ideal conditions for a rookie, so he ended up on the fourth row. In the early laps he twice nearly crashed, then staged a remarkable comeback from 17th to eighth, finishing just behind team-mate Franco Morbidelli, after setting the fastest lap.

"I did something I shouldn't do," grinned Quartararo. "I switched to time-attack mapping [qualifying mapping]. I said, okay, let's see what happens – if I destroy the tyre it's my problem."

The flying Frenchman's last two victims were Cal Crutchlow and Álex Rins, who had his worst result since Brno 2018. "We were missing something in the first part of the corner, from the moment I released the brakes," said the COTA winner. "If I tried to use more corner speed I lost the front."

CLOCKWISE FROM TOP LEFT | *Oliveira and Syahrin battled for the last few points; post-race showers; Zarco had a humbling weekend in front of his home crowd; the Márquez brothers made more history: the first sibling victors in MotoGP and Moto2; Aleix Espargaró passes Abraham, who was black-flagged; Rins had a strange weekend – somehow Le Mans robbed the GSX-RR of its greatest weapon: corner-entry speed.*

Honda-san's dream was finally fulfilled when Freddie Spencer took the 1983 500cc riders title aboard the NS500 two-stroke triple; Honda had had to go with the flow to conquer the two-stroke-dominated series. The NS500 won 14 GPs and was replaced by Honda's most successful race bike of all time, the NSR500 V4 two-stroke. In its numerous iterations between 1984 and 2001 the NSR won 132 Grands Prix, as well as ten riders world titles with Spencer, Wayne Gardner, Eddie Lawson, Mick Doohan, Alex Crivillé and Valentino Rossi.

Honda's first MotoGP bike, the RC211V was similarly dominant, taking 48 wins during the 990cc era, from 2002 to 2006. The subsequent 800cc RC212V scored 24 victories between 2007 and 2011. Márquez's Le Mans victory was the 1000cc RC213V's 72nd race win.

5 | FRANCE

SHARK HELMETS GRAND PRIX DE FRANCE
LE MANS
17/18/19 MAY

START LINE
SECTORS

SPEED TRAP
FL FINISH LINE

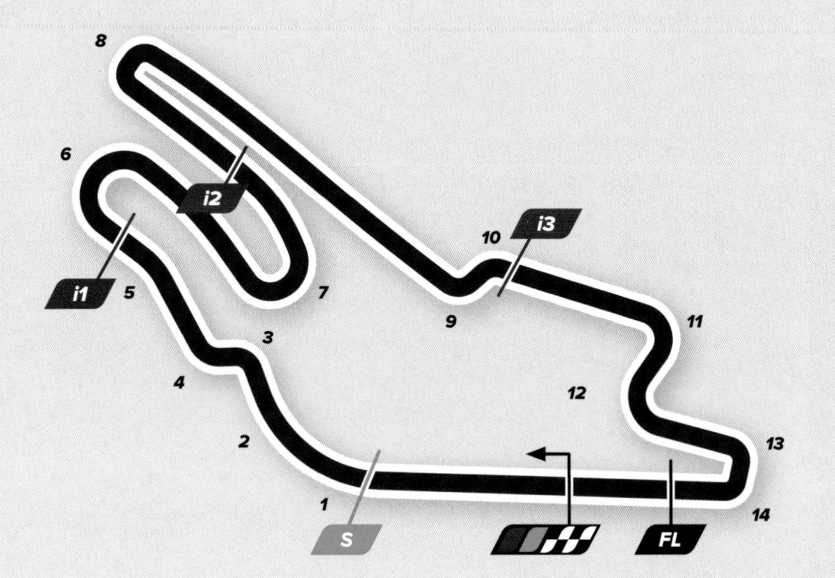

QUALIFYING RESULTS

	RIDER	NAT	TEAM	MACHINE	QP/TIME		GAP 1ST/PREV	
1	Marc Márquez	SPA	Repsol Honda Team	HONDA	Q2	1'40.952		
2	Danilo Petrucci	ITA	Mission Winnow Ducati	DUCATI	Q2	1'41.312	0.360	0.360
3	Jack Miller	AUS	Pramac Racing	DUCATI	Q2	1'41.366	0.414	0.054
4	Andrea Dovizioso	ITA	Mission Winnow Ducati	DUCATI	Q2	1'41.552	0.600	0.186
5	Valentino Rossi	ITA	Monster Energy Yamaha MotoGP	YAMAHA	Q2	1'41.655	0.703	0.103
6	Franco Morbidelli	ITA	Petronas Yamaha SRT	YAMAHA	Q2	1'41.681	0.729	0.026
7	Takaaki Nakagami	JPN	LCR Honda IDEMITSU	HONDA	Q2	1'42.059	1.107	0.378
8	Jorge Lorenzo	SPA	Repsol Honda Team	HONDA	Q2	1'42.067	1.115	0.008
9	Aleix Espargaró	SPA	Aprilia Racing Team Gresini	APRILIA	Q2	1'42.450	1.498	0.383
10	Fabio Quartararo	FRA	Petronas Yamaha SRT	YAMAHA	Q2	1'42.509	1.557	0.059
11	Maverick Viñales	SPA	Monster Energy Yamaha MotoGP	YAMAHA	Q2	1'42.555	1.603	0.046
12	Pol Espargaró	SPA	Red Bull KTM Factory Racing	KTM	FP2	1'31.923	0.495	
13	Francesco Bagnaia	ITA	Pramac Racing	DUCATI	Q1	1'39.982	*2.315	0.720
14	Johann Zarco	FRA	Red Bull KTM Factory Racing	KTM	Q1	1'40.029	*2.362	0.047
15	Cal Crutchlow	GBR	LCR Honda CASTROL	HONDA	Q1	1'40.114	*2.447	0.085
16	Miguel Oliveira	POR	Red Bull KTM Tech 3	KTM	Q1	1'40.385	*2.718	0.271
17	Karel Abraham	CZE	Reale Avintia Racing	DUCATI	Q1	1'40.482	*2.815	0.097
18	Joan Mir	SPA	Team SUZUKI ECSTAR	SUZUKI	Q1	1'40.606	*2.939	0.124
19	Álex Rins	SPA	Team SUZUKI ECSTAR	SUZUKI	Q1	1'40.706	*3.039	0.100
20	Tito Rabat	SPA	Reale Avintia Racing	DUCATI	Q1	1'41.351	*3.684	0.645
21	Hafizh Syahrin	MAL	Red Bull KTM Tech 3	KTM	Q1	1'41.717	*4.050	0.366
22	Andrea Iannone	ITA	Aprilia Racing Team Gresini	APRILIA	Q1	1'41.786	*4.119	0.069

** Gap to the fastest rider in the Q1 session   ** Went forward from Q1 to Q2   Track severity = Wear + Temperature + Load*

GRAND PRIX INFORMATION

TRACK INFORMATION			
2019 WINNER	Marc Márquez		
CIRCUIT LENGTH	4.2 km	2.6 miles	
LAPS	27		
RACE DISTANCE	113.0 KM	70.2 miles	
ALL TIME LAP RECORD	1'31.185	165.2 Km/h	Johann Zarco (2018)
BEST RACE LAP	1'32.309	163.2 Km/h	Maverick Viñales (2017)
RACE CONDITION	Dry		
AIR	15°C		
HUMIDITY	79%		
GROUND	19°C		

TYRE SELECTION

FRONT	
SOFT	WHITE
MEDIUM	GREY
HARD	YELLOW

L M R

REAR	
SOFT	WHITE
MEDIUM	GREY
HARD	YELLOW

< MILD — TRACK SEVERITY — SEVERE >

1 MARC MÁRQUEZ
Probably the most interesting factor in his latest win was his ability to be able to run the soft front. Yes, conditions were cool, but this was only the third or fourth time he'd run the soft in the Michelin era.

2 ANDREA DOVIZIOSO
Back on the podium after two consecutive fourth-place finishes. A good result, but he didn't have enough rear tyre left to take the fight to Márquez and then had to switch focus to defending second place from his team-mate.

3 DANILO PETRUCCI
Back on the podium for the first time since Le Mans 2018. Started from the front row for the time since Sachsenring 2018 but threw away the advantage in the early laps, so he spent much of the race fighting back from there.

4 JACK MILLER
Enjoyed the race and even more so passing Márquez and spending two laps at the front of the pack, even if this early speed cost him later in the race, when he didn't have the edge grip he needed to repeat his COTA podium.

5 VALENTINO ROSSI
A good ride but not the result he wanted. The positive was that he finished 4.5 seconds closer to the winner than he had at Jerez. On the other hand, the race proved to him that the 2019 M1 engine was no faster than the 2018 unit.

6 POL ESPARGARÓ
A remarkable effort from rider and team. They tried the carbon-fibre swingarm in a private test at Jerez and Espargaró immediately decided he must use it at Le Mans. Finished 15 seconds closer to the winner than at Jerez.

7 FRANCO MORBIDELLI
Another great race and another step closer to the leaders – just seven seconds behind the winner, even though he didn't have the start he had had at Jerez. Felt better than ever on his M1 and left Le Mans looking forward to Mugello.

8 FABIO QUARTARARO
There was no dream home MotoGP debut for the 20-year-old. But perhaps more importantly he coped superbly with the pressures of riding in front of his home crowd and used the race to learn more about tyre management.

9 CAL CRUTCHLOW
Didn't feel comfortable on the bike. Unlike Márquez was still struggling with the corner-entry issues that had affected him since COTA. Starting from 15th didn't help, so perhaps he did well just to stay on and get some points.

10 ÁLEX RINS
Had a horrible weekend that hurt his title hopes. Usually the GSX-RR's greatest strength is its corner-entry performance, but for some reason at Le Mans he kept losing the front when he entered corners aggressively.

RACE LAP CHART

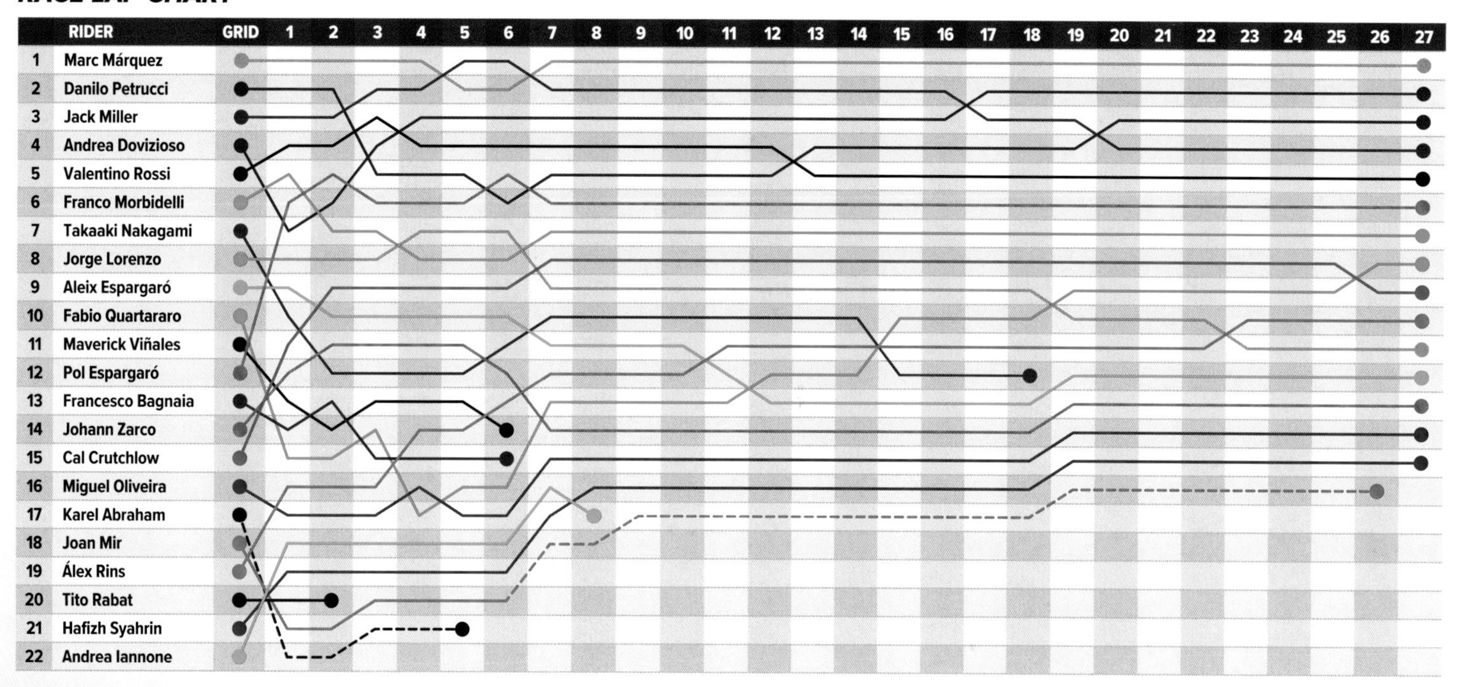

RACE RESULTS

	RIDER	NAT	TEAM	MACHINE	TIME	+ GAP	TYRES
1	Marc Márquez	SPA	Repsol Honda Team	HONDA	41'53.647		S/S
2	Andrea Dovizioso	ITA	Mission Winnow Ducati	DUCATI	41'55.631	1.984	S/S
3	Danilo Petrucci	ITA	Mission Winnow Ducati	DUCATI	41'55.789	2.142	S/S
4	Jack Miller	AUS	Pramac Racing	DUCATI	41'56.587	2.940	S/S
5	Valentino Rossi	ITA	Monster Energy Yamaha MotoGP	YAMAHA	41'56.700	3.053	S/S
6	Pol Espargaró	SPA	Red Bull KTM Factory Racing	KTM	41'59.582	5.935	S/S
7	Franco Morbidelli	ITA	Petronas Yamaha SRT	YAMAHA	42'00.834	7.187	S/S
8	Fabio Quartararo	FRA	Petronas Yamaha SRT	YAMAHA	42'02.086	8.439	S/S
9	Cal Crutchlow	GBR	LCR Honda CASTROL	HONDA	42'03.500	9.853	S/S
10	Álex Rins	SPA	Team SUZUKI ECSTAR	SUZUKI	42'07.356	13.709	S/S
11	Jorge Lorenzo	SPA	Repsol Honda Team	HONDA	42'08.650	15.003	S/S
12	Aleix Espargaró+	SPA	Aprilia Racing Team Gresini	APRILIA	42'23.159	29.512	S/S
13	Johann Zarco	FRA	Red Bull KTM Factory Racing	KTM	42'26.708	33.061	S/S
14	Hafizh Syahrin	MAL	Red Bull KTM Tech 3	KTM	42'29.128	35.481	S/S
15	Miguel Oliveira+	POR	Red Bull KTM Tech 3	KTM	42'29.691	36.044	S/S
16	Joan Mir	SPA	Team SUZUKI ECSTAR	SUZUKI	42'36.095	1 lap	S/S
NC	Takaaki Nakagami	JPN	LCR Honda IDEMITSU	HONDA	28'11.271	9 laps	M/S
NC	Andrea Iannone	ITA	Aprilia Racing Team Gresini	APRILIA	12'42.652	19 laps	S/S
NC	Maverick Viñales	SPA	Monster Energy Yamaha MotoGP	YAMAHA	9'29.312	21 laps	S/S
NC	Francesco Bagnaia	ITA	Pramac Racing	DUCATI	9'29.713	21 laps	S/S
NC	Tito Rabat	SPA	Reale Avintia Racing	DUCATI	3'17.678	25 laps	S/S
NC	Karel Abraham+	CZE	Reale Avintia Racing	DUCATI			S/S

+ FIM MotoGP Stewards Race penalties - Karel Abraham : black flag, Aleix Espargaro : 1.4 seconds penalty to be imposed at the end of the race, Miguel Oliveira : 1.5 seconds penalty to be imposed at the end of the race

CHAMPIONSHIP STANDINGS

	RIDER	NAT	TEAM	PTS
1	Marc Márquez	SPA	Repsol Honda Team	95
2	Andrea Dovizioso	ITA	Mission Winnow Ducati	87
3	Álex Rins	SPA	Team SUZUKI ECSTAR	75
4	Valentino Rossi	ITA	Monster Energy Yamaha MotoGP	72
5	Danilo Petrucci	ITA	Mission Winnow Ducati	57
6	Jack Miller	AUS	Pramac Racing	42
7	Cal Crutchlow	GBR	LCR Honda CASTROL	34
8	Franco Morbidelli	ITA	Petronas Yamaha SRT	34
9	Pol Espargaró	SPA	Red Bull KTM Factory Racing	31
10	Maverick Viñales	SPA	Monster Energy Yamaha MotoGP	30
11	Takaaki Nakagami	JPN	LCR Honda IDEMITSU	29
12	Fabio Quartararo	FRA	Petronas Yamaha SRT	25
13	Aleix Espargaró	SPA	Aprilia Racing Team Gresini	22
14	Jorge Lorenzo	SPA	Repsol Honda Team	16
15	Johann Zarco	FRA	Red Bull KTM Factory Racing	10
16	Francesco Bagnaia	ITA	Pramac Racing	9
17	Joan Mir	SPA	Team SUZUKI ECSTAR	8
18	Miguel Oliveira	POR	Red Bull KTM Tech 3	8
19	Stefan Bradl	GER	Team HRC	6
20	Andrea Iannone	ITA	Aprilia Racing Team Gresini	6
21	Hafizh Syahrin	MAL	Red Bull KTM Tech 3	2
22	Tito Rabat	SPA	Reale Avintia Racing	2
23	Karel Abraham	CZE	Reale Avintia Racing	
24	Bradley Smith	GBR	Aprilia Factory Racing	

11 JORGE LORENZO
The result wasn't much but he insisted there was light at the end of the tunnel: for the first time on the Honda he ended a day inside the top-five and qualified inside the top-eight. His race time was also his closest to the winner.

12 ALEIX ESPARGARÓ
Struggled to find grip, especially exiting the corners when the RS-GP didn't have the initial traction that his rivals seemed to have. Like 21 of the 22 starters chose a soft/soft tyre combination, due to the cold track temperature.

13 JOHANN ZARCO
The hero of the 2018 French GP had to make the best of what he had this time. He did score points, albeit 27 seconds behind his team-mate. Did everything he could to score his first KTM top-ten but simply didn't have the pace.

14 HAFIZH SYAHRIN
Scored his first points aboard his KTM RC16, so he left his team's home GP feeling happier than Zarco. Struggled to find a rhythm, then got into a good groove, finally bettering his team-mate when Oliveira made a mistake.

15 MIGUEL OLIVEIRA
Oliveira wasn't happy with 15th, because he lost 14th due to a 1.5-second penalty for cutting the Chemin aux Boeufs chicane. However, he did help make history: this was the first time four KTMs had finished in the MotoGP points.

16 JOAN MIR
A demoralising weekend for the rookie who had five crashes, including three on Sunday: two in morning warm-up and one on the warm-up lap. Had difficulty getting heat in the tyres, but at least he was relatively unscathed.

NC TAKAAKI NAKAGAMI
Was disappointed by his first no-score and DNF of the season. The Japanese had been running in tenth place until Rins came past him, then crashed heavily at turn 11 while trying to stay ahead of the older Espargaró brother.

NC ANDREA IANNONE
Following his nasty accident at Jerez, had to undergo a medical on Thursday. Was passed fit to ride, but his left-ankle injury worsened as the weekend went on. Started the race but withdrew after nine laps, hoping to get fit for Mugello.

NC MAVERICK VIÑALES
Another confusing weekend. The Spaniard was fastest in FP2 and again in FP3, but when the race started he sunk without trace, once again. He went backwards in the first few laps and was taken out by Bagnaia.

NC FRANCESCO BAGNAIA
Had a good race pace that had him fighting with Rins and Viñales in the early laps and confident of a second top-ten finish. Instead he had his second consecutive race crash, after tangling with Viñales.

NC TITO RABAT
Spent most of Friday and Saturday practice trying to improve rear grip and feel. Made some progress but it was all for nothing, because his GP18 was struck dead by an electronics glitch during the warm-up lap.

NC KAREL ABRAHAM
The Czech rider completed a horrible Sunday for the Avintia team. He crashed at the same place as Mir on the warm-up lap (either cold tyres or cold brakes) and started his race after the first lap was finished, so he was black-flagged.

REPSOL
riello ups
Lenovo
valsir
MICHELIN
REV'IT!
DAIKO
MISSION WINNOW

The decisive moment. Turn one, last lap: Márquez goes wide, Dovizioso dives inside, Petrucci seizes his chance.

6 | ITALY

GRAN PREMIO D'ITALIA OAKLEY
AUTODROMO INTERNAZIONALE DEL MUGELLO
31 MAY - 01/02 JUNE

PETRUCCI ENTERS THE PANTHEON

Petrucci won his first MotoGP race in breathtaking style and there's hardly been a more popular Grand Prix winner

Mugello is MotoGP's Holy of Holies. The strip of asphalt that wends its way up and down a verdant Tuscan valley is probably the best track in the championship, but the beauty of the surrounding area and the day-and-night frenzy of the fans camped on the hillsides make this MotoGP's most sparkling weekend.

The 2019 Mugello Grand Prix was the track's 35th and certainly one of its best, with blissful weather and an enthralling battle between Marc Márquez and Ducati that raged all weekend. And, at the end of it all, the most popular winner in a long time.

There was only one negative for the crowd: an off-form Valentino Rossi who started from his worst dry-weather grid position in more than a decade and then crashed out of last place. Not to worry: the fans who had brought arsenals of yellow smoke flares had also brought red flares, so they were ready to celebrate the success of the Bologna bullets.

Márquez rarely has the best of times at Mugello. The track doesn't really work for his technique and neither does it work well for the RC213V (or for its RC212V predecessor): going into this race Honda had won just twice in their previous dozen visits.

Of course, the world champion was keen to inflict a defeat on Ducati where it would hurt them most. Ducati's attempt to deny

CLOCKWISE, FROM TOP LEFT | *Espargaró used a revised RC16 engine in another strong ride; Luigi Dall'Igna had another carbon-fibre trick in his box; Rossi's special Mugello helmet was as classy as ever; Nakagami's ride to fifth on his year-old RC213V was a breakthrough performance; Dovizioso, Pirro and Petrucci rode Ducati streetbikes to the track; The locals had stocked up on red smoke flares, as well as yellow, just in case; Dovizioso had no option but to remove himself from the Marquez/Petrucci sandwich.*

'THERE WAS JUST ONE METRE OF SPACE ON THE INSIDE AND I PUT MY BIKE THERE'
DANILO PETRUCCI

him began during Q2, when wherever Márquez went there was always a couple of GP19s with him. But messing with the former 125cc and Moto2 champion is a risky business. Sure enough, at the end of Q2 he beat Ducati at their own game, with a perfectly timed run that used Andrea Dovizioso's draft to give him pole position.

Second was Fabio Quartararo, who compensated his M1's 10.2kmh/6.3mph top-speed handicap by maximising the bike's corner speed with new tyres and a clear track. Last man on the front row was Danilo Petrucci, who had told journalists earlier in the week that he would quit racing if he didn't win a race in 2019.

And what a race to win. The early laps were as wild as you'd expect at Mugello, with Jack Miller and Álex Rins getting stuck in with Márquez and the factory Ducatis. The world champion led, then suddenly found himself swamped as Miller barged past and Rins dived inside, demoting him to fifth.

By three-quarters distance this was still the lead group, but with Miller fifth and then setting the fastest lap, only to go down moments later.

That made it a straight four-way fight to the finish; all of the riders using the respective advantages of their machines in an attempt to make the difference. The Ducati had the most straight-line speed, the Honda changed direction quickest through Mugello's numerous esses sections and the Suzuki was strongest on corner entry.

The last lap and particularly the first corner of the last lap were unforgettable. Petrucci had led past the pits every time since half-distance, usually just a few hundredths in front. Then as they swept down Mugello's 355kmh/220mph start/finish to start the climactic last lap Dovizioso drafted past his team-mate, then Márquez used a double Ducati draft to slingshot back into the lead. But the world champion arrived at the end of the straight 11kmh/7mph faster than the previous lap, so he got a little sideways into San Donato and Dovizioso was on him in a flash. Neither of them quite found the apex, however, so Petrucci found for it for them.

"They braked really hard and I braked a little earlier, so I was very tight to the kerb," he said. "There was just one metre of space on the inside and I put my bike there. Andrea was closing the corner, but I was there. I'm so sorry for that pass! Andrea was the last person in the world I wanted to make pick up his bike, but today I had a good chance to win."

Dovizioso had no option to back out of it. "I tried to close the door as fast as I could, but Danilo arrived at that moment, so I had to pick up my bike very quickly to not touch him," he said. "But at the same moment Marc was there, so when I picked up my bike I had to be careful to keep some lean angle, because if I'd hit Marc I could've crashed."

ROSSI'S MISERABLE MUGELLO

Valentino Rossi had endured worse Mugello Grands Prix than his 20th premier-class outing at the track. The 2010 Italian GP was obviously his lowest ebb, when he left the track in a helicopter ambulance, with a badly broken right leg.

Apart from that injury, caused by a cold-tyre crash, 2019 was his worst home Grand Prix since he hit the world championship trail in 1996. Twelve months on from starting the 2018 race from pole position and finishing on the podium, the 40-year-old was out of the loop all weekend. Eighteenth fastest on Friday, between Tito Rabat and Andrea Iannone, he was 18th again in qualifying, with no real hope of accomplishing his old "rabbit

Petrucci's lunge had worked: he flew into turn two in the lead, with Márquez right behind, but wary of attacking.

"When I saw Danilo was first and Dovi was third I decided I must not try [to attack Petrucci], because we might both go wide and then Dovi would win the race, which would be worse for the championship," he said.

Dovizioso was out of ammunition anyway. "I had too little grip in the last lap to make something crazy, which is why Rins almost overtook me at the last corner."

The three-way battle at the front was so intense that it was easy to forget that Rins was right there and ready to seize the moment if the leaders did tangle. At the final corner, where Dovizioso ran wide while focusing on Márquez, Rins went inside to briefly take third place, but he didn't have the corner-exit grip to stay there.

Petrucci was overcome by his first Grand Prix victory at his 124th attempt. "Exiting the last corner I thought if this follows the path of my life I will leave the last corner in first place and cross the line in third. I changed into fourth... then fifth... waiting for the others to come past. Then I changed into sixth and when I crossed the line I started to scream, but I had no breath left to scream."

As Petrucci rode towards parc fermé he was mobbed all the way down pit lane. Ever the gentleman, he attributed his success to his team-mate. "I dedicate this victory to Andrea, who last winter adopted me like a brother," he said.

CLOCKWISE FROM TOP LEFT | *Rossi chases Mir, into the gravel; there was little relief for Lorenzo, until he left Mugello and boarded a plane to Japan; Bagnaia (in Lamborghini colours) was fast again and crashed out again; KTM technical director Sebastian Risse checks out another V4 MotoGP bike; Petrucci had waited all his life for this; Unusual scenes in pit lane – the race winner is mobbed by well-wishers*

out of a hat" trick on race day.

"We suffer," he said on Friday. "I don't feel comfortable with the bike. I don't have enough feeling to be fast, so I'm not able to ride very well and I'm slow in the corners."

Saturday was even worse. During FP3 he did his best to fight his way into the top-ten to go directly into to Q2, but it all went wrong at the end of the session. "On the second lap of my time attack I was fast enough for Q2, but unfortunately on the exit from Biondetti I got a big headshake and when I arrived at the last corner the brake lever came back to the handlebar."

Q1 was another disaster. He wanted to use Álex Rins for a tow but the Spaniard wouldn't have it, so both of them missed what should've been their last laps. "I wanted to wait for Rins, but he didn't want to make the lap, then I didn't want to make the lap, so I missed the flag by one second. But the problem wasn't that – I didn't have the potential for Q2."

There was no comfort on race day, either. Rossi collided with Joan Mir while pushing forward, putting them both in the gravel. This latest mishap might've broken the resilience of many, but not Rossi. He regained the track in last place and pushed hard to make time until he lost the front at Arrabbiata 2. Incredibly, his last flying lap was faster than that of the leader!

6 | ITALY

GRAN PREMIO D'ITALIA OAKLEY
AUTODROMO INTERNAZIONALE DEL MUGELLO
31 MAY - 01/02 JUNE

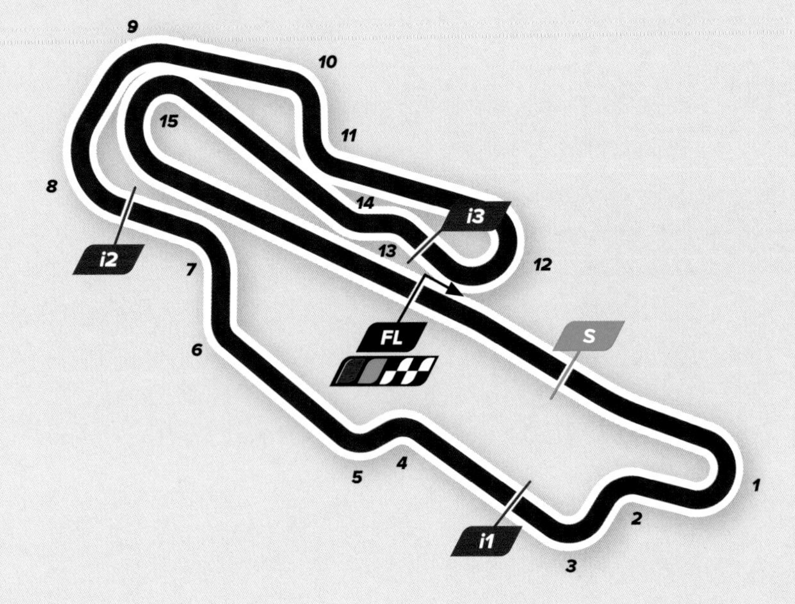

QUALIFYING RESULTS

	RIDER	NAT	TEAM	MACHINE	QP	TIME	GAP 1ST	GAP PREV
1	Marc Márquez	SPA	Repsol Honda Team	HONDA	Q2	1'45.519		
2	Fabio Quartararo	FRA	Petronas Yamaha SRT	YAMAHA	Q2	1'45.733	0.214	0.214
3	Danilo Petrucci	ITA	Mission Winnow Ducati	DUCATI	Q2	1'45.881	0.362	0.148
4	Franco Morbidelli	ITA	Petronas Yamaha SRT	YAMAHA	Q2	1'45.959	0.440	0.078
5	Jack Miller	AUS	Pramac Racing	DUCATI	Q2	1'46.029	0.510	0.070
6	Cal Crutchlow	GBR	LCR Honda CASTROL	HONDA	Q2	1'46.079	0.560	0.050
7	Maverick Viñales	SPA	Monster Energy Yamaha MotoGP	YAMAHA	Q2	1'46.181	0.662	0.102
8	Francesco Bagnaia	ITA	Pramac Racing	DUCATI	Q2	1'46.260	0.741	0.079
9	Andrea Dovizioso**	ITA	Mission Winnow Ducati	DUCATI	Q2	1'46.293	0.774	0.033
10	Takaaki Nakagami	JPN	LCR Honda IDEMITSU	HONDA	Q2	1'46.387	0.868	0.094
11	Pol Espargaró	SPA	Red Bull KTM Factory Racing	KTM	Q2	1'46.433	0.914	0.046
12	Michele Pirro**	ITA	Mission Winnow Ducati	DUCATI	Q2	1'46.638	1.119	0.205
13	Álex Rins	SPA	Team SUZUKI ECSTAR	SUZUKI	Q1	1'46.539	*0.261	0.256
14	Tito Rabat	SPA	Reale Avintia Racing	DUCATI	Q1	1'46.678	*0.400	0.139
15	Aleix Espargaró	SPA	Aprilia Racing Team Gresini	APRILIA	Q1	1'46.899	*0.621	0.221
16	Karel Abraham	CZE	Reale Avintia Racing	DUCATI	Q1	1'47.028	*0.750	0.129
17	Jorge Lorenzo	SPA	Repsol Honda Team	HONDA	Q1	1'47.135	*0.857	0.107
18	Valentino Rossi	ITA	Monster Energy Yamaha MotoGP	YAMAHA	Q1	1'47.184	*0.906	0.049
19	Johann Zarco	FRA	Red Bull KTM Factory Racing	KTM	Q1	1'47.394	*1.116	0.210
20	Joan Mir	SPA	Team SUZUKI ECSTAR	SUZUKI	Q1	1'47.519	*1.241	0.125
21	Hafizh Syahrin	MAL	Red Bull KTM Tech 3	KTM	Q1	1'48.222	*1.944	0.703
22	Miguel Oliveira	POR	Red Bull KTM Tech 3	KTM	Q1	1'48.235	*1.957	0.013
23	Andrea Iannone	ITA	Aprilia Racing Team Gresini	APRILIA	Q1	1'48.303	*2.025	0.068

** Gap to the fastest rider in the Q1 session   ** Went forward from Q1 to Q2   Track severity = Wear + Temperature + Load*

GRAND PRIX INFORMATION

TRACK INFORMATION			
2019 WINNER	Danilo Petrucci		
CIRCUIT LENGTH	5.2 km	3.26 miles	
LAPS	23		
RACE DISTANCE	120.6 KM	75.0 miles	
ALL TIME LAP RECORD	1'45.519	178.9 Km/h	Marc Márquez (2019)
BEST RACE LAP	1'47.639	175.4 Km/h	Marc Márquez (2013)
RACE CONDITION	Dry		
AIR	29°C		
HUMIDITY	33%		
GROUND	49°C		

TYRE SELECTION

FRONT	
SOFT	WHITE
MEDIUM	GREY
HARD	YELLOW

REAR	
SOFT	WHITE
MEDIUM	GREY
HARD	YELLOW

L M R

< MILD — TRACK SEVERITY — SEVERE >

1 DANILO PETRUCCI
Led more laps than anyone else and then had to brawl with the best of them at the end. His victory made him one of a select few riders to have won a premier-class race without graduating through the smaller Grand Prix classes.

2 MARC MÁRQUEZ
Not usually a great circuit for the Spaniard or the Honda, but a revised riding style and the 2019 RC213V's horsepower was very nearly enough for victory. This was another sign that there's no one stronger in MotoGP right now.

3 ANDREA DOVIZIOSO
Wasn't happy about getting beaten, or about losing four points to his main championship rival. His race went well, until the first corner of the last lap when he got squeezed out by his team-mate and by Márquez.

4 ÁLEX RINS
Missed the podium but was every bit as impressive as the top-three. The key was an epic first lap that took him from 13th to seventh, allowing him to use the GSX-RR's corner speed to get a sniff of a draft from the leaders.

5 TAKAAKI NAKAGAMI
A breakthrough ride from the Japanese contesting his second MotoGP season aboard a year-old RC213V. Changed his mind-set into riding "like an animal" in the first laps, so he would be close enough to chase the lead group.

6 MAVERICK VIÑALES
Once again went backwards from the start – from seventh on the grid to 12th after the first lap. It was the sixth lap before he started moving forward, but he didn't feel comfortable on the bike, because "the tyres were very slippery."

7 MICHELE PIRRO
Ducati's third consecutive Mugello victory was like another victory for the factory's chief test rider, who missed the 2018 race after a huge practice crash. Struggled with arm pump in the early stages. Made good progress later.

8 CAL CRUTCHLOW
Ran at the tail of the lead group during the early stages, looking like he was riding a sensible race strategy. But then he started going backwards. Michelin checked his rear tyre at the end of the race and found a small delamination.

9 POL ESPARGARÓ
Used another revised version of KTM's big-bang engine, designed to give the rear tyre an easier time. Maintained a decent pace throughout the race to finish three seconds closer to the winner than he had managed in 2018.

10 FABIO QUARTARARO
Chose the hard front but the race-day heat caused a problematic increase in tyre temperature, so he didn't have the feeling needed to attack the corners. Also suffered arm pump. After the race flew to Barcelona for surgery.

RACE LAP CHART

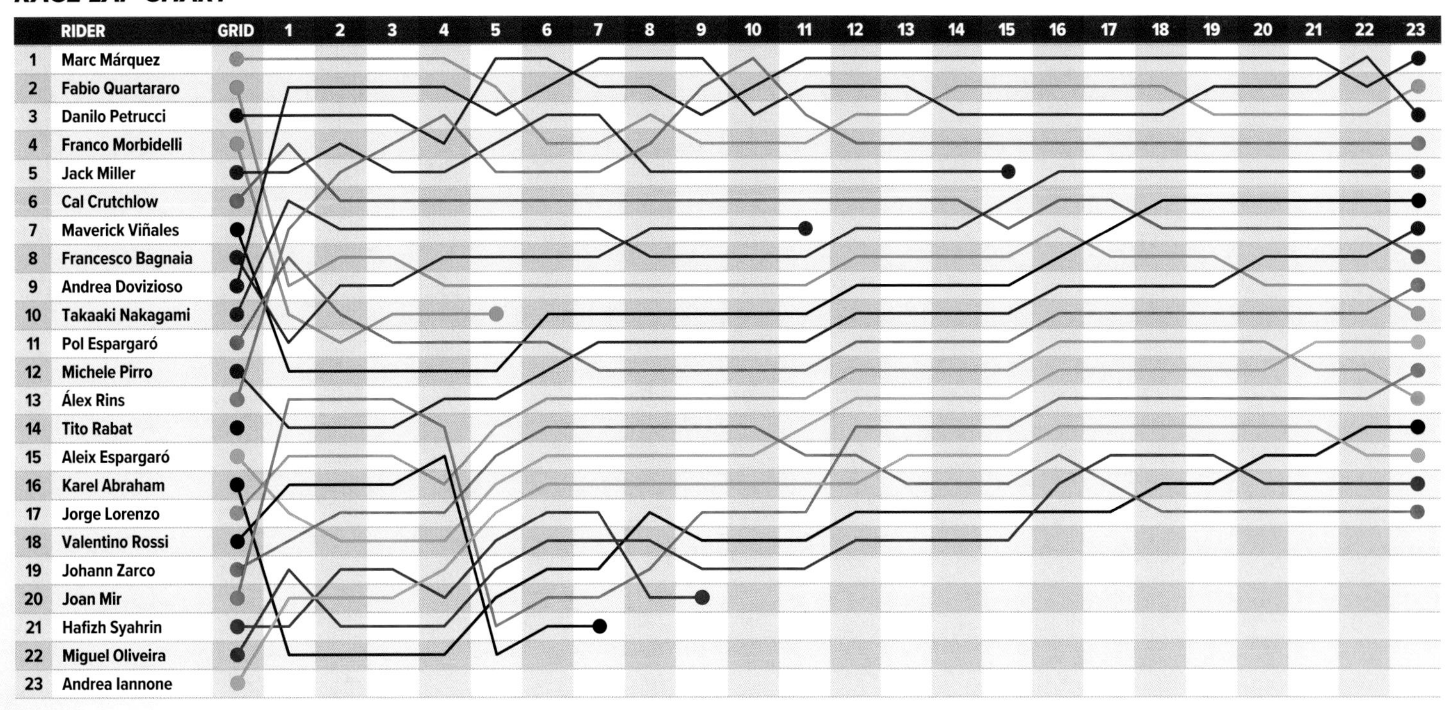

RACE RESULTS

	RIDER	NAT	TEAM	MACHINE	TIME	+GAP	TYRES
1	Danilo Petrucci	ITA	Mission Winnow Ducati	DUCATI	41'33.794		M/M
2	Marc Márquez	SPA	Repsol Honda Team	HONDA	41'33.837	0.043	H/H
3	Andrea Dovizioso	ITA	Mission Winnow Ducati	DUCATI	41'34.132	0.338	M/M
4	Álex Rins	SPA	Team SUZUKI ECSTAR	SUZUKI	41'34.329	0.535	H/M
5	Takaaki Nakagami	JPN	LCR Honda IDEMITSU	HONDA	41'40.329	6.535	M/M
6	Maverick Viñales	SPA	Monster Energy Yamaha MotoGP	YAMAHA	41'41.275	7.481	M/M
7	Michele Pirro	ITA	Mission Winnow Ducati	DUCATI	41'47.082	13.288	M/M
8	Cal Crutchlow	GBR	LCR Honda CASTROL	HONDA	41'47.731	13.937	H/M
9	Pol Espargaró	SPA	Red Bull KTM Factory Racing	KTM	41'50.327	16.533	M/M
10	Fabio Quartararo	FRA	Petronas Yamaha SRT	YAMAHA	41'51.788	17.994	H/M
11	Aleix Espargaró	SPA	Aprilia Racing Team Gresini	APRILIA	41'54.317	20.523	M/M
12	Joan Mir	SPA	Team SUZUKI ECSTAR	SUZUKI	41'54.338	20.544	H/M
13	Jorge Lorenzo	SPA	Repsol Honda Team	HONDA	41'54.607	20.813	M/M
14	Karel Abraham	CZE	Reale Avintia Racing	DUCATI	42'01.092	27.298	M/M
15	Andrea Iannone	ITA	Aprilia Racing Team Gresini	APRILIA	42'01.845	28.051	H/M
16	Miguel Oliveira	POR	Red Bull KTM Tech 3	KTM	42'03.895	30.101	M/M
17	Johann Zarco	FRA	Red Bull KTM Factory Racing	KTM	42'15.651	41.857	H/S
NC	Jack Miller	AUS	Pramac Racing	DUCATI	27'09.517	8 laps	M/M
NC	Francesco Bagnaia	ITA	Pramac Racing	DUCATI	19'58.251	12 laps	M/M
NC	Hafizh Syahrin	MAL	Red Bull KTM Tech 3	KTM	16'31.937	14 laps	M/M
NC	Valentino Rossi	ITA	Monster Energy Yamaha MotoGP	YAMAHA	12'52.709	16 laps	H/M
NC	Franco Morbidelli	ITA	Petronas Yamaha SRT	YAMAHA	9'08.316	18 laps	H/H
NC	Tito Rabat	SPA	Reale Avintia Racing	DUCATI			M/M

CHAMPIONSHIP STANDINGS

	RIDER	NAT	TEAM	PTS
1	Marc Márquez	SPA	Repsol Honda Team	115
2	Andrea Dovizioso	ITA	Mission Winnow Ducati	103
3	Álex Rins	SPA	Team SUZUKI ECSTAR	88
4	Danilo Petrucci	ITA	Mission Winnow Ducati	82
5	Valentino Rossi	ITA	Monster Energy Yamaha MotoGP	72
6	Jack Miller	AUS	Pramac Racing	42
7	Cal Crutchlow	GBR	LCR Honda CASTROL	42
8	Maverick Viñales	SPA	Monster Energy Yamaha MotoGP	40
9	Takaaki Nakagami	JPN	LCR Honda IDEMITSU	40
10	Pol Espargaró	SPA	Red Bull KTM Factory Racing	38
11	Franco Morbidelli	ITA	Petronas Yamaha SRT	34
12	Fabio Quartararo	FRA	Petronas Yamaha SRT	31
13	Aleix Espargaró	SPA	Aprilia Racing Team Gresini	27
14	Jorge Lorenzo	SPA	Repsol Honda Team	19
15	Joan Mir	SPA	Team SUZUKI ECSTAR	12
16	Johann Zarco	FRA	Red Bull KTM Factory Racing	10
17	Michele Pirro	ITA	Mission Winnow Ducati	9
18	Francesco Bagnaia	ITA	Pramac Racing	9
19	Miguel Oliveira	POR	Red Bull KTM Tech 3	8
20	Andrea Iannone	ITA	Aprilia Racing Team Gresini	7
21	Stefan Bradl	GER	Team HRC	6
22	Karel Abraham	CZE	Reale Avintia Racing	2
23	Hafizh Syahrin	MAL	Red Bull KTM Tech 3	2
24	Tito Rabat	SPA	Reale Avintia Racing	2
25	Bradley Smith	GBR	Aprilia Factory Racing	

11 ALEIX ESPARGARÓ
A collision with Zarco on the first lap relegated him to 17th position. He fought back well and took advantage of the various DNFs to nearly make it into the top-ten, despite a lack of front feel that made it hard work to overtake.

12 JOAN MIR
Twelfth position may not have been the best but this was the rookie's first points haul since he finished eighth in his debut ride at Losail. Could've made the top-ten but for a collision with Rossi that sent them both off the track.

13 JORGE LORENZO
There was no fairy-tale repeat of his dream first win with Ducati at the 2018 Italian GP. Continued making progress, but not enough. After the race travelled to Japan to visit HRC to work on ergonomic improvements.

14 KAREL ABRAHAM
Finally scored his first championship points of 2019, after finishing 16th in two of the previous three races. Struggled with grip like many others but got into the swing of riding the bike with sliding tyres and made a few overtakes.

15 ANDREA IANNONE
Took the last championship point, his first score since COTA. Despite some disagreement with his team-mate on development direction and pain from his Jerez crash he rode a good race, fending off Oliveira in the last few laps.

16 MIGUEL OLIVEIRA
Experimented with a thumb rear brake in practice but decided against continuing with it. The middle part of his race went well, but the early laps were compromised by a full tank and the later laps by a lack of grip.

17 JOHANN ZARCO
The only rider to choose the soft rear and paid the price. His plan was to have good speed in the early stages, so he could at least compare himself and his bike to his rivals. Said he learned plenty, which should help in the future.

NC JACK MILLER
Once again proved he can be as fast as anyone in MotoGP. Was with the lead group at three-quarters distance when he realised the leaders were pushing harder to break away. Crashed out while planning a move on Rins.

NC FRANCESCO BAGNAIA
Was the fastest man on track on lap two, then passed Viñales and Nakagami and set about chasing down Crutchlow. Crashed out while just behind the Briton at half-distance. This was his third consecutive race crash.

NC HAFIZH SYAHRIN
Felt good in the early stages but then came within an nth of losing the front and crashing at speed as he raced through the Arrabbiata section. Had several more close-run calls and decided it was better to retire than crash.

NC VALENTINO ROSSI
The only two positives were that his high-speed crash at Arrabbiata 2 didn't hurt him and that his pace at that point was good.

NC FRANCO MORBIDELLI
Was chasing rookies Bagnaia and Quartararo when he lost the front on lap six. However, once again proved he had good speed.

NC TITO RABAT
The weekend went well, until Sunday, when an electrical fault forced him to start from pit lane and retire after one lap.

ENEOS
MONSTER
46
Lenovo
NetApp
SKF
GIVI valsir

Lorenzo was in too hot and the first to crash, skittling the luckless Dovizioso. Moments later both Viñales and Rossi were collateral damage. And the season was changed forever.

GRAN PREMI MONSTER ENERGY DE CATALUNYA
CIRCUIT DE BARCELONA-CATALUNYA
14/15/16 JUNE

THE WORLD TURNED UPSIDE DOWN

Barcelona's lap-two pile-up allowed Márquez to cruise to victory and changed the whole championship

A few tenths of a second is a long time in MotoGP. That's all it took for Jorge Lorenzo, Andrea Dovizioso, Maverick Viñales and Valentino Rossi to turn upside down at Barcelona-Catalunya, along with the race for the 2019 MotoGP world championship.

The pile-up was a typical early race incident: a pack of riders funnelling into a downhill, first-gear corner. Things get tight, they get tighter still and suddenly it's skittles time.

There was no doubt who was at fault. On the second lap Lorenzo tried to out-brake third-placed Viñales into turn ten. Immediately ahead of them Marc Márquez had out-braked race-leader Dovizioso, who adjusted his line to prepare his classic undercut manoeuvre. All of a sudden, Lorenzo found himself in deep trouble.

The three-time MotoGP champion wasn't exactly out of control but he was out of options – either T-bone Dovizioso or brake harder and inevitably exceed the available grip. Sure enough he locked his front tyre and down he went, his RC213V skittling Dovizioso, then Viñales and finally Valentino Rossi, who had out-braked Danilo Petrucci.

None of the fallen were able to continue, which left Márquez in glorious isolation out front, initially unaware of the chaos that had

CLOCKWISE, FROM TOP LEFT *Viñales was fast, but it didn't matter; Rookie Quartararo dazzled with his second pole in four races; rookie Mir fought for his best result yet; Rossi missed the front row by 0.4 seconds but it was all in vain; Lorenzo was on the charge until it all went wrong; Bagnaia lost the front, again; Márquez's job was easier than he had dared expect; Zarco took his first KTM top-ten; Viñales gets launched by the fallen Honda and Ducati. The same fate is soon to befall Rossi.*

'JORGE WASN'T LUCID AT THAT MOMENT"
ANDREA DOVIZIOSO

erupted just metres behind his rear wheel. He rode freely to his fourth victory of the year, while Petrucci engaged in a frantic battle for second with Álex Rins and pole-starter Fabio Quartararo.

The man who paid the highest price for Lorenzo's misdemeanour was Dovizioso, who arrived at Catalunya 12 points behind Márquez and left 37 points adrift. In one fell swoop his championship aspirations had been derailed. And he wasn't happy.

"Jorge wasn't lucid at that moment," he said. "He wanted to overtake Maverick, but he didn't look where he was braking, because Maverick braked very late and Jorge braked later, so he arrived too fast and he was on the inside. The mistake wasn't too big but to make that move at that corner on the second lap is a big mistake."

Lorenzo, always outspoken when he gets taken out, apologised to his victims, some taking the apology better than others. "The biggest thing is that I made three riders who are fighting for the championship crash," he said. "I would've loved to have crashed alone. I've said sorry."

Rossi was the most philosophical. "This is racing – sometimes it happens," said the veteran who has seen it all; this was his 330th Grand Prix race!

Of course, the 40-year-old has been in Lorenzo's boots himself, most memorably at Jerez in 2011, when he took out Casey Stoner.

In fact the circumstances of the two accidents were very similar. Rossi went into the 2011 Spanish GP following a grim first few races with Ducati. In the race he saw his chance of getting his first decent result and got carried away. Lorenzo went into the 2019 Catalan GP following a grim first few races with Honda. After Mugello he flew to Japan, spending several days at HRC, working on ergonomic improvements to improve his braking performance. The result was a pair of appendages attached to the fuel-tank cover of his RC213V.

"I felt very good on the bike and I was recovering a lot in braking," added Lorenzo. "Probably I was excited, because I was feeling good and I felt I could go faster and faster."

Lorenzo didn't get all the blame. Rossi directed some of his ire at the corner itself. "This corner is like supermarket parking!" he said. "It's not a racetrack corner and it's in corners like this that it's easy for these things to happen."

Turn ten was rearranged during the 2016 Catalan GP, as part of an immediate redesign following the death of Moto2 rider Luis Salom at turn 12. Most riders still prefer the original, more open turn ten, but not Márquez.

"We have many other turns like this, like at Austin and in Austria," he said. "We changed the layout for safety because with the original turn the wall is very close – in 2015 I went into the gravel there and almost arrived in the wall."

HAPPY 70TH BIRTHDAY, MotoGP!

The story of motorcycling's world championships began on 13th June 1949, when Freddie Frith rode a Velocette KTT to victory in the Isle of Man Junior TT for 350cc machines. The first premier-class race, the Senior TT for 500cc bikes, took place on 17th June 1949, hours after the Lightweight TT for 250s.

Thus the 2019 Catalan MotoGP round was Grand Prix racing's 70th birthday. It was also the sport's 930th event. The occasion was marked by various commemorative events throughout the weekend. Before practice got underway several 2019 bikes were taken into Barcelona and photographed alongside machines from the early days of world-championship racing, including

Márquez's victory cruise was imperious, although he did admit to very nearly losing the front at turn five during the mid-stages of the race, so he wasn't exactly cruising. The big question concerned Dovizioso: could he have fought the champion for victory? His crew said yes – they had crunched the numbers on tyre wear and no one tends his tyres better.

However, Márquez also had a plan. "I knew in the first seven laps I would be very strong, when the track was very slippery, before there was more rubber laid down," he explained. "For that reason I chose the soft rear to push at the beginning and open the gap."

With Márquez four seconds ahead after ten laps the battle for second provided the main entertainment. It was a classic contest of straight-line speed versus corner speed. Petrucci had plenty of the former, while Quartararo and Rins exulted in the latter.

With seven laps to go Rins tried to pass Petrucci at turn one. The pair collided, Rins saving an almighty wobble, while Quartararo pounced on Petrucci for his first MotoGP podium, exactly a year after he had turned his career around with his first Grand Prix victory, in Moto2.

Petrucci's third consecutive podium moved him to within five points of Dovizioso and gave Ducati another headache. At Mugello, Petrucci had declared he would dedicate the rest of his season to helping Ducati win the title. Many assumed this meant he would ride shotgun to Dovizioso. But not at all.

"For sure we don't have team orders – if I have the chance to win I will try," he confirmed at Barcelona.

CLOCKWISE FROM TOP LEFT | *Pol Espargaró and the RC16 were strong again, six tenths off the winning pace; Iannone looked for help from above; Guintoli did sterling test work for Suzuki; a shattered Quartararo lets his first MotoGP podium sink in; Rabat scored his first top-ten since his Silverstone 2018 horror; Márquez celebrates his first home-race win since 2014.*

Marc Márquez's RC213V shot at Camp Nou football stadium, next to a Mondial 125, winner of the inaugural 125cc title.

On Thursday evening the entire MotoGP grid turned out in bowties and tuxedos. On Saturday recently appointed FIM president Jorge Viegas awarded several MotoGP stalwarts for their services to the sport: Dorna CEO Carmelo Ezpeleta, IRTA general secretary Mike Trimby, MSMA general secretary Takanao Tsubouchi and former FIM president Luigi Brenni.

Brenni was FIM president in the early 1980s when the sport was going through huge changes. Fittingly, Brenni was a spectator at the 1949 Isle of Man TT.

7 | CATALUNYA

GRAN PREMI MONSTER ENERGY DE CATALUNYA

CIRCUIT DE BARCELONA-CATALUNYA

14/15/16 JUNE

QUALIFYING RESULTS

	RIDER	NAT	TEAM	MACHINE	QP/TIME		GAP 1ST/PREV	
1	Fabio Quartararo	FRA	Petronas Yamaha SRT	YAMAHA	Q2	1'39.484		
2	Marc Márquez	SPA	Repsol Honda Team	HONDA	Q2	1'39.499	0.015	0.015
3	Maverick Viñales	SPA	Monster Energy Yamaha MotoGP	YAMAHA	Q2	1'39.710	0.226	0.211
4	Franco Morbidelli	ITA	Petronas Yamaha SRT	YAMAHA	Q2	1'39.711	0.227	0.001
5	Valentino Rossi	ITA	Monster Energy Yamaha MotoGP	YAMAHA	Q2	1'39.753	0.269	0.042
6	Andrea Dovizioso	ITA	Mission Winnow Ducati	DUCATI	Q2	1'39.777	0.293	0.024
7	Danilo Petrucci	ITA	Mission Winnow Ducati	DUCATI	Q2	1'39.844	0.360	0.067
8	Álex Rins	SPA	Team SUZUKI ECSTAR	SUZUKI	Q2	1'39.870	0.386	0.026
9	Cal Crutchlow	GBR	LCR Honda CASTROL	HONDA	Q2	1'40.151	0.667	0.281
10	Jorge Lorenzo	SPA	Repsol Honda Team	HONDA	Q2	1'40.199	0.715	0.048
11	Joan Mir	SPA	Team SUZUKI ECSTAR	SUZUKI	Q2	1'40.240	0.756	0.041
12	Pol Espargaró	SPA	Red Bull KTM Factory Racing	KTM	Q2	1'40.425	0.941	0.185
13	Francesco Bagnaia	ITA	Pramac Racing	DUCATI	Q1	1'40.167	*0.440	0.155
14	Jack Miller	AUS	Pramac Racing	DUCATI	Q1	1'40.271	*0.544	0.104
15	Karel Abraham	CZE	Reale Avintia Racing	DUCATI	Q1	1'40.349	*0.622	0.078
16	Takaaki Nakagami	JPN	LCR Honda IDEMITSU	HONDA	Q1	1'40.362	*0.635	0.013
17	Aleix Espargaró	SPA	Aprilia Racing Team Gresini	APRILIA	Q1	1'40.400	*0.673	0.038
18	Johann Zarco	FRA	Red Bull KTM Factory Racing	KTM	Q1	1'40.427	*0.700	0.027
19	Tito Rabat	SPA	Reale Avintia Racing	DUCATI	Q1	1'40.682	*0.955	0.255
20	Miguel Oliveira	POR	Red Bull KTM Tech 3	KTM	Q1	1'40.752	*1.025	0.070
21	Hafizh Syahrin	MAL	Red Bull KTM Tech 3	KTM	Q1	1'40.839	*1.112	0.087
22	Bradley Smith	GBR	Aprilia Racing Team	APRILIA	Q1	1'41.232	*1.505	0.393
23	Sylvain Guintoli	FRA	Team SUZUKI ECSTAR	SUZUKI	Q1	1'41.270	*1.543	0.038
24	Andrea Iannone	ITA	Aprilia Racing Team Gresini	APRILIA	Q1	1'41.748	*2.021	0.478

** Gap to the fastest rider in the Q1 session* *** Went forward from Q1 to Q2* *Track severity = Wear + Temperature + Load*

GRAND PRIX INFORMATION

TRACK INFORMATION			
2019 WINNER	Marc Márquez		
CIRCUIT LENGTH	4.6 km	2.88 miles	
LAPS	24		
RACE DISTANCE	111.0 km	69.1 miles	
ALL TIME LAP RECORD	1'38.680	168.8 Km/h	Jorge Lorenzo (2018)
BEST RACE LAP	1'40.021	166.5 Km/h	Jorge Lorenzo (2018)
RACE CONDITION	Dry		
AIR	26°C		
HUMIDITY	47%		
GROUND	51°C		

TYRE SELECTION

FRONT	
SOFT	WHITE
MEDIUM	GREY
HARD	YELLOW

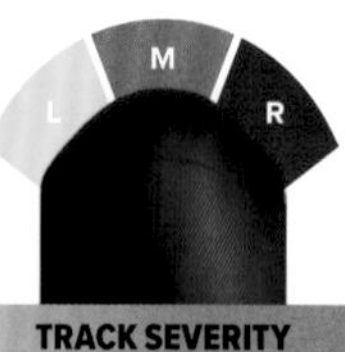

REAR	
SOFT	WHITE
MEDIUM	GREY
HARD	YELLOW

< MILD TRACK SEVERITY SEVERE >

1 MARC MÁRQUEZ
Expected a battle with at least Dovizioso, but his race was made much simpler by the lap-two skittles match at turn ten. After that he kept pushing to maintain his focus. A perfect day, after his brother had won the earlier Moto2 race.

2 FABIO QUARTARARO
Scored his first podium six weeks after he should've made the top-three at Jerez. And this despite a recent operation for arm pump. Had his first MotoGP fall in FP3, after 6800km/4200 miles of testing, practice and racing.

3 DANILO PETRUCCI
Enjoyed the battle with Quartararo and Rins, using the speed of his GP19 and refusing to be bullied in the corners, even though his rivals had the advantage there. A third consecutive podium was another big moment for the Italian.

4 ÁLEX RINS
Had impressive speed throughout – might he have been able to go with Márquez if he had got away with his compatriot? Struggled with Petrucci because his front tyre temperature rose too much while in the Ducati's draft.

5 JACK MILLER
Ducati's holeshot device helped him make a great start: from 14th to seventh on lap one. Ran with Petrucci's group for a few laps but didn't have the grip to stay with them. Briefly got ahead of Rins when he ran off at turn one.

6 JOAN MIR
Two weeks after his first points since Qatar came his first top-ten finish since Qatar. Chased Miller and Crutchlow for most of the race, until Crutchlow fell. Was still right in Miller's slipstream when they took the chequered flag.

7 POL ESPARGARÓ
Reined in his aggressive instincts to ride a perfectly precise race on a very slippery track, using a lot of electronics to help him maintain control. His race time was 20 seconds closer to the winner than at the 2018 Catalan GP!

8 TAKAAKI NAKAGAMI
Not as impressive a ride as Mugello, but proved himself in the tricky conditions, chasing Espargaró in the final stages. During Monday's test he got to try a 2019 RC213V; further proof that HRC take him very seriously.

9 TITO RABAT
This was a richly deserved first top-ten result since he suffered horrific leg injuries at Silverstone 2018. The local qualified 19th and like so many others took advantage of the lap-two pile-up to move up the finishing order.

10 JOHANN ZARCO
The Frenchman found that the slippery track made the KTM easier to ride. His first top-ten with KTM was also the first time he'd been within a second a lap of the winner since Qatar, but there were few smiles in his garage.

RACE LAP CHART

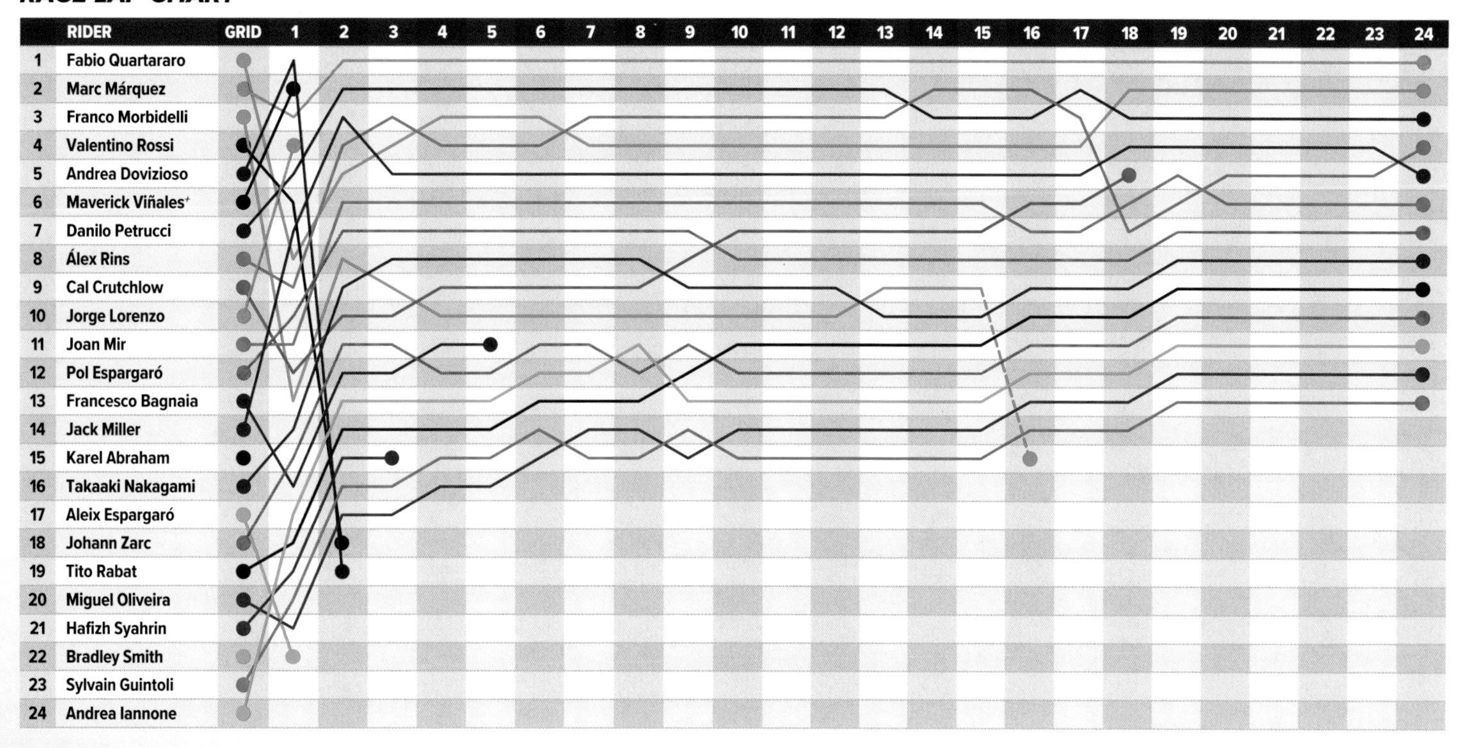

+ FIM MotoGP Stewards grid penalty - Maverick Viñales

RACE RESULTS

	RIDER	NAT	TEAM	MACHINE	TIME	+ GAP	TYRES
1	Marc Márquez	SPA	Repsol Honda Team	HONDA	40'31.175		H/M
2	Fabio Quartararo	FRA	Petronas Yamaha SRT	YAMAHA	40'33.835	2.660	S/M
3	Danilo Petrucci	ITA	Mission Winnow Ducati	DUCATI	40'35.712	4.537	S/S
4	Álex Rins	SPA	Team SUZUKI ECSTAR	SUZUKI	40'37.777	6.602	M/M
5	Jack Miller	AUS	Pramac Racing	DUCATI	40'38.045	6.870	S/M
6	Joan Mir	SPA	Team SUZUKI ECSTAR	SUZUKI	40'38.215	7.040	M/M
7	Pol Espargaró	SPA	Red Bull KTM Factory Racing	KTM	40'47.319	16.144	M/S
8	Takaaki Nakagami	JPN	LCR Honda IDEMITSU	HONDA	40'49.144	17.969	M/S
9	Tito Rabat	SPA	Reale Avintia Racing	DUCATI	40'53.836	22.661	M/M
10	Johann Zarco	FRA	Red Bull KTM Factory Racing	KTM	40'57.403	26.228	S/H
11	Andrea Iannone	ITA	Aprilia Racing Team Gresini	APRILIA	41'03.211	32.036	S/S
12	Miguel Oliveira	POR	Red Bull KTM Tech 3	KTM	41'15.841	44.666	M/M
13	Sylvain Guintoli	FRA	Team SUZUKI ECSTAR	SUZUKI	41'22.538	51.363	M/M
NC	Cal Crutchlow	GBR	LCR Honda CASTROL	HONDA	30'28.089	6 laps	M/M
NC	Franco Morbidelli	ITA	Petronas Yamaha SRT	YAMAHA	32'06.024	8 laps	S/H
NC	Francesco Bagnaia	ITA	Pramac Racing	DUCATI	8'35.942	19 laps	S/S
NC	Hafizh Syahrin	MAL	Red Bull KTM Tech 3	KTM	5'15.055	21 laps	M/M
NC	Valentino Rossi	ITA	Monster Energy Yamaha MotoGP	YAMAHA	4'20.286	22 laps	S/M
NC	Andrea Dovizioso	ITA	Mission Winnow Ducati	DUCATI	4'39.419	22 laps	S/S
NC	Maverick Viñales	SPA	Monster Energy Yamaha MotoGP	YAMAHA	1'46.084	23 laps	S/S
NC	Jorge Lorenzo	SPA	Repsol Honda Team	HONDA	1'46.625	23 laps	S/S
NC	Aleix Espargaró	SPA	Aprilia Racing Team Gresini	APRILIA	2'30.510	23 laps	M/S
NC	Karel Abraham	CZE	Reale Avintia Racing	DUCATI			M/M
NC	Bradley Smith	GBR	Aprilia Racing Team	APRILIA			M/S

CHAMPIONSHIP STANDINGS

	RIDER	NAT	TEAM	PTS
1	Marc Márquez	SPA	Repsol Honda Team	140
2	Andrea Dovizioso	ITA	Mission Winnow Ducati	103
3	Álex Rins	SPA	Team SUZUKI ECSTAR	101
4	Danilo Petrucci	ITA	Mission Winnow Ducati	98
5	Valentino Rossi	ITA	Monster Energy Yamaha MotoGP	72
6	Jack Miller	AUS	Pramac Racing	53
7	Fabio Quartararo	FRA	Petronas Yamaha SRT	51
8	Takaaki Nakagami	JPN	LCR Honda IDEMITSU	48
9	Pol Espargaró	SPA	Red Bull KTM Factory Racing	47
10	Cal Crutchlow	GBR	LCR Honda CASTROL	42
11	Maverick Viñales	SPA	Monster Energy Yamaha MotoGP	40
12	Franco Morbidelli	ITA	Petronas Yamaha SRT	34
13	Aleix Espargaró	SPA	Aprilia Racing Team Gresini	27
14	Joan Mir	SPA	Team SUZUKI ECSTAR	22
15	Jorge Lorenzo	SPA	Repsol Honda Team	19
16	Johann Zarco	FRA	Red Bull KTM Factory Racing	16
17	Miguel Oliveira	POR	Red Bull KTM Tech 3	12
18	Andrea Iannone	ITA	Aprilia Racing Team Gresini	12
19	Michele Pirro	ITA	Mission Winnow Ducati	9
20	Francesco Bagnaia	ITA	Pramac Racing	9
21	Tito Rabat	SPA	Reale Avintia Racing	9
22	Stefan Bradl	GER	Team HRC	6
23	Sylvain Guintoli	FRA	Team SUZUKI ECSTAR	3
24	Karel Abraham	CZE	Reale Avintia Racing	2
25	Hafizh Syahrin	MAL	Red Bull KTM Tech 3	2
26	Bradley Smith	GBR	Aprilia Factory Racing	

11 ANDREA DOVIZIOSO
Bettered his previous Aprilia best by one position, despite starting from last on the grid, due to a problem with his RS-GP's ride-by-wire in QP1. Chased Zarco during the early stages but then had a big drop in tyre performance.

12 MIGUEL OLIVEIRA
Started well but got caught up in the first-lap Smith/Aleix Espargaró incident, which forced him off the track and put him in last position. From there he rode his race, overtaking Guintoli for his fourth points haul of the year.

13 SYLVAIN GUINTOLI
Suzuki's test rider rode his second GP, in advance of the post-race tests. Used a revised frame and swingarm which he had tested at Brno a few days earlier. In FP1 there was so much less grip than at Brno he thought he had a puncture!

DNF CAL CRUTCHLOW
Crashed out with six laps to go while trying to make a pass on Miller. Was still struggling with the corner-entry problems he had had all season, so he locked the rear with the rear brake. Owned up that the tumble was his fault.

NC FRANCO MORBIDELLI
Rode in some discomfort from a nasty corner-entry highside on Saturday. Got a good start and had good speed but wasn't getting any feeling from the front brake, so when he started pushing harder he ran wide and slid off.

NC FRANCESCO BAGNAIA
Lost the front at the tricky downhill turn five while chasing Morbidelli in the early stages of the race. This was the Moto2 world champion's fifth crash in five races – one of those moments when it's important to keep your nerve.

NC HAFIZH SYAHRIN
Started from the seventh row of the grid and was in the point-scoring positions following the pile-up. However, his chances of taking his second points haul with KTM were ruined by an engine glitch that forced his retirement.

NC VALENTINO ROSSI
Two weeks after his Mugello misery he found his bike/tyre combination much more competitive, reflected by his second-row start. Sadly, his chances of fighting for the podium were ruined by the second-lap disaster.

NC MAVERICK VIÑALES
What luck. His strongest start since Jerez should've put him in the podium battle. Instead Lorenzo tried to out-brake him and took him out.

NC ANDREA DOVIZIOSO
Márquez was able to pass him because he was waiting for his rear tyre to come up to temperature. We all know what happened next.

NC JORGE LORENZO
Boosted by new ergonomics, this could've been a breakthrough. Instead his race turned into a disaster when he got boxed in on the brakes.

NC ALEIX ESPARGARÓ
Smith went down and collided with his team-mate. The Spaniard didn't crash but the impact damaged his left knee and he retired in agony.

NC KAREL ABRAHAM
Equalled his best qualifying performance so far, but it was all for nothing, because he fell at the tricky downhill turn seven, on lap one.

NC BRADLEY SMITH
Another test rider in the race to gather race data before Monday's post-race tests. But the Briton's efforts only lasted nine corners.

Viñales dominated at a favourite Yamaha track, where corner speed counts.

8 | NETHERLANDS

MOTUL TT ASSEN
TT CIRCUIT ASSEN
28/29/30 JUNE

VIÑALES MAKES IT WORK

Finally Maverick Viñales put together an almost perfect weekend – had the Spaniard turned the corner?

At last, the breakthrough. At the eighth time of trying Maverick Viñales and new crew chief Sergio Garcia won their first race together, and Yamaha's first since Phillip Island the previous October.

The 24-year-old's winning advantage of 4.8 seconds might suggest that he dominated Assen, but the race didn't go quite like that. He spent more than half the 26 laps battling with Marc Márquez and pole-starter Fabio Quartararo to make it to the front. And he might have had to keep battling if Márquez hadn't eased off because he really didn't need to take such risks, and because Quartararo slowed because he had post-surgery issues with his right arm.

Nonetheless Viñales was rightly delighted, not merely with his sixth MotoGP victory but with the manner of that victory.

"The best feeling is that we did the job from Friday to Sunday," he said, suggesting he had found a new way of working with Garcia. "After practice at Mugello we thought we had our maximum potential because practice was really good, but the set-up wasn't the best for the race. We needed to find more traction, which is what our bike needs. We found it at Catalunya and here. And finally we found a way that the race was the same as warm-up for us, so I could ride in the same way and that's the most important thing."

"THE BEST FEELING IS THAT WE DID THE JOB FROM FRIDAY TO SUNDAY"
MAVERICK VIÑALES

CLOCKWISE, FROM TOP LEFT | *Rossi's lowly grid position led to disaster; Gigi Dall'Igna dreamt of a mid-corner fix; Quartararo took his second consecutive pole; Iannone was getting the hang of the Aprilia; Lorenzo was out after a very nasty accident; the factory Ducatis raced each other to the finish; Viñales and his crew did great work in their garage; Quartararo led a MotoGP race for the first time; the race didn't produce a 2018 Assen rerun.*

If Assen was a breakthrough for Viñales it was just another chapter in Jorge Lorenzo's nightmare 2019 season. The former Yamaha rider crashed heavily in FP1, fracturing two vertebrae. After hospital treatment he was sent home wearing an upper body brace.

Grand Prix racing's oldest venue favours the sweet-handling Yamaha and Suzuki, which drive home their corner-speed advantage through sweeping, flowing twists and turns. At first it was Álex Rins and team-mate Joan Mir who led the race. Rins, who had beaten Viñales into second at Assen 2018, looked like he had the pace to break away, until he reached turn nine on lap three.

"Exiting turn eight I got a bit more wheelie than normal, then I braked a little harder for turn nine and lost the front completely," explained Rins after a rare error, abetted by the windy conditions. "I'm convinced my rhythm was good enough to fight for victory."

That put Mir into the lead of a MotoGP race for the first time, but the pressure soon told and a few corners later he left the door wide open. Quartararo didn't need a written invitation. This was also the first time the Frenchman had led a MotoGP race, but while he seemed perfectly relaxed his motorcycle was a nervous wreck. Each time he accelerated down the Veenslang straight towards turn six his M1 broke into a terrifying tank-slapper, giving him a stark choice: shut the gas or abandon ship.

Márquez and Viñales were now right on the youngster, who wasn't for giving up, even though his right arm most likely was. His post-Mugello arm-pump op hadn't been a concern at Catalunya, but Assen is one of MotoGP's most arduous circuits, even without a bike that's trying to unseat its rider.

Both Márquez and Viñales made mistakes as they chased after their young rival, possibly distracted by his dancing M1. Also, the pair were tripping over themselves in their efforts to get the upper hand; after all, neither is on the other's Christmas card list.

As the trio raced down Veenslang for the 16th time Quartararo had to shut the gas once more. Viñales swept ahead, while Márquez nearly tail-ended the Petronas Yamaha. Moments later at the daunting Ramshoek left he went past the rookie.

Quartararo now watched and learned as Márquez inched closer to the leader, taking all kinds of risks to stay with him. Most riders with a 37-point championship lead would've used that as an excuse to move away from the cliff edge, but not Márquez. He saw his points advantage as a good reason to keep dancing on that edge; for a while at least.

Although Márquez wanted to win the race he had chosen his tyres for the championship – using the soft rear, while Viñales went with the hard.

"I chose the soft because my strategy was to be with the Yamaha riders until lap 15, then maybe suffer the last laps and

HONDA CELEBRATES 60 YEARS

Here was another nod to the past in a season full of milestones. Two weeks after MotoGP celebrated its 70th birthday at Barcelona, Honda marked the 60th anniversary of its participation in world championship racing.

Honda veterans Mick Doohan and Kunimitsu Takahashi rode a lap of honour on two machines that spanned the company's six decades in Grands Prix. Doohan rode the NSR500 that Eddie Lawson took to the 1989 500cc title, while Takahashi rode the 125cc RC142 with which Honda made its world-class debut in the 1959 Isle of Man Ultra-Lightweight TT.

just survive," he said. "For me, the risk with the hard tyre was to have a slower pace and end up with [Andrea] Dovizioso."

Both Dovizioso and Danilo Petrucci had difficult races, way off the pace. "Here you have many long corners where you have to use corner speed and that's not our strong point," said Dovizioso, who left Assen 44 points behind Márquez.

His team-mate described the situation more eloquently. "The problem is that the Suzuki does one kilometre more around the lap, but they are faster because they don't have to do square off corners like us," said Petrucci. "The Suzuki can use all the track, which is impossible for us. If we enter very wide like them and try to find the apex at the last moment we miss the apex."

The Desmosedici riders suffered most at the end of the race, by which time the hot track had consumed their rear tyres. "The last ten laps were a nightmare," Petrucci added.

Franco Morbidelli got faster as the race went on, moving up from eighth at half-distance to nip past Petrucci as the Italian lined up a last-lap move on Dovizioso.

Cal Crutchlow was neither fast at the beginning nor the end. He had his best grip mid-race, which was good enough to get him past Mir but not good enough to keep Morbidelli behind him.

CLOCKWISE FROM TOP LEFT | *A little hilarity in the pre-event media conference; Viñales celebrates through the yellow haze; Márquez knew that second place was more than good enough; Syahrin and Bagnaia disputing the final points at the chicane; Viñales attributed his victory to a new mentality in his garage; no one could remember when two Suzukis last led a premier-class Grand Prix, but it would've been in the Kevin Schwantz era.*

Takahashi, who in 1961 became the first Japanese rider to win a GP race, still remembers Honda's pioneering years. "Arriving in Europe was a total shock, because everything was different," said the 79-year-old. "At that time Japan didn't have paved roads, whereas in Europe the roads were paved and proper race circuits were available, so the level of racing was totally, totally different."

Doohan wasn't exactly delighted to be reunited with the '89 NSR, which he rode during his pain-wracked rookie season. "I used to get scared hearing them revving up the bike in the pit box: Jeez, have I got to ride that thing?!" he laughed. "Winning the championship on that bike was a credit to Eddie, but for a rookie like me it was very intimidating."

8 | NETHERLANDS

MOTUL TT ASSEN
TT CIRCUIT ASSEN
28/29/30 JUNE

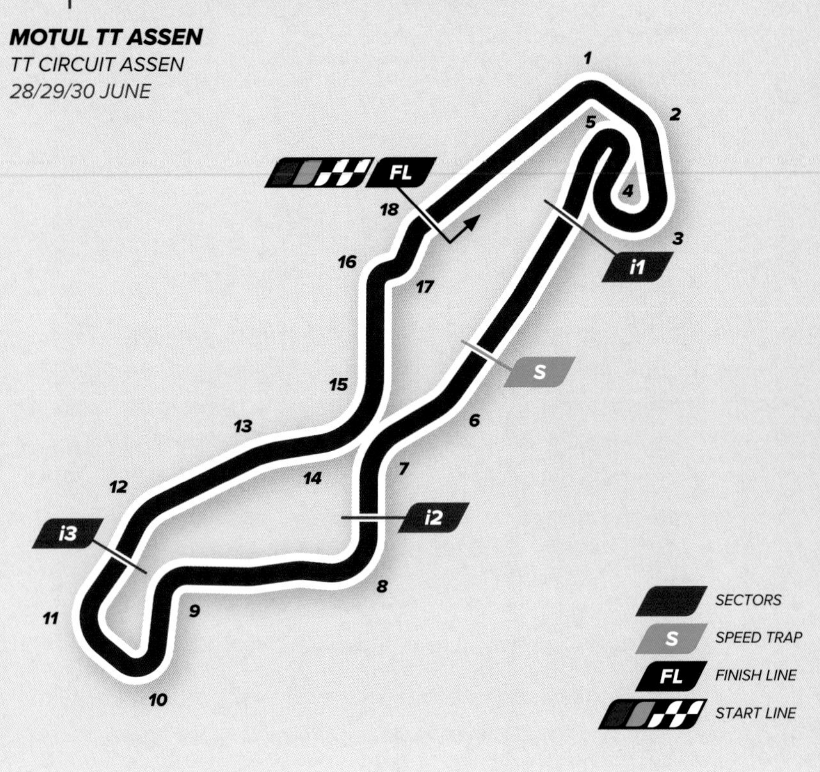

QUALIFYING RESULTS

	RIDER	NAT	TEAM	MACHINE	QP/TIME		GAP 1ST/PREV	
1	Fabio Quartararo	FRA	Petronas Yamaha SRT	YAMAHA	Q2	1'32.017		
2	Maverick Viñales	SPA	Monster Energy Yamaha MotoGP	YAMAHA	Q2	1'32.157	0.140	0.140
3	Álex Rins**	SPA	Team SUZUKI ECSTAR	SUZUKI	Q2	1'32.458	0.441	0.301
4	Marc Márquez	SPA	Repsol Honda Team	HONDA	Q2	1'32.731	0.714	0.273
5	Joan Mir	SPA	Team SUZUKI ECSTAR	SUZUKI	Q2	1'33.085	1.068	0.354
6	Cal Crutchlow	GBR	LCR Honda CASTROL	HONDA	Q2	1'33.228	1.211	0.143
7	Danilo Petrucci	ITA	Ducati Team	DUCATI	Q2	1'33.282	1.265	0.054
8	Takaaki Nakagami	JPN	LCR Honda IDEMITSU	HONDA	Q2	1'33.295	1.278	0.013
9	Franco Morbidelli	ITA	Petronas Yamaha SRT	YAMAHA	Q2	1'33.314	1.297	0.019
10	Jack Miller	AUS	Pramac Racing	DUCATI	Q2	1'33.323	1.306	0.009
11	Andrea Dovizioso	ITA	Ducati Team	DUCATI	Q2	1'33.692	1.675	0.369
12	Pol Espargaró**	SPA	Red Bull KTM Factory Racing	KTM	Q2	1'33.762	1.745	0.070
13	Francesco Bagnaia	ITA	Pramac Racing	DUCATI	Q1	1'33.221	*0.511	0.051
14	Valentino Rossi	ITA	Monster Energy Yamaha MotoGP	YAMAHA	Q1	1'33.466	*0.756	0.245
15	Aleix Espargaró	SPA	Aprilia Racing Team Gresini	APRILIA	Q1	1'33.547	*0.837	0.081
16	Karel Abraham	CZE	Reale Avintia Racing	DUCATI	Q1	1'33.583	*0.873	0.036
17	Miguel Oliveira	POR	Red Bull KTM Tech 3	KTM	Q1	1'33.706	*0.996	0.123
18	Johann Zarco	FRA	Red Bull KTM Factory Racing	KTM	Q1	1'33.776	*1.066	0.070
19	Hafizh Syahrin	MAL	Red Bull KTM Tech 33	KTM	Q1	1'33.869	*1.159	0.093
20	Andrea Iannone	ITA	Aprilia Racing Team Gresini	APRILIA	Q1	1'33.960	*1.250	0.091
21	Tito Rabat	SPA	Reale Avintia Racing	DUCATI	Q1	1'34.580	*1.870	0.620

** Gap to the fastest rider in the Q1 session* *** Went forward from Q1 to Q2* *Track severity = Wear + Temperature + Load*

GRAND PRIX INFORMATION

TRACK INFORMATION			
2019 WINNER	Maverick Viñales		
CIRCUIT LENGTH	4.5 km	2.82 miles	
LAPS	26		
RACE DISTANCE	118.1 km	73.3 miles	
ALL TIME LAP RECORD	1'32.017	177.6 Km/h	Fabio Quartararo (2019)
BEST RACE LAP	1'33.617	174.6 Km/h	Marc Márquez (2015)
RACE CONDITION	Dry		
AIR	25°C		
HUMIDITY	55%		
GROUND	44°C		

TYRE SELECTION

FRONT	
SOFT	WHITE
MEDIUM	GREY
HARD	YELLOW

REAR	
SOFT	WHITE
MEDIUM	GREY
HARD	YELLOW

L M R

< MILD — TRACK SEVERITY — SEVERE >

1 MAVERICK VIÑALES
His second win in 11 races seemed like something of a turning point – bit by bit the Spaniard was putting things back together after two very difficult years. Worked coolly and calmly from FP1, which is nearly always the secret.

2 MARC MÁRQUEZ
Always knew this could be a difficult weekend, so took the maximum possible and played the perfect championship strategy. Hard to know what his rivals can do when he can achieve second place at a so-so track for the Honda.

3 FABIO QUARTARARO
Fulfilled his childhood dream of leading a MotoGP race, but the combination of his recently operated right arm and a lack of machine stability didn't allow him to keep fighting. Nonetheless achieved his second consecutive podium.

4 ANDREA DOVIZIOSO
Considering the fact that he started from the fourth row and that the Ducati doesn't like Assen, fourth place was as good as he could expect; but that doesn't mean it made him happy. A 14-second deficit is no smiling matter.

5 FRANCO MORBIDELLI
Matched his best-ever fifth-place finish at COTA. Spent much of the race chasing Crutchlow, then found a better feeling with his bike and tyres, which helped him overtake the Briton, Mir and Petrucci in the final laps.

6 DANILO PETRUCCI
The hotter-than-usual Assen weather made life more difficult for the Ducati riders, who need good rear grip to exploit their power advantage. Lost fifth to Morbidelli at the final chicane when considering a move on his team-mate.

7 CAL CRUTCHLOW
This wasn't a bad salvage job from the Briton, who qualified on the third row of the grid, soon lost touch with the lead group and made a few mistakes, then got into a better groove, riding his fastest lap in the second half of the race.

8 JOAN MIR
Spent much of the race with the factory Ducatis, getting ahead of both Petrucci and Dovizioso on several occasions, using his GSX-RR's corner speed, but once his rear tyre went he decided discretion was the better part of valour.

9 JACK MILLER
Wasn't at all happy with his race, because he never had the rear grip he expected and needed. The Australian's pace dropped significantly after half-distance and he spent most of the 26 laps all on his lonesome.

10 ANDREA IANNONE
Finally, the Italian's first top-ten finish with Aprilia; thanks in part to improvements made at the Barcelona test and in part thanks to the RS-GP's easy handling. Very nearly caught Miller at the very end of the race.

RACE LAP CHART

----- *Dashed line: Lapped rider*

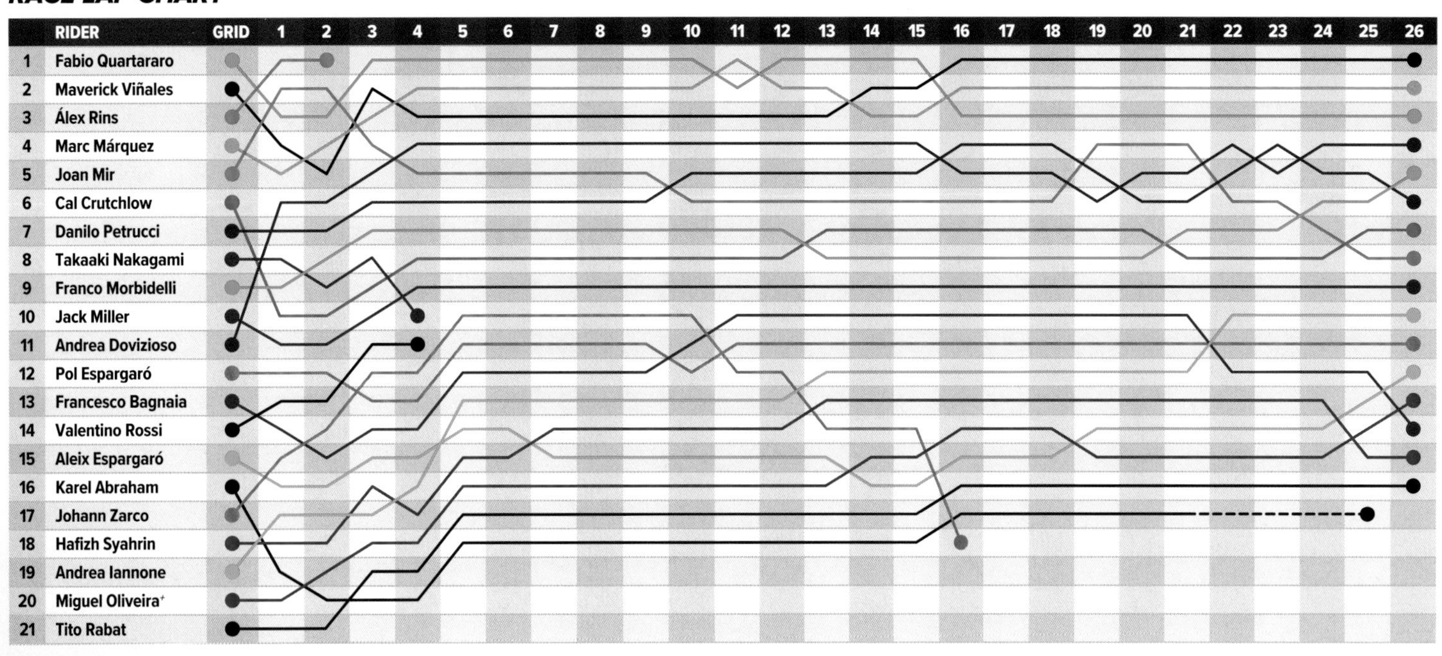

+ FIM MotoGP Stewards grid penalty - #88 Miguel Oliveira

RACE RESULTS

	RIDER	NAT	TEAM	MACHINE	TIME	+ GAP	TYRES
1	Maverick Viñales	SPA	Monster Energy Yamaha MotoGP	YAMAHA	40'55.415		M/H
2	Marc Márquez	SPA	Repsol Honda Team	HONDA	41'00.269	4.854	M/S
3	Fabio Quartararo	FRA	Petronas Yamaha SRT	YAMAHA	41'05.153	9.738	M/H
4	Andrea Dovizioso	ITA	Ducati Team	DUCATI	41'09.562	14.147	M/H
5	Franco Morbidelli	ITA	Petronas Yamaha SRT	YAMAHA	41'09.882	14.467	M/H
6	Danilo Petrucci	ITA	Ducati Team	DUCATI	41'10.209	14.794	M/H
7	Cal Crutchlow	GBR	LCR Honda CASTROL	HONDA	41'13.776	18.361	M/H
8	Joan Mir	SPA	Team SUZUKI ECSTAR	SUZUKI	41'19.683	24.268	H/S
9	Jack Miller	AUS	Pramac Racing	DUCATI	41'21.911	26.496	S/H
10	Andrea Iannone	ITA	Aprilia Racing Team Gresini	APRILIA	41'22.412	26.997	S/H
11	Pol Espargaró	SPA	Red Bull KTM Factory Racing	KTM	41'24.147	28.732	M/H
12	Aleix Espargaró	SPA	Aprilia Racing Team Gresini	APRILIA	41'29.510	34.095	M/S
13	Miguel Oliveira	POR	Red Bull KTM Tech 3	KTM	41'29.596	34.181	M/H
14	Francesco Bagnaia	ITA	Pramac Racing	DUCATI	41'29.664	34.249	S/H
15	Hafizh Syahrin	MAL	Red Bull KTM Tech 3	KTM	41'29.909	34.494	M/H
16	Tito Rabat	SPA	Reale Avintia Racing	DUCATI	41'43.772	48.357	M/H
17	Karel Abraham	CZE	Reale Avintia Racing	DUCATI	41'39.924	1 lap	M/S
NC	Johann Zarco	FRA	Red Bull KTM Factory Racing	KTM	25'53.816	10 laps	M/H
NC	Takaaki Nakagami	JPN	LCR Honda IDEMITSU	HONDA	6'26.973	22 laps	M/M
NC	Valentino Rossi	ITA	Monster Energy Yamaha MotoGP	YAMAHA	6'27.026	22 laps	M/H
NC	Álex Rins	SPA	Team SUZUKI ECSTAR	SUZUKI	3'14.410	24 laps	H/S

CHAMPIONSHIP STANDINGS

	RIDER	NAT	TEAM	PTS
1	Marc Márquez	SPA	Repsol Honda Team	160
2	Andrea Dovizioso	ITA	Ducati Team	116
3	Danilo Petrucci	ITA	Ducati Team	108
4	Álex Rins	SPA	Team SUZUKI ECSTAR	101
5	Valentino Rossi	ITA	Monster Energy Yamaha MotoGP	72
6	Fabio Quartararo	FRA	Petronas Yamaha SRT	67
7	Maverick Viñales	SPA	Monster Energy Yamaha MotoGP	65
8	Jack Miller	AUS	Pramac Racing	60
9	Pol Espargaró	SPA	Red Bull KTM Factory Racing	52
10	Cal Crutchlow	GBR	LCR Honda CASTROL	51
11	Takaaki Nakagami	JPN	LCR Honda IDEMITSU	48
12	Franco Morbidelli	ITA	Petronas Yamaha SRT	45
13	Aleix Espargaró	SPA	Aprilia Racing Team Gresini	31
14	Joan Mir	SPA	Team SUZUKI ECSTAR	30
15	Jorge Lorenzo	SPA	Repsol Honda Team	19
16	Andrea Iannone	ITA	Aprilia Racing Team Gresini	18
17	Johann Zarco	FRA	Red Bull KTM Factory Racing	16
18	Miguel Oliveira	POR	Red Bull KTM Tech 3	15
19	Francesco Bagnaia	ITA	Pramac Racing	11
20	Michele Pirro	ITA	Ducati Team	9
21	Tito Rabat	SPA	Reale Avintia Racing	9
22	Stefan Bradl	GER	Team HRC	6
23	Sylvain Guintoli	FRA	Team SUZUKI ECSTAR	3
24	Hafizh Syahrin	MAL	Red Bull KTM Tech 3	3
25	Karel Abraham	CZE	Reale Avintia Racing	2
26	Bradley Smith	GBR	Aprilia Factory Racing	

11 POL ESPARGARÓ
Spent the weekend handicapped by a right-hand injury sustained when he crashed heavily during the Barcelona tests. He therefore rode conservatively during the race, then spent the last few laps surviving as the pain increased.

13 MIGUEL OLIVEIRA
Part of the three-man group fighting for 12th, the Portuguese rookie got the better of team-mate Syahrin two laps from the finish and then pounced on the ailing Bagnaia on the final lap. This was his fifth MotoGP points score.

15 HAFIZH SYAHRIN
His best qualifying of the year should've yielded his best result, but it didn't quite turn out like that. Raced with the Aprilias, slotted in behind Iannone but lost grip and couldn't control it with the TC. His second points with KTM.

17 KAREL ABRAHAM
Not the best of days. Qualified 16th and was confident of scoring points. But the race didn't go well: got a bad start and couldn't get any feel from the tyres, then crashed and remounted to finish a lap down on the winner.

NC TAKAAKI NAKAGAMI
Was on course for his seventh top-ten from the first eight races when he was taken out by a hard-charging Rossi at turn eight. Both riders fell heavily at high speed, Nakagami hitting the air-fence and suffering concussion.

NC ÁLEX RINS
His first front-row start of the year suggested great things for the COTA winner. Looked like he had plans to make the break from the pack when he lost the front and crashed on lap three. A rare mistake from the youngster.

12 ALEIX ESPARGARÓ
Like his little brother, was still hurting from Barcelona, where he was rammed on the first lap of the race. His left leg injury made it particularly difficult to muscle his bike through Assen's numerous high-speed changes of direction.

14 FRANCESCO BAGNAIA
This, believe it or not, was the Moto2 champ's first finish since COTA. The rookie ran tenth from lap 11 to lap 21 but then ran into serious grip problems, his lap times dropping like a stone as he lost position after position.

16 TITO RABAT
After Barcelona underwent further surgery on his still problematic right leg and struggled with pain and strength – wrestling a Desmosedici around Assen isn't easy at the best of time. Was also hit by stability and brake issues.

NC JOHANN ZARCO
Crashed in FP2 at turn seven, where Lorenzo fell, but walked away. Ran tenth in the race but dropped back from half-distance until he was behind Syahrin. Withdrew because "I had the feeling I wasn't holding the bike anymore".

NC VALENTINO ROSSI
Seemed to have "pulled the rabbit out of the hat" again, with a warm-up settings change that found him more than half a second. Was fighting through from 14th on the grid when he lost the front and took out Nakagami.

DNS JORGE LORENZO
Lost the front at turn seven in the cool FP1 session. What should've been a fast but straightforward crash turned into something nastier when he flipped in the gravel trap and landed headfirst, fracturing his T6 and T8 vertebrae.

Márquez reached 66 degrees of lean at Sachsenring, so that no one could reach him.

9 | GERMANY

HJC HELMETS MOTORRAD GRAND PRIX DEUTSCHLAND

SACHSENRING

05/06/07 JULY

SPIN IT TO WIN IT

Marc Márquez knows how to ride the Sachsenring – it's a bit like a 270-horsepower dirt track for the world champ

No one in motorcycling's modern era has managed to do what Marc Márquez did at Sachsenring: win a tenth consecutive race across different classes at the same track. The last man to do such a thing was (of course) Giacomo Agostini, who won 13 successive races in the 500cc and 350cc classes at Imatra, Finland, between 1966 and 1973.

Márquez lives in different times, when races aren't won by several minutes but by a few seconds. And such is modern MotoGP that this 4.5-second victory was considered a walkover. In some ways it was: the Spaniard's fifth win of the year was his third biggest (after Argentina 2019 and Jerez 2018) since the rain-affected 2017 Czech GP.

It's no surprise that Termas and Sachsenring allow Márquez to wave goodbye to his rivals. They are both low-grip circuits where riders spend a lot of time on the edge of the tyres, which means lots of sliding, which is what Márquez does best, especially when he's turning left. Sachsenring accorded perfectly to his 2019 strategy: when everything is perfect, don't hang around to make a race of it, just disappear and remind people how good you are. In fact he'd already done a bit of that in practice, achieving an all-time record lean angle of 66 degrees.

"The plan was there and I followed it," he said. "The plan was to lead from the beginning to the end – just warm the tyres the first two laps, then push from lap three. We found the way in FP4, to be very precise with the electronics, the tyres and everything. I was convinced to race the hard rear, then on the grid, okay, we changed to the medium [which all riders agreed was harder than the hard]. It was the correct choice and it felt good."

Márquez didn't quite lead from start to finish. He got crossed-up off the line and had to ride around the outside of Fabio Quartararo into the treacherously negative-camber first corner. Then the pack almost disappeared from view as it raced through a thick fog of yellow smoke flares ignited by fans.

Maverick Viñales raced after the leader and momentarily got level as they swept downhill from Ralf Waldmann Kurve for the first time, with Álex Rins, Cal Crutchlow, Jack Miller, Danilo Petrucci and Quartararo fighting among themselves just behind.

Quartararo was the first to go. He slid off – his first MotoGP race crash – when he asked too much too soon of the right of his tyres as he sneaked past Petrucci at the turn-three right-hander on lap two. It wasn't his first big moment of the weekend. During practice he had partially dislocated his left shoulder controlling a vicious tank-slapper; the result of taking turn 11 at full gas!

On lap four Viñales went from hunter to hunted as Rins took second place at turn 12. The COTA winner was now the fastest man on track and set off after Márquez, who wasn't having any of it. Tyres fully warmed, the world champion upped his pace by seven tenths and was very soon all alone, while Rins made second place his own, leaving Viñales to battle for the last place on the podium with an on-form Crutchlow.

Then Rins lost the front as he peeled into Waldmann Kurve for the 19th time, throwing away a second podium finish in as many weekends. "I entered the corner just a couple of kilometres per hour faster than usual," he explained, still dizzy from the high-speed tumble.

Rins' exit took the pressure off Viñales and Crutchlow, because both men were now booked into the post-race prosecco soaking. Crutchlow did want second place but gave up after one near miss. "I lost the rear, off the throttle," he explained. "After that I said to Maverick, 'you can have it'. This is a special track – you slide a lot – which helps with the turning of our bike."

Viñales was convinced that this result proved his return to form, although he also finished on the podium at the 2018 Dutch and German rounds.

"It's a consequence of everyone, because I'm not alone, I'm in a team," he said. "We changed the mentality in the team. Also we changed the bike's geometry a bit. Now I can ride in my normal way and we've got consistency at tracks with grip and at tracks without grip. We've made that step."

CLOCKWISE, FROM TOP LEFT | *Crutchlow rode injured and loved it; Rookie Mir was turning things around after a tough start to the year; Quartararo finally fell off in a race; Márquez was imperious; the battle for third became the battle for second; Petrucci edged closer to Dovizioso in the championship; Rins made another big mistake; riders use a lot of elbow at Sachsenring; Lorenzo's replacement Bradl had a strong ride.*

‘THE PLAN WAS THERE AND I FOLLOWED IT’
MARC MÁRQUEZ

MotoGP'S ELECTRIC MILESTONE

History was made at Sachsenring when the first electric-powered motorcycle race took place at a Grand Prix event. The inaugural round of the Enel MotoE World Cup started the race-day action an hour earlier than usual and gave fans an extra race to enjoy, without rudely waking those who were sleeping in with a hangover.

Electric-vehicle racing has a huge future, so it made perfect sense for MotoGP to add an EV championship to its programme, five years after the hugely successful Formula E car series' first race. The first MotoE series started later than planned, following a fire during pre-season tests at Jerez. Energica worked miracles to rebuild the grid in time for a mock MotoE race weekend, staged at

The mood was much less bright in the Ducati garage. Petrucci, Andrea Dovizioso and Jack Miller crossed the line almost side by side and 16 seconds behind the winner, a deficit of more than a half a second a lap.

At Assen their problem was mid-corner turning, here it was lack of front-end loading through Sachsenring's huge, sweeping corners.

"Here you use a lot of lean angle for a lot of time," explained Petrucci. "There are only two or three hard braking areas and especially there are very, very long corners where we don't feel the front turning. From corners three to 11 you don't brake, you just close the throttle, so you don't load the front tyre. This is our weak point."

Joan Mir once again mixed it with the GP19s, chasing Miller over the line in seventh, two seconds ahead of Valentino Rossi, who was more confused than ever. At Sachsenring 2018 the veteran had chased home Márquez. This time Márquez's race time was three minutes slower, while Rossi was 20 seconds slower.

"If during today's race I was fast like last year but the other guys made a step and were 20 seconds faster, I'd say, hey, it's over," he said. "Sincerely in my mind I don't feel I've given up or I'm not concentrated or I don't have enough motivation, so I don't have a reason why I was 20 seconds slower than last year, so we must understand and recover."

CLOCKWISE FROM TOP LEFT | *Petrucci and other GP19 riders struggled to keep their front tyres planted, which gave him a nasty QP crash; another injury comeback/podium for Crutchlow; Mir and Miller chased home the factory Ducatis, while Rossi struggled more than ever; the crew that helped Márquez win his seventh consecutive MotoGP race at the 'Ring; Abraham chased Iannone; Alex Márquez helped big brother celebrate again.*

Valencia in June, which helped acclimatise the 18 riders and their teams to the format: free practice sessions and E-Pole qualifying on Friday and Saturday, then the race on Sunday.

Former World Supersport and Moto2 rider Niki Tuuli was the history maker at Sachsenring. The young Finn took pole position and the race win, less than a second ahead of Aprilia MotoGP tester Bradley Smith and former 125cc world champion Mike Di Meglio.

There was a neat parallel in commencing MotoE at Sachsenring. It was in this region that Grand Prix racing's first alternative power unit was born. The two-stroke engine, which gradually and entirely replaced four-strokes in Grand Prix racing during the 1960s and 1970s, was developed by DKW and MZ in the nearby town of Zschopau.

9 | GERMANY

HJC HELMETS MOTORRAD GRAND PRIX DEUTSCHLAND

SACHSENRING
05/06/07 JULY

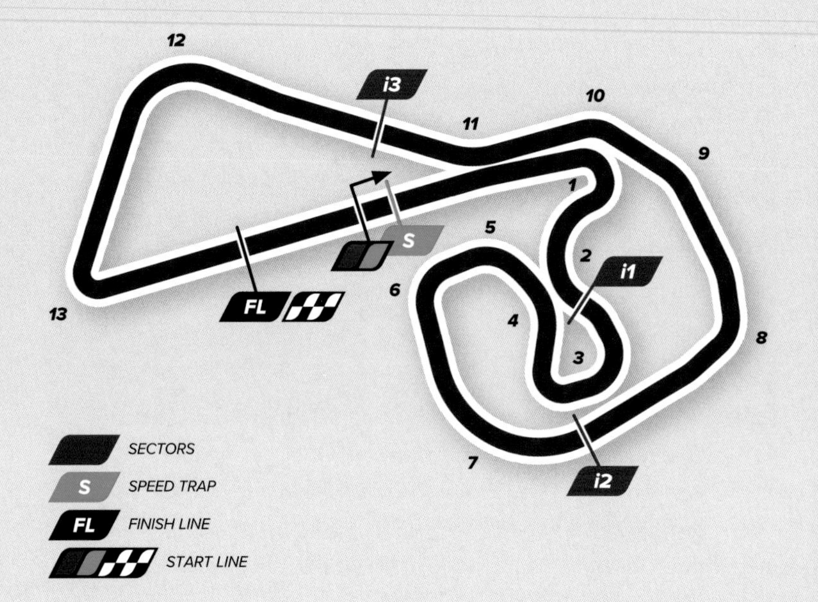

QUALIFYING RESULTS

	RIDER	NAT	TEAM	MACHINE	QP/TIME		GAP 1ST/PREV	
1	Marc Márquez	SPA	Repsol Honda Team	HONDA	Q2	1'20.195		
2	Fabio Quartararo	FRA	Petronas Yamaha SRT	YAMAHA	Q2	1'20.400	0.205	0.205
3	Maverick Viñales	SPA	Monster Energy Yamaha MotoGP	YAMAHA	Q2	1'20.406	0.211	0.006
4	Álex Rins	SPA	Team SUZUKI ECSTAR	SUZUKI	Q2	1'20.531	0.336	0.125
5	Jack Miller	AUS	Pramac Racing	DUCATI	Q2	1'20.690	0.495	0.159
6	Cal Crutchlow	GBR	LCR Honda CASTROL	HONDA	Q2	1'20.857	0.662	0.167
7	Franco Morbidelli	ITA	Petronas Yamaha SRT	YAMAHA	Q2	1'20.964	0.769	0.107
8	Pol Espargaró	SPA	Red Bull KTM Factory Racing	KTM	Q2	1'21.023	0.828	0.059
9	Joan Mir	SPA	Team SUZUKI ECSTAR	SUZUKI	Q2	1'21.061	0.866	0.038
10	Takaaki Nakagami	JPN	LCR Honda IDEMITSU	HONDA	Q2	1'21.104	0.909	0.043
11	Valentino Rossi	ITA	Monster Energy Yamaha MotoGP	YAMAHA	Q2	1'21.137	0.942	0.033
12	Danilo Petrucci	ITA	Ducati Team	DUCATI	Q2	1'21.486	1.291	0.349
13	Andrea Dovizioso	ITA	Ducati Team	DUCATI	Q1	1'21.105	*0.172	0.003
14	Stefan Bradl	GER	Repsol Honda Team	HONDA	Q1	1'21.227	*0.294	0.122
15	Aleix Espargaró	SPA	Aprilia Racing Team Gresini	APRILIA	Q1	1'21.313	*0.380	0.086
16	Andrea Iannone	ITA	Aprilia Racing Team Gresini	APRILIA	Q1	1'21.433	*0.500	0.120
17	Francesco Bagnaia	ITA	Pramac Racing	DUCATI	Q1	1'21.446	*0.513	0.013
18	Hafizh Syahrin	MAL	Red Bull KTM Tech 3	KTM	Q1	1'21.465	*0.532	0.019
19	Johann Zarco	FRA	Red Bull KTM Factory Racing	KTM	Q1	1'21.637	*0.704	0.172
20	Miguel Oliveira	POR	Red Bull KTM Tech 3	KTM	Q1	1'21.683	*0.750	0.046
21	Karel Abraham	CZE	Reale Avintia Racing	DUCATI	Q1	1'21.796	*0.863	0.113
22	Tito Rabat	SPA	Reale Avintia Racing	DUCATI	Q1	1'22.119	*1.186	0.323

** Gap to the fastest rider in the Q1 session* *** Went forward from Q1 to Q2* *Track severity = Wear + Temperature + Load*

GRAND PRIX INFORMATION

TRACK INFORMATION			
2019 WINNER	Marc Márquez		
CIRCUIT LENGTH	3.7 km	2.28 miles	
LAPS	30		
RACE DISTANCE	110.1 km	68.4 miles	
ALL TIME LAP RECORD	1'20.195	164.7 Km/h	Marc Márquez (2019)
BEST RACE LAP	1'21.228	162.6 Km/h	Marc Márquez (2019)
RACE CONDITION	Dry		
AIR	20°C		
HUMIDITY	44%		
GROUND	32°C		

OFFICIAL TIMEKEEPER

OFFICIAL MotoGP™ CLASS TYRE

TYRE SELECTION

FRONT	
SOFT	WHITE
MEDIUM	GREY
HARD	YELLOW

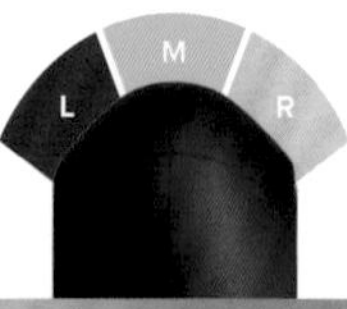

REAR	
SOFT	WHITE
MEDIUM	GREY
HARD	YELLOW

< MILD — TRACK SEVERITY — SEVERE >

1 MARC MÁRQUEZ
Ten out of ten pole positions, ten out of ten race wins and ten out of ten for the manner of his latest Sachsenring victory. The Spaniard was once again untouchable at his happiest hunting ground. Basically, no one else stood a chance.

2 MAVERICK VIÑALES
Was happy with second place because he knew Márquez would be just about unbeatable and because 45 points from two races was his best two-race score since he finished first and second in the 2017 French and Italians GPs.

3 CAL CRUTCHLOW
Another gritty performance from the Brit who injured his right knee in a freak cycling accident on the eve of practice. Would certainly have made a much more aggressive attack on Viñales if Rins' exit hadn't put him on the podium.

4 DANILO PETRUCCI
Recovered from a big Saturday crash at turn ten, when he asked too much of his bike's turning capability. Noted that all three GP19s finished together, suggesting that all three riders were riding the bike to its absolute limit.

5 ANDREA DOVIZIOSO
Passed by his team-mate with two laps to go, but was more concerned with the deficit to the race winner. On the other hand, went on holiday looking forward to more favourable tracks: Brno, Red Bull Ring, Silverstone and so on.

6 JACK MILLER
Fought with the lead group during the early stages, but couldn't maintain that kind of pace and ended up with his fellow GP19 riders. Wanted to make a move on the factory Ducati riders on the last lap but decided it was too risky.

7 JOAN MIR
For the third race in a row the rookie spent a lot of time wielding his fine-handling GSX-RR against the faster Ducatis. Made a few mistakes, from which he recovered but couldn't find a way past the three GP19s just ahead of him.

8 VALENTINO ROSSI
His speed in the Assen race, before his crash, gave him confidence for Sachsenring, but never had the speed. According to advice, chose the medium rear but this was a mistake, the tyre sliding around throughout the race.

9 FRANCO MORBIDELLI
Chose the same medium rear as Rossi and also found his performance compromised by the tyre. Fought as well as he could in the six-rider group comprising the Ducatis, Mir and Rossi but finished at the back.

10 STEFAN BRADL
His second race of the year, this time as Jorge Lorenzo substitute, not as HRC test rider, and once again acquitted himself very well against the full-timers. Tried HRC's carbon-coated frame again but raced the conventional alloy unit.

RACE LAP CHART

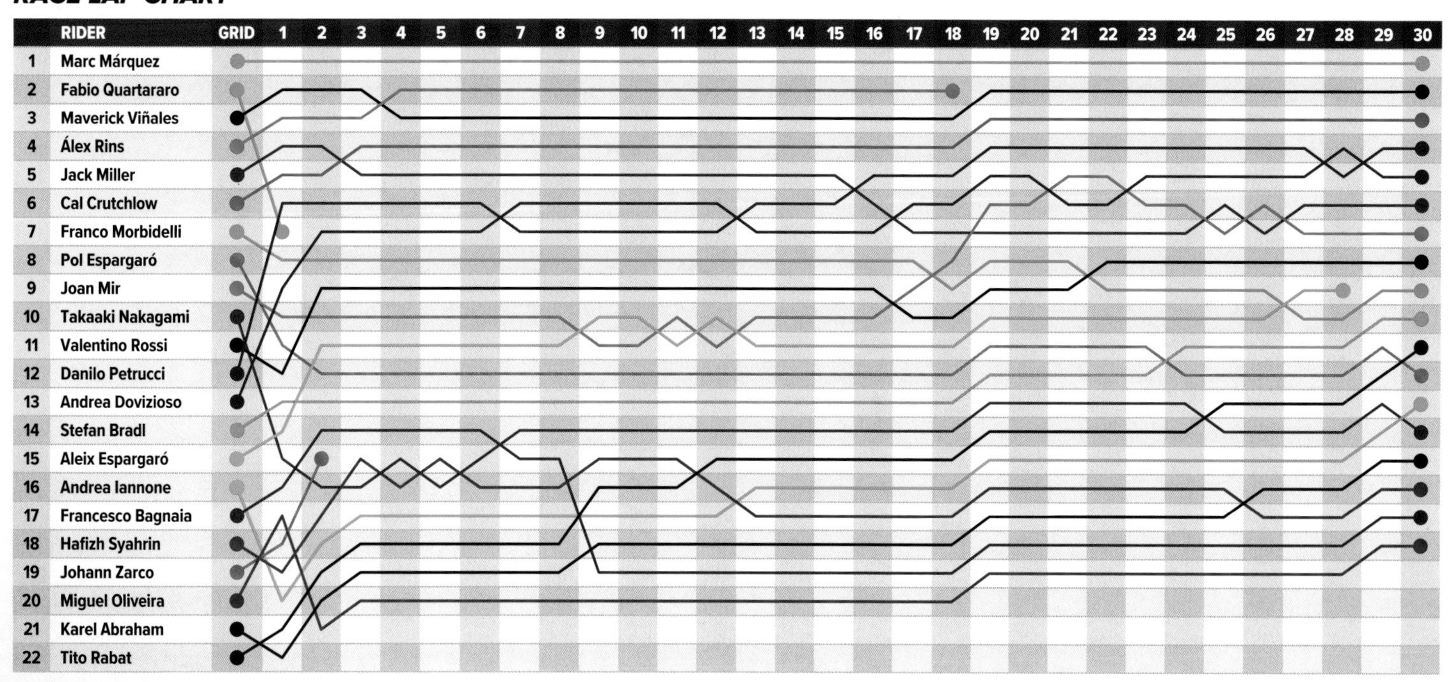

RACE RESULTS

	RIDER	NAT	TEAM	MACHINE	TIME	+ GAP	TYRES
1	Marc Márquez	SPA	Repsol Honda Team	HONDA	41'08.276		H/M
2	Maverick Viñales	SPA	Monster Energy Yamaha MotoGP	YAMAHA	41'12.863	4.587	M/H
3	Cal Crutchlow	GBR	LCR Honda CASTROL	HONDA	41'16.017	7.741	H/M
4	Danilo Petrucci	ITA	Ducati Team	DUCATI	41'24.853	16.577	M/H
5	Andrea Dovizioso	ITA	Ducati Team	DUCATI	41'24.945	16.669	M/H
6	Jack Miller	AUS	Pramac Racing	DUCATI	41'25.112	16.836	M/S
7	Joan Mir	SPA	Team SUZUKI ECSTAR	SUZUKI	41'25.432	17.156	M/H
8	Valentino Rossi	ITA	Monster Energy Yamaha MotoGP	YAMAHA	41'27.386	19.110	M/M
9	Franco Morbidelli	ITA	Petronas Yamaha SRT	YAMAHA	41'28.910	20.634	M/M
10	Stefan Bradl	GER	Repsol Honda Team	HONDA	41'30.984	22.708	M/S
11	Tito Rabat	SPA	Reale Avintia Racing	DUCATI	41'34.621	26.345	M/H
12	Pol Espargaró	SPA	Red Bull KTM Factory Racing	KTM	41'34.850	26.574	M/H
13	Andrea Iannone	ITA	Aprilia Racing Team Gresini	APRILIA	41'41.029	32.753	M/S
14	Takaaki Nakagami	JPN	LCR Honda IDEMITSU	HONDA	41'41.201	32.925	H/S
15	Karel Abraham	CZE	Reale Avintia Racing	DUCATI	41'46.210	37.934	M/H
16	Hafizh Syahrin	MAL	Red Bull KTM Tech 3	KTM	41'49.891	41.615	M/H
17	Francesco Bagnaia	ITA	Pramac Racing	DUCATI	42'04.465	56.189	M/H
18	Miguel Oliveira	POR	Red Bull KTM Tech 3	KTM	42'05.653	57.377	M/H
NC	Aleix Espargaró	SPA	Aprilia Racing Team Gresini	APRILIA	38'40.398	2 laps	H/H
NC	Álex Rins	SPA	Team SUZUKI ECSTAR	SUZUKI	24'38.068	12 laps	M/H
NC	Johann Zarco	FRA	Red Bull KTM Factory Racing	KTM	2'49.822	28 laps	M/H
NC	Fabio Quartararo	FRA	Petronas Yamaha SRT	YAMAHA	1'25.030	29 laps	M/M

CHAMPIONSHIP STANDINGS

	RIDER	NAT	TEAM	PTS
1	Marc Márquez	SPA	Repsol Honda Team	185
2	Andrea Dovizioso	ITA	Ducati Team	127
3	Danilo Petrucci	ITA	Ducati Team	121
4	Álex Rins	SPA	Team SUZUKI ECSTAR	101
5	Maverick Viñales	SPA	Monster Energy Yamaha MotoGP	85
6	Valentino Rossi	ITA	Monster Energy Yamaha MotoGP	80
7	Jack Miller	AUS	Pramac Racing	70
8	Fabio Quartararo	FRA	Petronas Yamaha SRT	67
9	Cal Crutchlow	GBR	LCR Honda CASTROL	67
10	Pol Espargaró	SPA	Red Bull KTM Factory Racing	56
11	Franco Morbidelli	ITA	Petronas Yamaha SRT	52
12	Takaaki Nakagami	JPN	LCR Honda IDEMITSU	50
13	Joan Mir	SPA	Team SUZUKI ECSTAR	39
14	Aleix Espargaró	SPA	Aprilia Racing Team Gresini	31
15	Andrea Iannone	ITA	Aprilia Racing Team Gresini	21
16	Jorge Lorenzo	SPA	Repsol Honda Team	19
17	Johann Zarco	FRA	Red Bull KTM Factory Racing	16
18	Miguel Oliveira	POR	Red Bull KTM Tech 3	15
19	Tito Rabat	SPA	Reale Avintia Racing	14
20	Stefan Bradl	GER	Team HRC	12
21	Francesco Bagnaia	ITA	Pramac Racing	11
22	Michele Pirro	ITA	Ducati Team	9
23	Sylvain Guintoli	FRA	Team SUZUKI ECSTAR	3
24	Karel Abraham	CZE	Reale Avintia Racing	3
25	Hafizh Syahrin	MAL	Red Bull KTM Tech 3	3
26	Bradley Smith	GBR	Aprilia Factory Racing	

11 TITO RABAT
Rode an excellent race from last position on the grid, achieving his second-best result since his return from injury. Felt good with his bike and tyres. Kept attacking throughout, passing Pol Espargaró for 11th on the last lap.

12 POL ESPARGARÓ
Achieved his second-best qualifying result of the year, only to be slowed at the start by an electronics glitch. Spent much of the race chasing his older brother, then ran out of rear tyre and had to wave the white flag.

13 ANDREA IANNONE
A worse result than the previous two races but this was the Italian's fourth consecutive points-scoring finish, continuing a general upward trend with the RS-GP since the Barcelona tests, following a grim start to the season.

14 TAKAAKI NAKAGAMI
The most heroic ride of the day. Was in a bad state after getting taken out at Assen, with a left-ankle injury that worsened over the weekend, requiring him to get around on crutches. Rode through the pain barrier for two points.

15 KAREL ABRAHAM
Helped the Avintia team achieve its first double-score finish of the season, coming back from two zero scores at Barcelona and Assen. Nearly crashed at turn 11 at the start of the race, which made him a bit gun-shy for a while.

16 HAFIZH SYAHRIN
Just missed out on a second consecutive points score. Like fellow RC16 rider Espargaró he suffered a major loss in grip. Days later Tech3 announced that it had signed KTM Moto2 star Brad Binder for the 2020 MotoGP season

18 FRANCESCO BAGNAIA
The Moto2 world champion's challenging rookie season continued with a heavy fall at the fast turn eight during FP1. Didn't ride again until Saturday, when he felt better on the bike, but struggled with his injuries in the race.

18 MIGUEL OLIVEIRA
Crashed out at turn three moments after Quartararo hit the ground there. Was able to get going again and ran a good pace, despite missing a winglet. Rode the fastest KTM lap of the race, 0.038 seconds faster than Espargaró.

NC ALEIX ESPARGARÓ
Rode a great race, chasing Rossi, Morbidelli and the second group. Was lining up an attack on Morbidelli when he lost the front at turn one, with just two laps remaining. A DNF, yes, but he was delighted to have been in the fight.

NC ÁLEX RINS
Rins is one of MotoGP's smoothest, most composed riders, so a second unforced error in as many races was unexpected. Perhaps the pressure of being a regular front-runner was starting to mess with his head a little.

NC JOHANN ZARCO
Another downbeat weekend for the Frenchman and another downbeat result. Had a nasty fall at Waldmann Kurve in morning warm-up, then during the race lost the front at turn three, which had already claimed two victims.

NC FABIO QUARTARARO
The man of the moment finally proved he's human, by sliding off while attacking Petrucci. Started from the front row for the fourth successive race but had a bad first lap, which probably made him a bit too impatient.

SHOEI
PULL&BEAR
GIVES YOU WINGS
BRNO
REPSOL
HONDA
One HEART.
Red Bull
Allianz
HRC
93
ENERGY
MICHELIN

This was a good moment for some Mick Doohan style domination: 25 years after the Aussie had won his first 500cc title at Brno, in August 1994

10 | CZECH REPUBLIC

MONSTER ENERGY GRAND PRIX ČESKÉ REPUBLIKY
AUTOMOTODROM BRNO
02/03/04 AUGUST

RELENTLESS

The world champion won again, stretching out his rivals just like former Repsol Honda hero Mick Doohan

This may have been the weekend where Marc Márquez's domination began to assume a Mick Doohan aura. Once again he controlled the race to his own liking and none of his rivals ever got close enough to give him any kind of hassle.

The Doohan link was particularly fitting at Brno, where the Australian won his first 500cc world title in August 1994. The synchronicity continued with Márquez reaching his first Doohan record. In qualifying the reigning world champion scored his 58th MotoGP pole position, equalling his forebear's all-time premier-class record. In the race he scored his 50th MotoGP win, making him one of only four men to reach the half-century, along with Doohan, Giacomo Agostini and Valentino Rossi.

If his sixth victory of 2019 looked totally under control, his sixth pole of the year was anything but. And all the more glorious for it. This was one of those moments when Márquez left his rivals slack-jawed in disbelief. Qualifying got underway on a damp track, so the Spaniard did his first run on rain tyres, then switched to a slick-equipped bike. When the rain returned minutes later it seemed his typically brave gamble had failed. But it hadn't. The rain kept falling and Márquez kept getting faster, his final lap 2.5 second quicker than anyone else, despite his bike slipping and sliding through the wettest parts of the track.

'THIS YEAR MARC CAN MAKE THE RACE IN FRONT AND CREATE A PROBLEM FOR EVERYBODY BECAUSE THE PACE IS SO HIGH.'
ANDREA DOVIZIOSO

CLOCKWISE, FROM TOP LEFT | *Dovizioso gave it everything he had; it was tense on the grid; Zarco scored KTM's first front row; then took out Mir and Morbidelli in the race; no one said it was going to be easy; Quartararo had his worst result since Le Mans; Race Direction discuss the 40-minute start delay; Viñales had a miserable weekend; riders who started from damp parts of the track were at a big disadvantage.*

"I don't understand how the track was dry for Marc, but not for the rest of us," deadpanned Danilo Petrucci, speaking for most of the grid.

Márquez won the race (shortened by a lap following a delay to allow the track to dry after a rain shower) by a slightly smaller margin, but who knows how fast he might have gone if he had been pushed? He led from start to finish, chased all the way by Andrea Dovizioso.

"I told myself, we will see when my tyres drop and when his tyres drop," he explained. "Dovi's dropped a little bit earlier than mine and this made the biggest difference around laps nine, ten and 11."

Márquez went into the race with a 58-point championship lead, which allowed him to await the start in complete serenity. "Before the race my points advantage gave me a different feeling. I was so calm because I knew that even if something happened, the advantage would still be there; a little bit smaller, but it would be there."

Dovizioso wore an air of resignation after the race. At Brno 2018 he had scored a famous victory, leading a Ducati one-two after a frantic battle with Márquez. This time he had nothing for his greatest rival. And he knew it.

"This year Marc made a step," he said. "He can accelerate a bit better and he's able to make most of the race in front of everybody and create a problem for everybody because the pace is so high. It's difficult. This year's tyres work in a slightly different way, so it's hard for anybody to stop him. I pushed so hard but I couldn't keep my speed until the end."

There were only two changes of position in the fight for podium places during the race; the first when Álex Rins took third place from Jack Miller after three laps, the second when Miller reclaimed the position two laps before the chequered flag.

This was another classic corner-speed versus straight-line-speed battle; or at least it was until the Suzuki had used up its rear tyre, by which time Miller had almost given up hope of achieving his first podium since COTA.

"I could see that his rear tyre wasn't very flash – with about five laps to go he started spinning all the way up the last hill to the braking zone," said the Australian. "I was gaining a lot, so I was like, I'll just wait. So I just waited it out, then passed him into turn one because he lost so much drive on the front straight. But he's able to hold such a tight line on the Suzuki that he ended up getting past me again."

Miller made it stick four corners later. He got so much more drive out of turn four that he got alongside Rins and made a block pass into turn five. Rins knew his podium hopes were finished, so he immediately looked over his shoulder to see if he might lose even more positions. He made it home in fourth place, even though Cal Crutchlow was gaining fast.

RINS FRONTS UP TO MÁRQUEZ

Every king must defend his castle. Márquez has made a good job of defending his since he came to MotoGP, only failing to repel the invaders on one occasion, in 2015, when HRC went the wrong way on engine spec.

Such domination takes a multitude of talents and a great back-up team. Márquez has everything he needs on track and in pit lane, but even that isn't enough. A rock-solid psyche is also required to withstand the pitiless pressure from factory, team, media and fans, and also to win mind games with rivals attacking your ramparts.

Over the years Márquez has dealt with Rossi, Jorge Lorenzo and Viñales. During 2019 Rins became a new threat to his crown, so

The Briton had made a hash of the rain-affected Q2 session, ending up on the fourth row. Once again he had podium pace, but he didn't make the podium. Stuck in the middle of the pack he was 4.5 seconds behind Márquez after five laps and only six down at the finish, despite losing time getting past Petrucci and Rossi.

This was Rossi's best result since May's French round, but there was little to smile about, because he finished nine seconds down on Márquez, three times his deficit at Le Mans.

"The guys that finished in front were faster than me, but in the end it was better than the last few races," he said, without enthusiasm.

Team-mate Maverick Viñales had an even worse day. After a win and a second place in the previous two rounds he had been aiming for his first MotoGP podium hat-trick. It wasn't to be. He went all the way back to 15th after the start due to excessive wheelspin – his grid slot was on a wet part of the track. Like Rossi he suffered from a lack of traction and a lack of horsepower at one of MotoGP's bigger racetracks. He finished tenth.

Ahead of the Spaniard were Fabio Quartararo, Petrucci and Takaaki Nakagami. Petrucci had his worst race of the year so far, like many perturbed by the changeable weekend weather that compromised set-up time and traction.

CLOCKWISE FROM TOP LEFT | *Miller chases Rins, Dovizioso and Márquez in the early laps; Márquez and crew celebrate six wins from ten races; Zarco was running out of road at KTM; Miller had to fight to the finish for his first podium since COTA; Rins was out of rear tyre by the final laps; no one could quite believe what they saw Márquez do in the rain-soaked Q2 session.*

the mind games between the pair began.

During the Le Mans pre-event media conference Rins explained how his heightened, post-COTA status led to more pressure. Márquez said that real pressure only begins when you're expected to win the world championship.

At Brno their rivalry made headlines when they clashed during qualifying. They were both on their first runs when Márquez ran wide on a damp patch at turn five, which let Jack Miller past. Márquez was slow through the next two corners, Rins squeezing inside at turn seven and clattering into the Honda.

Márquez gave chase to return the compliment by out-braking Rins at turn 13, then riding into pit lane, followed by his young compatriot. Incredibly, the quarrel continued in pit lane. Rins caught Márquez, nudged into the side of him again, the world champion pushing the Suzuki away with his left hand to avoid running into a tyre wall.

Márquez denied having seen Rins earlier in the lap. "I only saw Jack, so I tried to follow him because I know he had good pace. Then I went a bit too wide and there was a small space, but enough, and Rins ran into me," he said. "The funny thing was when we entered the box and the tyre wall was there and I didn't have the space because he was going that way. I don't know if that was intentional or not, but for me it wasn't important. I lose zero time on these sort of things."

Both were summoned to Race Direction, just to calm things down.

10 | CZECH REPUBLIC

MONSTER ENERGY GRAND PRIX ČESKÉ REPUBLIKY

AUTOMOTODROM BRNO

02/03/04 AUGUST

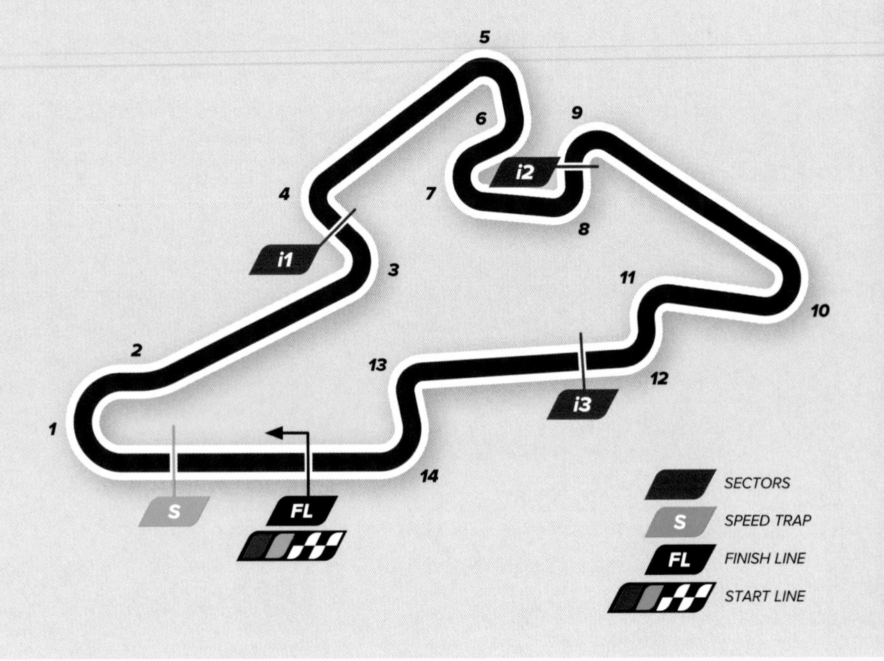

QUALIFYING RESULTS

	RIDER	NAT	TEAM	MACHINE	QP/TIME		GAP 1ST/PREV	
1	Marc Márquez	SPA	Repsol Honda Team	HONDA	Q2	2'02.753		
2	Jack Miller	AUS	Pramac Racing	DUCATI	Q2	2'05.277	2.524	2.524
3	Johann Zarco**	FRA	Red Bull KTM Factory Racing	KTM	Q2	2'05.351	2.598	0.074
4	Andrea Dovizioso	ITA	Ducati Team	DUCATI	Q2	2'05.590	2.837	0.239
5	Pol Espargaró**	SPA	Red Bull KTM Factory Racing	KTM	Q2	2'05.710	2.957	0.120
6	Álex Rins	SPA	Team SUZUKI ECSTAR	SUZUKI	Q2	2'06.172	3.419	0.462
7	Valentino Rossi	ITA	Monster Energy Yamaha MotoGP	YAMAHA	Q2	2'06.233	3.480	0.061
8	Danilo Petrucci	ITA	Ducati Team	DUCATI	Q2	2'06.457	3.704	0.224
9	Maverick Viñales	SPA	Monster Energy Yamaha MotoGP	YAMAHA	Q2	2'06.626	3.873	0.169
10	Fabio Quartararo	FRA	Petronas Yamaha SRT	YAMAHA	Q2	2'06.648	3.895	0.022
11	Cal Crutchlow	GBR	LCR Honda CASTROL	HONDA	Q2	2'07.123	4.370	0.475
12	Franco Morbidelli	ITA	Petronas Yamaha SRT	YAMAHA	Q2	2'09.404	6.651	2.281
13	Takaaki Nakagami	JPN	LCR Honda IDEMITSU	HONDA	Q1	2'05.265	*0.232	0.212
14	Francesco Bagnaia	ITA	Pramac Racing	DUCATI	Q1	2'05.286	*0.253	0.021
15	Sylvain Guintoli	FRA	Team SUZUKI ECSTAR	ECSTAR	Q1	2'05.551	*0.518	0.265
16	Miguel Oliveira	POR	Red Bull KTM Tech 3	KTM	Q1	2'05.763	*0.730	0.212
17	Stefan Bradl	GER	Repsol Honda Team	HONDA	Q1	2'05.974	*0.941	0.211
18	Aleix Espargaró	SPA	Aprilia Racing Team Gresini	APRILIA	Q1	2'06.284	*1.251	0.310
19	Joan Mir	SPA	Team SUZUKI ECSTAR	SUZUKI	Q1	2'06.554	*1.521	0.270
20	Karel Abraham	CZE	Reale Avintia Racing	DUCATI	Q1	2'06.898	*1.865	0.344
21	Hafizh Syahrin	MAL	Red Bull KTM Tech 3	KTM	Q1	2'07.155	*2.122	0.257
22	Tito Rabat	SPA	Reale Avintia Racing	DUCATI	Q1	2'07.315	2.282	0.160
23	Andrea Iannone	ITA	Aprilia Racing Team Gresini	APRILIA	Q1	2'07.923	*2.890	0.608

** Gap to the fastest rider in the Q1 session* *** Went forward from Q1 to Q2* *Track severity = Wear + Temperature + Load*

GRAND PRIX INFORMATION

TRACK INFORMATION			
2019 WINNER	Marc Márquez		
CIRCUIT LENGTH	5.4 km	3.36 miles	
LAPS	21		
RACE DISTANCE	113.5 km	70.6 miles	
ALL TIME LAP RECORD	1'54.596	169.7 Km/h	Marc Márquez (2016)
BEST RACE LAP	1'56.027	167.6 Km/h	Dani Pedrosa (2014)
RACE CONDITION	Wet		
AIR	23°C		
HUMIDITY	43%		
GROUND	28°C		

TYRE SELECTION

FRONT	
SOFT	WHITE
MEDIUM	GREY
HARD	YELLOW

REAR	
SOFT	WHITE
MEDIUM	GREY
HARD	YELLOW

< MILD — TRACK SEVERITY — SEVERE >

1 MARC MÁRQUEZ
Had everything under control. Chose the soft rear and pushed from start to finish, so that no one got close enough to even try passing him. As usual, pushed hardest as the tyres started to go.

2 ANDREA DOVIZIOSO
Said he was happy with second, but this was a track where he beat the world champion in 2018. Chose the medium rear in the hope it would help him attack at the end, but the plan didn't pan out.

3 JACK MILLER
The Australian's first 'real' dry MotoGP podium, with no one crashing ahead of him, as was the case at COTA. A well-deserved result which he had to fight for, hunting down Rins with style.

4 ÁLEX RINS
Was desperate for a podium after crashes at Assen and Sachsenring lost him two likely top-three results; but he ran out of rear tyre and fell easy victim to Miller. But at least he reached the flag.

5 CAL CRUTCHLOW
Paid the price for not making exactly the right call during the rain-affected Q2 qualifying session. Wasted time fighting his way through the pack and wasted his rear tyre at the same time.

6 VALENTINO ROSSI
Wasn't happy with his sixth-place result, continuing a run of fifth positions or lower going all the way back to Le Mans. However, felt that the track and set-up allowed him to ride his bike better.

7 FABIO QUARTARARO
This was the first race in which the rookie had to work hard to save his tyres and he was happy to have learned some lessons. Tried to chase Rossi for sixth but wasn't quite able to close the gap.

8 DANILO PETRUCCI
Frankly admitted this was his worst race of his season so far. Lacked useful dry practice, because he was slow on Friday, the weekend's driest day. Didn't have good grip from the beginning.

9 TAKAAKI NAKAGAMI
Like most riders he was unsettled by the 40-minute delay. Tried to follow his team-mate in the early laps but couldn't maintain that pace. Still suffering from the right shoulder he hurt at Assen.

10 MAVERICK VIÑALES
Just when he seemed to have found consistent pace he lost it again. Got a bad start on the damp part of the grid and then ran into his usual problem, a lack of grip compared to earlier in the weekend.

RACE LAP CHART

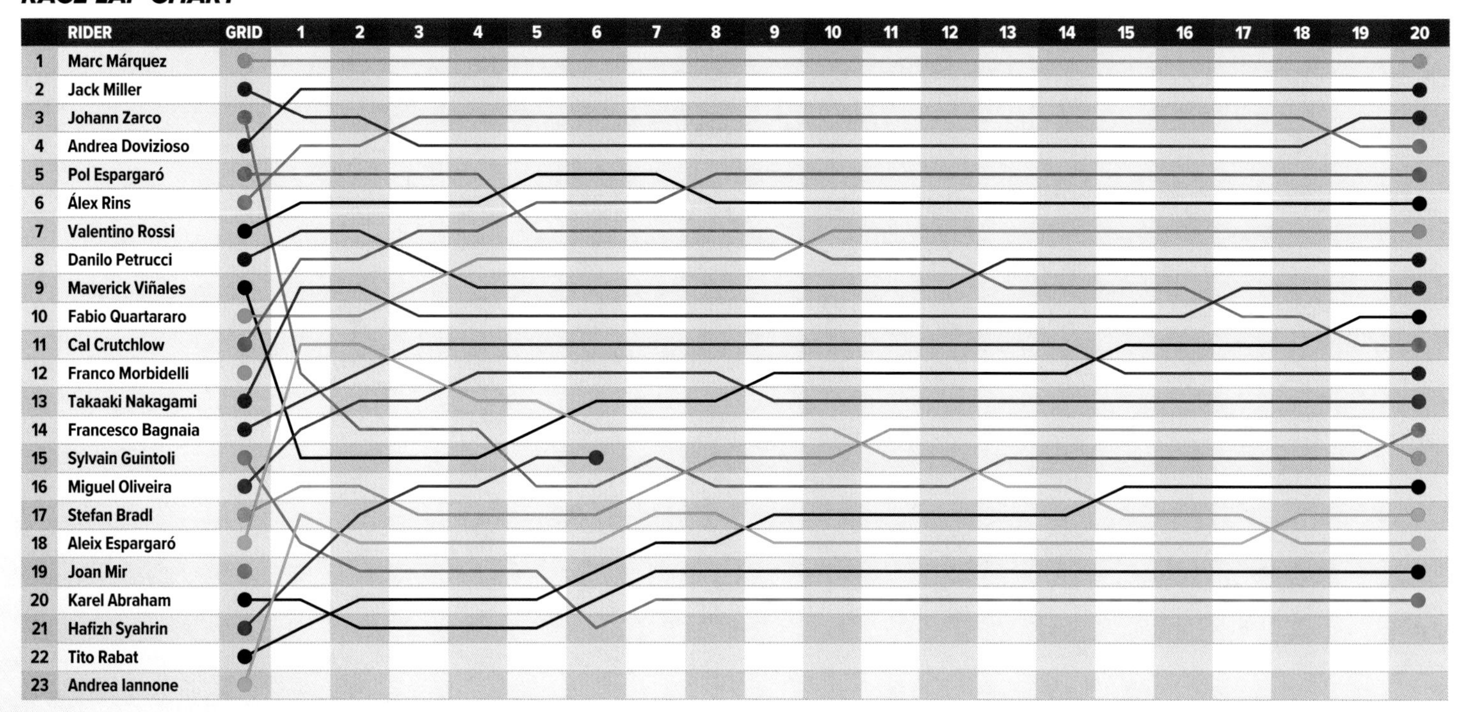

Start delayed and race distance shortened to 20 laps due to track conditions

RACE RESULTS

	RIDER	NAT	TEAM	MACHINE	TIME	+ GAP	TYRES
1	Marc Márquez	SPA	Repsol Honda Team	HONDA	39'24.430		H/S
2	Andrea Dovizioso	ITA	Ducati Team	DUCATI	39'26.882	2.452	M/M
3	Jack Miller	AUS	Pramac Racing	DUCATI	39'27.927	3.497	H/S
4	Álex Rins	SPA	Team SUZUKI ECSTAR	SUZUKI	39'29.288	4.858	M/S
5	Cal Crutchlow	GBR	LCR Honda CASTROL	HONDA	39'30.437	6.007	H/S
6	Valentino Rossi	ITA	Monster Energy Yamaha MotoGP	YAMAHA	39'33.513	9.083	M/S
7	Fabio Quartararo	FRA	Petronas Yamaha SRT	YAMAHA	39'36.522	12.092	M/S
8	Danilo Petrucci	ITA	Ducati Team	DUCATI	39'38.406	13.976	M/M
9	Takaaki Nakagami	JPN	LCR Honda IDEMITSU	HONDA	39'40.154	15.724	H/S
10	Maverick Viñales	SPA	Monster Energy Yamaha MotoGP	YAMAHA	39'40.988	16.558	M/S
11	Pol Espargaró	SPA	Red Bull KTM Factory Racing	KTM	39'42.664	18.234	M/S
12	Francesco Bagnaia	ITA	Pramac Racing	DUCATI	39'44.168	19.738	M/S
13	Miguel Oliveira	POR	Red Bull KTM Tech 3	KTM	39'46.969	22.539	M/S
14	Johann Zarco	FRA	Red Bull KTM Factory Racing	KTM	39'54.889	30.459	M/S
15	Stefan Bradl	GER	Repsol Honda Team	HONDA	39'54.930	30.500	M/S
16	Tito Rabat	SPA	Reale Avintia Racing	DUCATI	39'55.185	30.755	M/S
17	Andrea Iannone	ITA	Aprilia Racing Team Gresini	APRILIA	40'01.600	37.170	M/S
18	Aleix Espargaró	SPA	Aprilia Racing Team Gresini	APRILIA	40'01.773	37.343	M/M
19	Karel Abraham	CZE	Reale Avintia Racing	DUCATI	40'08.726	44.296	M/S
20	Sylvain Guintoli	FRA	Team SUZUKI ECSTAR	SUZUKI	40'13.368	48.938	M/S
NC	Hafizh Syahrin	MAL	Red Bull KTM Tech 3	KTM	11'59.511	14 laps	M/S
NC	Franco Morbidelli	ITA	Petronas Yamaha SRT	YAMAHA			M/S
NC	Joan Mir	SPA	Team SUZUKI ECSTAR	SUZUKI			M/S

CHAMPIONSHIP STANDINGS

	RIDER	NAT	TEAM	PTS
1	Marc Márquez	SPA	Repsol Honda Team	210
2	Andrea Dovizioso	ITA	Ducati Team	147
3	Danilo Petrucci	ITA	Ducati Team	129
4	Álex Rins	SPA	Team SUZUKI ECSTAR	114
5	Maverick Viñales	SPA	Monster Energy Yamaha MotoGP	91
6	Valentino Rossi	ITA	Monster Energy Yamaha MotoGP	90
7	Jack Miller	AUS	Pramac Racing	86
8	Cal Crutchlow	GBR	LCR Honda CASTROL	78
9	Fabio Quartararo	FRA	Petronas Yamaha SRT	76
10	Pol Espargaró	SPA	Red Bull KTM Factory Racing	61
11	Takaaki Nakagami	JPN	LCR Honda IDEMITSU	57
12	Franco Morbidelli	ITA	Petronas Yamaha SRT	52
13	Joan Mir	SPA	Team SUZUKI ECSTAR	39
14	Aleix Espargaró	SPA	Aprilia Racing Team Gresini	31
15	Andrea Iannone	ITA	Aprilia Racing Team Gresini	21
16	Jorge Lorenzo	SPA	Repsol Honda Team	19
17	Johann Zarco	FRA	Red Bull KTM Factory Racing	18
18	Miguel Oliveira	POR	Red Bull KTM Tech 3	18
19	Francesco Bagnaia	ITA	Pramac Racing	15
20	Tito Rabat	SPA	Reale Avintia Racing	14
21	Stefan Bradl	GER	Team HRC	13
22	Michele Pirro	ITA	Ducati Team	9
23	Sylvain Guintoli	FRA	Team SUZUKI ECSTAR	3
24	Karel Abraham	CZE	Reale Avintia Racing	3
25	Hafizh Syahrin	MAL	Red Bull KTM Tech 3	3
26	Bradley Smith	GBR	Aprilia Factory Racing	

11 POL ESPARGARÓ
Qualified an excellent fifth and kept a great rhythm for the first quarter of the race, but from that point he was battled straight-line wheelspin, so he couldn't go with Rossi, Petrucci and Crutchlow.

12 FRANCESCO BAGNAIA
His best result since COTA – and only his third points-scoring finish since that race – was part of a confidence-rebuilding exercise for the Italian. Chased Nakagami for half of the race.

13 MIGUEL OLIVEIRA
Another impressive ride from the rookie, who achieved his second best race time of the season so far, 22 seconds behind the winner. The Tech 3 bikes ran carbon-fibre swingarms for the first time.

14 JOHANN ZARCO
A bittersweet weekend: KTM's front-row start, then went backwards in the race, because he was on the damp side of the grid. Was happy to finish the race, after DNFing at Assen and Sachsenring.

15 STEFAN BRADL
As usual, was busy testing set-ups for HRC, so the lack of dry track time hurt him more than most riders. Expected a better result, but struggled with rear grip (like most riders) and turning.

16 TITO RABAT
Qualified poorly in 22nd, largely due to the weather, and was last at the end of the first lap, but fought back superbly in the race. He only missed scoring a point by two tenths of a second.

17 ANDREA IANNONE
Qualified 23rd and last in the rain-soaked Q1 session. His race was better, running a consistent pace with the soft rear tyre and passing his struggling team-mate three laps from the finish

18 ALEIX ESPARGARÓ
Had high hopes of a top-ten finish to make up for his Sachsenring disappointment. A lightning start made that a possibility. However, he suffered from straight-line wheelspin, even in higher gears.

19 KAREL ABRAHAM
There were no points for the local. Qualified 20th and aimed for the top-15, but it was not to be. Rose with his team-mate for a while, but then had the same the wheelspin problems that hurt so many.

20 SYLVAIN GUINTOLI
Suzuki's test rider contested his second race of the year, after Barcelona, but this time there were no points for him. Although he ended FP1 an impressive fifth fastest he didn't have the race pace.

DNF HAFIZH SYAHRIN
One of only three riders to choose the hard front. Had a great start, but on lap seven he lost the front and crashed.

DNF FRANCO MORBIDELLI
Qualified 12th and was confident of a good race, but Zarco took him out on lap one, with what he called an "inelegant" move.

DNF JOAN MIR
A victim of the skittle effect – got taken out by Morbidelli's fallen bike on lap one.

SHOEI
PULL&BEAR
GIVES YOU WINGS
REPSOL
93
SUOMY
DUCATI
valsir
Lenovo
04
Lenovo
DUCATI
Tiello

Dovizioso wields the executioner's axe at the last corner. His swingarm has broken Márquez's front-brake guard, which is in mid-air. If the guard hadn't snapped Márquez probably would've crashed.

11 | **AUSTRIA**

MYWORLD MOTORRAD GRAND PRIX VON ÖSTERREICH

RED BULL RING - SPIELBERG

09/10/11 AUGUST

EYE TO EYE CONTACT

The Márquez versus Dovizioso duels keep getting better – this time they made contact at the last turn as they fought for the win

The Red Bull Ring doesn't look like much of a racetrack: 4.3 kilometres (2.7 miles) long and only ten corners, three of which are dead slow and followed by long straights. In theory it shouldn't make for great racing.

And yet the track has provided epic encounters since MotoGP returned to the venue in 2016. The last three Austrian GPs have been unforgettable; and not in a good way for reigning MotoGP king Marc Márquez who has suffered three agonisingly close defeats at the hands of Ducati riders. In 2017 Andrea Dovizioso beat him by 0.176 seconds, in 2018 Jorge Lorenzo bettered him by 0.130 seconds and on this occasion he once again succumbed by 0.130 seconds, to Dovizioso.

This was supposed to be the year Márquez finally put an end to Ducati's Austrian monopoly. Everything seemed to point in this direction: for the first time Honda's RC213V had a fraction more speed than the Desmosedici, Márquez had stepped up his riding and he could pretty much throw caution to the wind, because he had such a big points advantage that he could risk a DNF.

Saturday only seemed to confirm that theory. His 59th pole position made him the most successful qualifier in premier-class

CLOCKWISE, FROM TOP LEFT | Nakagami and Morbidelli went at it for tenth place; Petrucci was still in a hole, despite appearances; Rins removes a tear-off; lap two, turn one: Quartararo leads Dovizioso, Miller, Rins, Márquez, Rossi and Nakagami; test-rider Michele Pirro was another pair of ears and eyes for Dovizioso; Quartararo was a wonder once again; the hills are alive with the sound of music.

"'THERE WAS A SMALL CONTACT AT THE LAST CORNER BUT THIS IS PART OF RACING AND I LIKE IT!'"

MARC MARQUEZ

history, four tenths quicker than Fabio Quartararo and almost half a second up on Dovizioso.

But Sunday was different, after overnight rain and a track temperature that dropped from Saturday's 51 degrees to 32 degrees. Márquez chose the medium rear and Dovizioso chose the soft. This was the reverse of their Brno choices and the result was also reversed. But only just.

Lap one, turn three gave a hint of what was to come. Márquez and Dovizioso were side by side into the first-gear right-hander, the Spaniard running such a deep defensive line that Dovizioso almost went straight, which allowed Quartararo into the lead, followed by Jack Miller and Álex Rins.

Rins didn't have the horsepower to survive at the front for more than a few corners. Miller hung on for a few laps. Then Dovizioso and Márquez set about hunting down Quartararo. On lap 26 they both used their speed advantage to power past the rookie.

Miller was the first of the lead group to overcook it, when he was right behind Quartararo and just ahead of Valentino Rossi, having his best ride since COTA. The two leaders soon dropped Quartararo and spent the last two thirds of the race brushing elbows on the straights, ducking and diving in the corners, seeking an advantage any which way.

On lap eight Márquez got ahead and stayed there for 11 laps, then with nine laps to go Dovizioso motored past on the start/finish. As he did so Márquez looked across at his rival. What was going on?

"Dovi was playing with me – he was closing the gas on the straights," explained Márquez. But surely you don't win races by cutting the throttle on the straights? In fact you can. "Twice I played on the straights," admitted Dovizioso. "Because if I overtake and stay next to him then I control the braking area."

This is how it works: you stay level and to the right of your rival approaching a right-hander, so the only way he can out-brake you is around the outside, which most likely won't work.

Dovizioso led the next nine laps, unable to break his rival, who finally pounced at turn seven with two laps to go. Now the pair's body language changed – it was win or bust from here on in. The Italian regained the lead at turn nine, only to lose it at turn ten, then retake it at turn one at the start of the penultimate lap. But he got in too hot, allowing Márquez to swoop past on the cutback. Five overtakes in five corners.

The start of the final lap was the same. Dovizioso led going into turn one, Márquez led going out, dancing on the edge, his front tyre juddering into every corner. Crucially Dovizioso had more rear grip, so as they accelerated out of turn eight for the last time he was on the Honda's rear tyre.

At turn ten he pounced, swinging the executioner's axe. He

A SILLY SEASON STORM

MotoGP's silly season – when often fanciful contract talk dominates the headlines – is these days usually a biannual affair, because most of the top riders have two-year contracts; in this case completing at the end of next season.

Thus the summer of 2019 was expected to be quiet on the contract front. And then the paddock landed in Austria...

Rumour had it that Ducati wanted to replace Jack Miller (on a one-plus-one-year deal at Pramac) with Jorge Lorenzo, who was struggling to get along with Honda's RC213V. Surely this was prime silly season bull? But no. On Thursday Miller revealed that Ducati and Lorenzo had talked. And he wasn't happy.

swept inside Márquez, who nearly crashed. Not because he had overdone it but because his front-brake guard was hooked onto Dovizioso's swingarm. Márquez was going, going, gone until the guard snapped, pinging into the sky; a nice souvenir for a marshal, no doubt.

"I was thinking I could stop my bike and come back on Dovi like he did on me two years ago here," explained the world champion, who had enjoyed the race more than the result. "There is always respect between us two and there was just a small contact at the last corner, but this is part of racing and I like it!"

Dovizioso had once again beaten Márquez the Merciless at the final corner. He was overjoyed, if a bit surprised. "I didn't prepare the last corner like that – it isn't my style, but a lot of things had happened during the race," he said. "The temperature changed from yesterday, so we made a different tyre choice. Maybe that had an effect. When Marc overtook me and pushed to make a gap I could see his rear tyre was dropping too much. In braking he was better than me, but with the rear grip I had I could stay with him and make that crazy last corner."

Quartararo completed the podium, six seconds down, after another storming ride, resisting pressure from factory Yamaha riders Rossi and Maverick Viñales. Rins was next, two tenths behind his compatriot.

This was a huge improvement for Yamaha following their disastrous 2018 Austrian GP, although much of the improvement was thanks to Michelin's decision to deploy its hard-construction Buriram rear slick, which really suits the YZR-M1.

CLOCKWISE FROM TOP LEFT | *Rookies Bagnaia and Oliveira impressed in the battle for seventh; Carmelo Ezpeleta donned his usual local dress; thriller Miller was all action as usual; the Red Bull Ring is spectacular in every way; rarely has victory tasted so sweet; Dovizioso and the rest of the pack chase leader Quartararo on lap two.*

"The news hit me like a tonne of bricks," said the Aussie, who felt he was being stabbed in the back.

Of course, there was also the small matter of Lorenzo's two-year HRC deal. By the end of the weekend the storm had blown over: Lorenzo would stay at Honda, Miller at Pramac.

But there was more. On Saturday evening Johann Zarco requested a meeting with KTM management and told them he wouldn't ride their RC16 in 2020. "I've given everything, but with like a handbrake inside me," he said. KTM made the split public on Monday. "The team tried relentlessly to mould the RC16 to his requirements," they said. "While Pol [Espargaró] made regular Q2 qualification appearances and persistently vied for top-ten results."

11 | AUSTRIA

MYWORLD MOTORRAD GRAND PRIX VON ÖSTERREICH

RED BULL RING - SPIELBERG

09/10/11 AUGUST

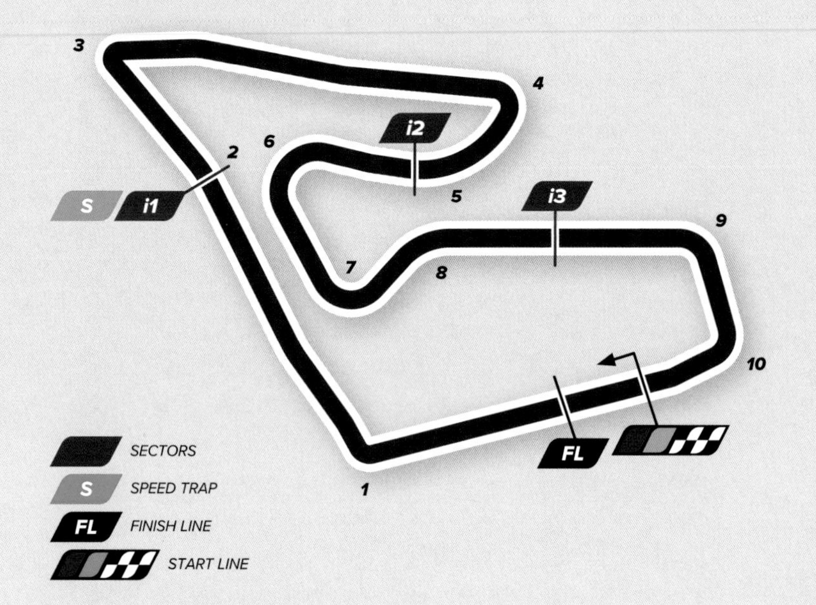

QUALIFYING RESULTS

	RIDER	NAT	TEAM	MACHINE	QP/TIME		GAP 1ST/PREV	
1	Marc Márquez	SPA	Repsol Honda Team	HONDA	Q2	1'23.027		
2	Fabio Quartararo	FRA	Petronas Yamaha SRT	YAMAHA	Q2	1'23.461	0.434	0.434
3	Andrea Dovizioso	ITA	Ducati Team	DUCATI	Q2	1'23.515	0.488	0.054
4	Maverick Viñales	SPA	Monster Energy Yamaha MotoGP	YAMAHA	Q2	1'23.523	0.496	0.008
5	Francesco Bagnaia	ITA	Pramac Racing	DUCATI	Q2	1'23.652	0.625	0.129
6	Takaaki Nakagami	JPN	LCR Honda IDEMITSU	HONDA	Q2	1'23.669	0.642	0.017
7	Álex Rins	SPA	Team SUZUKI ECSTAR	SUZUKI	Q2	1'23.681	0.654	0.012
8	Jack Miller	AUS	Pramac Racing	DUCATI	Q2	1'23.688	0.661	0.007
9	Cal Crutchlow	GBR	LCR Honda CASTROL	HONDA	Q2	1'23.754	0.727	0.066
10	Valentino Rossi	ITA	Monster Energy Yamaha MotoGP	YAMAHA	Q2	1'23.817	0.790	0.063
11	Pol Espargaró	SPA	Red Bull KTM Factory Racing	KTM	Q2	1'23.866	0.839	0.049
12	Danilo Petrucci	ITA	Ducati Team	DUCATI	Q2	1'23.964	0.937	0.098
13	Miguel Oliveira	POR	Red Bull KTM Tech 3	KTM	Q1	1'24.130	*0.301	0.202
14	Franco Morbidelli	ITA	Petronas Yamaha SRT	YAMAHA	Q1	1'24.270	*0.441	0.140
15	Tito Rabat	SPA	Reale Avintia Racing	DUCATI	Q1	1'24.389	*0.560	0.119
16	Johann Zarco	FRA	Red Bull KTM Factory Racing	KTM	Q1	1'24.392	*0.563	0.003
17	Karel Abraham	CZE	Reale Avintia Racing	DUCATI	Q1	1'24.423	*0.594	0.031
18	Andrea Iannone	ITA	Aprilia Racing Team Gresini	APRILIA	Q1	1'24.526	*0.697	0.103
19	Aleix Espargaró	SPA	Aprilia Racing Team Gresini	APRILIA	Q1	1'24.749	*0.920	0.223
20	Hafizh Syahrin	MAL	Red Bull KTM Tech 3	KTM	Q1	1'24.759	*0.930	0.010
21	Stefan Bradl	GER	Repsol Honda Team	HONDA	Q1	1'25.020	*1.191	0.261

GRAND PRIX INFORMATION

TRACK INFORMATION			
2019 WINNER	Andrea Dovizioso		
CIRCUIT LENGTH	4.3 km	2.68 miles	
LAPS	28		
RACE DISTANCE	120.9 km	75.0 miles	
ALL TIME LAP RECORD	1'23.027	187.2 Km/h	Marc Márquez (2019)
BEST RACE LAP	1'23.827	185.4 Km/h	Andrea Dovizioso (2019)
RACE CONDITION	Dry		
AIR	23°C		
HUMIDITY	70%		
GROUND	32°C		

TYRE SELECTION

FRONT	
SOFT	WHITE
MEDIUM	GREY
HARD	YELLOW

REAR	
SOFT	WHITE
MEDIUM	GREY
HARD	YELLOW

< MILD — TRACK SEVERITY — SEVERE >

** Gap to the fastest rider in the Q1 session   ** Went forward from Q1 to Q2   Track severity = Wear + Temperature + Load*

1 ANDREA DOVIZIOSO
Ducati's number one really needed this, his first win since Qatar. As usual, strategy was a vital part of his 14th MotoGP victory. He made the right tyre choice and worked out exactly what he had to do to beat Márquez.

2 MARC MÁRQUEZ
Came up 0.130 seconds short, exactly matching his 2018 deficit to Lorenzo. Had such a points advantage that he risked racing a new carbon-coated frame, aero and swingarm device for the first time, gathering vital data for the future.

3 FABIO QUARTARARO
Rode perfectly, responding to a threatening Rossi, who was just three tenths behind at one stage. Used the race to play with tyre life, working hard to avoid wheelspin, especially at the long double right, turns four and five.

4 VALENTINO ROSSI
When a nine-time world champion says fourth place is a good result, you know he's been in trouble for some time. In fact this was his best result since COTA and proved that Yamaha were making small steps forward.

5 MAVERICK VIÑALES
Tried an all-new set-up to reduce wheelspin, but the changes had the opposite effect in the cooler race conditions, destroying his rear tyre. Was at least happy that his race time was 20 seconds faster than his 2018 Austrian GP.

6 ÁLEX RINS
Red Bull Ring is a brute horsepower track, where a fine-handling chassis doesn't help much. Thus the GSX-RR couldn't give its best, so Rins was content to have been twice as close to the winner as on his previous visit.

7 FRANCESCO BAGNAIA
The Moto2 champ continued his steady comeback from a miserable run of four consecutive DNFs with his best MotoGP qualifying (fifth quickest) and race result so far. During the final laps he had to work hard to resist Oliveira.

8 MIGUEL OLIVEIRA
The ever-improving rookie was the fastest KTM rider in the race, scoring his first MotoGP top-ten finish, almost ten seconds in front of factory KTM rider Zarco. A very impressive performance from the cool-headed rookie.

9 DANILO PETRUCCI
Still struggling to regain the form of his three consecutive podiums at Le Mans, Mugello and Barcelona. Started from row four, after a mistake in Q2, then got caught up in Crutchlow's crash which dropped him to 13th.

10 FRANCO MORBIDELLI
Suffered a mysterious problem throughout the weekend – couldn't get his bike stopped as well as his fellow Yamaha riders – which put him 14th on the grid. Made steady progress in the race but this was his worst 2019 result so far.

RACE LAP CHART

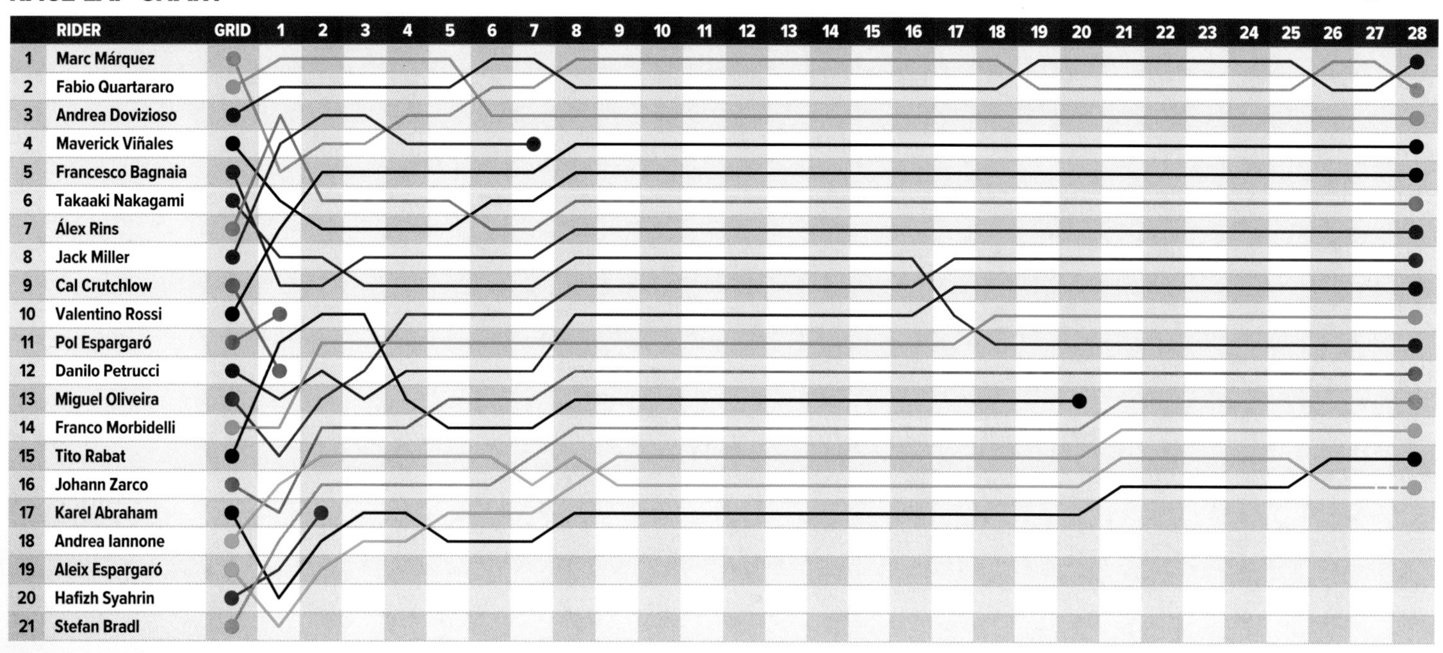

RACE RESULTS

	RIDER	NAT	TEAM	MACHINE	TIME	+ GAP	TYRES
1	Andrea Dovizioso	ITA	Ducati Team	DUCATI	39'34.771		M/S
2	Marc Márquez	SPA	Repsol Honda Team	HONDA	39'34.984	0.213	M/M
3	Fabio Quartararo	FRA	Petronas Yamaha SRT	YAMAHA	39'40.888	6.117	M/S
4	Valentino Rossi	ITA	Monster Energy Yamaha MotoGP	YAMAHA	39'42.490	7.719	M/M
5	Maverick Viñales	SPA	Monster Energy Yamaha MotoGP	YAMAHA	39'43.445	8.674	M/M
6	Álex Rins	SPA	Team SUZUKI ECSTAR	SUZUKI	39'43.466	8.695	M/M
7	Francesco Bagnaia	ITA	Pramac Racing	DUCATI	39'50.792	16.021	M/M
8	Miguel Oliveira	POR	Red Bull KTM Tech 3	KTM	39'50.977	16.206	H/S
9	Danilo Petrucci	ITA	Ducati Team	DUCATI	39'52.121	17.350	M/M
10	Franco Morbidelli	ITA	Petronas Yamaha SRT	YAMAHA	39'55.281	20.510	M/M
11	Takaaki Nakagami	JPN	LCR Honda IDEMITSU	HONDA	39'57.044	22.273	H/S
12	Johann Zarco	FRA	Red Bull KTM Factory Racing	KTM	40'00.274	25.503	M/M
13	Stefan Bradl	GER	Repsol Honda Team	HONDA	40'06.733	31.962	H/M
14	Aleix Espargaró	SPA	Aprilia Racing Team Gresini	APRILIA	40'09.512	34.741	H/S
15	Karel Abraham	CZE	Reale Avintia Racing	DUCATI	40'22.880	48.109	M/S
16	Andrea Iannone	ITA	Aprilia Racing Team Gresini	APRILIA	39'46.598	1 lap	M/M
NC	Tito Rabat	SPA	Reale Avintia Racing	DUCATI	28'34.686	8 laps	H/M
NC	Jack Miller	AUS	Pramac Racing	DUCATI	9'58.670	21 laps	M/S
NC	Hafizh Syahrin	MAL	Red Bull KTM Tech 3	KTM	2'59.364	26 laps	H/S
NC	Pol Espargaró	SPA	Red Bull KTM Factory Racing	KTM	1'30.967	27 laps	H/S
NC	Cal Crutchlow	GBR	LCR Honda CASTROL	HONDA	1'31.293	27 laps	M/M

CHAMPIONSHIP STANDINGS

	RIDER	NAT	TEAM	PTS
1	Marc Márquez	SPA	Repsol Honda Team	230
2	Andrea Dovizioso	ITA	Ducati Team	172
3	Danilo Petrucci	ITA	Ducati Team	136
4	Álex Rins	SPA	Team SUZUKI ECSTAR	124
5	Valentino Rossi	ITA	Monster Energy Yamaha MotoGP	103
6	Maverick Viñales	SPA	Monster Energy Yamaha MotoGP	102
7	Fabio Quartararo	FRA	Petronas Yamaha SRT	92
8	Jack Miller	AUS	Pramac Racing	86
9	Cal Crutchlow	GBR	LCR Honda CASTROL	78
10	Takaaki Nakagami	JPN	LCR Honda IDEMITSU	62
11	Pol Espargaró	SPA	Red Bull KTM Factory Racing	61
12	Franco Morbidelli	ITA	Petronas Yamaha SRT	58
13	Joan Mir	SPA	Team SUZUKI ECSTAR	39
14	Aleix Espargaró	SPA	Aprilia Racing Team Gresini	33
15	Miguel Oliveira	POR	Red Bull KTM Tech 3	26
16	Francesco Bagnaia	ITA	Pramac Racing	24
17	Johann Zarco	FRA	Red Bull KTM Factory Racing	22
18	Andrea Iannone	ITA	Aprilia Racing Team Gresini	21
19	Jorge Lorenzo	SPA	Repsol Honda Team	19
20	Stefan Bradl	GER	Team HRC	16
21	Tito Rabat	SPA	Reale Avintia Racing	14
22	Michele Pirro	ITA	Ducati Team	9
23	Karel Abraham	CZE	Reale Avintia Racing	4
24	Sylvain Guintoli	FRA	Team SUZUKI ECSTAR	3
25	Hafizh Syahrin	MAL	Red Bull KTM Tech 3	3
26	Bradley Smith	GBR	Aprilia Factory Racing	

11 TAKAAKI NAKAGAMI
Raced the hard/soft tyre combination he had used in practice, but it didn't work the same in the cooler conditions, leaving him with little feeling and grip from the front, especially turning into corners. And the problem only got worse.

12 JOHANN ZARCO
Not easy to maintain your focus when you've just agreed to leave your team, but he managed it, with one of his best rides on the RC16. Enjoyed himself in the early laps while in a good group and got that adrenaline feeling back.

13 STEFAN BRADL
His fourth MotoGP race of the year was compromised by a problematic Saturday, which left him last on the grid. Then the damp warm-up prevented him from testing alternative settings. However, kept his full house of points scores.

14 ALEIX ESPARGARÓ
Horsepower matters at Red Bull Ring more than anywhere else, so this was never going to be an easy weekend for Aprilia. And it got much worse for the Spaniard at turn three on lap one when several collisions relegated him to last.

15 KAREL ABRAHAM
His third points score from the first 11 races of the season, but the Czech rider didn't rate this as one of his better races. He didn't make a great start and then ran into rear-grip issues. Ended up the last un-lapped rider.

16 ANDREA IANNONE
Qualified 18th and spent the early stages chasing his team-mate. The pair caught Bradl, but neither had the pace to overcome the Honda rider. Ran into a technical problem with three laps to go and got lapped by the leaders.

DNF TITO RABAT
Grew stronger throughout the weekend as his crew improved the set-up of his GP18, then got a good start from 15th on the grid. Was chasing Zarco when he had a big moment and had to abandon ship due to a wrist injury.

DNF JACK MILLER
Rode a great first third of the race, chasing the leading three riders, only to lose the front at turn nine on lap eight. Disappointed because he felt he had the pace to better Quartararo. Rode the third-fastest lap of the race.

DNF HAFIZH SYAHRIN
Crashed out on lap three while just behind Bradl. Went down at the first-gear turn three but it was a heavy tumble, which left him concussed. He was taken to hospital for further checks. This was his second DNF in two Sundays.

DNF POL ESPARGARÓ
KTM's main hope for its home race. Qualified 11th and had the potential for another top-ten. But an electronics glitch stopped his bike at turn three on lap two. Rabat clipped his rear, then Crutchlow hit Rabat and fell.

DNF CAL CRUTCHLOW
The Briton qualified ninth and thought he could do better in the race, but he was out of luck. A victim of the domino effect on the second lap, he fell at the dead-slow turn three. Damage to a handlebar stopped him continuing.

DNF JOAN MIR
A non-starter in this race, following a huge crash during post-Czech GP testing at Brno. Fell at close to top speed at the entry to turn one; his bike clearing the air-fence and service road. Was too battered about to race.

GoPro

Márquez has run out of rubber and road, and Rins knows it!

12 | GREAT BRITAIN

GOPRO BRITISH GRAND PRIX
SILVERSTONE CIRCUIT
23/24/25 AUGUST

0.013 SECONDS 'TWIXT HEAVEN AND HELL

Rins and Márquez set Silverstone alight with the fourth-closest finish in Grand Prix history

It would be difficult to imagine a more extreme reversal of fortunes than Silverstone 2018 and Silverstone 2019: from miserable weather and no racing to a summer heatwave and the fourth-closest finish in more than 70 years of premier-class Grand Prix racing.

The 2019 British Grand Prix – 70 years after the World Championships got underway at the 1949 Isle of Man TT – needed something special after the events of the previous year. And it got it.

Following the difficulties during MotoGP's previous visit – when racing was cancelled due to poor track conditions – the entire circuit had been resurfaced, with the work undertaken by Italian company Dromo, which had already been involved at Sepang, Mugello, Misano and Termas de Rio Hondo.

The extra grip transformed the circuit into what it should be: a daunting, high-speed, old-school racetrack that rewards the brave. Riders loved the new Silverstone but the grippier asphalt presented them with a dilemma: how to square the circle of 280 horsepower engines and 20 laps at around 175km/h (109mph).

Marc Márquez knew tyre life would once again be key. On Saturday afternoon the 26-year-old had achieved his 60th

‘RINS LOST THE REAR, I SHUT THE THROTTLE TO AVOID HIM AND MADE A BIG HIGHSIDE’
FABIO QUARTARARO

CLOCKWISE, FROM TOP LEFT | *Dovizioso rams Quartararo’s fallen M1; Crutchlow struggled with a blistered tyre; Dovizioso’s survival was a testament to modern riding kit; Viñales gave chase after losing time in the pile-up; Guintoli raced as well as he had tested for Suzuki; Lorenzo had a humbling comeback; best-mates Miller and Crutchlow battled; Full fuel tanks and sparks – Dovizioso’s GP19 is set to ignite.*

MotoGP pole position ahead of Valentino Rossi and Jack Miller, but he knew the race would be another matter. His pre-race comments turned out to be prophetic.

"Tyre consumption is a bit of an issue for us," he said. "Our target is to push at the beginning to try to have as small a group as possible. Of course, if you push at the beginning you will have less tyre at the end, but our target is the championship, not the race."

The sun-baked crowd's expectations of another multi-rider Silverstone dogfight ended ten seconds into the race, when Fabio Quartararo crashed at the first corner, his Petronas YZR-M1 a launch pad for Andrea Dovizioso, who hit the bike amidships and flew several metres. The Italian's Alpinestars data recorded an impact of 35g, but he escaped with concussion and bruising. He was stretchered away, while Quartararo walked away. Modern riding gear is great.

Márquez did exactly what he said he would do – he pushed from the start to stretch the pack and it was soon obvious that only one man could match his pace. This was the first real duel between the world champion and Álex Rins, just three weeks after their Brno contretemps.

As is usually the case when duelling riders use two very different motorcycles the contest was fascinating. The RC213V is a point-and-squirt bike built for tighter 21st century racetracks, while the GSX-RR is more of an old-school GP bike, totally at home at old-school tracks like Silverstone, which is where it took its first victory, with Maverick Viñales in 2016. Thus Rins was able to stay with Márquez's faster bike, the youngster occasionally hanging back into corners, so he could use his mid-corner advantage to close the gap on the exit.

Márquez's plan to reduce the group had worked perfectly – he had distilled the pack to himself and one rival.

Rins was happy to let the champion do the work, Márquez's RC213V shaking, kicking and squirming through Silverstone's high-speed kinks and turns, proving he wasn't cruising. Rins lead briefly just before half-distance, but seemed a little lost with the vast expanse of Silverstone all to himself, so Márquez fired back in front six corners later.

For the next ten laps Rins once again held station, although he nearly destroyed his race with three laps to go when he looked behind exiting Stowe and nearly crashed at the next corner.

He made his first real attack at turn 15 on the last lap. At least he thought it was the last lap. Márquez immediately counter-attacked but had used all of his grip, so that Rins could ride gloriously around the outside at Woodcote to cross the line 0.001 seconds ahead. Rins immediately realised he hadn't won the race and gathered himself together to do the same all over again.

Márquez's final lap was all about blocking, but once again he didn't have the speed where he really needed it, through

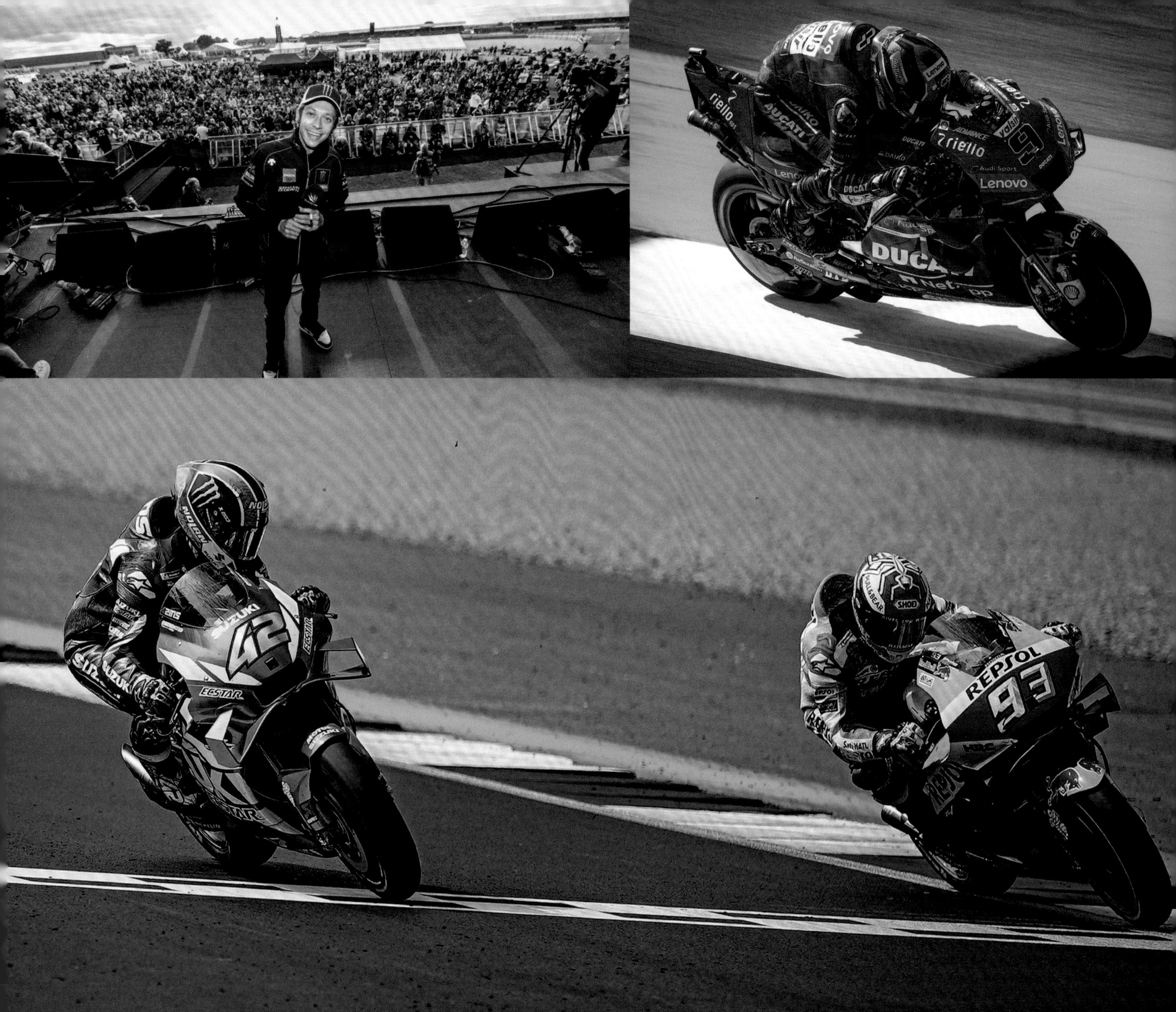

WHY THE LAP RECORD WAS BROKEN BY 1.6 SECONDS

Silverstone could not afford another 2018, so for the second consecutive year the entire circuit was fully resurfaced. After the disaster of 2018, circuit managing director Stuart Pringle engaged the services of Italian racetrack experts Dromo.

Dromo boss Jarno Zafelli has a somewhat obsessive approach to cooking and laying asphalt. He had been at the 2018 British GP, working with one of the factories, so he was able to start work at Silverstone the morning after the washout.

Pringle explained Dromo's approach. "They are very specific in

Woodcote. Indeed this time he had a big slide that sent him wide and allowed Rins to cut through on the inside for a brilliant victory.

The 23-year-old was ecstatic. Márquez – beaten by a smidgen for the second race in a row – was anything but. This was Rins' second MotoGP victory, but the first not gifted to him by the leader crashing out. He had played his game perfectly, rolling the dice on the last corner. Twice!

"I felt comfortable behind him, I was trying to play, with just one chance to win at the last corner," he said. "I was stronger than him in the first sectors, but in the last sector he was much faster than me, with all the accelerations. I was lucky to cut a lot of metres at the last corner, otherwise he would've beaten me."

No surprise that Márquez preferred to talk about his increased championship lead. "In the last laps Rins was more fresh, but I achieved my target – we arrived here 58 points in front and now we have 78."

Unlike those ahead of him, Viñales had to shut the throttle to avoid the Quartararo/Dovizioso pile-up. He made it past Rossi into third on lap seven, then stalked the leaders, narrowing the gap from 2.4 seconds to just six tenths.

"I took the maximum from the bike and I couldn't ask for more because this track is one of the worst for our engine," he said.

Rossi ran into rear-tyre issues, along with Cal Crutchlow and Jack Miller. The combination of the ultra-grippy new asphalt and a very un-British 44-degree track temperature caused some tyres to blister badly. Rossi lost 10.4 seconds to his team-mate in the last half of the race.

***CLOCKWISE FROM TOP LEFT** | Rossi drew the crowds at the 30th Day Of Champions event; Petrucci had another gloomy weekend; Quartararo and manager Eric Mahé watch the race from their garage; Rossi was right there in the early laps; Márquez is a genius at hiding disappointment; Rins can see he's won!*

their technical requirements," he said. "Tarmac [Silverstone's asphalting contractors] had to buy two brand-new planer machines of a specific make, model and type, according to Dromo's request. They cost £500,000 each."

"Dromo planed as much as 140mm off the old surface, remodelled the track in CAD and built in camber at various points to get rid of rainwater. They also put a slight crown in the middle of the track at the end of Hangar straight [where several riders – including Tito Rabat – crashed during the British GP due to aquaplaning]. They laid two courses of new asphalt: a 30mm pad-coat [lower coat], then a 40mm wearing course [topcoat]."

Zafelli was happy with his work at Silverstone – the lap record was broken by 1.6 seconds. "The track has good grip, the riders get a good feeling from the tyres, both with Michelin in MotoGP and with Dunlop in Moto2 and Moto3," he said. "And there's been a very low crash rate."

Most important of all, the riders were happy. "Last year the track was like a motocross track, so we must congratulate the circuit for the job they've done," said lap-record-breaker Marc Márquez.

The smoother asphalt opened up the circuit for riders, so they could use all the track available, instead of searching for the fast line through the bumps.

"With good grip and no bumps you have to approach most of the corners in a completely different way, using completely different lines," explained Andrea Dovizioso. "I was losing a lot of tenths in a few corners until we found the right lines and gained some tenths."

12 | GREAT BRITAIN

GOPRO BRITISH GRAND PRIX
SILVERSTONE CIRCUIT
23/24/25 AUGUST

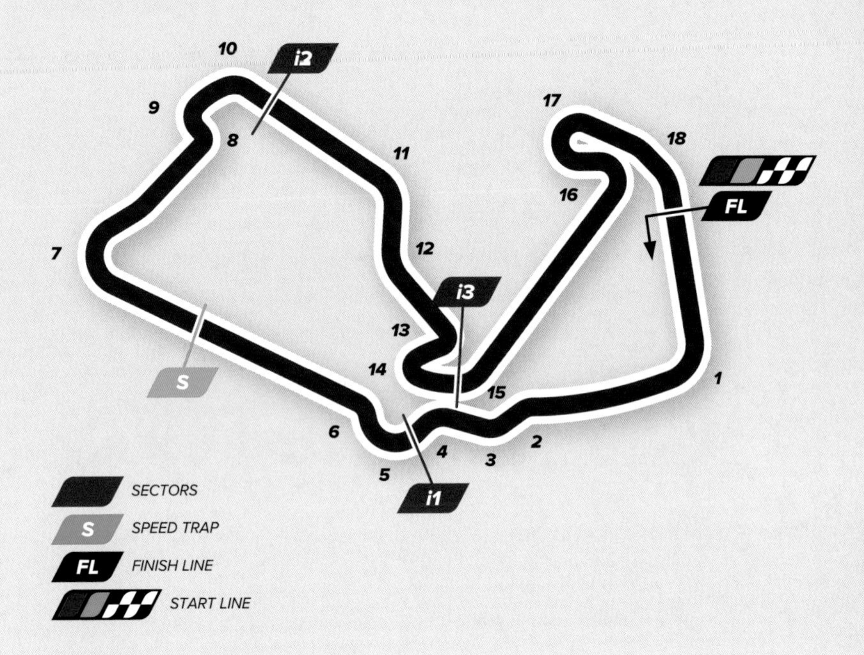

QUALIFYING RESULTS

	RIDER	NAT	TEAM	MACHINE	QP/TIME		GAP 1ST/PREV	
1	Marc Márquez	SPA	Repsol Honda Team	HONDA	Q2	1'58.168		
2	Valentino Rossi	ITA	Monster Energy Yamaha MotoGP	YAMAHA	Q2	1'58.596	0.428	0.428
3	Jack Miller	AUS	Pramac Racing	DUCATI	Q2	1'58.602	0.434	0.006
4	Fabio Quartararo	FRA	Petronas Yamaha SRT	YAMAHA	Q2	1'58.612	0.444	0.010
5	Álex Rins	SPA	Team SUZUKI ECSTAR	SUZUKI	Q2	1'58.670	0.502	0.058
6	Maverick Viñales	SPA	Monster Energy Yamaha MotoGP	YAMAHA	Q2	1'58.762	0.594	0.092
7	Andrea Dovizioso	ITA	Ducati Team	DUCATI	Q2	1'58.762	0.594	0.000
8	Franco Morbidelli	ITA	Petronas Yamaha SRT	YAMAHA	Q2	1'59.096	0.928	0.334
9	Cal Crutchlow	GBR	LCR Honda CASTROL	HONDA	Q2	1'59.243	1.075	0.147
10	Takaaki Nakagami	JPN	LCR Honda IDEMITSU	HONDA	Q2	1'59.427	1.259	0.184
11	Danilo Petrucci	ITA	Ducati Team	DUCATI	Q2	1'59.487	1.319	0.060
12	Aleix Espargaró	SPA	Aprilia Racing Team Gresini	APRILIA	Q2	1'59.620	1.452	0.133
13	Pol Espargaró	SPA	Red Bull KTM Factory Racing	KTM	Q1	1'59.549	*0.605	0.359
14	Johann Zarco	FRA	Red Bull KTM Factory Racing	KTM	Q1	1'59.648	*0.704	0.099
15	Miguel Oliveira	POR	Red Bull KTM Tech 3	KTM	Q1	1'59.758	*0.814	0.110
16	Tito Rabat	SPA	Reale Avintia Racing	DUCATI	Q1	1'59.916	*0.972	0.158
17	Andrea Iannone	ITA	Aprilia Racing Team Gresini	APRILIA	Q1	2'00.240	*1.296	0.324
18	Francesco Bagnaia	ITA	Pramac Racing	DUCATI	Q1	2'00.362	*1.418	0.122
19	Sylvain Guintoli	FRA	Team SUZUKI ECSTAR	ECSTAR	Q1	2'00.660	*1.716	0.298
20	Hafizh Syahrin	MAL	Red Bull KTM Tech 3	KTM	Q1	2'00.700	*1.756	0.040
21	Jorge Lorenzo	SPA	Repsol Honda Team	HONDA	Q1	2'01.562	*2.618	0.862
22	Karel Abraham	CZE	Reale Avintia Racing	DUCATI	Q1	2'04.845	*5.901	3.283

GRAND PRIX INFORMATION

TRACK INFORMATION			
2019 WINNER	Álex Rins		
CIRCUIT LENGTH	5.9 km	3.67 miles	
LAPS	20		
RACE DISTANCE	118.0 km	73.4 miles	
ALL TIME LAP RECORD	1'58.168	179.7 Km/h	Marc Márquez (2019)
BEST RACE LAP	1'59.936	177.0 Km/h	Marc Márquez (2019)
RACE CONDITION	Dry		
AIR	31°C		
HUMIDITY	27%		
GROUND	44°C		

TYRE SELECTION

FRONT	
SOFT	WHITE
MEDIUM	GREY
HARD	YELLOW

REAR	
SOFT	WHITE
MEDIUM	GREY
HARD	YELLOW

< MILD — TRACK SEVERITY — SEVERE >

** Gap to the fastest rider in the Q1 session   ** Went forward from Q1 to Q2   Track severity = Wear + Temperature + Load*

1 ÁLEX RINS
This was a breakthrough win for Rins and he knew it. The usually quiet, retiring youngster climbed to the top step of the podium screaming his battle cry: "Vamos!". He saved his tyres and played Márquez perfectly.

2 MARC MÁRQUEZ
Once again, didn't need to fight for the win but he did, because that's what he does. Of course, he could've let Rins lead, but that might've allowed Viñales to join the battle. Had his first crash since Le Mans in FP2.

3 MAVERICK VIÑALES
Lost very nearly a second on the first lap to the Quartararo/Dovizioso pile-up and finished six tenths down on Rins. There was no doubt that he had the pace, at a fast, flowing track that suits the Suzuki and Yamaha.

4 VALENTINO ROSSI
Was the last rider ahead of the Turn One accident, so he was right with the leaders for the first few laps. Second quickest in qualifying, his podium hopes were dashed in the second half of the race by a blistered rear tyre.

5 FRANCO MORBIDELLI
His best result since Assen ended a run of so-so results and followed two not-so-easy days of practice and qualifying. His feeling improved as the race went on and he won an entertaining battle with Crutchlow.

6 CAL CRUTCHLOW
Spent the early laps fighting with Morbidelli and then best-mate Miller, but couldn't find the grip he had had in practice. Ran into tyre blistering issues in the closing stages and was very nearly beaten by Petrucci.

7 DANILO PETRUCCI
Lost a lot of time and positions due to the Turn One crash. Thirteenth after one lap he worked his way forward, then in the second half found he had more grip than most, allowing him to chase Crutchlow home.

8 JACK MILLER
Had a nightmare start: had to avoid the crash and his holeshot device jammed, giving his GP19 the geometry of a chopper for the first few corners. His rear tyre blistered, putting him in the same situation as Crutchlow.

9 POL ESPARGARÓ
Everyone apart from the top three was a long way back in this race, so KTM's top rider was happy enough with ninth place, chasing a factory Ducati and Honda, less than two seconds behind Crutchlow in sixth.

10 ANDREA IANNONE
The Italian's second top-ten result with Aprilia came at a track that allowed him to use the RS-GP's strong points – easy handling and manoeuvrability – to full effect. Made a good start, which helped a lot.

RACE LAP CHART

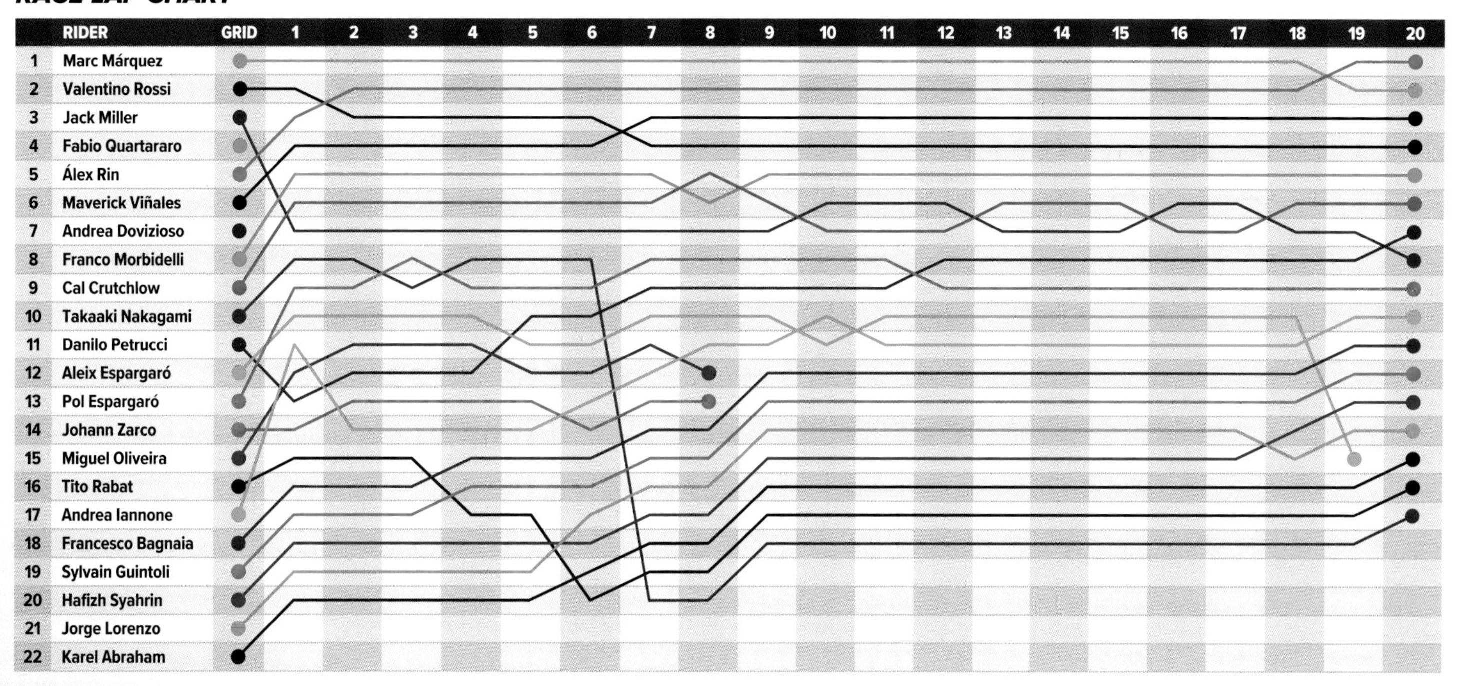

RACE RESULTS

	RIDER	NAT	TEAM	MACHINE	TIME	+GAP	TYRES
1	Álex Rins	SPA	Team SUZUKI ECSTAR	SUZUKI	40'12.79		H/H
2	Marc Márquez	SPA	Repsol Honda Team	HONDA	40'12.812	0.013	H/H
3	Maverick Viñales	SPA	Monster Energy Yamaha MotoGP	YAMAHA	40'13.419	0.620	H/H
4	Valentino Rossi	ITA	Monster Energy Yamaha MotoGP	YAMAHA	40'24.238	11.439	H/H
5	Franco Morbidelli	ITA	Petronas Yamaha SRT	YAMAHA	40'25.908	13.109	H/H
6	Cal Crutchlow	GBR	LCR Honda CASTROL	HONDA	40'31.968	19.169	H/H
7	Danilo Petrucci	ITA	Ducati Team	DUCATI	40'32.481	19.682	H/H
8	Jack Miller	AUS	Pramac Racing	DUCATI	40'33.117	20.318	H/H
9	Pol Espargaró	SPA	Red Bull KTM Factory Racing	KTM	40'33.878	21.079	H/H
10	Andrea Iannone	ITA	Aprilia Racing Team Gresini	APRILIA	40'37.943	25.144	H/H
11	Francesco Bagnaia	ITA	Pramac Racing	DUCATI	40'53.116	40.317	H/H
12	Sylvain Guintoli	FRA	Team SUZUKI ECSTAR	SUZUKI	40'58.277	45.478	M/H
13	Hafizh Syahrin	MAL	Red Bull KTM Tech 3	KTM	41'07.582	54.783	H/H
14	Jorge Lorenzo	SPA	Repsol Honda Team	HONDA	41'09.450	56.651	M/M
15	Karel Abraham	CZE	Reale Avintia Racing	DUCATI	41'42.081	89.282	M/H
16	Tito Rabat	SPA	Reale Avintia Racing	DUCATI	41'44.515	91.716	H/H
17	Takaaki Nakagami	JPN	LCR Honda IDEMITSU	HONDA	41'53.219	100.420	H/M
NC	Aleix Espargaró	SPA	Aprilia Racing Team Gresini	APRILIA	39'10.162	1 lap	H/H
NC	Miguel Oliveira	POR	Red Bull KTM Tech 3	KTM	16'17.802	12 laps	H/H
NC	Johann Zarco	FRA	Red Bull KTM Factory Racing	KTM	16'18.287	12 laps	H/H
NC	Fabio Quartararo	FRA	Petronas Yamaha SRT	YAMAHA			M/H
NC	Andrea Dovizioso	ITA	Ducati Team	DUCATI			H/H

CHAMPIONSHIP STANDINGS

	RIDER	NAT	TEAM	PTS
1	Marc Márquez	SPA	Repsol Honda Team	250
2	Andrea Dovizioso	ITA	Ducati Team	172
3	Álex Rins	SPA	Team SUZUKI ECSTAR	149
4	Danilo Petrucci	ITA	Ducati Team	145
5	Maverick Viñales	SPA	Monster Energy Yamaha MotoGP	118
6	Valentino Rossi	ITA	Monster Energy Yamaha MotoGP	116
7	Jack Miller	AUS	Pramac Racing	94
8	Fabio Quartararo	FRA	Petronas Yamaha SRT	92
9	Cal Crutchlow	GBR	LCR Honda CASTROL	88
10	Franco Morbidelli	ITA	Petronas Yamaha SRT	69
11	Pol Espargaró	SPA	Red Bull KTM Factory Racing	68
12	Takaaki Nakagami	JPN	LCR Honda IDEMITSU	62
13	Joan Mir	SPA	Team SUZUKI ECSTAR	39
14	Aleix Espargaró	SPA	Aprilia Racing Team Gresini	33
15	Francesco Bagnaia	ITA	Pramac Racing	29
16	Andrea Iannone	ITA	Aprilia Racing Team Gresini	27
17	Miguel Oliveira	POR	Red Bull KTM Tech 3	26
18	Johann Zarco	FRA	Red Bull KTM Factory Racing	22
19	Jorge Lorenzo	SPA	Repsol Honda Team	21
20	Stefan Bradl	GER	Team HRC	16
21	Tito Rabat	SPA	Reale Avintia Racing	14
22	Michele Pirro	ITA	Ducati Team	9
23	Sylvain Guintoli	FRA	Team SUZUKI ECSTAR	7
24	Hafizh Syahrin	MAL	Red Bull KTM Tech 3	6
25	Karel Abraham	CZE	Reale Avintia Racing	5
26	Bradley Smith	GBR	Aprilia Factory Racing	1

11 FRANCESCO BAGNAIA
Had high hopes for the race after a good run in FP4, but had a disastrous Q1 qualifying session that put him 18th on the grid. Ended the first lap in 16th and was more than happy with 11th in the circumstances.

12 SYLVAIN GUINTOLI
Replaced Joan Mir, who was still recovering from his huge crash during post-Czech GP tests at Brno. This was the Frenchman's best result from his three races so far. Was as delighted with Rins' result as he was for his own.

13 HAFIZH SYAHRIN
This was the Malaysian's best KTM result so far. Admitted that he took too long to get up to speed in the race – but this shouldn't have come as a surprise for someone who had crashed out of the last two GPs.

14 JORGE LORENZO
Climbed aboard his RC213V for the first time since his horrible Assen crash. His injured vertebrae gave him pain and his lack of muscle strength also caused him problems. Most of all, he knew he couldn't afford to crash.

15 KAREL ABRAHAM
Had a torrid time, with crashes in FP1, FP2 and FP3. Was so battered about that he was nearly ruled out of the race. Considered retiring due to the pain, but the number of DNFs made it worth sticking at it.

16 TITO RABAT
Qualified 16th and a strong warm-up outing had the Spaniard – who had that horror smash at Silverstone 2018 – full of optimism for the race. He was trying to overtake Guintoli at Village when he locked the front and crashed.

17 TAKAAKI NAKAGAMI
Crashed on lap seven at Brooklands as he let go of the brake and got on the throttle. He was going very well at the time – in front of the Espargaró brothers, Petrucci and Oliveira. Remounted, but ended up last.

DNF ALEIX ESPARGARÓ
The lanky Spaniard was out of luck again after another good ride. Spent much of the race battling with his brother, his team-mate and Petrucci. Then with two laps to go his RS-GP slowed and finally gave up the ghost.

DNF MIGUEL OLIVEIRA
Started from 15th on the grid, but after all the early exits he felt he had a realistic chance of making it into the top-ten at the finish. Was chasing Iannone, Aleix Espargaró and Danilo Petrucci when Zarco slammed into him.

DNF JOHANN ZARCO
Didn't make any more friends at KTM when he made an over-optimistic lunge on Oliveira at the dead-slow Loop just before half-distance. In trying to take 12th place from the Portuguese he took them both out.

DNF ANDREA DOVIZIOSO
After the race the top-three discussed the fact that Dovizioso might've had the best race pace in the circumstances. But once again the Italian got taken out by another rider. Was lucky to escape with minor injuries.

DNF FABIO QUARTARARO
Rins got a bit sideways at the first corner, Quartararo shut the throttle to avoid him and got highsided. He too was lucky to get away largely unhurt. Might he have won his first MotoGP race without the crash?

PETRONAS
Visit Malaysia
BARRACUDA
PETRONAS
YAMAHA
withu
REPSOL
HONDA
SHOEI
PULL&BEAR
BARRACUDA
PETRONAS
PETRONAS
Visit Malaysia
YAMAHA
PETRONAS

13 | SAN MARINO

GP OCTO DI SAN MARINO E DELLA RIVIERA DI RIMINI

MISANO WORLD CIRCUIT MARCO SIMONCELLI

13/14/15 SEPTEMBER

MASTER BEATS APPRENTICE, JUST

Quartararo had his best ride yet at Misano, pushing the world champion all the way

There was plenty for the media to be excited about at Misano. First, the announcement that Aprilia's Andrea Iannone and his brother Angelo will manage Romano Fenati, at the very track where the youngster got into so much trouble last year. Then on Saturday afternoon MotoGP's biggest stars Marc Márquez and Valentino Rossi had their first clash in quite a while. Some journalists hardly knew what to do with themselves.

The real story of the weekend was somewhat less of a thrill. Some months before the MotoGP weekend the Misano track was shot-peened in an attempt to improve grip. The idea was to decrease the asphalt's macro-roughness and increase its micro-roughness. In other words, fracturing the aggregate in the bitumen to create sharper-edged stones that would offer more grip. In fact the process decreased grip, so much so that the 2019 race was 20 seconds slower than the 2018 edition.

The search for traction dominated all three days of the event. Most people thought the lack of grip would mostly hurt the corner-speed bikes – the inline-four Yamaha and Suzuki – because these machines use the edge of their tyres to achieve their big cornering arcs. In fact riders of the point-and-squirt bikes – the V4 Honda and Ducati – suffered most because they couldn't brake deep or accelerate early. With one exception, of course.

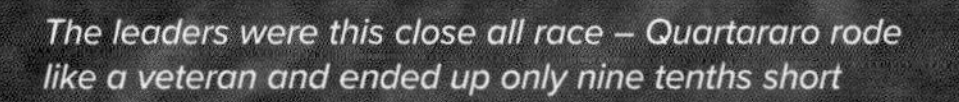

The leaders were this close all race – Quartararo rode like a veteran and ended up only nine tenths short

Incredibly, Yamaha had their best weekend in years: the first

CLOCKWISE, FROM TOP LEFT *Márquez and Quartararo 'debrief' in parc fermé, Viñales flirts with the green in Q2; life didn't get any easier for Lorenzo; Mir made a strong return from his Brno smash; Misano was so slippery it claimed 69 fallers, including Crutchlow in the race; Morbidelli charges past Syahrin in practice; former 250cc world champion Marco Melandri was a visitor; Dovizioso's race was 33 seconds slower than 2018; Espargaró celebrates KTM's first dry-track front row with KTM's Pit Beirer, Mike Leitner and Paul Trevathan.*

'THIS IS AMAZING – THANKS TO THOSE THAT PUT IN ALL THE HOURS, EFFORT AND SWEAT!'

POL ESPARGARÓ

time four YZR-M1s had finished in the top-five since Aragon 2012. This must've pleased company president Yoshihiro Hadaka, making a rare visit to a European race. With Hadaka came various parts, including Yamaha's first carbon-fibre swingarm, a Suzuki-style twin-pipe exhaust and a Ducati-style front-wheel fairing. Finally, Yamaha were fighting back.

"Since the beginning of this season something has changed," said Rossi. "We have a lot of different people from Europe and especially from Japan. It looks like now we feel the effect."

However, it wasn't Rossi who kept Hadaka on the edge of his seat throughout the race. Once again it was Fabio Quartararo who squeezed the maximum out of the M1. The 20-year-old qualified on the front row, alongside Maverick Viñales and Pol Espargaró, who chased Viñales in Q2 to score KTM's first dry-track top-three grid slot.

Viñales led, but not for long, struggling as usual with a full tank. On lap three Quartararo swept past him into the 250km/h (155mph) Turn 11 and one lap later Márquez was also past. From here it was a straight duel between the rookie and the champ.

Three weeks earlier Márquez had done all the work at Silverstone, only to lose out on the last lap, so he wasn't going to make the same mistake. He stalked the leader lap after lap, mostly just a couple of metres behind, awaiting his moment. Quartararo was amazing. He had never led a race for this long and yet he never wavered or faltered.

However, Márquez didn't look like he was struggling to keep up and when he made his move, into Turn One on the last lap, it was a straightforward pass. But that didn't stop Quartararo counter-attacking three corners later. Márquez knew he had to get back in front quickly, so he threw his RC213V inside the M1 at Turn Eight, front end weaving, rear tyre in the air, smoke pouring off the sole of his left boot.

"Fabio rides the Yamaha in a very good way – very precise all the time – and especially in the fast corners he's very, very fast," said Márquez. "That's why I got him before Turn 11 because if I was behind him there I would've lost the race."

Both riders had watched the earlier Moto2 race, which Augusto Fernandez had won on the last lap by barging past Fabio Di Giannantonio at Turn 14, so Márquez defended his line at the hairpin like his life depended on it and Quartararo very nearly tailgated him in the process.

After the race Quartararo was overcome by mixed emotions: sadness at getting beaten but overjoyed to be racing with the greatest. Then an ominous warning...

"We are gaining experience because every time we go a track it's new for us," he said. "Next year, from FP1 at every track we will already have some references."

TAVULLIA WORSHIPS THE KING

Before Valentino Rossi became king of MotoGP he was boss of the roads around his hometown of Tavullia. The mischievous teenager and his friends spent their days hurtling their scooters through the streets of the ancient hill town and down the twisting roads to the seaside, no doubt attracting the opprobrium of the locals and the police.

On the Wednesday before the 2019 San Marino Grand Prix the situation in Tavullia was somewhat different. Rossi rode his Yamaha YZR-M1 MotoGP bike – with open exhaust, no lights and so on – through the town, where the police were kept busy keeping the adoring locals and visiting fans at bay. It was dream come true,

Perhaps the secret to his speed at Misano was his ability to save front-end slides, a bit like Márquez.

"Fabio doesn't use his elbows like Marc, but he feels the slide very, very early, so it's reaction time and control," explained Petronas SRT team manager Wilco Zeelenberg. "He lets the bike come up maybe half a degree, then he can save it. Fabio rides the bike the same way as Jorge [Lorenzo] rode it. He trusts the front end, more than the other Yamaha riders. But there's also a difference between Fabio and Jorge: basically Fabio doesn't care. Sometimes he overrides the bike like Marc to find the limit and he controls that and he doesn't complain. Jorge sometimes struggled because he wanted the bike to be smooth and behave the way he wanted, without any movements."

Viñales came on strong in the later laps but once again he couldn't quite close the gap. Rossi finished fourth for the third consecutive race, just bettering his VR46 protégé Franco Morbidelli and Andrea Dovizioso, whose race time was 33 seconds slower than his 2018-winning time.

"We can't use the grip we usually have in the traction [acceleration] area," Dovizioso explained. "And if we try to be aggressive in the middle of the corner we lose the front very easily."

Espargaró was next, six seconds behind Dovizioso, riding brilliantly aboard an RC16 that was starting to benefit from the input of test-rider Dani Pedrosa. Johann Zarco finished 12 seconds further back, in what turned out to be his last race with KTM. Two days later the factory told him that he had been exempted from all MotoGP duties.

CLOCKWISE FROM TOP LEFT | *Rossi thanks his fan club while Márquez relishes an important 'away' victory; Suzuki win the pit-lane helmet race every time; Aprilia had a sad home race: Espargaró 12th, Iannone injured; Quartararo and Viñales shared the podium, as they had at Assen; no one knew it yet but this was Zarco's last KTM ride; yellow was definitely the colour.*

he said, to ride his Grand Prix bike through his hometown, where his VR46 Academy, Motor Ranch and merchandising operation employs more than 80 people, many of them locals.

Sadly, Rossi's race weekend didn't quite go to plan. The most talked-about moment of his 396th GP was probably his Q2 clash with Marc Márquez. Both men were on their final qualifying laps when the youngster swept past Rossi at the hyper-fast Turn 11, then Rossi dived past Márquez three corners later.

"I stayed more inside to try and overtake him at the hairpin but I arrived wide, so we lost the chance to improve my lap time," he said.

In fact both riders had their laps cancelled, because Rossi had exceeded track limits at Turn Six and Márquez on the exit of Turn 11.

13 | SAN MARINO

GP OCTO DI SAN MARINO E DELLA RIVIERA DI RIMINI
MISANO WORLD CIRCUIT MARCO SIMONCELLI
13/14/15 SEPTEMBER

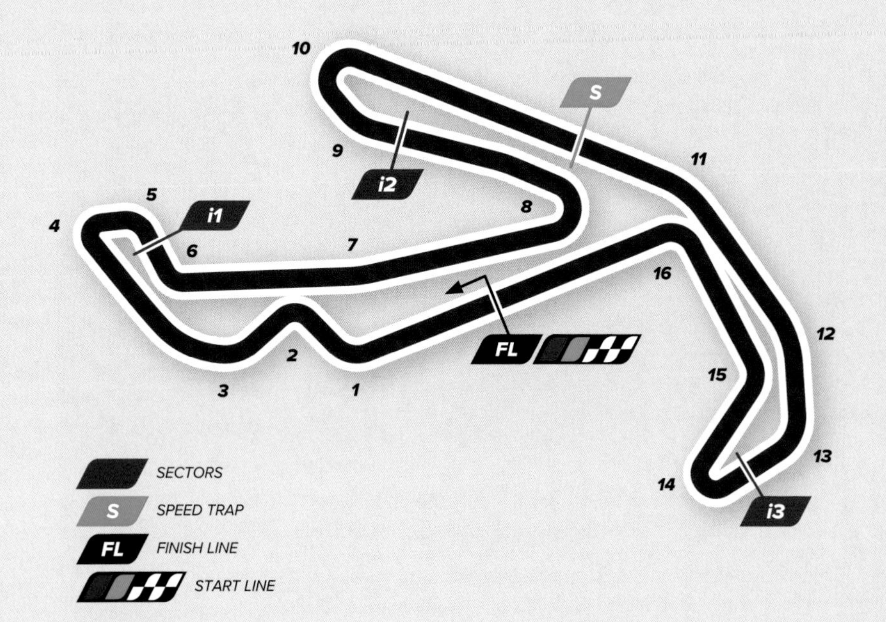

QUALIFYING RESULTS

	RIDER	NAT	TEAM	MACHINE	QP/TIME		GAP 1ST/PREV	
1	Maverick Viñales	SPA	Monster Energy Yamaha MotoGP	YAMAHA	Q2	1'32.265		
2	Pol Espargaró	SPA	Red Bull KTM Factory Racing	KTM	Q2	1'32.560	0.295	0.295
3	Fabio Quartararo	FRA	Petronas Yamaha SRT	YAMAHA	Q2	1'32.571	0.306	0.011
4	Franco Morbidelli	ITA	Petronas Yamaha SRT	YAMAHA	Q2	1'32.710	0.445	0.139
5	Marc Márquez	SPA	Repsol Honda Team	HONDA	Q2	1'32.742	0.477	0.032
6	Andrea Dovizioso	ITA	Ducati Team	DUCATI	Q2	1'33.038	0.773	0.296
7	Valentino Rossi	ITA	Monster Energy Yamaha MotoGP	YAMAHA	Q2	1'33.079	0.814	0.041
8	Johann Zarco	FRA	Red Bull KTM Factory Racing	KTM	Q2	1'33.123	0.858	0.044
9	Álex Rins	SPA	Team SUZUKI ECSTAR	SUZUKI	Q2	1'33.265	1.000	0.142
10	Joan Mir	SPA	Team SUZUKI ECSTAR	SUZUKI	Q2	1'33.431	1.166	0.166
11	Takaaki Nakagami	JPN	LCR Honda IDEMITSU	HONDA	Q2	1'33.449	1.184	0.018
12	Michele Pirro	ITA	Ducati Team	DUCATI	Q2	1'33.461	1.196	0.012
13	Francesco Bagnaia	ITA	Pramac Racing	DUCATI	Q1	1'33.488	*0.341	0.003
14	Cal Crutchlow	GBR	LCR Honda CASTROL	HONDA	Q1	1'33.516	*0.369	0.028
15	Aleix Espargaró	SPA	Aprilia Racing Team Gresini	APRILIA	Q1	1'33.522	*0.375	0.006
16	Jack Miller	AUS	Pramac Racing	DUCATI	Q1	1'33.571	*0.424	0.049
17	Danilo Petrucci	ITA	Ducati Team	DUCATI	Q1	1'33.630	*0.483	0.059
18	Jorge Lorenzo	SPA	Repsol Honda Team	HONDA	Q1	1'33.777	*0.630	0.147
19	Miguel Oliveira	POR	Red Bull KTM Tech 3	KTM	Q1	1'34.162	*1.015	0.385
20	Hafizh Syahrin	MAL	Red Bull KTM Tech 3	KTM	Q1	1'34.322	*1.175	0.160
21	Karel Abraham	CZE	Reale Avintia Racing	UCATI	Q1	1'34.401	*1.254	0.079
22	Tito Rabat	SPA	Reale Avintia Racing	DUCATI	Q1	1'34.904	*1.757	0.503
23	Andrea Iannone	ITA	Aprilia Racing Team Gresini	APRILIA	FP2	1'34.381	1.606	

** Gap to the fastest rider in the Q1 session ** Went forward from Q1 to Q2 Track severity = Wear + Temperature + Load*

GRAND PRIX INFORMATION

TRACK INFORMATION			
2019 WINNER	Marc Márquez		
CIRCUIT LENGTH	4.2 km	2.63 miles	
LAPS	27		
RACE DISTANCE	114.1 km	71.0 miles	
ALL TIME LAP RECORD	1'31.629	166.0 Km/h	Jorge Lorenzo (2018)
BEST RACE LAP	1'32.678	164.1 Km/h	Andrea Dovizioso (2018)
RACE CONDITION	Dry		
AIR	26°C		
HUMIDITY	54%		
GROUND	39°C		

TYRE SELECTION

FRONT	
SOFT	WHITE
MEDIUM	GREY
HARD	YELLOW

REAR	
SOFT	WHITE
MEDIUM	GREY
HARD	YELLOW

L M R

< MILD — TRACK SEVERITY — SEVERE >

1 MARC MÁRQUEZ
For the third consecutive race the reigning world champion fought for the lead lap after lap – and finally this time victory was his. Number 93 left Misano with a 93-point advantage and the championship all but out of anyone's reach.

2 FABIO QUARTARARO
When a young rookie gets beaten on the last lap and says it's the best day of his life, you know he's got the right attitude. The Frenchman was delighted to have his first real race with Márquez and learned plenty along the way.

3 MAVERICK VIÑALES
A second consecutive podium result convinced the Assen winner that Yamaha's recent progress, especially with electronics set-up, was finally making a difference for him. "We are starting to understand many things."

4 VALENTINO ROSSI
Scored his third fourth-place finish in a row, 11 seconds behind his team-mate, so quite a long way from the home podium he so desperately wanted. Spent much of the race with protégé Morbidelli. Lacked corner-exit grip.

5 FRANCO MORBIDELLI
Another fifth-place finish proved that the first member of the VR46 Academy was regaining speed and confidence after a mid-season slump. This was his 100th GP, six years after his made his debut in the 2013 Misano Moto2 race.

6 ANDREA DOVIZIOSO
Last year's Misano winner had very little to smile about this time. The Ducati suffered badly on the slippery asphalt, so he couldn't attack the corners and when he caught Rossi and Morbidelli it was too risky to try overtaking.

7 POL ESPARGARÓ
KTM's best weekend so far had the Spaniard qualify a remarkable second fastest and finish seventh, after chasing Rossi and Dovizioso. Revised frame stiffness – via removing the upper-rear engine bolts – helped the RC16's turning.

8 JOAN MIR
Returned to racing for the first time since his huge Brno crash. Found it easy to get back in the groove. Qualified on the third row next to his team-mate and rode a strong race, although he wasn't comfortable with his bike set-up.

9 JACK MILLER
Like the other Ducati riders spent the weekend skating around on the sketchy surface. During the race he got ahead of Mir but in the final laps he had no answer to Suzuki's rookie. Was happy to leave Misano with a few points.

10 DANILO PETRUCCI
Another so-so result, the Italian admitting that his weight is a problem both for his riding technique and bike performance. "And I can't lose 15 kilos to be like Andrea." Rins' crash returned him to third in the championship.

RACE LAP CHART

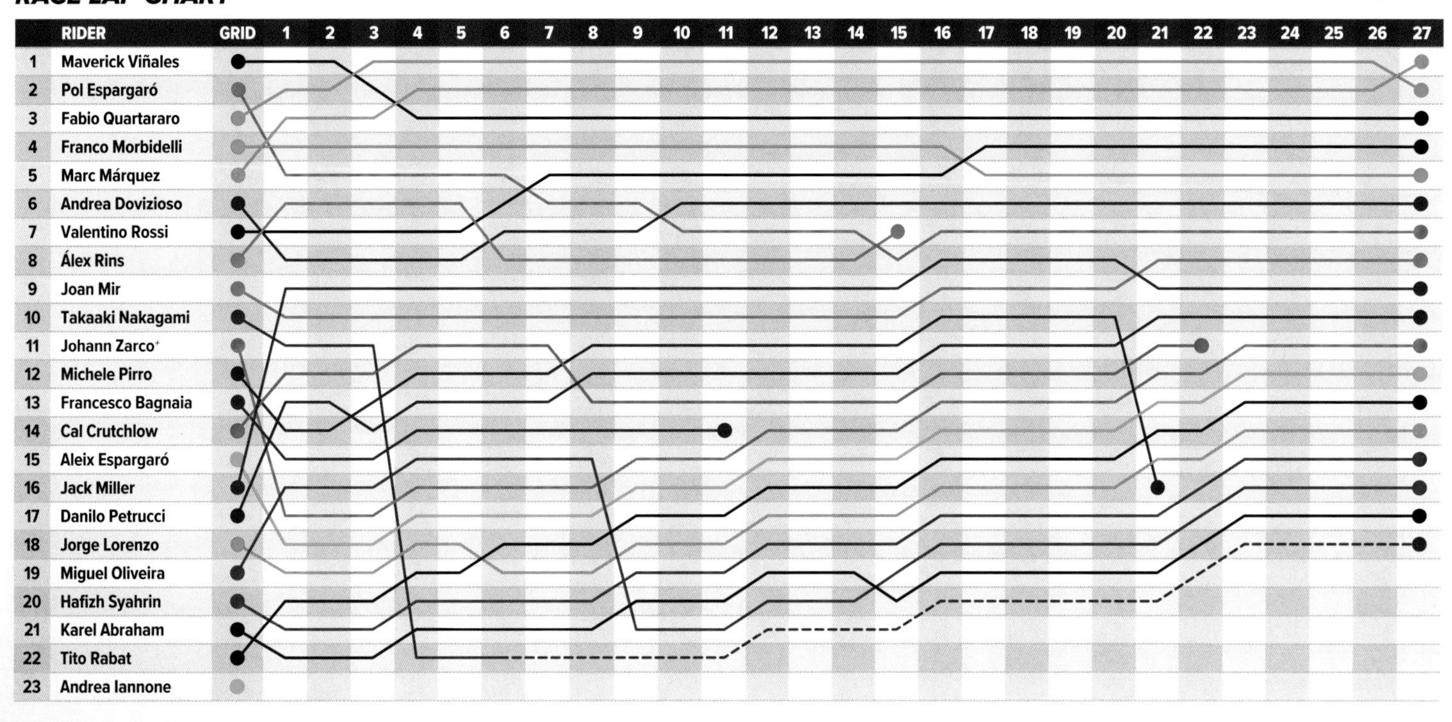

+ FIM MotoGP Stewards grid penalty - #5 Johann Zarco

RACE RESULTS

	RIDER	NAT	TEAM	MACHINE	TIME	+ GAP	TYRES
1	Marc Márquez	SPA	Repsol Honda Team	HONDA	42'25.163		M/M
2	Fabio Quartararo	FRA	Petronas Yamaha SRT	YAMAHA	42'26.066	0.903	M/M
3	Maverick Viñales	SPA	Monster Energy Yamaha MotoGP	YAMAHA	42'26.799	1.636	M/M
4	Valentino Rossi	ITA	Monster Energy Yamaha MotoGP	YAMAHA	42'37.823	12.660	M/M
5	Franco Morbidelli	ITA	Petronas Yamaha SRT	YAMAHA	42'37.937	12.774	M/M
6	Andrea Dovizioso	ITA	Ducati Team	DUCATI	42'38.907	13.744	M/M
7	Pol Espargaró	SPA	Red Bull KTM Factory Racing	KTM	42'45.213	20.050	M/M
8	Joan Mir	SPA	Team SUZUKI ECSTAR	SUZUKI	42'47.675	22.512	M/M
9	Jack Miller	AUS	Pramac Racing	DUCATI	42'51.717	26.554	M/M
10	Danilo Petrucci	ITA	Ducati Team	DUCATI	42'56.619	31.456	M/M
11	Johann Zarco	FRA	Red Bull KTM Factory Racing	KTM	42'57.551	32.388	S/M
12	Aleix Espargaró	SPA	Aprilia Racing Team Gresini	APRILIA	42'59.640	34.477	M/M
13	Tito Rabat	SPA	Reale Avintia Racing	DUCATI	43'00.488	35.325	M/M
14	Jorge Lorenzo	SPA	Repsol Honda Team	HONDA	43'12.410	47.247	S/S
15	Hafizh Syahrin	MAL	Red Bull KTM Tech 3	KTM	43'27.443	62.280	M/M
16	Miguel Oliveira	POR	Red Bull KTM Tech 3	KTM	43'32.994	67.831	M/S
17	Karel Abraham	CZE	Reale Avintia Racing	DUCATI	43'49.829	84.666	M/M
18	Takaaki Nakagami	JPN	LCR Honda IDEMITSU	HONDA	43'07.607	1 lap	M/M
NC	Cal Crutchlow	GBR	LCR Honda CASTROL	HONDA	35'00.485	5 laps	M/M
NC	Michele Pirro	ITA	Ducati Team	DUCATI	33'42.043	6 laps	M/M
NC	Álex Rins	SPA	Team SUZUKI ECSTAR	SUZUKI	23'45.558	12 laps	M/M
NC	Francesco Bagnaia	ITA	Pramac Racing	DUCATI	17'35.661	16 laps	M/M

CHAMPIONSHIP STANDINGS

	RIDER	NAT	TEAM	PTS
1	Marc Márquez	SPA	Repsol Honda Team	275
2	Andrea Dovizioso	ITA	Ducati Team	182
3	Danilo Petrucci	ITA	Ducati Team	151
4	Álex Rins	SPA	Team SUZUKI ECSTAR	149
5	Maverick Viñales	SPA	Monster Energy Yamaha MotoGP	134
6	Valentino Rossi	ITA	Monster Energy Yamaha MotoGP	129
7	Fabio Quartararo	FRA	Petronas Yamaha SRT	112
8	Jack Miller	AUS	Pramac Racing	101
9	Cal Crutchlow	GBR	LCR Honda CASTROL	88
10	Franco Morbidelli	ITA	Petronas Yamaha SRT	80
11	Pol Espargaró	SPA	Red Bull KTM Factory Racing	77
12	Takaaki Nakagami	JPN	LCR Honda IDEMITSU	62
13	Joan Mir	SPA	Team SUZUKI ECSTAR	47
14	Aleix Espargaró	SPA	Aprilia Racing Team Gresini	37
15	Francesco Bagnaia	ITA	Pramac Racing	29
16	Andrea Iannone	ITA	Aprilia Racing Team Gresini	27
17	Johann Zarco	FRA	Red Bull KTM Factory Racing	27
18	Miguel Oliveira	POR	Red Bull KTM Tech 3	26
19	Jorge Lorenzo	SPA	Repsol Honda Team	23
20	Tito Rabat	SPA	Reale Avintia Racing	17
21	Stefan Bradl	GER	Team HRC	16
22	Michele Pirro	ITA	Ducati Team	9
23	Sylvain Guintoli	FRA	Team SUZUKI ECSTAR	7
24	Hafizh Syahrin	MAL	Red Bull KTM Tech 3	7
25	Karel Abraham	CZE	Reale Avintia Racing	5
26	Bradley Smith	GBR	Aprilia Factory Racing	

11 JOHANN ZARCO
Didn't know it at the time but this was his last race with KTM. Had a good qualifying, then had to wait for his medium rear to come in during the race. Seventeenth on lap one he gained positions via passes and crashes.

12 ALEIX ESPARGARÓ
Qualified 15th, then lost a few positions at the start, so he had his work cut out. Spent the entire race chasing Zarco's KTM. The pattern was the same throughout: the Aprilia was better on the brakes, the KTM on acceleration.

13 TITO RABAT
A mechanical problem during qualifying left the Spaniard last on the grid, so just getting points would be a huge challenge. Rode aggressively in the early laps, then found further promotion through rivals crashing out.

14 JORGE LORENZO
His second race following his return from his Assen back injury didn't go as well as Silverstone: a very slippery track is not ideal for a rider who cannot afford to crash. Felt a bit stronger on the bike but back pain was still a problem.

15 HAFIZH SYAHRIN
To finish first, first you must finish, and to score points, first you must finish. This was the Malaysian's fourth points score with KTM after qualifying 20th. Had "a strange feeling during all the race" but finished nonetheless.

16 MIGUEL OLIVEIRA
Suffered with the right shoulder he injured at Silverstone, then crashed on lap nine due to an overheating front tyre, which raised tyre pressure. Remounted and set a good pace, finishing five seconds behind his team-mate.

17 KAREL ABRAHAM
The Czech rider was sick all weekend and needed help from the Clinica Mobile to make the start. His main issue in the race was lack of physical strength, so he had to give up the chase and focus on making it to the finish.

18 TAKAAKI NAKAGAMI
The 2018 RC213V rider, who had scored points at nine of the first 11 races, crashed and remounted for the second consecutive race. Got a dash warning that front-tyre pressure was getting too high but kept pushing anyway.

DNF CAL CRUTCHLOW
The Briton had struggled at the pre-race Misano tests and had his worst weekend of the year, qualifying 15th and crashing out. Was genuinely surprised to fall because he didn't think he was going fast enough to crash!

DNF MICHELE PIRRO
Ducati's test rider had his second GP of the year, but there was none of the joy of Mugello. Was running a good race in tenth place, just ahead of Petrucci, when he lost the front at Turn 14 with seven laps to go.

DNF ÁLEX RINS
Qualified eighth, made some passes but exceeded track limits. Fell before he took his long-lap penalty.

DNF FRANCESCO BAGNAIA
His hopes of a good home race were spoiled by a lack of front-end grip that had him crash out.

DNS ANDREA IANNONE
The Italian was one of 69 crashers when he fell at Turn 14, during FP4, injuring his left shoulder.

MICHELIN
MICHELIN

Like a boss: this win wasn't as big as Termas but it was big enough.

14 | ARAGÓN

GRAN PREMIO MICHELIN® DE ARAGÓN
MOTORLAND ARAGÓN
20/21/22 SEPTEMBER

MÁRQUEZ WINS IN SPLENDID ISOLATION

After three crazy-close races the champion checked out at one of his favourite tracks

Marc Márquez had a lot to think about during the two-hour drive from his home in Cervera to MotorLand Aragón. Still very much in his mind were his agonising final-corner defeats at Red Bull Ring and Silverstone, and his race-long Misano duel for victory with a rookie.

Never mind his 93-point lead, he desperately wanted to re-establish his dominance. And Aragón would give him the perfect opportunity to do that. The spectacular hillside track is ideal Márquez territory: it turns left, like Sachsenring and COTA, where he is just about unbeatable, and the layout is dominated by the kind of fast, sweeping corners that reward the brave. Not for nothing had he won on his previous three visits.

Márquez laid down the law in FP1, which he finished 1.6 seconds faster than his nearest challenger, prompting these words from Jack Miller, who had completed the outing a solid fifth quickest.

"I came in at the end of the session and it was all high fives from the boys. They were like, good session, mate! Then I looked at the screens and I saw I was f**king two seconds off. Good? That's good? F**king hell, it hurts, it hurts."

And it continued hurting for everyone over the next two and half days. No one came close to bettering Márquez's FP1 time

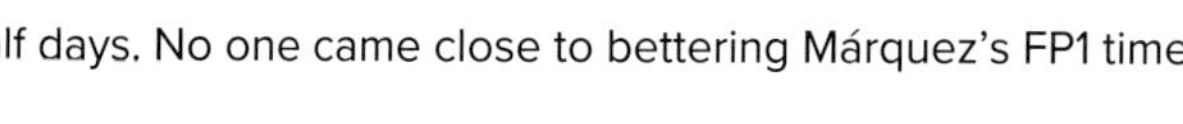

'ONCE ANDREA CAME PAST ME I UNDERSTOOD WHAT TO DO"
JACK MILLER

CLOCKWISE, FROM TOP LEFT | Aleix Espargaro and the Aprilia were in their element; Rossi had his worst result so far; Marquez nailed the holeshot and enjoyed his third home win of 2019; Iannone also used his RS-GP well, beating Petrucci; did Viñales seek divine guidance in his tyre choice? Mika Kallio raced again, for the first time in 15 months; the Marquez brothers tried being Casey Stoner; when Dovizioso got past Miller the Aussie learned plenty about the Italian's tyre-conservation skills.

in FP2, FP3 or FP4; not even the man himself when he topped qualifying!

There is no such thing as a foregone conclusion in MotoGP – as Márquez had proved at COTA – but no one had the pace to race with him. By three-quarters distance he was six seconds ahead of the chasing pack, easing off in the final laps to win by 4.8 seconds.

"My main target here was to be focused, patient and not push too much," he said. "The experience of Austin was always in my head, so I just kept going, trying to manage the gap, because what I learned in Austin is that it doesn't matter if you win by 12 seconds, four seconds, or one second. Most important is the 25 points."

While the local hero rode off into the distance the battle for the last two podium positions provided the entertainment. Maverick Viñales had qualified third fastest behind Fabio Quartararo, passed Miller on lap eight and by halfway seemed to have made second place his own, which would've given him his first three MotoGP podium results in a row.

But then things changed. Viñales had chosen the hard rear, while his pursuers Miller and Andrea Dovizioso had gone with the soft, like Márquez.

"The temperature was cooler today, which opened the door for us to use the soft rear," explained Dovizioso, who came on strong in the second half, passing Miller and then attacking the ailing Viñales.

Miller had the best seat in the house to see what was going on. "When Maverick passed me he had a lot of spin and a lot of smoke," explained the Australian. "He started to spin the tyre more and at the end of the race he had no rubber left on the left side."

The science is straightforward, if counterintuitive: the soft rear has better grip, so it spins less, while the hard has less grip, so it spins more, so it doesn't last as long.

Miller learned plenty while chasing Dovizioso, the master of throttle control and tyre conservation. "Andrea was a little tighter than me in a few corners and getting better acceleration," he added. "Whereas, typical me, I was going into corners too fast, running wide and opening the throttle a bit too early. Once he came past me I understood what to do, especially at the top of the hill – Turns Four, Five and Six – where he was really hugging the kerb, getting a lot more grip than me coming out and using a heap less torque and a lot less metres."

Dovizioso took Viñales with three laps to go, while Miller got him on the last lap. "With four laps to go I felt the drop of the tyre and I nearly crashed two or three times, losing the rear off the gas," explained the Spaniard.

All four Yamaha riders used the hard rear, which also compromised the results of Quartararo and Rossi. Franco Morbidelli was taken out by an overeager Álex Rins on the first lap.

ZARCO OUT, WITH IMMEDIATE EFFECT

Johann Zarco got the call from KTM three days before Aragón practice was due to begin. "They explained they would prefer to stop with me immediately," he said, while visiting the Aragón paddock as a spectator.

The decision came as a surprise to the Frenchman, who five weeks earlier had told his employers he wanted to terminate their two-year contract at the end of 2019, because "I didn't want to live again this difficult feeling on the bike".

KTM motorsport manager Pit Beirer explained his decision at Aragón on Friday. "We have 100 people at the factory and 34 at the racetrack. When you are getting nowhere [with one rider] it's

Rossi finished eighth, 23 seconds down, his worst result of the year so far. "I had a big, big drop from the rear after five laps, so I had to slow down," he said. "I was sliding very much and when you slide on the edge of the tyre you damage the tyre more, so we need to find a solution."

Márquez wasn't the only hero of the day. Aleix Espargaró rode an epic race to seventh, five hundredths of a second behind Cal Crutchlow and five seconds off the podium. The Aprilia RS-GP always goes well at Aragón, indeed on Saturday the factory had both its riders in Q2 for the first time ever, despite a top-speed handicap of 8.3km/h (5.2mph) against the fastest bike, Dovizioso's 346.1km/h (214.9mph) GP19.

"Where we always suffer is stopping the bike in a straight line," explained Espargaró. "The problem is that we don't have enough load on the rear during hard braking, so the engine-braking doesn't work well enough, so we cannot reduce speed fast enough. But Aragón is one of the few tracks in the world where you are already braking with 25 or 30 degrees of lean in almost every braking area, so the rear tyre is pushing into the asphalt, so we can stop the bike better."

The result was a much-needed boost for the struggling Aprilia camp. "Here it's been important to make the team happy and take some positive energy into the next races, because everyone in Aprilia is suffering because this isn't a good year for us," he added.

CLOCKWISE FROM TOP LEFT | *Viñales overtook Miller on lap eight, only for Miller to repass him on the only lap that matters; Dovizioso needed this after the disasters of Silverstone and Misano; Rins with Smith and Abraham after taking out Morbidelli on lap one; another impressive ride from Thriller; Rabat passes the struggling Lorenzo; Petrucci still missed the speed he had enjoyed earlier in the year.*

very difficult to keep everybody motivated to keep working. We need to prepare the future – I cannot leave 50 percent of the project unused and not going forward with the bike.

"It's a sad moment for us. We struggled from the first day when Johann threw a leg over our bike at Valencia [in November 2018]. It was a surprise that it was immediately difficult for him to reach the level of Pol [Espargaró]. From that first moment Johann started crashing when he started pushing.

"I'm not happy that we couldn't supply the bike he wanted, but also that he couldn't make a step to help the bike at a moment when it's not at the very top. He puts so much stress on himself when things aren't going easy and that's what he was always looking for – that easy-riding feeling.

"We have learned there are two different characters of bikes in MotoGP. There are the bikes that are easier to ride and there are the bikes that need to be ridden with a different riding style, which are the bikes you need to win races.

"To me it wasn't clear when we signed Johann that there would be such a difference between the two bikes, just from riding style. Before he joined us, we saw what Johann could do on a year-old bike. What we saw was this: what a fighter! He didn't care what he had, he just took his bike and went faster. We saw that and said, wow, that's the guy we need!"

Zarco was replaced by Mika Kallio, who's been with the RC16 project since the start.

14 | ARAGÓN

GRAN PREMIO MICHELIN® DE ARAGÓN
MOTORLAND ARAGÓN
20/21/22 SEPTEMBER

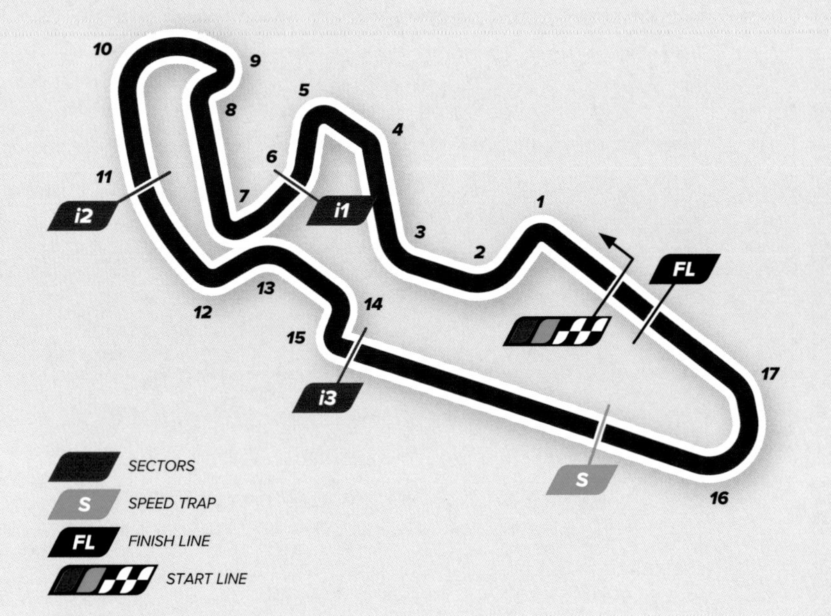

QUALIFYING RESULTS

	RIDER	NAT	TEAM	MACHINE	QP/TIME		GAP 1ST/PREV	
1	Marc Márquez	SPA	Repsol Honda Team	HONDA	Q2	1'47.009		
2	Fabio Quartararo	FRA	Petronas Yamaha SRT	YAMAHA	Q2	1'47.336	0.327	0.327
3	Maverick Viñales	SPA	Monster Energy Yamaha MotoGP	YAMAHA	Q2	1'47.472	0.463	0.136
4	Jack Miller	AUS	Pramac Racing	DUCATI	Q2	1'47.658	0.649	0.186
5	Aleix Espargaró	SPA	Aprilia Racing Team Gresini	APRILIA	Q2	1'47.733	0.724	0.075
6	Valentino Rossi	ITA	Monster Energy Yamaha MotoGP	YAMAHA	Q2	1'48.015	1.006	0.282
7	Cal Crutchlow	GBR	LCR Honda CASTROL	HONDA	Q2	1'48.322	1.313	0.307
8	Franco Morbidelli	ITA	Petronas Yamaha SRT	YAMAHA	Q2	1'48.372	1.363	0.050
9	Joan Mir	SPA	Team SUZUKI ECSTAR	SUZUKI	Q2	1'48.458	1.449	0.086
10	Andrea Dovizioso	ITA	Ducati Team	DUCATI	Q2	1'48.608	1.599	0.150
11	Andrea Iannone	ITA	Aprilia Racing Team Gresini	APRILIA	Q2	1'49.240	2.231	0.632
12	Pol Espargaro	SPA	Red Bull KTM Factory Racing	KTM	FP2	1'48.392	1.523	
13	Álex Rins	SPA	Team SUZUKI ECSTAR	SUZUKI	Q1	1'48.449	*0.157	0.119
14	Takaaki Nakagami	JPN	LCR Honda IDEMITSU	HONDA	Q1	1'48.477	*0.185	0.028
15	Danilo Petrucci	ITA	Ducati Team	DUCATI	Q1	1'48.682	*0.390	0.205
16	Francesco Bagnaia	ITA	Pramac Racing	DUCATI	Q1	1'48.748	*0.456	0.066
17	Miguel Oliveira	POR	Red Bull KTM Tech 3	KTM	Q1	1'48.827	*0.535	0.079
18	Tito Rabat	SPA	Reale Avintia Racing	DUCATI	Q1	1'48.916	*0.624	0.089
19	Mika Kallio	FIN	Red Bull KTM Factory Racing	KTM	Q1	1'49.085	*0.793	0.169
20	Jorge Lorenzo	SPA	Repsol Honda Team	HONDA	Q1	1'49.282	*0.990	0.197
21	Hafizh Syahrin	MAL	Red Bull KTM Tech 3	KTM	Q1	1'49.315	*1.023	0.033
22	Karel Abraham	CZE	Reale Avintia Racing	DUCATI	Q1	1'49.517	*1.225	0.202
23	Bradley Smith	GBR	Aprilia Racing Team	APRILIA	Q1	1'49.756	*1.464	0.239

** Gap to the fastest rider in the Q1 session   ** Went forward from Q1 to Q2   Track severity = Wear + Temperature + Load*

GRAND PRIX INFORMATION

TRACK INFORMATION			
2019 WINNER	Marc Márquez		
CIRCUIT LENGTH	5.1 km	3.15 miles	
LAPS	23		
RACE DISTANCE	116.8 km	72.5 miles	
ALL TIME LAP RECORD	1'46.635	171.4 Km/h	Marc Márquez (2015)
BEST RACE LAP	1'48.120	169.0 Km/h	Jorge Lorenzo (2015)
RACE CONDITION	Dry		
AIR	27°C		
HUMIDITY	46%		
GROUND	32°C		

TYRE SELECTION

FRONT	
SOFT	WHITE
MEDIUM	GREY
HARD	YELLOW

L M R

REAR	
SOFT	WHITE
MEDIUM	GREY
HARD	YELLOW

< MILD — TRACK SEVERITY — SEVERE >

1 MARC MÁRQUEZ
Never even looked out of control, except when he fell at Turn Eight during FP4, when he was trying a hard front. His race strategy was perfect – medium front/soft rear – and he made it look easy, although of course it never is.

2 ANDREA DOVIZIOSO
Needed to get back on the podium after his disasters at Silverstone and Misano. Did so with a typically well calculated weekend – chose the correct tyres and his race pace was strong and well controlled throughout.

3 JACK MILLER
His third podium of the season so far and his best so far. A second-row start was where it all began. He ran second for the first seven laps, ahead of Quartararo and Viñales, then took third from Viñales with a fine last lap.

4 MAVERICK VIÑALES
Worked hard from his front-row start but much of his hard work was wasted by an incorrect tyre choice. There was no doubt he had the pace for the podium but the hard tyre gave too much wheelspin, so it didn't last.

5 FABIO QUARTARARO
Rode a remarkable Q2 lap to qualify a close second behind Márquez and had the pace to finish in the top-three, just like Viñales. But had the wrong tyre just like Viñales, so he ran out of traction in all the left-handers.

6 CAL CRUTCHLOW
After a miserable time at Misano was delighted to be back at a track with some grip. Started from the third row of the grid and had a busy first few laps. Spent much of the race in successful pursuit of Aleix Espargaró.

7 ALEIX ESPARGARÓ
This was the result that Aprilia needed after months of little reward for their hard work. The RS-GP always works well at Aragón and the Spaniard said he could've done even better with more confidence in the front tyre.

8 VALENTINO ROSSI
Didn't have the pace of fellow M1 riders Viñales and Quartararo, so he knew a podium result was out of reach. His race was further spoiled by the same hard-rear tyre choice, which lost a lot of grip after the first five laps.

9 ÁLEX RINS
Once again didn't qualify well, which was most likely why he got too aggressive on the first lap, which had him ramming and taking out Morbidelli in a big way at Turn 12. He was lucky to get away with a long-lap penalty.

10 TAKAAKI NAKAGAMI
Struggled with rear grip, so didn't qualify as well as usual, then lost time with a big wheelie away from the grid and more time when he ran off the track while attacking Petrucci. All in all, a top-ten finish was a good result.

RACE LAP CHART

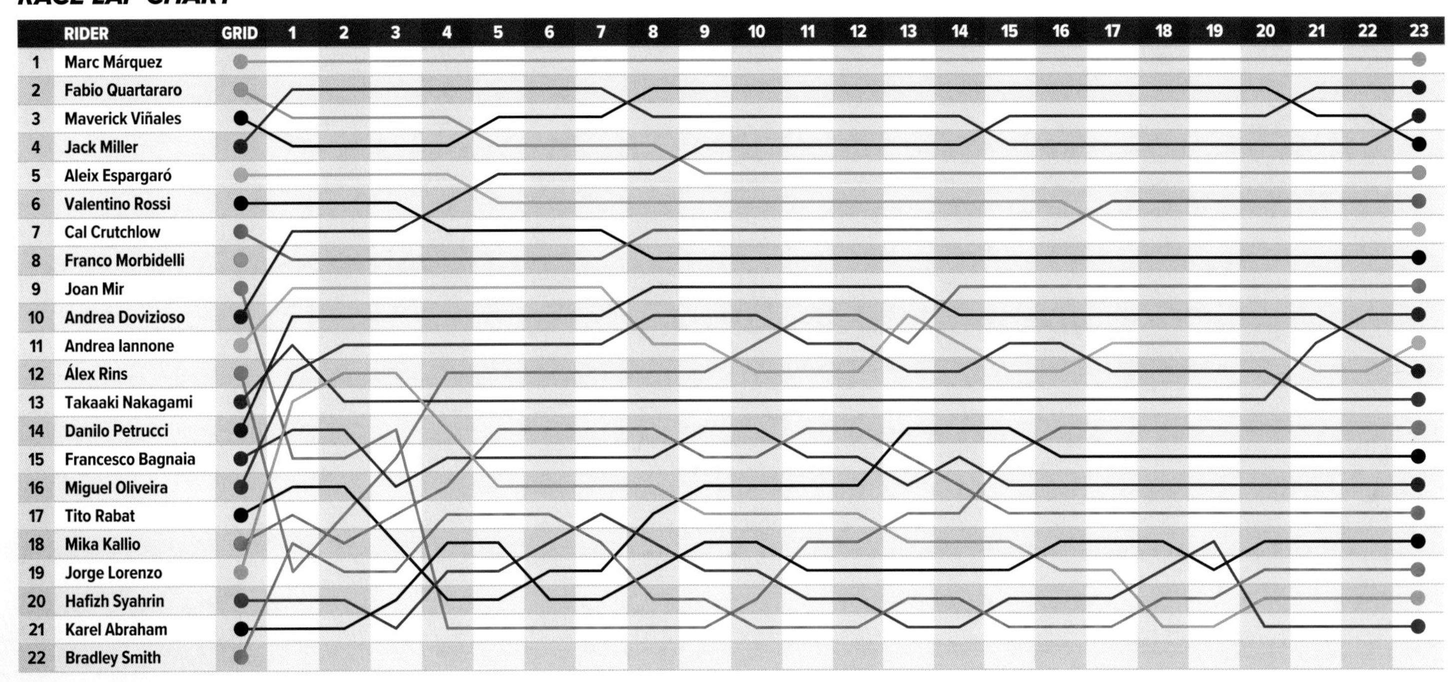

RACE RESULTS

	RIDER	NAT	TEAM	MACHINE	TIME	+GAP	TYRES
1	Marc Márquez	SPA	Repsol Honda Team	HONDA	41'57.221		M/S
2	Andrea Dovizioso	ITA	Ducati Team	DUCATI	42'02.057	4.836	M/S
3	Jack Miller	AUS	Pramac Racing	DUCATI	42'02.651	5.430	M/S
4	Maverick Viñales	SPA	Monster Energy Yamaha MotoGP	YAMAHA	42'03.032	5.811	M/H
5	Fabio Quartararo	FRA	Petronas Yamaha SRT	YAMAHA	42'06.145	8.924	M/H
6	Cal Crutchlow	GBR	LCR Honda CASTROL	HONDA	42'07.611	10.390	M/S
7	Aleix Espargaró	SPA	Aprilia Racing Team Gresini	APRILIA	42'07.662	10.441	M/S
8	Valentino Rossi	ITA	Monster Energy Yamaha MotoGP	YAMAHA	42'20.844	23.623	M/S
9	Álex Rins	SPA	Team SUZUKI ECSTAR	SUZUKI	42'25.219	27.998	M/H
10	Takaaki Nakagami	JPN	LCR Honda IDEMITSU	HONDA	42'28.463	31.242	M/S
11	Andrea Iannone	ITA	Aprilia Racing Team Gresini	APRILIA	42'29.845	32.624	M/S
12	Danilo Petrucci	ITA	Ducati Team	DUCATI	42'30.264	33.043	M/H
13	Miguel Oliveira	POR	Red Bull KTM Tech 3	KTM	42'30.284	33.063	M/S
14	Joan Mir	SPA	Team SUZUKI ECSTAR	SUZUKI	42'30.584	33.363	M/H
15	Tito Rabat	SPA	Reale Avintia Racing	DUCATI	42'33.579	36.358	M/S
16	Francesco Bagnaia	ITA	Pramac Racing	DUCATI	42'38.516	41.295	M/S
17	Mika Kallio	FIN	Red Bull KTM Factory Racing	KTM	42'40.204	42.983	H/H
18	Karel Abraham	CZE	Reale Avintia Racing	DUCATI	42'41.101	43.880	M/S
19	Bradley Smith	GBR	Aprilia Racing Team	APRILIA	42'41.500	44.279	M/S
20	Jorge Lorenzo	SPA	Repsol Honda Team	HONDA	42'43.308	46.087	M/S
21	Hafizh Syahrin	MAL	Red Bull KTM Tech 3	KTM	42'44.529	47.308	M/S
NC	Franco Morbidelli	ITA	Petronas Yamaha SRT	YAMAHA			M/H

CHAMPIONSHIP STANDINGS

	RIDER	NAT	TEAM	PTS
1	Marc Márquez	SPA	Repsol Honda Team	300
2	Andrea Dovizioso	ITA	Ducati Team	202
3	Álex Rins	SPA	Team SUZUKI ECSTAR	156
4	Danilo Petrucci	ITA	Ducati Team	155
5	Maverick Viñales	SPA	Monster Energy Yamaha MotoGP	147
6	Valentino Rossi	ITA	Monster Energy Yamaha MotoGP	137
7	Fabio Quartararo	FRA	Petronas Yamaha SRT	123
8	Jack Miller	AUS	Pramac Racing	117
9	Cal Crutchlow	GBR	LCR Honda CASTROL	98
10	Franco Morbidelli	ITA	Petronas Yamaha SRT	80
11	Pol Espargaró	SPA	Red Bull KTM Factory Racing	77
12	Takaaki Nakagami	JPN	LCR Honda IDEMITSU	68
13	Joan Mir	SPA	Team SUZUKI ECSTAR	49
14	Aleix Espargaró	SPA	Aprilia Racing Team Gresini	46
15	Andrea Iannone	ITA	Aprilia Racing Team Gresini	32
16	Francesco Bagnaia	ITA	Pramac Racing	29
17	Miguel Oliveira	POR	Red Bull KTM Tech 3	29
18	Johann Zarco	FRA	Red Bull KTM Factory Racing	27
19	Jorge Lorenzo	SPA	Repsol Honda Team	23
20	Tito Rabat	SPA	Reale Avintia Racing	18
21	Stefan Bradl	GER	Team HRC	16
22	Michele Pirro	ITA	Ducati Team	9
23	Sylvain Guintoli	FRA	Team SUZUKI ECSTAR	7
24	Hafizh Syahrin	MAL	Red Bull KTM Tech 3	7
25	Karel Abraham	CZE	Reale Avintia Racing	5
26	Bradley Smith	GBR	Aprilia Factory Racing	
27	Mika Kallio	FIN	Red Bull KTM Factory Racing	

11 ANDREA IANNONE
Gritted his teeth to ride the race in severe pain from the shoulder he injured at Misano. Used the RS-GP's strengths at Aragón to battle with Petrucci, Rins and Oliveira for a while, but slowed as he lost strength and grip.

12 DANILO PETRUCCI
His first 2019 finish outside the top-ten dropped him to fourth overall on points, still looking for answers to regain the form he had had earlier in the season. Made the mistake of choosing the hard rear for the race.

13 MIGUEL OLIVEIRA
The rookie enjoyed the race, battling for some time with more experienced riders on faster bikes. Took the chequered flag just two hundredths of a second behind Petrucci, despite also choosing the hard-option rear.

14 JOAN MIR
Was another rider to choose the hard rear and pay the price. Lacking grip, he ran wide several times in the opening laps, losing a wing when he made contact with a rival, just as Rins had when he hit Morbidelli.

15 TITO RABAT
Achieved his sixth world championship points score, despite going backwards to second to last in the early laps. Left Aragón aiming to work hard on electronics settings to give him more grip in the all-important first few laps.

16 FRANCESCO BAGNAIA
Decided to race with the soft rear, but still struggled with grip. The Italian rookie was still in confidence-building mode, desperate to get a full race of data after crashing out at Misano, his first DNF since Barcelona.

17 MIKA KALLIO
KTM's replacement for Johann Zarco had a lot of catching up to do in his first race since Barcelona 2018 and after a five-month layoff due to a nasty knee injury. Was happy enough with his progress throughout the weekend.

18 KAREL ABRAHAM
Still not fully recovered from recent injury the Czech rider finished the first lap in last place and worked hard to steadily work his way forward throughout the race, crossing the finish line less than a second behind Kallio.

19 BRADLEY SMITH
Aprilia's test rider had his fourth MotoGP race outing of the year, in advance of a private test session at Aragón a few days after the GP. Took a gamble with an experimental set-up for the race, which didn't make his race easy.

20 JORGE LORENZO
Was knocking on the door of the top-ten during the first few laps, but then lost rear grip. Tried to get around the issue by riding as smoothly as possible but that didn't really work. Once again, he couldn't afford to crash.

21 HAFIZH SYAHRIN
Tried to find a rhythm that would take him to Kallio, but ran into the gravel trap at Turn 12, which put him last.

DNF FRANCO MORBIDELLI
Confident of a good race, then Rins walloped into him on lap one. Was lucky to come out of that uninjured.

DNF POL ESPARGARÓ
Days after his heroics at Misano, broke a wrist in an off-throttle highside in FP4. Flew home to have the injury plated.

This is going to hurt: it's Friday morning and Márquez is on his way to hospital. To race and win after this proved the king has a lot of grit.

15 | THAILAND

PTT THAILAND GRAND PRIX
CHANG INTERNATIONAL CIRCUIT
04/05/06 OCTOBER

IS IT A BIRD, IS IT A PLANE?

No, it's superman! Márquez's recovery from a monster highside to race and take championship victory was the stuff of legend

At 11am on Friday Marc Márquez was strapped to a stretcher in an ambulance, on his way to Buriram Hospital. An hour and a half later Repsol Honda team manager Alberto Puig called a media scrum in the paddock to inform journalists and TV crews of his rider's medical condition.

It seemed like something out of an old movie: at the very moment the king is to receive his crown everything collapses around him.

Márquez had suffered an almighty off-throttle highside during the out-lap of his final run in FP1. He was on brand-new tyres, but they were of the softest compound, the track temperature was 36 degrees and (according to his sector times) he wasn't even pushing. Whatever, as he tipped into Turn Seven the rear tyre lost grip, then found it again, flicking him so high into the sky that Pol Espargaró thought about riding beneath him to break his fall.

It wasn't just the highside – with 26g impact – that was scary. While Márquez tumbled across the asphalt his RC213V took flight behind him, smashing itself to pieces, way too close for comfort.

"It was a strange crash," he said. "Maybe the tyres weren't ready, maybe I was on a dirty part of the track."

MotoGP medical director Doctor Angel Charte explained the

CLOCKWISE, FROM TOP LEFT | *Throttle closed, Márquez gets pinged over the highside; remarkably his RC213V suffered more damage than he did; Rossi should be on the cover, really; Morbidelli had started to show consistent speed; Petrucci still couldn't find his; Pol Espargaró rides out to try his plated left wrist; Miller is about to make a very big mistake; Quartararo fist bumps his crew on his way to another pole.*

'I WANTED TO TRY AT THE LAST CORNER – OTHERWISE I WON'T SLEEP UNTIL JAPAN'

FABIO QUARTARARO

aftermath. "Marc normally gets up quickly, but this time he stayed lying where the accident happened, because the impact was very hard and he couldn't breathe. We did some x-rays in the medical centre and it was unclear if there was some kind of injury to his vertebrae, so we decided to go to hospital to scan his entire spine."

The MRI scan was clear, so Márquez returned to the paddock, climbed gingerly aboard his RC213V and rode the sixth fastest lap in FP2, less than half a second behind pace-setter Fabio Quartararo. Why do this? Because you must convince both yourself and everyone else of your impregnability.

The following day Márquez qualified third fastest, two tenths behind Quartararo, who took his fourth MotoGP pole position, both of them falling at the bumpy Turn Five as they tried to better their times. Maverick Viñales ended up between them on the front row.

Quartararo was favourite to take his first MotoGP victory. Misano had proved he was ready to win and he had an advantage at Buriram. Michelin equipped riders with special rear slicks, only used at Buriram and Red Bull Ring, where the Frenchman had scored an unlikely third place.

These tyres featured a stiffer construction and harder central compound to resist heat build-up caused by frequent low-gear, straight-line acceleration. Like last year, the tyres helped the Yamahas more than any other bike.

Quartararo and Márquez quickly dropped Viñales, just as they'd done at Misano. After half-distance Viñales was sometimes faster than the two men ahead of him, but the gap was too big to bridge.

By lap ten of 26 the rookie was almost seven tenths ahead of the champ. Perhaps Márquez was hurting from Friday, perhaps this time he would let it go. Just this once. But no. With ten laps to go he was right on the YZR-M1's rear wheel, giving Quartararo no room to breathe, no chance to relax, just like Misano.

"At one point I said, okay, if he doesn't slow down it will be impossible," said Márquez. "So I said, okay, give up or try: push for two laps at the maximum and if I'm okay, I will be ready to win the race. I pushed for two laps, then I said, okay, now it's time to relax, to cool down, because I was on the limit with the front tyre."

Quartararo's corner speed was stunning, but the Honda's top-end advantage kept Márquez in the game, even though Yamaha had given its new hero those extra 500rpm he had been lacking all year. During the last four laps Márquez was prodding, probing and planning.

On the final lap he got level on the main straight and out-braked Quartararo into Turn Three, front end squirming, nearly running wide. Through the next left-handers he opened a small gap, but in the final sector Quartararo was right back on him, all set for a do-or-die final corner.

MÁRQUEZ SNOOKERS THEM ALL

This was Márquez's earliest championship wrap-up. In his five previous title-winning seasons he secured the title at Valencia, Motegi, Motegi, Valencia and Motegi. Once again the celebrations were elaborate. Last time in Japan it was arcade videogaming, this time it was potting the eight-ball on a pool table, to mark his eighth world title across all classes. And he had no doubt that this was his best championship yet, wrapping up the title without a single finish outside the top two.

"In 2014 I won ten races in a row, but back then there was a big difference in the level of the different bikes," he said. "Now the category is very competitive – four manufacturers can fight for victory in a race.

"We were very consistent. Especially we focused on our weak points and we recovered something in those weak points, so we could survive our difficult races in a very good way. Maybe if you check the results you will say it was an easy year, but believe me, to manage the pressure, to manage the fact that everybody is waiting for you to fail, that everybody is looking at you to win or looking at you to beat you isn't easy.

"I want to say thanks to all my team, because for a rider it's easy to stick to your mission, but for a team of a lot of people it's not easy to keep the same mentality and the same concentration. But they

The attack came very late, both riders with their rear wheels in the air, Márquez just about to tip into Turn 12 when Quartararo came juddering past. All Márquez had to do was exactly what he had done to Andrea Dovizioso in 2018: wait for his rival to miss the apex, then perform the undercut. He was already celebrating as he wheelied over the line, while his dismayed victim held his head in his hands.

For the second time in three days MotoGP's reigning king had convinced both himself and everyone else of his impregnability.

"I wanted to try something at the last corner – otherwise I won't sleep until Japan," said Quartararo, who didn't find much grip on the inside line. "I overtook him, then I saw his front wheel again. It was frustrating but we did an amazing race and we will try again."

Viñales took the flag 1.2 seconds behind the runner-up, while Dovizioso ended up a distant, dejected fourth, with the distant, niggling hope of beating Márquez to the title finally over, for the third year running.

"It's painful, because if your goal is to win the championship it didn't happen," said Dovizioso. "So it's the same as the last two years, but even harder, because this season Marc created an even bigger gap. He has been so strong since his first year in MotoGP and he is so smart. Year by year, he understands his limits and becomes better and better."

Dovizioso spent the first half of the race under pressure from Franco Morbidelli and the second half from Álex Rins, who once again had to fight his way through from the fourth row of the grid.

CLOCKWISE FROM TOP LEFT | *Márquez has already won the dash to the finish line; Viñales was happy with his third podium in four races; Crutchlow had a horrible weekend; cooling down on the podium – Quartararo had given it his all; Rossi uses all his front-suspension stroke; Márquez celebrated his eighth world title in high-flying style.*

are able to do it, and this is one of the most important things.

"I expected everything this season. I just didn't expect Fabio to be at his level. I expected Dovi to be very consistent, Viñales to be very fast in some races and maybe Suzuki. The most important thing for us is that in some races the Ducati was the bike, in others the Suzuki, in others the Yamaha, but we were always there.

"Next year Fabio will be a very tough contender for the championship. Every year there are new names and different situations. Sometimes you can be very good, but the bike isn't in the best condition; or the bike is really good, but you are not in the best condition. Finding this compromise is so difficult."

15 | THAILAND

PTT THAILAND GRAND PRIX

CHANG INTERNATIONAL CIRCUIT

04/05/06 OCTOBER

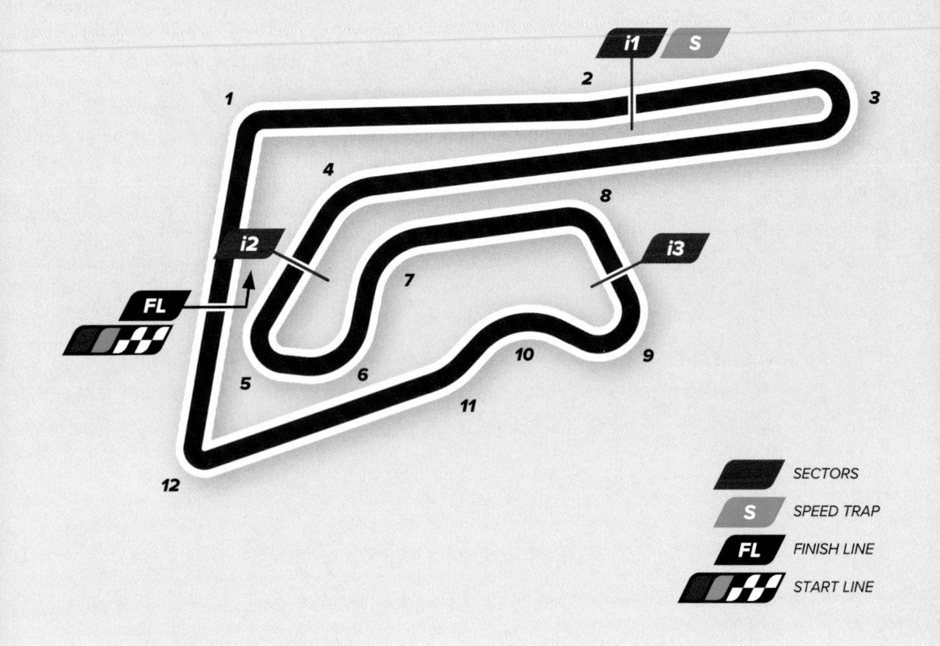

QUALIFYING RESULTS

	RIDER	NAT	TEAM	MACHINE	QP/TIME		GAP 1ST/PREV	
1	Fabio Quartararo	FRA	Petronas Yamaha SRT	YAMAHA	Q2	1'29.719		
2	Maverick Viñales	SPA	Monster Energy Yamaha MotoGP	YAMAHA	Q2	1'29.825	0.106	0.106
3	Marc Márquez	SPA	Repsol Honda Team	HONDA	Q2	1'29.931	0.212	0.106
4	Franco Morbidelli	ITA	Petronas Yamaha SRT	YAMAHA	Q2	1'30.431	0.712	0.500
5	Danilo Petrucci	ITA	Ducati Team	DUCATI	Q2	1'30.522	0.803	0.091
6	Jack Miller	AUS	Pramac Racing	DUCATI	Q2	1'30.597	0.878	0.075
7	Andrea Dovizioso	ITA	Ducati Team	DUCATI	Q2	1'30.692	0.973	0.095
8	Joan Mir	SPA	Team SUZUKI ECSTAR	SUZUKI	Q2	1'30.735	1.016	0.043
9	Valentino Rossi	ITA	Monster Energy Yamaha MotoGP	YAMAHA	Q2	1'30.741	1.022	0.006
10	Álex Rins	SPA	Team SUZUKI ECSTAR	SUZUKI	Q2	1'30.778	1.059	0.037
11	Pol Espargaro	SPA	Red Bull KTM Factory Racing	KTM	Q2	1'31.065	1.346	0.287
12	Aleix Espargaró	SPA	Aprilia Racing Team Gresini	APRILIA	Q2	1'31.258	1.539	0.193
13	Cal Crutchlow	GBR	LCR Honda CASTROL	HONDA	Q1	1'30.969	*0.284	0.013
14	Takaaki Nakagami	JPN	LCR Honda IDEMITSU	HONDA	Q1	1'31.388	*0.703	0.419
15	Francesco Bagnaia	ITA	Pramac Racing	DUCATI	Q1	1'31.416	*0.731	0.028
16	Andrea Iannone	ITA	Aprilia Racing Team Gresini	APRILIA	Q1	1'31.428	*0.743	0.012
17	Miguel Oliveira	POR	Red Bull KTM Tech 3	KTM	Q1	1'31.499	*0.814	0.071
18	Tito Rabat	SPA	Reale Avintia Racing	DUCATI	Q1	1'31.554	*0.869	0.055
19	Jorge Lorenzo	SPA	Repsol Honda Team	HONDA	Q1	1'31.605	*0.920	0.051
20	Karel Abraham	CZE	Reale Avintia Racing	DUCATI	Q1	1'31.773	*1.088	0.168
21	Mika Kallio	FIN	Red Bull KTM Factory Racing	KTM	Q1	1'31.849	*1.164	0.076
22	Hafizh Syahrin	MAL	Red Bull KTM Tech 3	KTM	Q1	1'31.979	*1.294	0.130

** Gap to the fastest rider in the Q1 session   ** Went forward from Q1 to Q2   Track severity = Wear + Temperature + Load*

GRAND PRIX INFORMATION

TRACK INFORMATION			
2019 WINNER	Marc Márquez		
CIRCUIT LENGTH	4.6 km	2.83 miles	
LAPS	26		
RACE DISTANCE	118.4 km	73.6 miles	
ALL TIME LAP RECORD	1'29.719	182.7 Km/h	Fabio Quartararo (2019)
BEST RACE LAP	1'30.904	180.3 Km/h	Marc Márquez (2019)
RACE CONDITION	Dry		
AIR	31°C		
HUMIDITY	58%		
GROUND	48°C		

TYRE SELECTION

FRONT	
SOFT	WHITE
MEDIUM	GREY
HARD	YELLOW

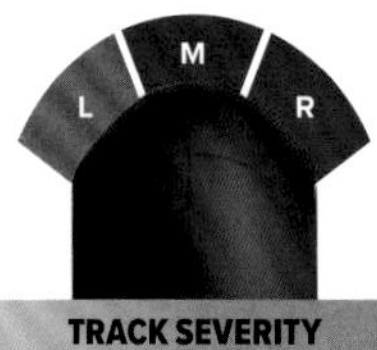

REAR	
SOFT	WHITE
MEDIUM	GREY
HARD	YELLOW

< MILD — TRACK SEVERITY — SEVERE >

1 MARC MÁRQUEZ
What a weekend, from jumping off his RC213V on Friday morning to jumping off his eight-ball pool table on Sunday afternoon. This was Márquez at his best, leaving rivals wondering what they must do to beat him.

2 FABIO QUARTARARO
For the second time in three races the rookie made the champion work as hard as he's ever worked. Perhaps he should've let Márquez past to study him, but other than that this was another perfect ride

3 MAVERICK VIÑALES
So near but so far. Once again. If he hadn't lost that smidgen of performance from laps six to 14 he might have been in the fight for victory. The usual questions: was it the full fuel tank, the rear tyre or the rider?

4 ANDREA DOVIZIOSO
The GP19 would be a missile at Buriram but for the twisting final two sectors, which negate the bike's braking and acceleration advantage from the earlier sectors. Was happy with fourth. Possibly not a good sign.

5 ÁLEX RINS
Compromised his Sunday performance by another fourth-row start, because he still lacks that single-lap intensity. Recovered well, from eighth on the first lap to cross the finish line just two tenths behind Dovizioso.

6 FRANCO MORBIDELLI
His third top-six finish in a row confirmed the good direction the Italian and his crew had found since August's British GP. Knew he had to examine the data of his team-mate and Viñales to work out how to go faster.

7 JOAN MIR
Suzuki's rookie out-qualified his team-mate for the second race in a row and ran a good pace until his lack of fitness told in the heat; the result of not riding or training for several weeks after his huge Brno shunt.

8 VALENTINO ROSSI
The week after he announced that he would change crew chief for 2020 the seven-time MotoGP champion was still looking for an answer to the same problem: a big drop in rear grip from about one-third race distance.

9 DANILO PETRUCCI
Fifth on the grid was his best Saturday performance since Mugello, where, of course, he won. Qualifying was the weekend's high point, because he lacked pace in the early laps, so he lost contact with the leading groups.

10 TAKAAKI NAKAGAMI
Struggled during practice and qualifying, which put him 14th on the grid, his worst starting position since COTA. Found a little more pace in the race and moved forward, resisting pressure from Bagnaia throughout.

RACE LAP CHART

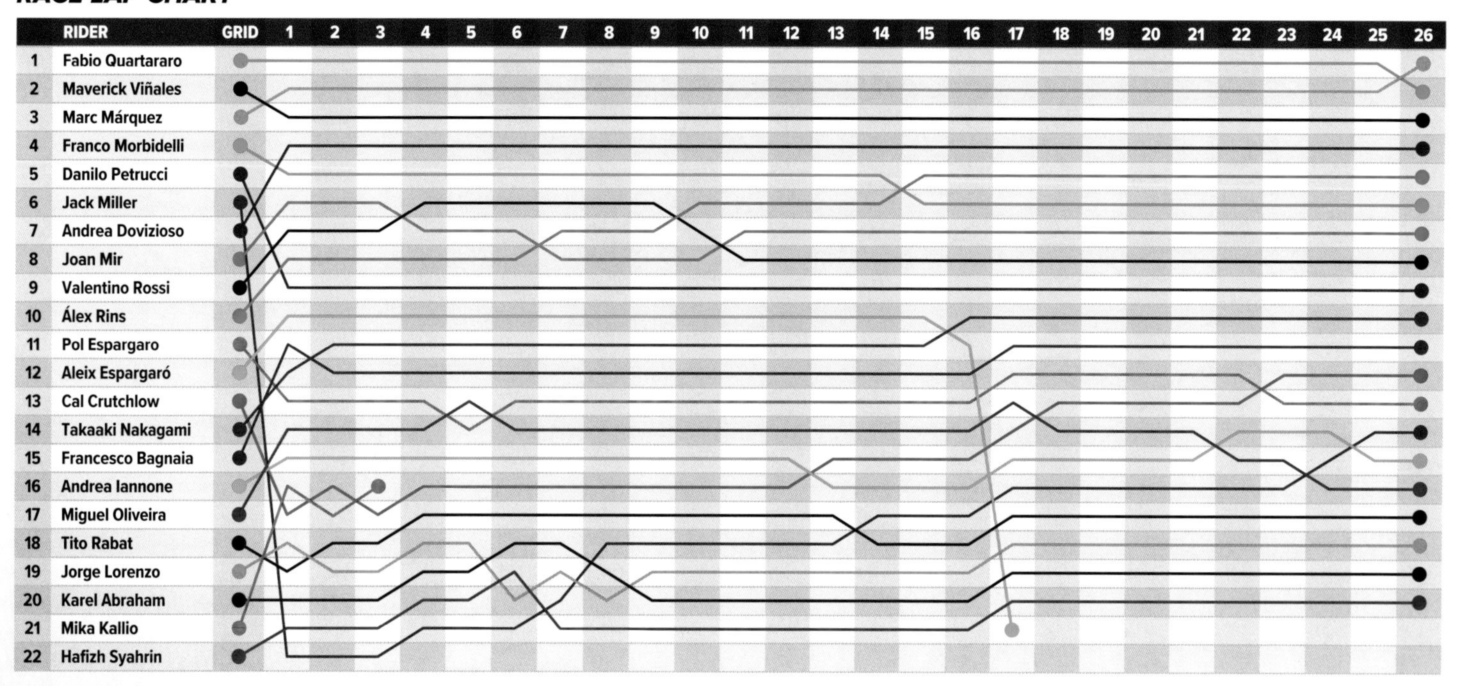

RACE RESULTS

	RIDER	NAT	TEAM	MACHINE	TIME	+ GAP	TYRES
1	Marc Márquez	SPA	Repsol Honda Team	HONDA	39'36.223		H/S
2	Fabio Quartararo	FRA	Petronas Yamaha SRT	YAMAHA	39'36.394	0.171	H/S
3	Maverick Viñales	SPA	Monster Energy Yamaha MotoGP	YAMAHA	39'37.603	1.380	H/S
4	Andrea Dovizioso	ITA	Ducati Team	DUCATI	39'47.441	11.218	H/S
5	Álex Rins	SPA	Team SUZUKI ECSTAR	SUZUKI	39'47.672	11.449	H/S
6	Franco Morbidelli	ITA	Petronas Yamaha SRT	YAMAHA	39'50.689	14.466	H/S
7	Joan Mir	SPA	Team SUZUKI ECSTAR	SUZUKI	39'54.952	18.729	H/S
8	Valentino Rossi	ITA	Monster Energy Yamaha MotoGP	YAMAHA	39'55.385	19.162	H/S
9	Danilo Petrucci	ITA	Ducati Team	DUCATI	39'59.648	23.425	H/S
10	Takaaki Nakagami	JPN	LCR Honda IDEMITSU	HONDA	40'05.646	29.423	H/S
11	Francesco Bagnaia	ITA	Pramac Racing	DUCATI	40'06.326	30.103	H/S
12	Cal Crutchlow	GBR	LCR Honda CASTROL	HONDA	40'09.439	33.216	H/S
13	Pol Espargaro	SPA	Red Bull KTM Factory Racing	KTM	40'11.890	35.667	H/S
14	Jack Miller	AUS	Pramac Racing	DUCATI	40'15.959	39.736	H/S
15	Andrea Iannone	ITA	Aprilia Racing Team Gresini	APRILIA	40'16.261	40.038	H/S
16	Miguel Oliveira	POR	Red Bull KTM Tech 3	KTM	40'16.359	40.136	H/S
17	Tito Rabat	SPA	Reale Avintia Racing	DUCATI	40'20.812	44.589	H/S
18	Jorge Lorenzo	SPA	Repsol Honda Team	HONDA	40'30.946	54.723	M/S
19	Karel Abraham	CZE	Reale Avintia Racing	DUCATI	40'32.235	56.012	H/S
20	Hafizh Syahrin	MAL	Red Bull KTM Tech 3	KTM	40'37.654	61.431	H/S
NC	Aleix Espargaró	SPA	Aprilia Racing Team Gresini	APRILIA	26'37.817	9 laps	H/S
NC	Mika Kallio	FIN	Red Bull KTM Factory Racing	KTM	4'44.870	23 laps	H/S

CHAMPIONSHIP STANDINGS

	RIDER	NAT	TEAM	PTS
1	Marc Márquez	SPA	Repsol Honda Team	325
2	Andrea Dovizioso	ITA	Ducati Team	215
3	Álex Rins	SPA	Team SUZUKI ECSTAR	167
4	Maverick Viñales	SPA	Monster Energy Yamaha MotoGP	163
5	Danilo Petrucci	ITA	Ducati Team	162
6	Valentino Rossi	ITA	Monster Energy Yamaha MotoGP	145
7	Fabio Quartararo	FRA	Petronas Yamaha SRT	143
8	Jack Miller	AUS	Pramac Racing	119
9	Cal Crutchlow	GBR	LCR Honda CASTROL	102
10	Franco Morbidelli	ITA	Petronas Yamaha SRT	90
11	Pol Espargaró	SPA	Red Bull KTM Factory Racing	80
12	Takaaki Nakagami	JPN	LCR Honda IDEMITSU	74
13	Joan Mir	SPA	Team SUZUKI ECSTAR	58
14	Aleix Espargaró	SPA	Aprilia Racing Team Gresini	46
15	Francesco Bagnaia	ITA	Pramac Racing	34
16	Andrea Iannone	ITA	Aprilia Racing Team Gresini	33
17	Miguel Oliveira	POR	Red Bull KTM Tech 3	29
18	Johann Zarco	FRA	Red Bull KTM Factory Racing	27
19	Jorge Lorenzo	SPA	Repsol Honda Team	23
20	Tito Rabat	SPA	Reale Avintia Racing	18
21	Stefan Bradl	GER	Team HRC	16
22	Michele Pirro	ITA	Ducati Team	9
23	Sylvain Guintoli	FRA	Team SUZUKI ECSTAR	7
24	Hafizh Syahrin	MAL	Red Bull KTM Tech 3	7
25	Karel Abraham	CZE	Reale Avintia Racing	5
26	Bradley Smith	GBR	Aprilia Factory Racing	
27	Mika Kallio	FIN	Red Bull KTM Factory Racing	

11 FRANCESCO BAGNAIA
The 2018 Moto2 champ scored his first points since Silverstone after a solid race with an aggressive start and a strong finish. Rode his best lap after half-distance and missed his third MotoGP top-ten by seven tenths.

12 CAL CRUTCHLOW
Another grim weekend for the Briton, not dissimilar to Misano. He qualified 14th and didn't get much better in the race. Struggled with a front-brake problem in the early stages, most likely due to overheating.

13 POL ESPARGARÓ
A heroic weekend from the Spaniard, who rode with a recently broken and plated left wrist. Underwent 24/7 physiotherapy and electrical stimulation therapy. Went through from Q1 to Q2 and scored points.

14 JACK MILLER
The Aussie was Ducati's fastest rider during free practice and qualified on the second row. Probably had the pace to go with Dovizioso, but hit the kill switch on the grid and had to start the race from pit lane.

15 ANDREA IANNONE
The Aprilia's lack of horsepower told during the first part of the track – basically a drag race – forcing the Italian to over-stress the front tyre trying to make up the deficit. This was his ninth points score on the RS-GP.

16 MIGUEL OLIVEIRA
The Portuguese continued to struggle with the shoulder injury that had been inflicted upon him at Silverstone, especially during hard-braking. Was in the points until the final laps when Miller and Iannone came past.

17 TITO RABAT
The Spaniard's hopes of scoring points at three consecutive races for the first time since his Silverstone 2018 accident came to nothing. Struggled throughout practice to find a bike set-up that gave him a decent race pace.

18 JORGE LORENZO
The three-time MotoGP world king's plan to get faster step-by-step, race-by-race, didn't come to fruition. Struggled in the heat, especially with braking. His average lap time was 2.1 seconds behind his team-mate.

19 KAREL ABRAHAM
Aimed for his first points since the British Grand Prix but came up 16 seconds short. Suffered more than most in the heat and humidity. Had an issue with the throttle that finally dropped him behind Lorenzo.

20 HAFIZH SYAHRIN
Struggled with a mysterious loss of horsepower – possibly heat-related – that left him unable to use the slipstream of his rivals. Days later announced he would return to Moto2 in 2020 with the Ángel Nieto team.

DNF ALEIX ESPARGARÓ
Made it into Q2 for the fifth time in 2019 and spent the first half of the race battling with Petrucci for ninth place, at Aprilia's worst track of the championship. Was distraught when an electrical problem stopped him.

DNF MIKA KALLIO
The Finn found his RC16 gave better grip with a full tank, but his second race outing of the year didn't end well. He was with Iannone and Crutchlow, just outside the championship points, when he crashed out on lap four.

The king of 2019 and the rookie of 2019: Márquez was already sizing up Quartararo for 2020.

MOTUL GRAND PRIX OF JAPAN
TWIN RING MOTEGI
18/19/20 OCTOBER

HONDA'S HOME-RACE JOY

Two weeks after securing the riders' title Márquez won the constructors' title for Honda at its own track

Honda had a lot riding on this race. For the first time Marc Márquez travelled to Honda's home race with the MotoGP crown already in his pocket. Cue a celebratory visit to HRC HQ in Asaka, followed by several events at Motegi to mark Honda's 60th Grand Prix anniversary. Finally, and most importantly, Márquez was expected to secure the constructors' title, a landmark 25th for Honda, under the watchful gaze of Honda Motor president and CEO Takahiro Hachigo. No pressure...

But everyone knows that Márquez feeds on pressure. He has that power to transform the kind of stress that would crush most human beings into a kind of magic force that makes him even stronger, like he's a character from a Marvel comic. Then again, all the greats have this power; it's what separates them from everyday folk.

Márquez rides in the wheel tracks of two of those greats: former Honda stars Mick Doohan and Jim Redman. At Motegi he had the chance to equal Doohan as Honda's most successful premier-class rider. He also got the chance to talk with Redman, who was at the event to help Honda celebrate its history. Redman won Honda's first premier-class race in 1966 and might have won that year's world title if he hadn't suffered career-ending injuries in a huge accident at Spa-Francorchamps.

'WITH ONE AND A HALF LAPS TO GO THE FUEL ALARM CAME ON'

MARC MARQUEZ

CLOCKWISE, FROM TOP LEFT *Dovizioso was dogged in his pursuit of Quartararo - he needed just one more lap; Viñales couldn't get the better of Dovizioso's GP19; Crutchlow fought well to beat Rins and Morbidelli; Rossi on the grid - hear no evil?; Miller getting too greedy with the throttle; Morbidelli heads out for his first front-row start since Jerez; Bagnaia offers some rider coaching to Abraham in wet practice; Aleix Espargaró leads the traditional pre-event minibike race, but little brother Pol was the winner; Marquez empties his RC213V's fuel tank.*

"I'm so happy to see that riders no longer have to worry about the biggest thing we had to worry about in the 1960s," said the 88-year-old. "Back then the circuits were mostly road circuits, so we were riding between houses and shops and everything, so if you made a mistake you usually died."

Márquez and the rest of the grid had no worries about crashing into houses and shops at Motegi; their main concern was running out of fuel. The mostly stop-and-go circuit, built by Honda in 1998 as a 50th birthday present to itself, is one of MotoGP's thirstiest venues, along with Losail and Red Bull Ring.

Therefore more effort than usual was spent on fuel maps, but the end result was much the same. Márquez scored a tenth pole and a tenth win of 2019, his dominance taking on a Doohan-like eminence. Back in Doohan's heyday the Australian's rivals were so psyched out by his relentless speed that they woke up on Sunday mornings wondering who was going to get second. Many of Márquez's rivals must ask themselves the same question on race days.

Márquez considered two different strategies for Sunday: let someone else lead, so he could hide in their slipstream to save fuel, or push to build a gap, then manage his advantage.

A rainy Saturday had minimised practice time, and the sun and track temperatures were already dropping before the late 3pm start. This convinced Fabio Quartararo and Maverick Viñales to switch to the soft-option rear, while Márquez stuck with the medium.

Quartararo's strategy was obvious: go like hell from the start, so he could get in front and use the Yamaha's corner-speed to break Márquez. The rookie did indeed get past the world champion on the first lap, using his superior corner speed out of Turn Six to pounce at Turn Seven. Márquez knew he mustn't give Quartararo the benefit of a clear track, so he immediately counter-attacked at the hairpin, where the Frenchman nearly fell.

Nevertheless Quartararo gave furious chase, making all kinds of shapes with his M1, but to no avail. "Marc was super-fast – I was really on the limit trying to follow him."

By two-thirds distance the gap had grown to 2.6 seconds and, instead of worrying about the man in front, Quartararo needed to watch his back. Andrea Dovizioso had also chosen the medium rear and was moving forward at quite a rate.

The 2017 Motegi winner overtook Jack Miller and Franco Morbidelli, then spent many laps resisting Viñales: point-and-squirt-bike versus corner-speed bike. Viñales swarmed all over the Ducati, but Dovizioso's blocking tactics were too good and sometimes Viñales wasted chances through frustration.

"Maverick tried to overtake many times, so I tried to close the door, stop in the middle of the corner and accelerate better," said Dovizioso.

SUZUKI TEST TEAM SANCTIONED FOR TESTING

The MotoGP regulations book is a weighty tome that gets heavier every year. Way back in 1999, in the dying days of the simpler two-strokes, the book numbered 97 pages. The 2019 edition consisted of no fewer than 352 pages.

So perhaps Suzuki's test team could be forgiven its minor indiscretion at Motegi. The European-based squad, which has done so much to make Suzuki a winning force once again, equipped rider Sylvain Guintoli with prototype 2020 GSX-RR engines, which he had tested at Motegi a few weeks previously.

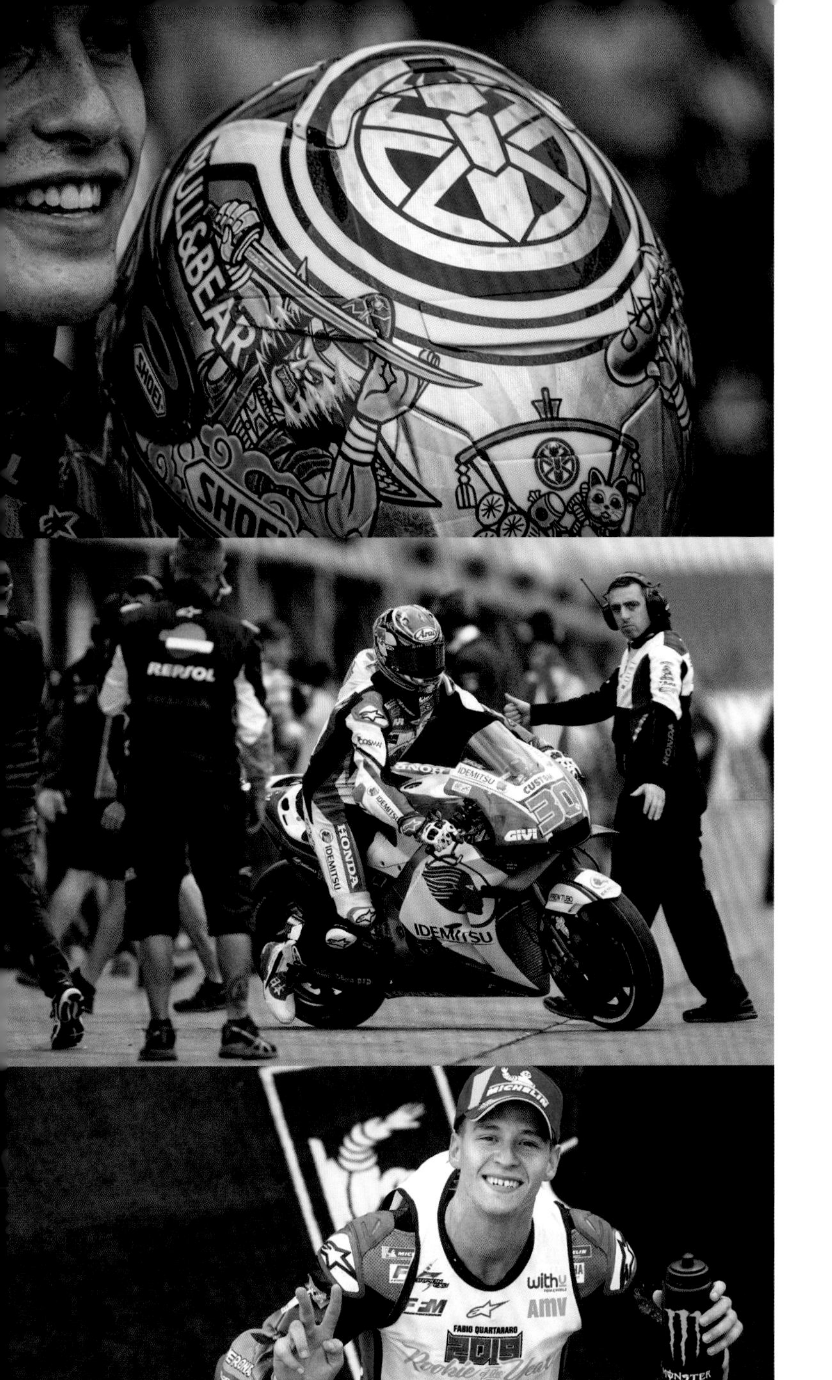

Finally, the soft rear tyres of both Yamahas were past their best, allowing the Italian to drop Viñales and close further on Quartararo.

"I was fast because I took too many risks – I braked like a stupid rider; I lost the front too many times!" added Dovizioso who finished less than half second behind Quartararo and 1.3 seconds behind the winner, his most impressive ride since Austria.

More surprising was that Márquez's lead evaporated in the last two laps – he was running low on fuel! "With one and a half laps to go the fuel alarm was on the dashboard," he said. "That means there's three laps of fuel left, so I tried to manage the situation." He crossed the line just eight tenths in front.

Quartararo's second place was his third in four races. More importantly it was the first time he had really followed Márquez and therefore been able to study him.

"I analysed Marc's lines," he said. "In the first corner I started using the same line as him and that helped me quite a lot to save the tyres, even if at the end we struggled. Even so we managed to get good lap times in another way."

Viñales took fourth, well ahead of Cal Crutchlow, Franco Morbidelli and Álex Rins who took the flag side by side. Crutchlow was delighted with his best ride since Brno, after miserable weekends at Misano and Buriram. He got the better of Rins after a long tussle and grabbed fifth from Morbidelli by out-dragging him from the final corner. The Italian wasn't best pleased – he had started from the front row for the first time since Jerez and expected a better result.

CLOCKWISE FROM TOP LEFT | *There was no magic fix for Lorenzo – he fought Abraham and Syahrin for 17th; Dovizioso was on the podium for the second time in three races; Márquez wore a samurai-inspired helmet to Japanese victory; this was Nakagami's last race of 2019; the last rider to wrap up the rookie title so early was Márquez in 2013; we are the champions: Márquez and HRC's technical director Takeo Yokoyama celebrate more history for HRC.*

On Friday night MotoGP technical director Danny Aldridge heard Guintoli praising the new engine and immediately realised something was amiss: wild-card entries must use current approved engines, unless their factory enjoys the benefit of engine concessions, which allow them to use more engines of different specifications during the season.

Hence the feverish Saturday-morning activity in Guintoli's garage as his crew removed the 2020 prototype engines from his GSX-RRs and fitted them with 2019 engines.

"It was a mistake, a misinterpretation of the rules," explained the Frenchman, whose times from FP1 and FP2 were nullified.

Aldridge believes there could be a rethink about this engine regulation, which would seem to discourage test teams from taking part in MotoGP championship races to evaluate their latest work in the white heat of competition. Racing is always much more demanding than testing, so it always gives teams and factories a much better idea about the value of the work they are undertaking.

"It's an MSMA rule which is all about cost-cutting," said Aldridge. "Also, the factories don't want a wild-card rider coming to an event with a much better engine that might interfere with the championship, so test teams have to use the same engine spec as the full-time teams. It's the same with aero rules – the MSMA doesn't want wild cards turning up and trying different aero packages all the time."

16 | JAPAN

MOTUL GRAND PRIX OF JAPAN

TWIN RING MOTEGI

18/19/20 OCTOBER

QUALIFYING RESULTS

	RIDER	NAT	TEAM	MACHINE	QP/TIME		GAP 1ST/PREV	
1	Marc Márquez	SPA	Repsol Honda Team	HONDA	Q2	1'45.763		
2	Franco Morbidelli	ITA	Petronas Yamaha SRT	YAMAHA	Q2	1'45.895	0.132	0.132
3	Fabio Quartararo	FRA	Petronas Yamaha SRT	YAMAHA	Q2	1'45.944	0.181	0.049
4	Maverick Viñales	SPA	Monster Energy Yamaha MotoGP	YAMAHA	Q2	1'46.090	0.327	0.146
5	Cal Crutchlow	GBR	LCR Honda CASTROL	HONDA	Q2	1'46.189	0.426	0.099
6	Jack Miller	AUS	Pramac Racing	DUCATI	Q2	1'46.337	0.574	0.148
7	Andrea Dovizioso	ITA	Ducati Team	DUCATI	Q2	1'46.410	0.647	0.073
8	Danilo Petrucci	ITA	Ducati Team	DUCATI	Q2	1'46.427	0.664	0.017
9	Aleix Espargaró	SPA	Aprilia Racing Team Gresini	APRILIA	Q2	1'46.558	0.795	0.131
10	Valentino Rossi	ITA	Monster Energy Yamaha MotoGP	YAMAHA	Q2	1'46.558	0.795	
11	Álex Rins	SPA	Team SUZUKI ECSTAR	SUZUKI	Q2	1'46.600	0.837	0.042
12	Joan Mir	SPA	Team SUZUKI ECSTAR	SUZUKI	Q2	1'46.616	0.853	0.016
13	Takaaki Nakagami	JPN	LCR Honda IDEMITSU	HONDA	Q1	1'46.998	*0.303	0.034
14	Francesco Bagnaia	ITA	Pramac Racing	DUCATI	Q1	1'47.594	*0.899	0.596
15	Pol Espargaro	SPA	Red Bull KTM Factory Racing	KTM	Q1	1'47.654	*0.959	0.060
16	Miguel Oliveira	POR	Red Bull KTM Tech 3	KTM	Q1	1'47.894	*1.199	0.240
17	Mika Kallio	FIN	Red Bull KTM Factory Racing	KTM	Q1	1'47.979	*1.284	0.085
18	Karel Abraham	CZE	Reale Avintia Racing	DUCATI	Q1	1'48.121	*1.426	0.142
19	Jorge Lorenzo	SPA	Repsol Honda Team	HONDA	Q1	1'48.492	*1.797	0.371
20	Hafizh Syahrin	MAL	Red Bull KTM Tech 3	KTM	Q1	1'48.522	*1.827	0.030
21	Sylvain Guintoli	FRA	Team SUZUKI ECSTAR	SUZUKI	Q1	1'49.186	*2.491	0.664
22	Andrea Iannone	ITA	Aprilia Racing Team Gresini	APRILIA	Q1	1'49.243	*2.548	0.057
23	Tito Rabat	SPA	Reale Avintia Racing	DUCATI	FP2	1'47.158	2.394	

** Gap to the fastest rider in the Q1 session* *** Went forward from Q1 to Q2* *Track severity = Wear + Temperature + Load*

GRAND PRIX INFORMATION

TRACK INFORMATION			
2019 WINNER	Marc Márquez		
CIRCUIT LENGTH	4.8 km	2.98 miles	
LAPS	24		
RACE DISTANCE	115.2 km	71.5 miles	
ALL TIME LAP RECORD	1'43.790	166.5 Km/h	Jorge Lorenzo (2015)
BEST RACE LAP	1'45.350	164.0 Km/h	Jorge Lorenzo (2014)
RACE CONDITION	Dry		
AIR	21°C		
HUMIDITY	76%		
GROUND	27°C		

TYRE SELECTION

FRONT	
SOFT	WHITE
MEDIUM	GREY
HARD	YELLOW

L M R

REAR	
SOFT	WHITE
MEDIUM	GREY
HARD	YELLOW

< MILD — TRACK SEVERITY — SEVERE >

1 MARC MÁRQUEZ
Another masterpiece from the master. Rode a perfect race, building enough of a lead to keep him ahead of his rivals even when he started running low on fuel. Even so, that fuel alarm on his dash must've given him a fright!

2 FABIO QUARTARARO
Rode his first Japanese GP as a Yamaha rider still resisting calls to sign for the factory from 2021. Instead kept his focus entirely on his motorcycle and his riding, which added up to victory in the Rookie of the Year contest.

3 ANDREA DOVIZIOSO
Márquez and Quartararo rode their best laps on laps five and three; Dovizioso rode his on lap 23. With less fuel and the medium rear tyre his GP19 felt better as the race went on. One lap more and he may have got Quartararo.

4 MAVERICK VIÑALES
Again showed he had found speed and more importantly consistency. This was the first time he had scored five consecutive top-four finishes since joining Yamaha in 2017! Got very frustrated trying to pass Dovizioso.

5 CAL CRUTCHLOW
His first top-five result since Brno, six races earlier, suggested that the Briton was digging himself out of the hole he'd fallen into. Managed his tyres well in the first half of the race, so he could charge hard in the second half.

6 FRANCO MORBIDELLI
Team-manager Wilco Zeelenberg said that the Italian "has seen the light now, understanding how to ride this bike in the best way". He scored his second front-row start, but in the race had less grip than during practice.

7 ÁLEX RINS
The same old story: couldn't find enough one-lap qualifying speed, which put him on the fourth row for the third consecutive race. Rode the third fastest race lap, but his pace was wasted by skirmishes in the early laps.

8 JOAN MIR
Came within 0.016 seconds of out-qualifying his team-mate for the second GP in a row and chased him throughout the race. At half-distance the gap between them was 3.2 seconds, at the flag it was just 1.3 seconds.

9 DANILO PETRUCCI
Had struggled with an overheating rear tyre at earlier races, so his crew changed the balance of his GP19, which only caused front-tyre overheating issues at Motegi. Once he had cooled the front tyre his pace did improve a bit.

10 JACK MILLER
Expected a great race after showing good pace in practice and great speed in qualifying. Had a go at breaking away with Márquez and Quartararo and looked good, until he lost rear grip and went backwards at a rapid rate.

RACE LAP CHART

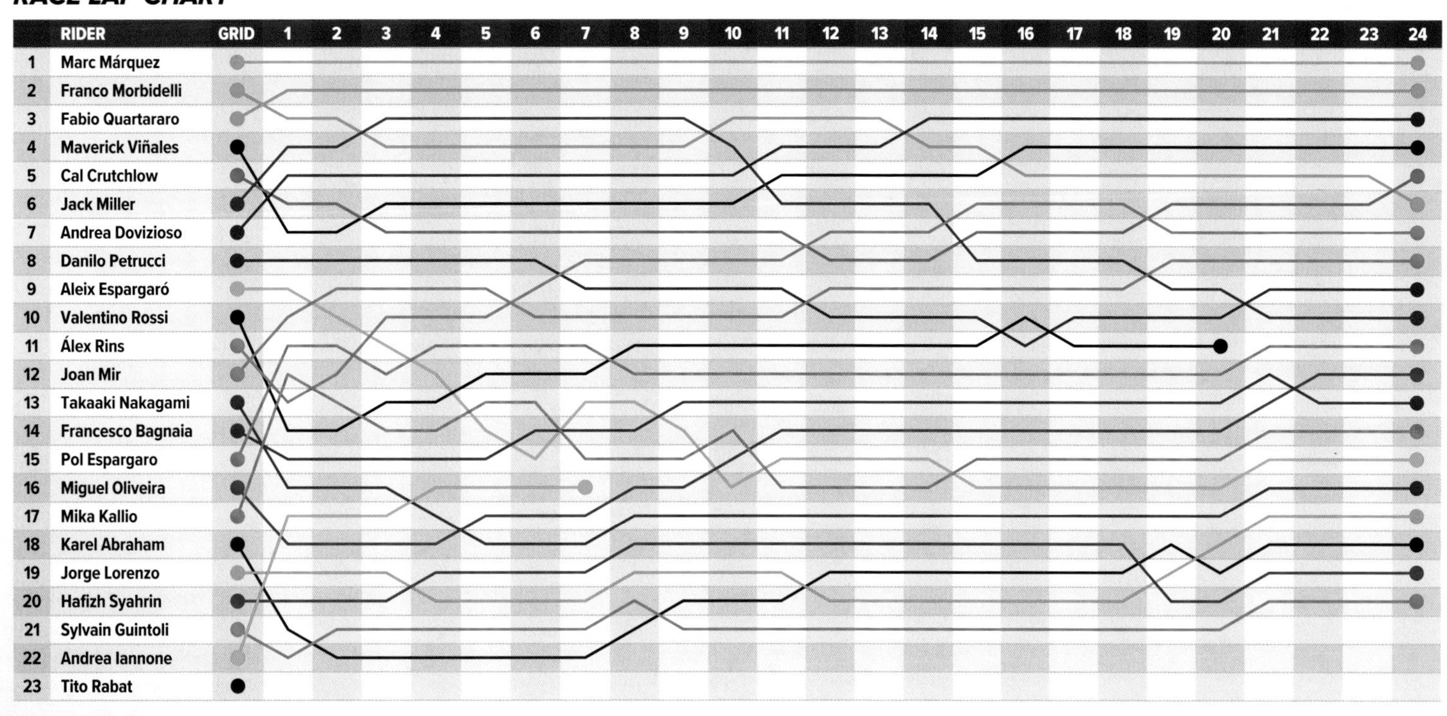

RACE RESULTS

	RIDER	NAT	TEAM	MACHINE	TIME	+GAP	TYRES
1	Marc Márquez	SPA	Repsol Honda Team	HONDA	42'41.492		M/M
2	Fabio Quartararo	FRA	Petronas Yamaha SRT	YAMAHA	42'42.362	0.870	M/S
3	Andrea Dovizioso	ITA	Ducati Team	DUCATI	42'42.817	1.325	S/M
4	Maverick Viñales	SPA	Monster Energy Yamaha MotoGP	YAMAHA	42'44.100	2.608	M/S
5	Cal Crutchlow	GBR	LCR Honda CASTROL	HONDA	42'50.632	9.140	M/M
6	Franco Morbidelli	ITA	Petronas Yamaha SRT	YAMAHA	42'50.679	9.187	M/S
7	Álex Rins	SPA	Team SUZUKI ECSTAR	SUZUKI	42'50.798	9.306	M/M
8	Joan Mir	SPA	Team SUZUKI ECSTAR	SUZUKI	42'52.187	10.695	M/M
9	Danilo Petrucci	ITA	Ducati Team	DUCATI	42'55.708	14.216	S/M
10	Jack Miller	AUS	Pramac Racing	DUCATI	43'00.401	18.909	S/S
11	Pol Espargaro	SPA	Red Bull KTM Factory Racing	KTM	43'07.046	25.554	M/S
12	Miguel Oliveira	POR	Red Bull KTM Tech 3	KTM	43'09.362	27.870	M/M
13	Francesco Bagnaia	ITA	Pramac Racing	DUCATI	43'11.475	29.983	S/S
14	Mika Kallio	FIN	Red Bull KTM Factory Racing	KTM	43'12.724	31.232	M/S
15	Aleix Espargaró	SPA	Aprilia Racing Team Gresini	APRILIA	43'14.038	32.546	M/S
16	Takaaki Nakagami	JPN	LCR Honda IDEMITSU	HONDA	43'18.974	37.482	S/M
17	Jorge Lorenzo	SPA	Repsol Honda Team	HONDA	43'21.902	40.410	M/M
18	Karel Abraham	CZE	Reale Avintia Racing	DUCATI	43'24.950	43.458	M/S
19	Hafizh Syahrin	MAL	Red Bull KTM Tech 3	KTM	43'27.698	46.206	M/M
20	Sylvain Guintoli	FRA	Team SUZUKI ECSTAR	SUZUKI	43'31.727	50.235	M/M
NC	Valentino Rossi	ITA	Monster Energy Yamaha MotoGP	YAMAHA	35'48.024	4 laps	M/M
NC	Andrea Iannone	ITA	Aprilia Racing Team Gresini	APRILIA	12'42.954	17 laps	M/S

CHAMPIONSHIP STANDINGS

	RIDER	NAT	TEAM	PTS
1	Marc Márquez	SPA	Repsol Honda Team	350
2	Andrea Dovizioso	ITA	Ducati Team	231
3	Álex Rins	SPA	Team SUZUKI ECSTAR	176
4	Maverick Viñales	SPA	Monster Energy Yamaha MotoGP	176
5	Danilo Petrucci	ITA	Ducati Team	169
6	Fabio Quartararo	FRA	Petronas Yamaha SRT	163
7	Valentino Rossi	ITA	Monster Energy Yamaha MotoGP	145
8	Jack Miller	AUS	Pramac Racing	125
9	Cal Crutchlow	GBR	LCR Honda CASTROL	113
10	Franco Morbidelli	ITA	Petronas Yamaha SRT	100
11	Pol Espargaró	SPA	Red Bull KTM Factory Racing	85
12	Takaaki Nakagami	JPN	LCR Honda IDEMITSU	74
13	Joan Mir	SPA	Team SUZUKI ECSTAR	66
14	Aleix Espargaró	SPA	Aprilia Racing Team Gresini	47
15	Francesco Bagnaia	ITA	Pramac Racing	37
16	Miguel Oliveira	POR	Red Bull KTM Tech 3	33
17	Andrea Iannone	ITA	Aprilia Racing Team Gresini	33
18	Johann Zarco	FRA	Red Bull KTM Factory Racing	27
19	Jorge Lorenzo	SPA	Repsol Honda Team	23
20	Tito Rabat	SPA	Reale Avintia Racing	18
21	Stefan Bradl	GER	Team HRC	16
22	Michele Pirro	ITA	Ducati Team	9
23	Sylvain Guintoli	FRA	Team SUZUKI ECSTAR	7
24	Hafizh Syahrin	MAL	Red Bull KTM Tech 3	7
25	Karel Abraham	CZE	Reale Avintia Racing	5
26	Mika Kallio	FIN	Red Bull KTM Factory Racing	2
27	Bradley Smith	GBR	Aprilia Factory Racing	

11 POL ESPARGARÓ
Riders spend a lot of the time hard on the brakes at Motegi, which can't have been pleasant for the Spaniard, with his recently plated left wrist. As always, gritted his teeth and came home with points and lots of data for KTM.

12 MIGUEL OLIVEIRA
An impressive fight from the rookie, who came through from 18th on the first lap after losing out in the chaos of the first few corners. Later had a good pace, confirming that his Silverstone shoulder injury was finally getting better.

13 FRANCESCO BAGNAIA
Another points-scoring finish from the 2018 Moto2 champion. Tried to go with Rossi, overtaking Kallio and Aleix Espargaró in the process which took him to 13th. Congratulated Quartararo for the Rookie of the Year title after the race.

14 MIKA KALLIO
Scored his first points since returning to racing at Misano, battling with Oliveira for a while. Was happy with his riding but this was the weekend when KTM told him he hadn't done enough to get a race contract for 2020.

15 ALEIX ESPARGARÓ
Possibly the toughest day in Aprilia's toughest 2019 season. Espargaró started superbly, completing the first lap in ninth, at a track that doesn't flatter the RS-GP. But then ran into a technical problem. Did well to finish in the points.

16 TAKAAKI NAKAGAMI
Announced before the race that this would be his last of 2019 because his right shoulder injury, from when Rossi took him out at Assen, was worsening. Afterwards underwent surgery to be ready for 2020 pre-season testing.

17 JORGE LORENZO
Qualified 19th and finished 40 seconds behind his team-mate, but surprisingly the former champion felt positive because he started to enjoy riding the bike again and was braking later than usual in the second half of the race.

18 KAREL ABRAHAM
The Czech rider was chasing his first points score since the British Grand Prix but the race didn't go his way. Started from 18th, then a technical problem dropped him to last place, from which he fought back to finish in 18th.

19 HAFIZH SYAHRIN
Started from 20th place on the grid and spent much of the 24 laps battling with the weakened Nakagami, but his pace dropped considerably in the final quarter of the race, when he was overtaken by Abraham and then Lorenzo.

20 SYLVAIN GUINTOLI
Suzuki's test rider spent several days at Motegi a few weeks before the race and impressed everyone in the wet FP3 session when he was fifth fastest. Rode a consistent rhythm in the race, gathering vital data for Rins and Mir.

DNF VALENTINO ROSSI
Lost time after the start when he was "in the middle of the chaos". Worked hard from 14th to briefly take tenth, then fell at Turn One.

DNF ANDREA IANNONE
Had a technical problem with a new engine, like his team-mate, but Iannone's issue caused him to crash out in the early stages.

DNS TITO RABAT
Decided not to race due to injury and engine issues – he would've had to start from pit lane for exceeding his engine allocation.

REPSOL
93
YAMAHA

17 | AUSTRALIA

PRAMAC GENERAC AUSTRALIAN MOTORCYCLE GP
PHILLIP ISLAND
25/26/27 OCTOBER

TO FINISH FIRST, FIRST YOU MUST FINISH

Viñales did everything he could for a second consecutive Phillip Island win, but this time Márquez was on his case

Every MotoGP bike has its good racetracks and its bad racetracks. Aprilia's 2019 RS-GP led a race for the first time at Phillip Island, seven days after its worst Sunday of the year at Motegi. The previous October Yamaha's YZR-M1 won its only race of the year at the fast and flowing old-school Australian track, using its corner speed to excellent effect.

Honda's RC213V is supposed to work best around tighter, more modern layouts, but if you are Marc Márquez or Cal Crutchlow, there are ways and means to make it work around Phillip Island.

"The Honda is good around here because we can slide the bike to make it turn," said Crutchlow.

Nevertheless, Maverick Viñales was favourite to repeat his 2018 success after taking pole in an extraordinary Sunday morning qualifying session, postponed from Saturday, when 50kmh/30mph winds lashed the seaside circuit. During FP4 the wind caused Miguel Oliveira to fall at the end of the start/finish. After the rookie's accident the session was red-flagged and qualifying cancelled.

On Sunday afternoon Viñales was on a mission. He carved his way through from sixth on lap one to take the lead on lap ten of 27 and stay there almost, but not quite, to the end.

Viñales said he braked ten metres late in his effort to retake the lead from Márquez, and this was the result.

CLOCKWISE, FROM TOP LEFT | *Aleix Espargaró helped Aprilia to its first MotoGP double top ten; Bagnaia is all eyes in wet practice - in the race he finally showed his true potential; Lorenzo has his worst race ever; Márquez toyed with Viñales lap after lap; Zarco made the most of his Honda lifeline; Rossi led his 400th GP but then went backwards; Miller doing his best to look like Ned Kelly; the Aussie outlaw sweeps around Phillip Island with Dovizioso and Rins; Crutchlow and Iannone lead the early change.*

'I SAID TO LUCY BEFORE I CAME HERE – I'M SCARED AND WORRIED"

CAL CRUTCHLOW

His nemesis stalked him all the way, slotting into second place on lap ten, when the two Spaniards took over the running from Cal Crutchlow and Andrea Iannone, who reminded the world that he and Aprilia are still very much around.

Márquez already had his game plan. When Viñales took the lead from Crutchlow the champion immediately pounced on his fellow HRC rider, the pair colliding heavily.

"I stayed on the bike but my left glove was half off," laughed Crutchlow afterwards. "I was trying to get it back on for a lap – I was going down the straight passing Iannone, trying to rub it back onto my hand!"

Crutchlow tried to go with the new leaders but couldn't because he had chosen the hard rear, which gave more wheelspin than their softs. From that moment the race was a two-man duel.

Lap after lap Márquez shadowed Viñales, who knew what was coming. As the pair sped out of the super-fast final corner for the penultimate time Márquez used his 4.7kmh/2.9mph top-speed advantage to saunter into the lead before the start/finish line.

Viñales now switched into win-it-or-bin-it mode. "I planned to push at the maximum in sector three and overtake in Turn Ten – go in without brakes to see what happened. Today was a race to win, not to be second. I had the chance, so I tried."

As he came over the top of Lukey Heights and flicked from left to right for Turn Ten he locked the rear and his M1 spat him off. Márquez continued to take his fifth win in a row.

"I crashed but I'm satisfied that I gave my best every lap and what else can I say?" he said. Later he added, "the problem was that I braked maybe ten metres later than normal!"

Yamaha's disappointment was Australia's delight, because a long way behind the leaders Jack Miller had been winning a big battle for fourth place.

"You never want to see anyone else crash, but it is what it is," said Miller, who found himself promoted to third just a few hundred metres from the finish. "As I came over Turn Nine I saw the dust and my heart race probably jumped up about 50 beats per minute, so I was right to the inside at Ten and 11, then as I went between the two last corners I switched to full power mode to make sure no one came past me on the front straight."

Thirty years after Wayne Gardner won the inaugural Phillip Island GP and seven years after Casey Stoner took his final victory at the track the Aussie crowd had another local hero to cheer.

Best mates 'Thriller' and 'Crutch' were on the podium together for the first time and made the most of it. Miller had wanted to look special for his home race; so he asked an Italian designer to make him look like Ned Kelly, a 19th century Aussie outlaw who wore homemade armour, but there must've been a bit of a misunderstanding...

ROSSI'S MAGICAL MILESTONE: 400 GPs!

Motorcycle racing started in the 1890s. Grand Prix racing started in the 1920s. World Championship racing started in 1949. Since then there have been about 940 Grand Prix events.

At Phillip Island Valentino Rossi contested his 400th world championship Grand Prix. That means the 40-year-old has contested more than 40 percent of the sport's events. That is a mind-boggling statistic.

Rossi has become so used to making history that he hardly takes notice when he surpasses another record. But at Phillip Island the nine-times world champion desperately wanted to celebrate

"I called Jack before the race and said, listen, just follow me, I'm going," said Crutchlow, who led six laps in the early stages. "Then when I saw his leathers I thought my call hadn't been the best idea because he looked like Bulletman – I'm coming through!"

Crutchlow's race, a year after the Turn One accident left him with a badly broken right ankle that threatened his career, was heroic.

"I've never had a crash that I've thought about – just get back on and don't really care," he said after his third podium of 2019. "But this one has haunted me for a year, honestly. I said to Lucy [Mrs Crutchlow] before I came here – I'm scared and worried. And if you're thinking about it, you never know if it's going to happen again."

Viñales had laid down such a rapid pace that Márquez took the flag 11 seconds ahead of Crutchlow and 14 ahead of Miller; his biggest win of the year. His strategy had been clear.

"I use this strategy when I'm not the fastest one on the track," he said. "Maverick was nearly one second faster than me in qualifying, but I knew that if I took some risks for a few laps to understand the way to follow him it would be enough. That's what I did with Quartararo in Thailand."

Miller was chased over the line by a pack of no fewer than seven riders: Pecco Bagnaia, Joan Mir, Iannone, Andrea Dovizioso, Valentino Rossi, Álex Rins and Aleix Espargaró. Those eight men were covered by just two second at the flag. Phillip Island had once again justified its reputation for creating thrilling multi-rider skirmishes; but this time the biggest battle of the race didn't happen at the front.

CLOCKWISE FROM TOP LEFT | *They let Miller and Quartararo out on the Aussie roads; no one, including Petrucci, enjoyed the weather; Jeremy Burgess, legendary crew chief to Rossi and Mick Doohan, was a popular visitor; Márquez was up to his usual antics in practice – obviously he didn't crash; Mir rode an inspired race; local hero Miller takes to the top of the podium to do a 'shoey'.*

his historic 400th Grand Prix from the podium at one of his favourite circuits.

It wasn't to be, but Rossi enjoyed himself anyway, battling in the midst of an eight-rider skirmish for fourth place, which turned into the battle for the final podium place when team-mate Maverick Viñales crashed out.

Years ago, Rossi's former crew chief Jeremy Burgess explained that the fundamental difference between the Italian and his previous multiple world champion Mick Doohan was that Doohan only raced to win, while Rossi races to enjoy himself.

Inevitably, Rossi had never even dreamed that he would reach the milestone of 400 GPs when he started racing bikes in the early 1990s.

"It's something you don't expect, but especially when I was younger and in general through my career I never had a clear idea of what had happened or how long I'd raced," he said. "When I was 17 I already saw guys that were 25-years-old and it felt like they were my grandfather! Now I am 40, imagine! But it's a good achievement, which I didn't expect because I didn't know what to expect when I started my career."

Despite his best efforts 2019 turned into his worst-ever season. But he still had no interest in quitting. "About motivation, for sure when you have good results everything is easier, because you enjoy racing more," he added. "If you are in a difficult moment the motivation is to try to come back from that and to try to be strong again."

17 | AUSTRALIA

PRAMAC GENERAC AUSTRALIAN MOTORCYCLE GP
PHILLIP ISLAND
25/26/27 OCTOBER

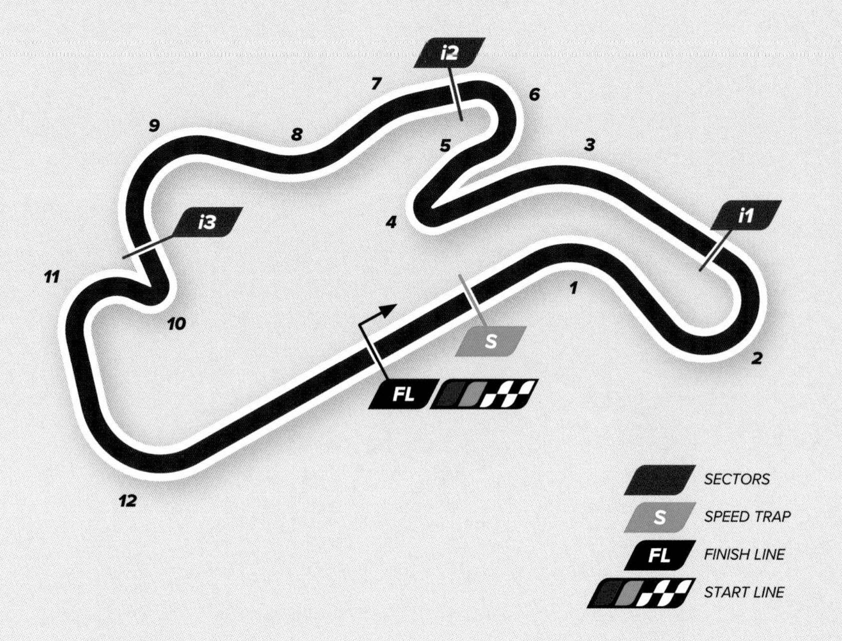

QUALIFYING RESULTS

	RIDER	NAT	TEAM	MACHINE	QP/TIME		GAP 1ST/PREV	
1	Maverick Viñales	SPA	Monster Energy Yamaha MotoGP	YAMAHA	Q2	1'28.492		
2	Fabio Quartararo	FRA	Petronas Yamaha SRT	YAMAHA	Q2	1'29.043	0.551	0.551
3	Marc Márquez	SPA	Repsol Honda Team	HONDA	Q2	1'29.216	0.724	0.173
4	Valentino Rossi	ITA	Monster Energy Yamaha MotoGP	YAMAHA	Q2	1'29.243	0.751	0.027
5	Danilo Petrucci	ITA	Ducati Team	DUCATI	Q2	1'29.339	0.847	0.096
6	Cal Crutchlow	GBR	LCR Honda CASTROL	HONDA	Q2	1'29.535	1.043	0.196
7	Aleix Espargaró	SPA	Aprilia Racing Team Gresini	APRILIA	Q2	1'29.558	1.066	0.023
8	Andrea Iannone	ITA	Aprilia Racing Team Gresini	APRILIA	Q2	1'29.581	1.089	0.023
9	Jack Miller	AUS	Pramac Racing	DUCATI	Q2	1'29.615	1.123	0.034
10	Andrea Dovizioso	ITA	Ducati Team	DUCATI	Q2	1'29.667	1.175	0.052
11	Franco Morbidelli	ITA	Petronas Yamaha SRT	YAMAHA	Q2	1'29.716	1.224	0.049
12	Álex Rins	SPA	Team SUZUKI ECSTAR	SUZUKI	Q2	1'29.947	1.455	0.231
13	Joan Mir	SPA	Team SUZUKI ECSTAR	SUZUKI	Q1	1'29.712	*0.763	0.157
14	Johann Zarco	FRA	LCR Honda IDEMITSU	HONDA	Q1	1'30.008	*1.059	0.296
15	Francesco Bagnaia	ITA	Pramac Racing	DUCATI	Q1	1'30.075	*1.126	0.067
16	Karel Abraham	CZE	Reale Avintia Racing	DUCATI	Q1	1'30.165	*1.216	0.090
17	Pol Espargaro	SPA	Red Bull KTM Factory Racing	KTM	Q1	1'30.180	*1.231	0.015
18	Mika Kallio	FIN	Red Bull KTM Factory Racing	KTM	Q1	1'30.495	*1.546	0.315
19	Jorge Lorenzo	SPA	Repsol Honda Team	HONDA	Q1	1'31.179	*2.230	0.684
20	Hafizh Syahrin	MAL	Red Bull KTM Tech 3	KTM	Q1	1'31.285	*2.336	0.106
21	Tito Rabat	SPA	Reale Avintia Racing	DUCATI	Q1	1'31.941	*2.992	0.656

** Gap to the fastest rider in the Q1 session   ** Went forward from Q1 to Q2   Track severity = Wear + Temperature + Load*

GRAND PRIX INFORMATION

TRACK INFORMATION			
2019 WINNER	Marc Márquez		
CIRCUIT LENGTH	4.4 km	2.76 miles	
LAPS	27		
RACE DISTANCE	120.1 km	74.5 miles	
ALL TIME LAP RECORD	1'27.899	182.1 Km/h	Jorge Lorenzo (2013)
BEST RACE LAP	1'28.108	181.7 Km/h	Marc Márquez (2013)
RACE CONDITION	Dry		
AIR	16°C		
HUMIDITY	63%		
GROUND	30°C		

TYRE SELECTION

FRONT	
SOFT	WHITE
MEDIUM	GREY
HARD	YELLOW

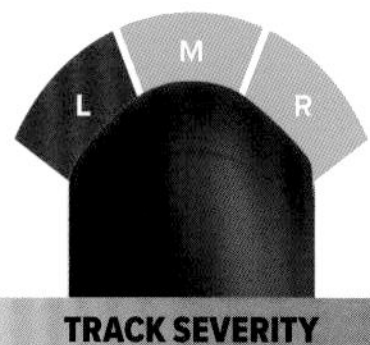

REAR	
SOFT	WHITE
MEDIUM	GREY
HARD	YELLOW

< MILD   TRACK SEVERITY   SEVERE >

1 MARC MÁRQUEZ
A fifth win in a row was an impressive achievement from a rider who knew he wasn't the fastest man on the racetrack. Took some risks to go with Viñales, then knew he had the horsepower to help him make the winning move.

2 CAL CRUTCHLOW
Twelve months on from his Turn One horror smash this was a well-deserved reward for the Briton's never-say-die attitude. He rode as hard as always and the fact that the RC213V works at Phillip Island made the difference.

3 JACK MILLER
The Aussie youth dirt track champion battled like crazy for his first home MotoGP podium and enjoyed every minute of the crowd's adulation. He later said he would never forget the day and he almost certainly never will

4 FRANCESCO BAGNAIA
Phillip Island allows riders to use a more natural style, which is why rookies often go so well there. This was by far the 2018 Moto2 champion's best ride of the season, missing the podium by just half a second.

5 JOAN MIR
Like fellow rookie Bagnaia, revelled in the track's easy-flowing layout. Fought through from 13th on the grid to join the battle for what turned out to be the last podium place. Proved once again that he's making big steps forward.

6 ANDREA IANNONE
The first Aprilia rider to lead a premier-class GP since Jeremy McWilliams led the British GP in 2000. He adores the track and should have won there in 2018. A collision lost him a winglet which made his RS-GP less stable.

7 ANDREA DOVIZIOSO
Chose the hard-option rear slick which turned out to be the wrong choice. Rode well in the eight-rider group that spent most of the race disputing fourth. Ran so short of grip he lost two positions on the last lap.

8 VALENTINO ROSSI
Wanted to celebrate his 400th Grand Prix from the podium. Was happy that he had been in the fight for the top three at one of MotoGP's most enjoyable tracks and at his most competitive since Misano. But still needed more

9 ÁLEX RINS
His fourth consecutive start from the fourth row once again stifled his race. Incredibly he worked his way up to fourth place at half-distance but he had asked too much from his tyres and later dropped to the back of the group

10 ALEIX ESPARGARÓ
Completed an historic weekend for Aprilia: the first time the factory had had two riders in the top ten of a MotoGP grid and the first time it had had two in the top-ten result. The Spaniard likened the battle for third to a Moto3 race!

RACE LAP CHART

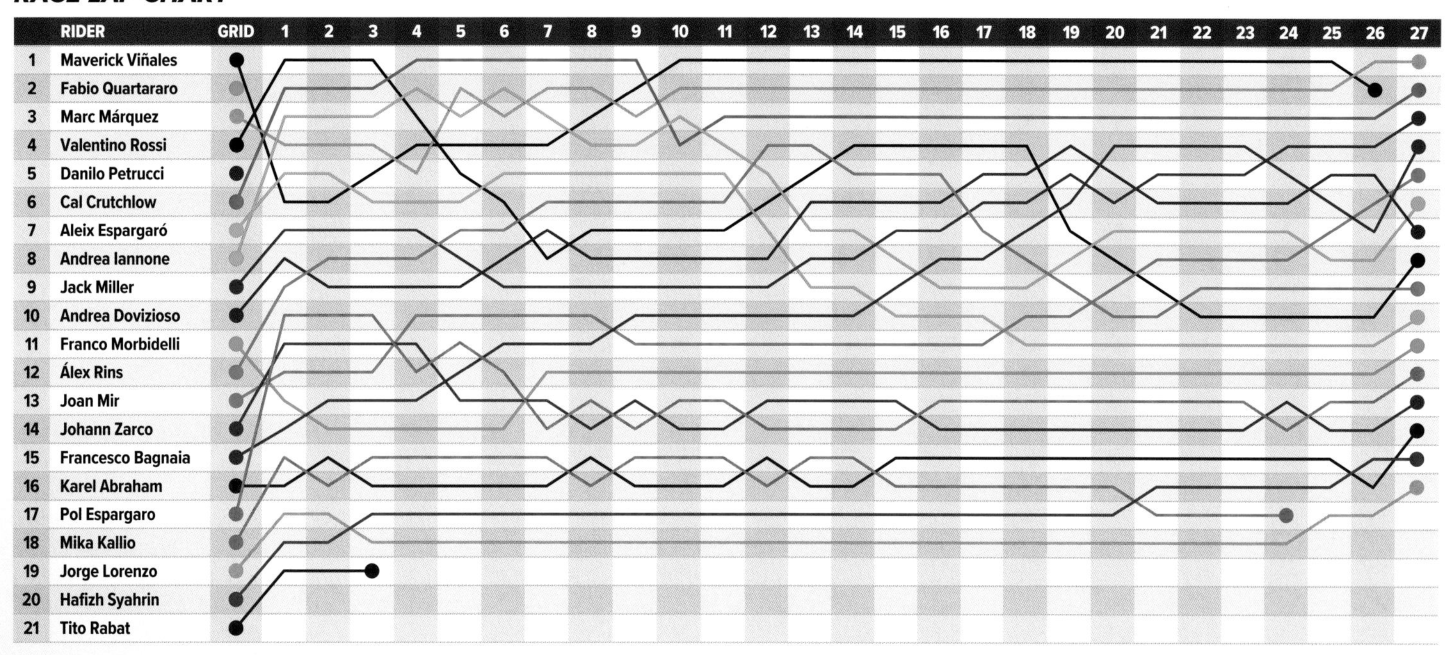

RACE RESULTS

	RIDER	NAT	TEAM	MACHINE	TIME	+ GAP	TYRES
1	Marc Márquez	SPA	Repsol Honda Team	HONDA	40'43.729		H/S
2	Cal Crutchlow	GBR	LCR Honda CASTROL	HONDA	40'55.142	11.413	H/H
3	Jack Miller	AUS	Pramac Racing	DUCATI	40'58.228	14.499	M/H
4	Francesco Bagnaia	ITA	Pramac Racing	DUCATI	40'58.283	14.554	M/H
5	Joan Mir	SPA	Team SUZUKI ECSTAR	SUZUKI	40'58.546	14.817	M/H
6	Andrea Iannone	ITA	Aprilia Racing Team Gresini	APRILIA	40'59.009	15.280	H/S
7	Andrea Dovizioso	ITA	Ducati Team	DUCATI	40'59.023	15.294	M/H
8	Valentino Rossi	ITA	Monster Energy Yamaha MotoGP	YAMAHA	40'59.570	15.841	M/S
9	Álex Rins	SPA	Team SUZUKI ECSTAR	SUZUKI	40'59.761	16.032	M/H
10	Aleix Espargaró	SPA	Aprilia Racing Team Gresini	APRILIA	41'00.319	16.590	M/S
11	Franco Morbidelli	ITA	Petronas Yamaha SRT	YAMAHA	41'07.874	24.145	M/S
12	Pol Espargaro	SPA	Red Bull KTM Factory Racing	KTM	41'10.383	26.654	M/H
13	Johann Zarco	FRA	LCR Honda IDEMITSU	HONDA	41'10.487	26.758	M/S
14	Karel Abraham	CZE	Reale Avintia Racing	DUCATI	41'28.641	44.912	M/S
15	Hafizh Syahrin	MAL	Red Bull KTM Tech 3	KTM	41'28.697	44.968	M/H
16	Jorge Lorenzo	SPA	Repsol Honda Team	HONDA	41'49.774	66.045	M/S
NC	Maverick Viñales	SPA	Monster Energy Yamaha MotoGP	YAMAHA	39'12.021	1 lap	S/S
NC	Mika Kallio	FIN	Red Bull KTM Factory Racing	KTM	36'58.452	3 laps	M/H
NC	Tito Rabat	SPA	Reale Avintia Racing	DUCATI	4'49.459	24 laps	M/S
NC	Fabio Quartararo	FRA	Petronas Yamaha SRT	YAMAHA			M/H
NC	Danilo Petrucci	ITA	Ducati Team	DUCATI			M/H

CHAMPIONSHIP STANDINGS

	RIDER	NAT	TEAM	PTS
1	Marc Márquez	SPA	Repsol Honda Team	375
2	Andrea Dovizioso	ITA	Ducati Team	240
3	Álex Rins	SPA	Team SUZUKI ECSTAR	183
4	Maverick Viñales	SPA	Monster Energy Yamaha MotoGP	176
5	Danilo Petrucci	ITA	Ducati Team	169
6	Fabio Quartararo	FRA	Petronas Yamaha SRT	163
7	Valentino Rossi	ITA	Monster Energy Yamaha MotoGP	153
8	Jack Miller	AUS	Pramac Racing	141
9	Cal Crutchlow	GBR	LCR Honda CASTROL	133
10	Franco Morbidelli	ITA	Petronas Yamaha SRT	105
11	Pol Espargaró	SPA	Red Bull KTM Factory Racing	89
12	Joan Mir	SPA	Team SUZUKI ECSTAR	77
13	Takaaki Nakagami	JPN	LCR Honda IDEMITSU	74
14	Aleix Espargaró	SPA	Aprilia Racing Team Gresini	53
15	Francesco Bagnaia	ITA	Pramac Racing	50
16	Andrea Iannone	ITA	Aprilia Racing Team Gresini	43
17	Miguel Oliveira	POR	Red Bull KTM Tech 3	33
18	Johann Zarco	FRA	LCR Honda IDEMITSU	30
19	Jorge Lorenzo	SPA	Repsol Honda Team	23
20	Tito Rabat	SPA	Reale Avintia Racing	18
21	Stefan Bradl	GER	Team HRC	16
22	Michele Pirro	ITA	Ducati Team	9
23	Hafizh Syahrin	MAL	Red Bull KTM Tech 3	8
24	Sylvain Guintoli	FRA	Team SUZUKI ECSTAR	7
25	Karel Abraham	CZE	Reale Avintia Racing	7
26	Mika Kallio	FIN	Red Bull KTM Factory Racing	2
27	Bradley Smith	GBR	Aprilia Factory Racing	

11 FRANCO MORBIDELLI
Struggled to match the fastest around this harum-scarum racetrack in qualifying, after feeling better in free practice. The Italian soon dropped off the back of the eight-rider group ahead of him for his worst finish since Qatar.

12 POL ESPARGARÓ
Was at a loss to explain the RC16's poor performance, apart from the fact that the ever-changing weather hurt KTM more than rival factories who had more experience in all conditions. Main problem was a lack of grip and traction.

13 JOHANN ZARCO
A big weekend, subbing for Takaaki Nakagami. Had to learn the Honda in scary conditions at an unforgiving track. Ironically, got involved in a scrap with former KTM team-mate Espargaró, who was determined not to be beaten.

14 KAREL ABRAHAM
Spent the race disputing position with Kallio and Syahrin. Eventually Kallio pulled into the pits, just before the Czech rider nearly crashed, letting Syahrin past. Finally Abraham repassed the Malaysian for two championship points.

15 HAFIZH SYAHRIN
Spent a considerable part of the race trying to find some feeling from his hard rear tyre. Once he had found his rhythm he managed to pass Kallio into Turn One, but didn't have enough to defend his position from Abraham.

16 JORGE LORENZO
The most humbling outing for the former world champion since he returned from injury at Silverstone. Couldn't find the confidence to push in the cold, windy conditions. Finished one minute six seconds behind his team-mate.

DNF MAVERICK VIÑALES
So near but so far. Had the pace to win the race, but not to beat the world champion, who had a decent advantage on the start/finish. Unhappy to crash but happy that he had once again shown race-winning speed.

DNF MIKA KALLIO
The fastest two riders chose the soft rear, so it wasn't long before the Finn realised he had done wrong by choosing the hard rear. Eventually he destroyed the rear tyre and then the front, so he had no option to withdraw from the race.

DNF TITO RABAT
Badly hampered by the hand he injured before the Japanese GP. The injury prevented him from starting the race at Motegi and prevented him from finishing at Phillip Island, forcing him into the pits after just three laps completed.

DNF DANILO PETRUCCI
Achieved only his second row-two start since Mugello, so was understandably fired up for the race. Chose the hard rear, went wide at Turn Two when Márquez came past and got pinged over the highside, hurting an ankle.

DNF FABIO QUARTARARO
Invigorated by second-place finishes in Thailand and Japan he came to Phillip Island dreaming of success at a track that favours the M1. Had a big crash on Friday, made the front row, only to get taken out by a flying Petrucci.

DNS MIGUEL OLIVEIRA
The rookie's terrifying crash at the end of the start/finish during FP4 left him unable to race due to swelling in his left hand and the pain in his right wrist. Underwent MRI scans in the hope he would be able to race the next weekend in Malaysia.

MICHELIN
MICHELIN

Victory to Viñales, pole position to Quartararo and lap record to Rossi – who said the M1 was no good?

SHELL MALAYSIA MOTORCYCLE GRAND PRIX
SEPANG INTERNATIONAL CIRCUIT
01/02/03 NOVEMBER

A YAMAHA RENAISSANCE

Finally, Yamaha dominated an entire MotoGP weekend, while Viñales made up for his Phillip Island faux pas

Not for two and a half years had Yamaha so comprehensively dominated a MotoGP weekend: race victory, front-row lock-out and a new lap record.

The last Grand Prix the Iwata factory ruled like that was Le Mans 2017, when Maverick Viñales won the race and set a new lap record after starting from pole position alongside Valentino Rossi and Johann Zarco.

That was Viñales' last win of 2017 and the start of Yamaha's drift into the doldrums. The 24-year-old's Malaysian victory suggested the factory was working its way out of the slump because, despite his Phillip Island crash, this was Viñales' strongest run of results since he first joined Yamaha.

But it wasn't just Viñales. Pole went to Fabio Quartararo – his fifth of the year – while team-mate Franco Morbidelli completed the front row at Petronas SRT's home race.

There were various reasons for Yamaha's resurgence. "When Maverick first arrived in 2017 he was very fast at every circuit, then when he struggled we tried to improve the setting, but sometimes that made confusion," explained Takahiro Tsumi, Yamaha's MotoGP group manager. "Finally at the Barcelona tests we found a good base setting, so now he can get back his feeling on the bike. If the bike doesn't change during the weekend he can concentrate on adapting himself to each situation."

‘WE FOLLOW OUR OWN WAY AND IT SEEMS TO WORK’
MAVERICK VIÑALES

CLOCKWISE, FROM TOP LEFT *Morbidelli’s hopes of a first podium came to nothing; Dovizioso once again used his skills to repulse a better-handling inline-four; there’s a huge buzz about MotoGP in South East Asia; Rossi really enjoyed himself; Zarco was undone by Mir; Mir slices inside Petrucci and takes aim at Zarco; Quartararo was delighted with his fifth pole; a lonely Viñales is a fast Viñales; Miller rode around Morbidelli to lead into Turn One.*

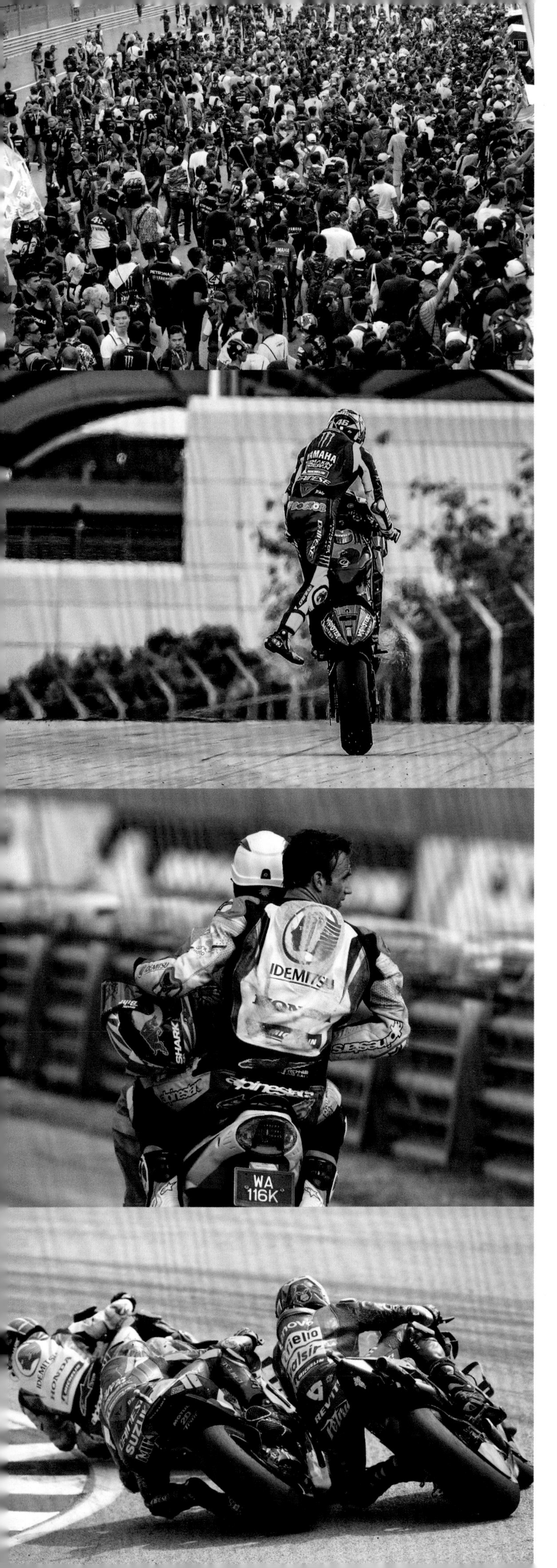

Quartararo's team manager Wilco Zeelenberg believed the 2019 M1 engine had a lot to do with it. "Most of all it's the engine that helps by giving us traction, which is what we needed last year," he said. "Pretty much all our problems last year were because the engine was wrong. The way it made power didn't find traction, the electronics weren't the biggest problem."

Viñales had also changed, thanks to off-season advice from a sports psychiatrist that improved his mentality. "I'm now very concentrated on myself," he explained. "We don't try to compare so much with the other riders. We follow our own way and it seems to work."

And yet he admitted he had been boosted by the arrival of Quartararo. "If you have a Yamaha in front it's always good to help you understand the way to ride the bike and how to improve."

On Saturday that's not what Marc Márquez thought. Going for a sixth consecutive victory he followed Quartararo in Q2, aiming to use the rookie's speed to improve his lap time, while at the same time psyching him out. It didn't work.

Every time Quartararo closed the throttle to shake off his shadow, Márquez did the same. They rode a whole lap like that and when the rookie returned to full speed Márquez went with him, with disastrous consequences: a huge highside at Turn Two.

"I saw it and knew exactly what Marc had done," said Jack Miller. "The left side of the rear tyre is quite hard here, so it got too cold and the bike highsided him. He's generally the master tactician, but today it came back and bit him on the arse."

The crash left the world champion badly beaten up and 11th on the grid, his worst grid slot since Mugello 2015 when he struggled through free practice and qualified 13th. On Saturday evening at Sepang he re-watched the start of that race, when he carved his way through to fourth in the first ten corners.

This first lap was just as impressive. By Turn Two he was up to sixth, at Turn Three he took Quartararo and at Turn 15 he swept inside the GP19s of Miller and Andrea Dovizioso. From 11th to second in one lap, but try as he might he had nothing for Viñales, who took the lead from Miller on the first lap and was already 1.3 seconds ahead by lap three.

Every so often Márquez did inch closer, but he made a couple of mistakes, while Viñales was able to make the most of Sepang's sweeping corners, which allow the Yamaha to exploit its mid-corner poise to build excellent exit speed.

"The Ducati has got big horsepower and the Honda has got big horsepower," explained Miller. "But the Yamaha can get onto the straights quickly, especially from that long right-hander before the back straight."

From half-distance the crowd's attention switched to the battle for third between Dovizioso and Rossi. This was yet another V4

REST IN PEACE AFRIDZA MUNANDAR

Racing went ahead under the darkest of clouds at Sepang, following the death of Indonesian youngster Afridza Munandar after a crash in Saturday's Idemitsu Asia Talent Cup race.

Munandar had been one of the stars of the 2019 ATC championship. The 20-year-old won ATC races at the Thailand World Superbike round in March and at a Malaysian national superbike event at Sepang in June. He also took podium results in ATC races at October's Thai and Japanese MotoGP rounds.

Munandar fell at Turn Ten on the first lap of the race and was struck by another rider. He underwent immediate medical

versus inline-four duel that played out in the usual way – Rossi should've been faster through the corners but the quicker Ducati was always in his way.

Rossi danced on the edge during the final laps. "I tried my maximum because the difference between third and fourth is very big!" he said. His maximum wasn't quite enough, but he had the satisfaction of the new lap record; not bad for a 40-year-old racing in 32-degree heat and 60 percent humidity. "I'm very happy to be strong here, because this is physically the hardest race of season," he said

Álex Rins managed to put his GSX-RR on the third row this time, but that still left him with too much work to do. Seventh on lap one he picked off Morbidelli and Miller, then closed on Rossi but never got close enough to attack.

Miller had his own V4 versus inline-four duels, with Rins and team-mate Joan Mir, colliding with both of them.

"The Suzuki turns well, so I guess it's inviting for them to make moves like that, especially in the off-camber hairpin [Turn 15] where you need to square it off, which leaves a bit of space," said the Aussie.

And what of Quartararo? Sepang seemed like his best chance of a win, but his front tyre overheated. "The pressure got really high, so I didn't have the grip to stop the bike, I was always running wide," said the Frenchman who got the better of Miller to take seventh, three seconds behind his team-mate.

CLOCKWISE FROM TOP LEFT | *Márquez chases Miller after the champ's astonishing first lap; Iannone was one of several to suffer from an overheating and over-pressurised front tyre; Crutchlow was another, his race ending the same way; again, Rins might've made the podium if he had qualified better; recently crowned Moto2 champion Alex Márquez greets big brother; Rossi congratulates the winner.*

treatment at the track and was flown by helicopter to hospital in Kuala Lumpur, but sadly succumbed to his injuries.

Márquez paid eloquent tribute to Munandar, who he knew from his frequent visits to the vast Astra Honda facilities in Indonesia.

"Today is an emotional day because yesterday we lost Munandar," he said after the MotoGP race. "He was a young talent. I knew him because he's from Astra Honda, where we went many times. We cannot forget that everybody here realises the risks we take on the track. We take these risks to achieve our goals, for those sweet moments, so when we achieve our goals we need to enjoy them. Today we enjoyed racing for him because he was also looking for these moments. He was pushing, riding with his passion and he will always be the most special rider of this Grand Prix."

Munandar started racing in motocross, before moving to roadracing. He was well known in Indonesia for riding underbone machines for Astra Honda in the national Motorprix series. He contested his first Asia Talent Cup season in 2018. His number four has now been retired from the championship.

The Asia Talent Cup was created by Dorna in 2014 as part of its Road to MotoGP programme to help young riders from Asia and Oceania develop their skills and make their way into world-class competition. The ATC has already brought Somkiat Chantra, Ai Ogura, Can Öncü, Ayumu Sasaki, Kaito Toba and others into the Moto2 and Moto3 world championships.

18 | MALAYSIA

START LINE
SECTORS

SPEED TRAP
FINISH LINE

SHELL MALAYSIA MOTORCYCLE GRAND PRIX

SEPANG INTERNATIONAL CIRCUIT
01/02/03 NOVEMBER

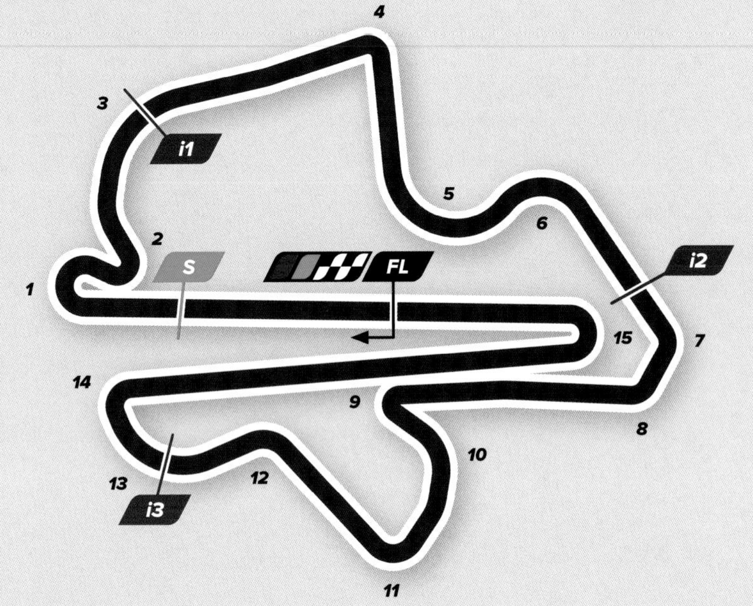

QUALIFYING RESULTS

	RIDER	NAT	TEAM	MACHINE	QP/TIME		GAP 1ST/PREV	
1	Fabio Quartararo	FRA	Petronas Yamaha SRT	YAMAHA	Q2	1'58.303		
2	Maverick Viñales	SPA	Monster Energy Yamaha MotoGP	YAMAHA	Q2	1'58.406	0.103	0.103
3	Franco Morbidelli	ITA	Petronas Yamaha SRT	YAMAHA	Q2	1'58.432	0.129	0.026
4	Jack Miller	AUS	Pramac Racing	DUCATI	Q2	1'58.725	0.422	0.293
5	Cal Crutchlow	GBR	LCR Honda CASTROL	HONDA	Q2	1'58.951	0.648	0.226
6	Valentino Rossi	ITA	Monster Energy Yamaha MotoGP	YAMAHA	Q2	1'59.000	0.697	0.049
7	Álex Rins	SPA	Team SUZUKI ECSTAR	SUZUKI	Q2	1'59.090	0.787	0.090
8	Danilo Petrucci	ITA	Ducati Team	DUCATI	Q2	1'59.097	0.794	0.007
9	Johann Zarco	FRA	LCR Honda IDEMITSU	HONDA	Q2	1'59.139	0.836	0.042
10	Andrea Dovizioso	ITA	Ducati Team	DUCATI	Q2	1'59.173	0.870	0.034
11	Marc Márquez	SPA	Repsol Honda Team	HONDA	Q2	1'59.178	0.875	0.005
12	Francesco Bagnaia	ITA	Pramac Racing	DUCATI	Q2	1'59.640	1.337	0.462
13	Joan Mir	SPA	Team SUZUKI ECSTAR	SUZUKI	Q1	1'59.374	*0.158	0.038
14	Aleix Espargaró	SPA	Aprilia Racing Team Gresini	APRILIA	Q1	1'59.435	*0.219	0.061
15	Pol Espargaro	SPA	Red Bull KTM Factory Racing	KTM	Q1	1'59.812	*0.596	0.377
16	Karel Abraham	CZE	Reale Avintia Racing	DUCATI	Q1	2'00.072	*0.856	0.260
17	Andrea Iannone	ITA	Aprilia Racing Team Gresini	APRILIA	Q1	2'00.205	*0.989	0.133
18	Jorge Lorenzo	SPA	Repsol Honda Team	HONDA	Q1	2'00.478	*1.262	0.273
19	Mika Kallio	FIN	Red Bull KTM Factory Racing	KTM	Q1	2'00.644	*1.428	0.166
20	Hafizh Syahrin	MAL	Red Bull KTM Tech 3	KTM	Q1	2'01.045	*1.829	0.401

* Gap to the fastest rider in the Q1 session   ** Went forward from Q1 to Q2   Track severity = Wear + Temperature + Load

GRAND PRIX INFORMATION

TRACK INFORMATION			
2019 WINNER	Maverick Viñales		
CIRCUIT LENGTH	5.5 km	3.44 miles	
LAPS	20		
RACE DISTANCE	110.9 km	68.8 miles	
ALL TIME LAP RECORD	1'58.303	168.6 Km/h	Fabio Quartararo (2019)
BEST RACE LAP	1'59.661	166.7 Km/h	Valentino Rossi (2019)
RACE CONDITION	Dry		
AIR	32°C		
HUMIDITY	60%		
GROUND	44°C		

OFFICIAL TIMEKEEPER

OFFICIAL MotoGP™ CLASS TYRE

TYRE SELECTION

FRONT	
SOFT	WHITE
MEDIUM	GREY
HARD	YELLOW

REAR	
SOFT	WHITE
MEDIUM	GREY
HARD	YELLOW

L M R

< MILD   TRACK SEVERITY   SEVERE >

1 MAVERICK VIÑALES
Made amends for his last-lap crash at Phillip Island the previous Sunday in fine style. Made sure he got to the front as soon as possible, so he could ride his own race. Dedicated his victory to Afridza Munandar.

2 MARC MÁRQUEZ
Rated his first lap as his best-ever, which says a lot! However, his aggression in the early laps overused his tyres, so he soon knew he had no chance of catching Viñales. Also remembered Munandar on the podium.

3 ANDREA DOVIZIOSO
The 2016 and 2017 Sepang winner chased Márquez, then spent the second half of the race keeping Rossi behind him. The battle was similar to his duel with Viñales at Motegi and once again he came out on top.

4 VALENTINO ROSSI
So close yet so far from the podium. But the oldest rider in the race was delighted that he had ridden the fastest lap in MotoGP's most gruelling race. Burned the edge of his tyres while trying to better Dovizioso.

5 ÁLEX RINS
Finished second to Márquez at Sepang 2018, so had high hopes of another podium. Lost a winglet when he collided with Miller, but nevertheless managed to get very close to attacking Rossi and Dovizioso.

6 FRANCO MORBIDELLI
Once again a first MotoGP podium eluded him, when he really thought he had a top-three finish in him. Was fastest in FP3 and FP4 but lacked acceleration in the race and had to override his M1 on the brakes.

7 FABIO QUARTARARO
Showed such stunning speed on Friday and topped qualifying. Seemed destined to delight Malaysian sponsors Petronas in the race but it wasn't to be. His front tyre pressure got too high which slowed him.

8 JACK MILLER
Led the first 11 corners from the second row of the grid, but struggled with his soft front from lap three. Had several rivals barge into him during the race. Lap by lap the tyre got worse until he was just surviving.

9 DANILO PETRUCCI
Still walking with the aid of a crutch after his big Phillip Island crash and struggled through the race with a back injury sustained in that accident. Did what he could until slowed by a very strong vibration from the rear.

10 JOAN MIR
The rookie said this was physically his toughest-ever race, not due to the tropical weather but because he couldn't breathe well due to the lung he hurt in his Brno crash. Got a long-lap penalty for taking out Zarco.

RACE LAP CHART

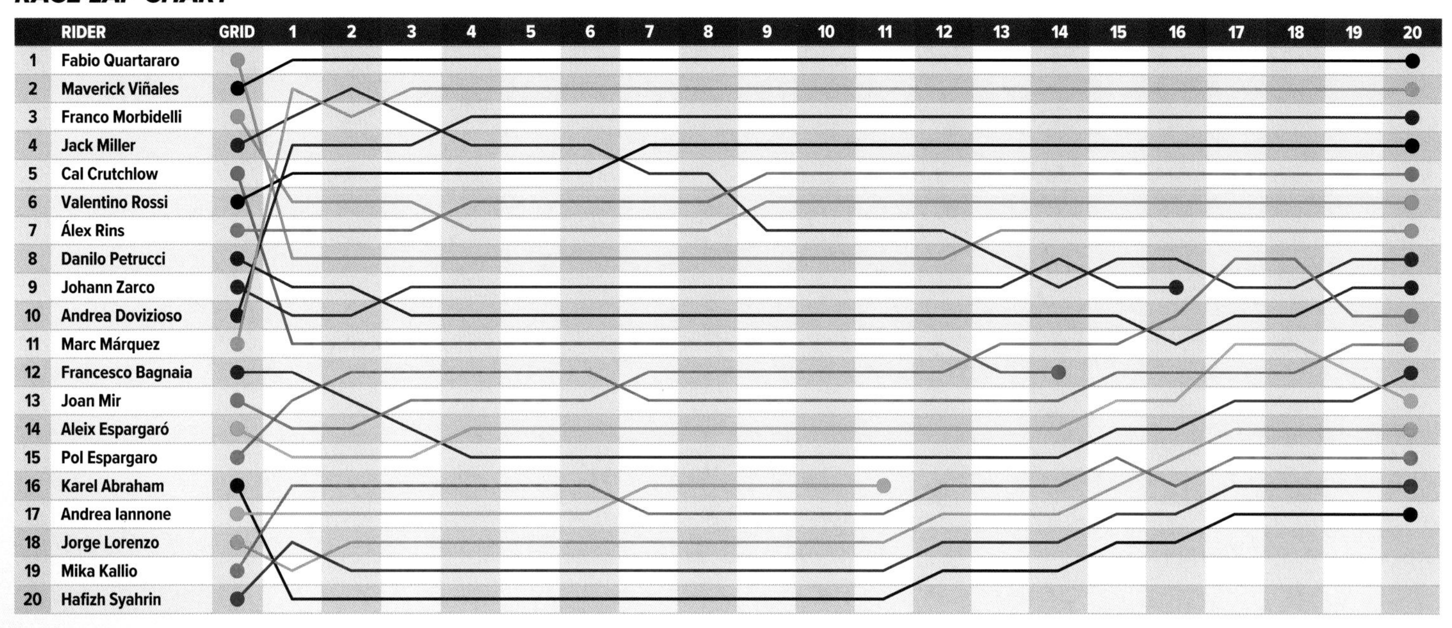

RACE RESULTS

	RIDER	NAT	TEAM	MACHINE	TIME	+GAP	TYRES
1	Maverick Viñales	SPA	Monster Energy Yamaha MotoGP	YAMAHA	40'14.632		M/M
2	Marc Márquez	SPA	Repsol Honda Team	HONDA	40'17.691	3.059	M/S
3	Andrea Dovizioso	ITA	Ducati Team	DUCATI	40'20.243	5.611	S/S
4	Valentino Rossi	ITA	Monster Energy Yamaha MotoGP	YAMAHA	40'20.597	5.965	M/M
5	Álex Rins	SPA	Team SUZUKI ECSTAR	SUZUKI	40'20.982	6.350	M/M
6	Franco Morbidelli	ITA	Petronas Yamaha SRT	YAMAHA	40'24.625	9.993	M/M
7	Fabio Quartararo	FRA	Petronas Yamaha SRT	YAMAHA	40'27.496	12.864	M/S
8	Jack Miller	AUS	Pramac Racing	DUCATI	40'31.884	17.252	S/S
9	Danilo Petrucci	ITA	Ducati Team	DUCATI	40'34.405	19.773	M/M
10	Joan Mir	SPA	Team SUZUKI ECSTAR	SUZUKI	40'37.486	22.854	M/M
11	Pol Espargaro	SPA	Red Bull KTM Factory Racing	KTM	40'39.453	24.821	M/M
12	Francesco Bagnaia	ITA	Pramac Racing	DUCATI	40'44.883	30.251	M/M
13	Aleix Espargaró	SPA	Aprilia Racing Team Gresini	APRILIA	40'45.079	30.447	M/M
14	Jorge Lorenzo	SPA	Repsol Honda Team	HONDA	40'48.847	34.215	M/M
15	Mika Kallio	FIN	Red Bull KTM Factory Racing	KTM	40'49.093	34.461	M/M
16	Hafizh Syahrin	MAL	Red Bull KTM Tech 3	KTM	40'58.951	44.319	S/M
17	Karel Abraham	CZE	Reale Avintia Racing	DUCATI	41'01.975	47.343	M/S
NC	Johann Zarco	FRA	LCR Honda IDEMITSU	HONDA	32'24.377	4 laps	M/M
NC	Cal Crutchlow	GBR	LCR Honda CASTROL	HONDA	28'23.231	6 laps	M/M
NC	Andrea Iannone	ITA	Aprilia Racing Team Gresini	APRILIA	22'26.032	9 laps	M/M

CHAMPIONSHIP STANDINGS

	RIDER	NAT	TEAM	PTS
1	Marc Márquez	SPA	Repsol Honda Team	395
2	Andrea Dovizioso	ITA	Ducati Team	256
3	Maverick Viñales	SPA	Monster Energy Yamaha MotoGP	201
4	Álex Rins	SPA	Team SUZUKI ECSTAR	194
5	Danilo Petrucci	ITA	Ducati Team	176
6	Fabio Quartararo	FRA	Petronas Yamaha SRT	172
7	Valentino Rossi	ITA	Monster Energy Yamaha MotoGP	166
8	Jack Miller	AUS	Pramac Racing	149
9	Cal Crutchlow	GBR	LCR Honda CASTROL	133
10	Franco Morbidelli	ITA	Petronas Yamaha SRT	115
11	Pol Espargaró	SPA	Red Bull KTM Factory Racing	94
12	Joan Mir	SPA	Team SUZUKI ECSTAR	83
13	Takaaki Nakagami	JPN	LCR Honda IDEMITSU	74
14	Aleix Espargaró	SPA	Aprilia Racing Team Gresini	56
15	Francesco Bagnaia	ITA	Pramac Racing	54
16	Andrea Iannone	ITA	Aprilia Racing Team Gresini	43
17	Miguel Oliveira	POR	Red Bull KTM Tech 3	33
18	Johann Zarco	FRA	LCR Honda IDEMITSU	30
19	Jorge Lorenzo	SPA	Repsol Honda Team	25
20	Tito Rabat	SPA	Reale Avintia Racing	18
21	Stefan Bradl	GER	Team HRC	16
22	Michele Pirro	ITA	Ducati Team	9
23	Hafizh Syahrin	MAL	Red Bull KTM Tech 3	8
24	Sylvain Guintoli	FRA	Team SUZUKI ECSTAR	7
25	Karel Abraham	CZE	Reale Avintia Racing	7
26	Mika Kallio	FIN	Red Bull KTM Factory Racing	3
27	Bradley Smith	GBR	Aprilia Factory Racing	

11 POL ESPARGARÓ
Turned the bike upside down after struggling in Japan and Australia, then switched to an old engine configuration, all without success. Struggled with grip and suspension pump on the hot, greasy track

12 FRANCESCO BAGNAIA
Was confused and frustrated by a serious lack of rear grip, which prevented him taking advantage of the Ducati's horsepower. His fastest race lap was no better than his best lap from the opening FP1 session.

13 ALEIX ESPARGARÓ
Started from 14th and was unable to move forward much from there. Spent much of the race with two faster bikes – Bagnaia's Ducati and Espargaró's KTM – so he was unable to ride the race and pace that he wanted.

14 JORGE LORENZO
His gap to the winner was about half what it had been in Australia, so that was a positive. Was four seconds off his goal of a 30-second gap to the winner. Struggled with turbulence from other bikes in the early laps.

15 MIKA KALLIO
Made it into the championship points for the second time since his return as Zarco's replacement. Couldn't get the best out of his tyres and couldn't stay with his rivals through the many fast sections of the track.

16 HAFIZH SYAHRIN
One year after his triumphant top-ten finish at Sepang on an M1 the local hero had the usual demanding race on his RC16. Tried to go with Lorenzo and Kallio but simply didn't have enough speed to do that.

17 KAREL ABRAHAM
The Czech rider ended up last after a couple of incidents with rivals. Had a torrid start to the race – collided with Kallio which put him in last-place - then ran off the track and into the gravel while riding with Lorenzo.

DNF JOHANN ZARCO
After the horrid Phillip Island weather Sepang gave Zarco a chance to get to grips with his 2018 RC213V. He did very well: qualified ninth and was running ninth in the closing stages when Mir took him out.

DNF CAL CRUTCHLOW
From hero at Phillip Island to zero at Sepang. Had no grip in the race, so he was locking the rear, which then caused him to lock the front. Fell at the hairpin, his first fall since he crashed out of the San Marino GP.

DNF ANDREA IANNONE
Chased Bagnaia for a points-scoring result, until he lost the front at the tight Turn Nine at half distance. Blamed the fall on excessive front tyre pressure, caused by overheating the tyre while drafting rivals.

DNS MIGUEL OLIVEIRA
Went out in FP1, six days after his huge Phillip Island accident, but couldn't ride, so withdrew from the race and flew to Europe for surgery on his right shoulder, first damaged when he got taken out at Silverstone.

DNS TITO RABAT
Withdrew from the Australian GP due to a right hand injury and decided not to compete at Sepang. Instead he flew home to Spain, where he began rehabilitation work to get as strong as possible for Valencia.

MICHELIN
REPSOL
HONDA
Satu HATI
MICHELIN
YUASA
alpinestars
MARQUEZ

GRAN PREMIO MOTUL DE LA COMUNITAT VALENCIANA
CIRCUIT RICARDO TORMO
15/16/17 NOVEMBER

Márquez pops the podium prosecco for the 18th time in 2019 and is kind enough to share it with mechanic Javier Ortiz

MÁRQUEZ ENDS 2019 ON A HIGH

Conditions were tricky at Valencia, but Márquez won anyway at the end of a weekend dominated by paddock gossip

MotoGP arrived at Valencia expecting a quiet weekend – the traditional season-ending fireworks excluded. After all, the MotoGP, Moto2 and Moto3 riders' and constructors' titles had all been decided, so this was merely the last race before testing for the 2020 season commenced two days later.

All that changed on Thursday morning when Jorge Lorenzo dropped his retirement bombshell. The news even caught Repsol Honda team-mate Marc Márquez by surprise as he ate his breakfast in the HRC hospitality unit.

The news was a surprise, but not a shock. Lorenzo had been haunted by his Assen back injuries since he returned to action at Silverstone. The paddock isn't a sentimental place, so the first question on most people's minds didn't concern Lorenzo's plans for retirement but who would replace him?

Cal Crutchlow, Álex Márquez, Takaaki Nakagami and Johann Zarco were the names churning around the rumour mill. And then there were more rumours thrown into the mill: Zarco to replace Jack Miller at Pramac Ducati, while Miller would replace Danilo Petrucci in the factory team.

"I think a lot of rumours get made up when it's a slow weekend," said Miller. "I saw on the internet a photo of me talking with

CLOCKWISE, FROM TOP LEFT *Lorenzo's swansong caused a stir; Viñales hurries through the late autumn sunshine; Crutchlow ended the season in the gravel; Miller's ride was his best-ever; the Espargaró brothers head out for a fun family feud; the hunter and the hunted, again; Rossi didn't have a great end to his 20th premier-class season; Miller keeps Rins and Dovizioso at bay; burning rubber through Turn 13.*

'I UNDERSTOOD THE WIND WAS PUSHING HARD AT TURNS SIX AND 11'

MARC MÁRQUEZ

Davide [Tardozzi, Ducati's factory team manager] between the trucks. The caption said we were talking about my 2020 contract, but it was just Davide telling me not to destroy my rear tyre."

In the race Miller certainly didn't destroy his rear tyre. He chased home Márquez and Fabio Quartararo, finishing just 3.3 seconds behind the winner. In some ways it was the most impressive ride of the year.

"This weekend has been a real statement of what we've learned throughout this season," said the Aussie after his fifth podium of 2019, achieved in very tricky conditions.

Valencia may be MotoGP's slowest racetrack but that doesn't make it easy, especially when a chill autumnal wind blows across the circuit and the track measures a wintry 16 degrees - a mere 28 degrees cooler than Sepang. Valencia is further complicated by its very asymmetric anti-clockwise layout, which makes the few right-handers particularly treacherous.

These were the big concerns floating through the minds of Márquez, Quartararo, Miller and the rest as they sat on the grid awaiting the start. Most of them had watched the earlier Moto2 and Moto3 races, which claimed a total of 16 crashes. They all knew they would be riding a knife edge as they worked to get their tyres up to a temperature that gave them enough grip and enough feel.

"I saw some strange crashes in Moto2," said Márquez, whose victory sealed the triple crown of riders', constructors' and teams' titles for Honda. "So I went into pit lane to check the wind direction and I immediately understood that the wind was pushing very hard at Turns Six and 11, so I was a bit careful at those corners because it was easy to lose the front."

Márquez didn't look like he was taking things easy. He got a bad start from the front row, completed the first lap in fifth, then overtook Andrea Dovizioso, Álex Rins and Miller on lap two. It took him another seven laps to catch Quartararo and sweep past him at Turn 11.

Both of his closest pursuers struggled with the south westerly wind. Miller most of all. "Turn Six was very bad and I nearly crashed between Turns 11 and 12, completely straight up and down. It was quite scary."

Some people had pole-starter Quartararo down as race favourite, but not the man himself. "We are really good in qualifying but we knew Marc had a much better pace than us," said the 20-year-old. "I wasn't even thinking about victory, just the podium."

Miller occasionally edged closer to Quartararo, encouraged by Dovizioso, who was getting closer in fourth, the Italian in turn trying to keep Rins at bay. "It was a fast race and the boys were pushing," added Miller. "But it kind of makes you spin a bit when you're chewing the handlebars and you see Marc cruising ahead!"

LORENZO SAYS HIS GOODBYES

Three-time MotoGP king Jorge Lorenzo decided to retire after a torrid, injury-marred season, during which he struggled to adapt to the RC213V that dominated the championship with Márquez on board.

By Barcelona he was making progress, but the day after his first-lap crash in the race he fell heavily during testing and four days later had another huge crash during FP1 at Assen.

That was the moment that finished a career which started on his 15th birthday at Jerez in 2002, included 297 Grand Prix starts, five world titles and 68 victories. Only Valentino Rossi,

At the finish Dovizioso was nine tenths behind the Pramac GP19 and less than two tenths in front of Rins, whose result was largely thanks to a lightning-fast getaway which took him from eighth on the grid to third at the first corner.

Sepang winner Maverick Viñales was the surprise of the race. His pace during practice suggested he would be in the podium fight, but once again he struggled with rear grip. At least he secured third overall, albeit with half the points of the champion.

Márquez's 12th victory of 2019 gave him a total of 420 points, an all-time record. And he finished the season 151 points ahead of runner-up Dovizioso, another all-time record, bettering Valentino Rossi's 147-point advantage over Marco Melandri in 2005.

Rossi completed his 20th season in the premier-class in eighth place, a very significant 22.9 seconds behind the winner. The treacherous conditions were no doubt part of his problem. Turn Six alone claimed three victims in quick succession – Danilo Petrucci, Zarco and impressive first-timer Iker Lecuona. Zarco was lucky to escape with a sore ankle after Lecuona's KTM hit him in the gravel trap.

CLOCKWISE FROM TOP LEFT | *Álex Márquez started his MotoGP career in the post-race tests; the Márquez brothers and Lorenzo Dalla Porta celebrate their titles; Petrucci was one of several victims of the chilly conditions; Márquez was the oldest rider on the podium; Lecuona had an impressive MotoGP debut; pit lane greets Lorenzo at the end of his 297th and last Grand Prix.*

Giacomo Agostini, Ángel Nieto, Mike Hailwood and Márquez have won more GPs.

"The bike never felt natural to me, but I never lost hope, I kept working with the team, thinking that it was a matter of time before everything was in the right place," said Lorenzo. "Then when I was starting to see some light at the end of the tunnel I had a nasty crash in the Montmeló tests, then some days later I crashed again at Assen. I have to admit that when I was rolling through the gravel I thought to myself, 'okay Jorge, is this really worth it, after what I've achieved? I'm done with it; I don't want to race anymore.' But then I got home and decided to give it a try again. But the truth is from that moment the hill became so high for me that I wasn't able to find the motivation to keep trying to climb this mountain."

The two fractured vertebrae he sustained at Assen continued to trouble him, both physically and psychologically. No doubt he made the decision to retire and then changed his mind a hundred times between June and November. But when he crossed the Valencia finish line in 13th place all the emotions were positive.

"I felt happy, completely free," he said. "Now I want to sleep more, eat more, spend more time with my family and friends and travel the world."

He was last seen at Valencia at 4am on Monday morning, singing karaoke with Márquez in the post-MotoGP awards party.

19 | VALENCIA

GRAN PREMIO MOTUL DE LA COMUNITAT VALENCIANA
CIRCUIT RICARDO TORMO
15/16/17 NOVEMBER

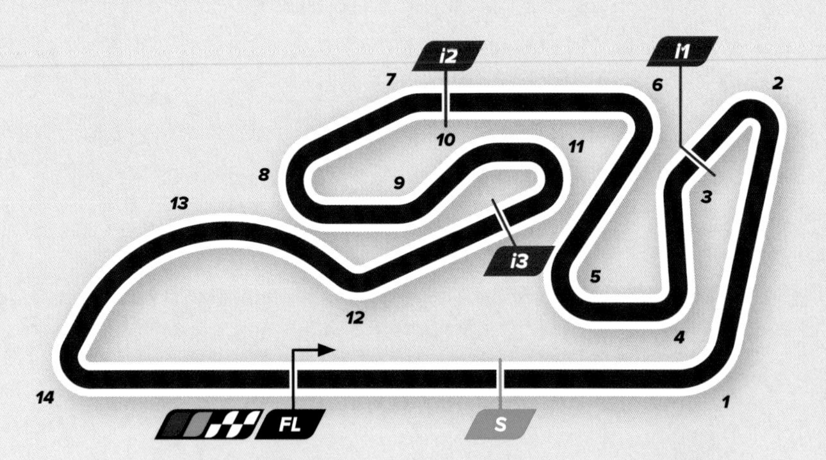

QUALIFYING RESULTS

	RIDER	NAT	TEAM	MACHINE	QP/TIME		GAP 1ST/PREV	
1	Fabio Quartararo	FRA	Petronas Yamaha SRT	YAMAHA	Q2	1'29.978		
2	Marc Márquez	SPA	Repsol Honda Team	HONDA	Q2	1'30.010	0.032	0.032
3	Jack Miller	AUS	Pramac Racing	DUCATI	Q2	1'30.086	0.108	0.076
4	Maverick Viñales	SPA	Monster Energy Yamaha MotoGP	YAMAHA	Q2	1'30.178	0.200	0.092
5	Franco Morbidelli	ITA	Petronas Yamaha SRT	YAMAHA	Q2	1'30.449	0.471	0.271
6	Andrea Dovizioso	ITA	Ducati Team	DUCATI	Q2	1'30.511	0.533	0.062
7	Joan Mir	SPA	Team SUZUKI ECSTAR	SUZUKI	Q2	1'30.573	0.595	0.062
8	Álex Rins	SPA	Team SUZUKI ECSTAR	SUZUKI	Q2	1'30.595	0.617	0.022
9	Cal Crutchlow	GBR	LCR Honda CASTROL	HONDA	Q2	1'30.726	0.748	0.131
10	Danilo Petrucci	ITA	Ducati Team	DUCATI	Q2	1'30.771	0.793	0.045
11	Pol Espargaró	SPA	Red Bull KTM Factory Racing	KTM	Q2	1'30.908	0.930	0.137
12	Valentino Rossi	ITA	Monster Energy Yamaha MotoGP	YAMAHA	Q2	1'30.954	0.976	0.046
13	Johann Zarco	FRA	LCR Honda IDEMITSU	HONDA	Q1	1'30.826	*0.288	0.283
14	Michele Pirro	ITA	Ducati Team	DUCATI	Q1	1'30.949	*0.411	0.123
15	Aleix Espargaró	SPA	Aprilia Racing Team Gresini	APRILIA	Q1	1'30.972	*0.434	0.023
16	Jorge Lorenzo	SPA	Repsol Honda Team	HONDA	Q1	1'31.295	*0.757	0.323
17	Mika Kallio	FIN	Red Bull KTM Factory Racing	KTM	Q1	1'31.383	*0.845	0.088
18	Tito Rabat	SPA	Reale Avintia Racing	DUCATI	Q1	1'31.507	*0.969	0.124
19	Iker Lecuona	SPA	Red Bull KTM Tech 3	KTM	Q1	1'31.658	*1.120	0.151
20	Andrea Iannone	ITA	Aprilia Racing Team Gresini	APRILIA	Q1	1'31.714	*1.176	0.056
21	Karel Abraham	CZE	Reale Avintia Racing	DUCATI	Q1	1'31.815	*1.277	0.101
22	Hafizh Syahrin	MAL	Red Bull KTM Tech 3	KTM	Q1	1'31.839	*1.301	0.024

** Gap to the fastest rider in the Q1 session   ** Went forward from Q1 to Q2   Track severity = Wear + Temperature + Load*

GRAND PRIX INFORMATION

TRACK INFORMATION			
2019 WINNER	Marc Márquez		
CIRCUIT LENGTH	4.0 km	2.49 miles	
LAPS	27		
RACE DISTANCE	108.1 km	67.2 miles	
ALL TIME LAP RECORD	1'29.401	161.2 Km/h	Jorge Lorenzo (2016)
BEST RACE LAP	1'31.116	158.2 Km/h	Marc Márquez (2019)
RACE CONDITION	Dry		
AIR	15°C		
HUMIDITY	44%		
GROUND	16°C		

TYRE SELECTION

FRONT	
SOFT	WHITE
MEDIUM	GREY
HARD	YELLOW

REAR	
SOFT	WHITE
MEDIUM	GREY
HARD	YELLOW

< MILD   TRACK SEVERITY   SEVERE >

1 MARC MÁRQUEZ
Quartararo looked like he had the pace to win but the world champion was relentless in his pursuit, as always. This time he didn't shadow the Frenchman, as he had done at Misano and Buriram, but quickly got ahead and disappeared.

2 FABIO QUARTARARO
Grabbed the lead from Miller at the second corner and looked like he might finally escape for his first MotoGP victory. In fact he knew that Márquez had the pace to come and get him, so he was happy enough with second.

3 JACK MILLER
Didn't want to lead from the start but with the Ducati holeshot device couldn't help it. Once he was in third he settled into a superb rhythm, probably his best-ever, so that Dovizioso never even got close enough to attack.

4 ANDREA DOVIZIOSO
Started from sixth and knew he would have to fight all the way if he wanted to finish his season on the podium. His attempts to catch Miller weren't helped by the fact that he had to use defending lines to keep ahead of Rins.

5 ÁLEX RINS
From eighth on the grid to third at the first corner, then dropped two places when Márquez and Dovizioso blasted past on the start/finish. His main aim was to take third overall from Viñales. He didn't make it, by only six points.

6 MAVERICK VIÑALES
His Yamaha was struck by the old rear-grip issues. These were a worry because although his practice pace suggested he might challenge for the podium his biggest concern was keeping Rins in sight to take third overall.

7 JOAN MIR
Couldn't find the same feeling that he had enjoyed during Friday and Saturday, so didn't get to end his rookie season on a high. Spent most of the race chasing Viñales but never managed to get within a second of the Yamaha.

8 VALENTINO ROSSI
A poor qualifying strategy put him 12th, his third worst grid slot of the year. Started well but couldn't make any impression on those ahead because, like Viñales, he struggled to find enough rear grip from the cold asphalt.

9 ALEIX ESPARGARÓ
Scored his second top-ten in three races after a great battle with his younger brother. At the flag they were separated by 0.27 seconds! This was a good result after he had three crashes within four hours during Saturday practice.

10 POL ESPARGARÓ
Wasn't happy about getting beaten by an Aprilia, even if his brother was on it. Didn't have the turning, grip or traction to deal with the easier-handling Italian V4. Missed KTM's first top-ten championship finish by 15 points.

RACE LAP CHART

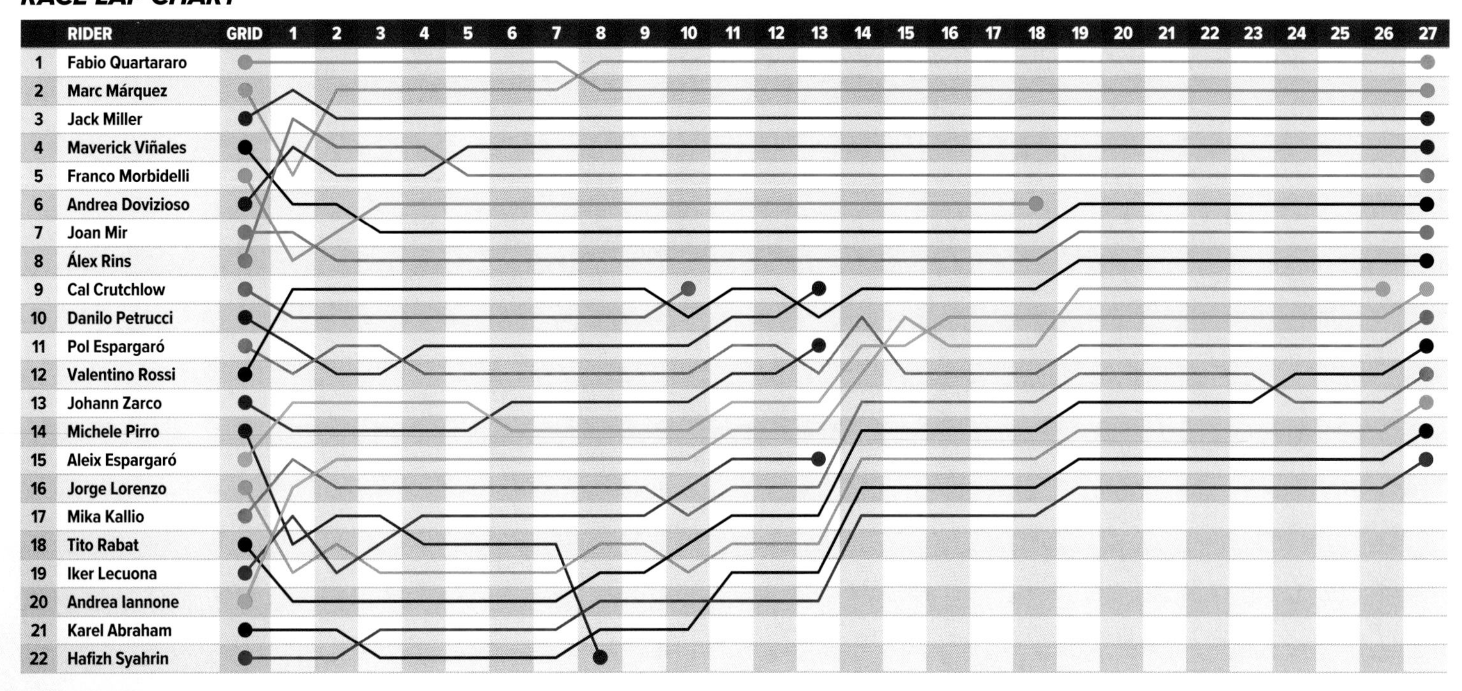

RACE RESULTS

	RIDER	NAT	TEAM	MACHINE	TIME	+GAP	TYRES
1	Marc Márquez	SPA	Repsol Honda Team	HONDA	41'21.469		M/H
2	Fabio Quartararo	FRA	Petronas Yamaha SRT	YAMAHA	41'22.495	1.026	M/H
3	Jack Miller	AUS	Pramac Racing	DUCATI	41'23.878	2.409	M/H
4	Andrea Dovizioso	ITA	Ducati Team	DUCATI	41'24.795	3.326	M/H
5	Álex Rins	SPA	Team SUZUKI ECSTAR	SUZUKI	41'24.977	3.508	M/S
6	Maverick Viñales	SPA	Monster Energy Yamaha MotoGP	YAMAHA	41'30.298	8.829	M/H
7	Joan Mir	SPA	Team SUZUKI ECSTAR	SUZUKI	41'32.091	10.622	M/S
8	Valentino Rossi	ITA	Monster Energy Yamaha MotoGP	YAMAHA	41'44.461	22.992	M/H
9	Aleix Espargaró	SPA	Aprilia Racing Team Gresini	APRILIA	41'54.173	32.704	M/S
10	Pol Espargaro	SPA	Red Bull KTM Factory Racing	KTM	41'54.442	32.973	M/H
11	Tito Rabat	SPA	Reale Avintia Racing	DUCATI	42'04.264	42.795	M/S
12	Mika Kallio	FIN	Red Bull KTM Factory Racing	KTM	42'07.201	45.732	M/S
13	Jorge Lorenzo	SPA	Repsol Honda Team	HONDA	42'12.513	51.044	M/S
14	Karel Abraham	CZE	Reale Avintia Racing	DUCATI	42'26.340	64.871	M/S
15	Hafizh Syahrin	MAL	Red Bull KTM Tech 3	KTM	42'37.956	76.487	M/S
NC	Andrea Iannone	ITA	Aprilia Racing Team Gresini	APRILIA	40'20.804	1 lap	M/S
NC	Franco Morbidelli	ITA	Petronas Yamaha SRT	YAMAHA	27'39.166	9 laps	M/H
NC	Danilo Petrucci	ITA	Ducati Team	DUCATI	20'04.178	14 laps	M/S
NC	Johann Zarco	FRA	LCR Honda IDEMITSU	HONDA	20'08.462	14 laps	M/H
NC	Iker Lecuona	SPA	Red Bull KTM Tech 3	KTM	20'15.159	14 laps	M/S
NC	Cal Crutchlow	GBR	LCR Honda CASTROL	HONDA	15'26.863	17 laps	M/H
NC	Michele Pirro	ITA	Ducati Team	DUCATI	12'47.135	19 laps	M/S

CHAMPIONSHIP STANDINGS

	RIDER	NAT	TEAM	PTS
1	Marc Márquez	SPA	Repsol Honda Team	420
2	Andrea Dovizioso	ITA	Ducati Team	269
3	Maverick Viñales	SPA	Monster Energy Yamaha MotoGP	211
4	Álex Rins	SPA	Team SUZUKI ECSTAR	205
5	Fabio Quartararo	FRA	Petronas Yamaha SRT	192
6	Danilo Petrucci	ITA	Ducati Team	176
7	Valentino Rossi	ITA	Monster Energy Yamaha MotoGP	174
8	Jack Miller	AUS	Pramac Racing	165
9	Cal Crutchlow	GBR	LCR Honda CASTROL	133
10	Franco Morbidelli	ITA	Petronas Yamaha SRT	115
11	Pol Espargaró	SPA	Red Bull KTM Factory Racing	100
12	Joan Mir	SPA	Team SUZUKI ECSTAR	92
13	Takaaki Nakagami	JPN	LCR Honda IDEMITSU	74
14	Aleix Espargaró	SPA	Aprilia Racing Team Gresini	63
15	Francesco Bagnaia	ITA	Pramac Racing	54
16	Andrea Iannone	ITA	Aprilia Racing Team Gresini	43
17	Miguel Oliveira	POR	Red Bull KTM Tech 3	33
18	Johann Zarco	FRA	LCR Honda IDEMITSU	30
19	Jorge Lorenzo	SPA	Repsol Honda Team	28
20	Tito Rabat	SPA	Reale Avintia Racing	23
21	Stefan Bradl	GER	Team HRC	16
22	Michele Pirro	ITA	Ducati Team	9
23	Hafizh Syahrin	MAL	Red Bull KTM Tech 3	9
24	Karel Abraham	CZE	Reale Avintia Racing	9
25	Sylvain Guintoli	FRA	Team SUZUKI ECSTAR	7
26	Mika Kallio	FIN	Red Bull KTM Factory Racing	7
27	Bradley Smith	GBR	Aprilia Factory Racing	
28	Iker Lecuona	SPA	Red Bull KTM Tech 3	

11 TITO RABAT
Ended the final race of his comeback season with his best finish since July's German Grand Prix, albeit largely thanks to the hefty crash rate. Was happy with his pace and the result, even if he spent most of the race all alone.

12 MIKA KALLIO
The high number of DNFs gave the Finn his best result since he took over Zarco's RC16s at September's Aragon GP. Like many other riders he struggled to get good feel and grip from his tyres in the cold conditions.

13 JORGE LORENZO
Had felt much happier in the heat of Sepang, where he could feel his tyres properly, but with little feel in the wintry conditions at Valencia he didn't feel confident enough to ride any faster than 1.7 seconds off his team-mate.

14 KAREL ABRAHAM
Had a bad start with technical problems that lost him time and places in the early laps. Once he got ahead of Syahrin he had a lonely race behind Lorenzo, but was happy enough to take his sixth points score of the season.

15 HAFIZH SYAHRIN
Completed his two seasons in MotoGP by scoring the last world championship point. In typical Syahrin style he apologised profusely to his crew for not bringing home the results he had hoped for during 2019.

DNF ANDREA IANNONE
Started from 20th and made great progress to pass the Espargaró brothers and move into ninth with eight laps to go. But without their bikes ahead of him to warm his front tyre he lost the front between Turns Nine and Ten.

DNF FRANCO MORBIDELLI
Got into a strong and fast groove. Passed Mir and Viñales, then set his sights on Rins. Crashed at Turn Four, blaming the fall on the fact that he had no one in front of him to help keep his front tyre up to temperature.

DNF DANILO PETRUCCI
Like his team-mate he knew he needed a good result to win the teams' championship. But his holeshot device failed to engage and he was 11th after lap one. Passed Rossi for ninth at half-distance, then fell at the tricky Turn Six.

DNF JOHANN ZARCO
Knew it was going to be a long and difficult race. Was right on one point, not on the other. Lost the front at Turn Six moments after Petrucci and was then knocked over by the bike of Lecuona who fell just behind him.

DNF IKER LECUONA
Tech 3's 2020 Syahrin replacement was drafted in to replace Miguel Oliveira. The teenager did a sterling job all weekend, making it through Friday and Saturday without a single fall. Was in the points when he fell at Turn Six.

DNF CAL CRUTCHLOW
Had just passed Rossi and had his heart set on chasing down Mir when he lost the front going into the high-speed Turn One.

DNF MICHELE PIRRO
Ducati's test rider wasn't in good shape for his third race of 2019. Had nausea and pulled in when his blood pressure dropped.

DNF FRANCESCO BAGNAIA
Had a freak fall at the end of pit lane during the FP3 session which left him with concussion and a micro fracture in his left wrist.

THE RESULTS

Official MotoGP Timing by **TISSOT**
www.motogp.com

MotoGP™ WORLD CHAMPIONSHIP CLASSIFICATION

	RIDER	NAT	POINTS	QAT	ARG	AME	ESP	FRA	ITA	CAT	NED	GER	CZE	AUT	GBR	RSM	ARA	THA	JPN	AUS	MAL	VAL
1	Marc Márquez	SPA	420	20	25	-	25	25	20	25	20	25	25	20	20	25	25	25	25	25	20	25
2	Andrea Dovizioso	ITA	269	25	16	13	13	20	16	-	13	11	20	25	-	10	20	13	16	9	16	13
3	Maverick Viñales	SPA	211	9	-	5	16	-	10	-	25	20	6	11	16	16	13	16	13	-	25	10
4	Álex Rins	SPA	205	13	11	25	20	6	13	13	-	-	13	10	25	-	7	11	9	7	11	11
5	Fabio Quartararo	FRA	192	0	8	9	-	8	6	20	16	-	9	16	-	20	11	20	20	-	9	20
6	Danilo Petrucci	ITA	176	10	10	10	11	16	25	16	10	13	8	7	9	6	4	7	7	-	7	-
7	Valentino Rossi	ITA	174	11	20	20	10	11	-	-	-	8	10	13	13	13	8	8	-	8	13	8
8	Jack Miller	AUS	165	-	13	16	-	13	-	11	7	10	16	-	8	7	16	2	6	16	8	16
9	Cal Crutchlow	GBR	133	16	3	-	8	7	8	-	9	16	11	-	10	-	10	4	11	20	-	-
10	Franco Morbidelli	ITA	115	5	-	11	9	9	-	-	11	7	-	6	11	11	-	10	10	5	10	-
11	Pol Espargaró	SPA	100	4	6	8	3	10	7	9	5	4	5	-	7	9	-	3	5	4	5	6
12	Joan Mir	SPA	92	8	-	0	-	0	4	10	8	9	-	-	-	8	2	9	8	11	6	9
13	Takaaki Nakagami	JPN	74	7	9	6	7	-	11	8	-	2	7	5	0	0	6	6	0	-	-	-
14	Aleix Espargaró	SPA	63	6	7	-	5	4	5	-	4	-	0	2	-	4	9	-	1	6	3	7
15	Francesco Bagnaia	ITA	54	-	2	7	-	-	-	-	2	0	4	9	5	-	0	5	3	13	4	-
16	Andrea Iannone	ITA	43	2	0	4	-	-	1	5	6	3	0	0	6	-	5	1	-	10	-	-
17	Miguel Oliveira	POR	33	0	5	2	0	1	0	4	3	0	3	8	-	0	3	0	4	-	-	-
18	Johann Zarco	FRA	30	1	1	3	2	3	0	6	-	-	2	4	-	5	-	-	-	3	-	-
19	Jorge Lorenzo	SPA	28	3	4	-	4	5	3	-	-	-	-	-	2	2	0	0	0	0	2	3
20	Tito Rabat	SPA	23	0	-	1	1	-	-	7	0	5	0	-	0	3	1	0	-	-	-	5
21	Stefan Bradl	GER	16	-	-	-	6	-	-	-	-	6	1	3	-	-	-	-	-	-	-	-
22	Michele Pirro	ITA	9	-	-	-	-	-	9	-	-	-	-	-	-	-	-	-	-	-	-	-
23	Hafizh Syahrin	MAL	9	0	0	0	0	2	-	-	1	0	-	-	3	1	0	0	0	1	0	1
24	Karel Abraham	CZE	9	0	-	0	0	-	2	-	0	1	0	1	1	0	0	0	0	2	0	2
25	Sylvain Guintoli	FRA	7	-	-	-	-	-	-	3	-	-	0	-	4	-	-	-	0	-	-	-
26	Mika Kallio	FIN	7	-	-	-	-	-	-	-	-	-	-	-	-	-	0	-	2	-	1	4
27	Bradley Smith	GBR	0	7	-	-	-	0	-	-	-	-	-	-	-	-	0	-	-	-	-	-
28	Iker Lecuona	SPA	0	-	-	-	-	-	-	-	-	-	-	-	-	-	-	-	-	-	-	0

CONSTRUCTORS

	MANUFACTURER	POINTS	QAT	ARG	AME	ESP	FRA	ITA	CAT	NED	GER	CZE	AUT	GBR	RSM	ARA	THA	JPN	AUS	MAL	VAL
1	Honda	426	20	25	6	25	25	20	25	20	25	25	20	20	25	25	25	25	25	20	25
2	Yamaha	321	11	20	20	16	11	10	20	25	20	10	16	16	20	13	20	20	8	25	20
3	Ducati	318	25	16	16	13	20	25	16	13	13	20	25	9	10	20	13	16	16	16	16
4	Suzuki	234	13	11	25	20	6	13	13	8	9	13	10	25	8	7	11	9	11	11	11
5	KTM	111	4	6	8	3	10	7	9	5	4	5	8	7	9	3	3	5	4	5	6
6	Aprilia	88	6	7	4	5	4	5	5	6	3	-	2	6	4	9	1	1	10	3	7

TEAMS

	TEAM	POINTS	QAT	ARG	AME	ESP	FRA	ITA	CAT	NED	GER	CZE	AUT	GBR	RSM	ARA	THA	JPN	AUS	MAL	VAL
1	Repsol Honda Team	458	23	29	-	29	30	23	25	20	31	26	23	22	27	25	25	25	25	22	28
2	Ducati Team	445	35	26	23	24	36	41	16	23	24	28	32	9	16	24	20	23	9	23	13
3	Monster Energy Yamaha MotoGP	385	20	20	25	26	11	10	-	25	28	16	24	29	29	21	24	13	8	38	18
4	Petronas Yamaha SRT	307	5	8	20	9	17	6	20	27	7	9	22	11	31	11	30	30	5	19	20
5	Team SUZUKI ECSTAR	301	21	11	25	20	6	17	23	8	9	13	10	29	8	9	20	17	18	17	20
6	Pramac Racing	219	-	15	23	-	13	-	11	9	10	20	9	13	7	16	7	9	29	12	16
7	LCR Honda	210	23	12	6	15	7	19	8	9	18	18	5	10	-	16	10	11	23	-	-
8	Red Bull KTM Factory Racing	134	5	7	11	5	13	7	15	5	4	7	4	7	14	-	3	7	4	6	10
9	Aprilia Racing Team Gresini	106	8	7	4	5	4	6	5	10	3	-	2	6	4	14	1	1	16	3	7
10	Red Bull KTM Tech 3	42	-	5	2	-	3	-	4	4	-	3	8	3	1	3	-	4	1	-	1
11	Reale Avintia Racing	32	-	-	1	1	-	2	7	-	6	-	1	1	3	1	-	-	2	-	7

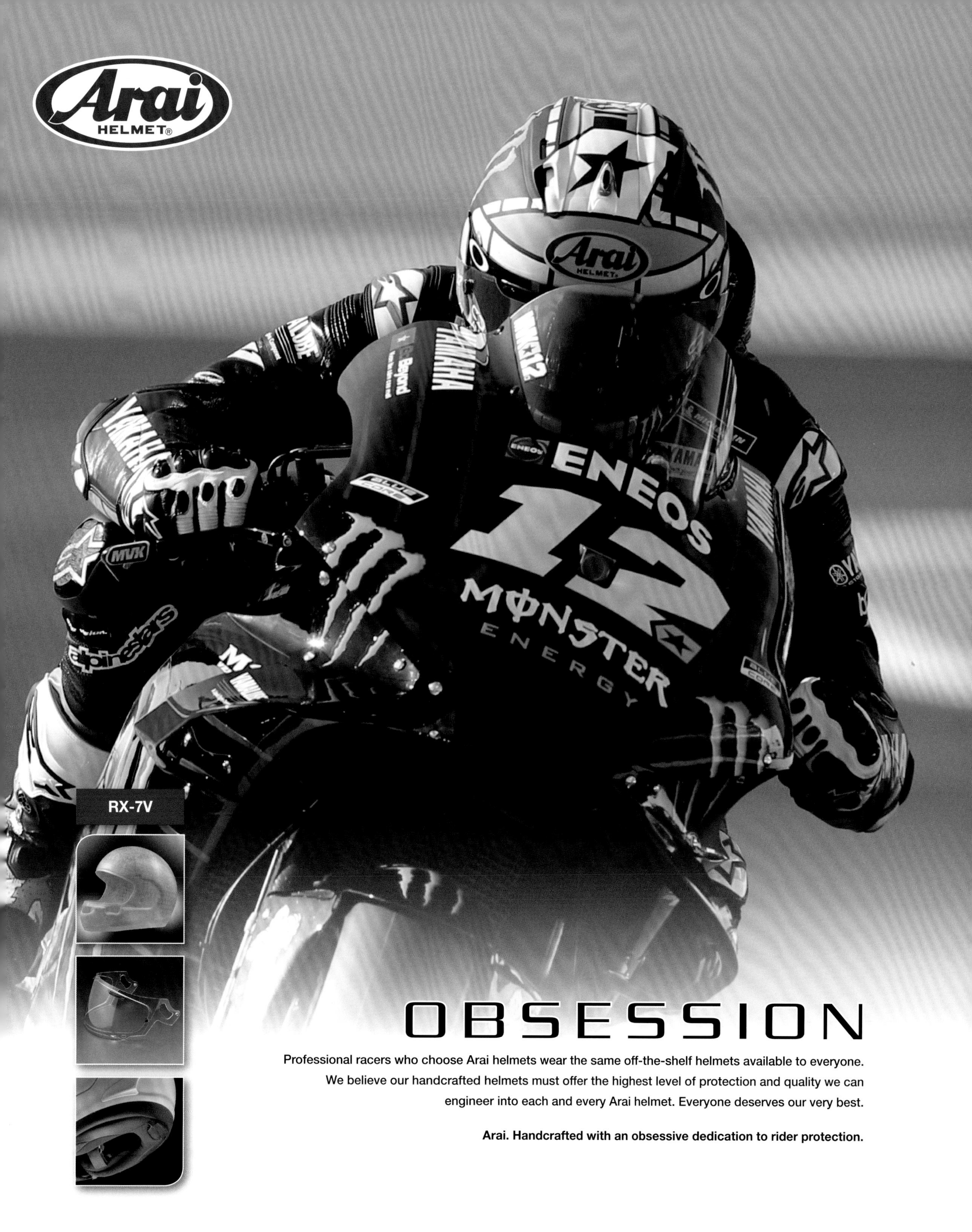
Arai HELMET®
RX-7V
OBSESSION
Professional racers who choose Arai helmets wear the same off-the-shelf helmets available to everyone.
We believe our handcrafted helmets must offer the highest level of protection and quality we can engineer into each and every Arai helmet. Everyone deserves our very best.
Arai. Handcrafted with an obsessive dedication to rider protection.
araihelmet.eu
THE CONSISTENT PURSUIT OF GAINS IN PROTECTION

ÁLEX MÁRQUEZ: TRIUMPH'S FIRST WORLD CHAMPION

Faster Triumph engines and fatter Dunlop tyres made Moto2 better than ever in 2019. Álex Márquez won the title, but it was a near-run thing

The 2019 Moto2 world championship was a season of three eras: the Lorenzo Baldassarri era, the Álex Márquez era and the Brad Binder era.

MotoGP's intermediate class underwent its biggest technical change since 2010, when it was transformed from an open 250cc category to Grand Prix racing's first spec-engine class. In 2019 out went Honda's CBR600 four-cylinder engine and in came Triumph's 765cc triple. Also new was Magneti software, introduced to educate up-and-coming riders in the ways of electronic rider controls.

Whenever there's a major rewrite of technical rules there's always a period of instability, as riders and teams grapple with new challenges.

After the first few races of the Triumph-powered championship, Baldassarri (Flexbox HP 40 Kalex) seemed favourite to make it three VR46 Moto2 champions in a row. The 22-year-old Italian won three of the first four races on his Kalex, entered by double 250cc world champion Sito Pons.

But everything changed when the Moto2 paddock returned to Europe. At Jerez, Dunlop equipped the grid with its bigger-section rear slick, designed to handle the extra power and torque of the larger-capacity Triumph engine. Riders had

CLOCKWISE, FROM TOP LEFT *Luthi leads Márquez at Le Mans as Locatelli goes flying; Martin's crew fix his crashed KTM; Fernandez was a revelation, most of the time; Luthi was delighted to be back after a bruising rookie MotoGP season; Kalex took its seventh consecutive constructors title; Navarro and Fernandez were the new kids in town; Márquez with team owner Marc van der Straten, before his move to MotoGP; Gardner was occasionally on fire; Binder knows how to ride out of shape.*

evaluated the tyre during pre-season testing, but they contested the first three races with the 2018 rear tyre, designed for the CBR600 engine.

Baldassarri won again at Jerez – the last time he stood on the podium all year. The man on the charge was Márquez (EG 0,0 Marc VDS Kalex). The 23-year-old younger brother of the MotoGP king qualified a close second at Jerez and had the pace to win, but was taken out at the first corner.

Two weeks later at Le Mans he dominated, taking over from early leader and COTA victor Tom Luthi (Dynavolt Intact GP Kalex), while learning plenty from the Swiss rider who had returned to Moto2 after a torrid 2018 in MotoGP.

"At Le Mans I did three laps behind Tom and I learned a lot," revealed Márquez. "I said, wow, I need to pick up the bike and make some metres, because he was doing that so well. With the bigger contact patch from the new rear tyre and the pick-up, the acceleration is really, really good."

Márquez's first win since Motegi 2017 made history: it was the first time that brothers had won the main and intermediate races on the same day. He won again at Mugello and Barcelona and was on his way.

"With the extra torque of the Triumph engine my riding style comes more naturally," he explained. "I have corner speed when I need to use corner speed, but in slow corners, where I need to stop the bike and pick it up, this engine works much better for my lines and for my style."

The real key to Márquez's new-found speed was the fatter rear tyre. "During pre-season we worked a lot with Dunlop's new 200 rear. All riders had only one or two of these tyres. Most of them focused on time attacks. But then the tyre dropped quite a lot and it was difficult to keep the lap time, so we worked a lot on race simulations."

Márquez topped the podium again at Sachsenring and Brno, a perfect run of what should've been five straight wins spoiled by a DNF at Assen, where he got wiped out by Baldassarri. That let the Italian's team-mate Augusto Fernandez through for his first Grand Prix victory and moved Luthi into the championship lead, for all of seven days.

Kalex was even more dominant than it had been during Moto2's Honda years. The German company won the first ten races of 2019, its conventional aluminium beam frame working perfectly with the taller, torquier Triumph triple.

Crucially, Márquez found he could race with a softer front tyre, a vital benefit for someone who had crashed 71 times during the previous four Moto2 seasons. But this improvement was thanks to engine-braking more than chassis performance.

"The soft front tyre gives me a lot more feedback, especially on edge grip," explained Márquez, who almost halved his crash rate

CLOCKWISE FROM TOP LEFT *Binder shows rookie team-mate Martin the way; Gardner takes out Márquez at Jerez; Fernandez and Binder get down to it; Marini was back to his winning ways in Thailand; Speed Up's carbon-fibre swingarm caused controversy; KTM built seven different chassis to get Binder winning again; the parc fermé at Sepang; Marini looks big on a Moto2 bike; champ Márquez smoking in Malaysia.*

from 2018. "It's frame geometry, plus the extra engine-braking and balance of the Triumph engine. With the Honda engine it was difficult to stop the bike with the soft front, but with the Triumph you can manage better, so the soft front tyre works."

The 2019 season changed eras for the second time a week after Márquez's first victory at Brno. Binder (Red Bull KTM Ajo) had had a disastrous start to Moto2's Triumph age, but despite KTM announcing its withdrawal from the class the Austrian factory put its full weight behind Binder's team and started moving forward. At Assen the 24-year-old South African scored his first podium of the year and at Red Bull Ring he took his first win.

A huge amount of work had gone into that success. KTM equipped Binder with no fewer than seven different chassis during 2019. The seventh arrived at Brno, but was worse than the previous iteration, so Binder reverted to version number six at Red Bull Ring and stuck with that for the rest of the year.

"It was tough," said Binder, who in July signed to ride KTM MotoGP bikes in 2020. "At the first pre-season test I came in after my first run and said, 'guys, we need to go back to the drawing board because this thing doesn't work'. As soon as you tipped over onto full lean the rear wheel literally started to jump, then the whole bike started."

Binder was on chassis number three when he lined up for the season-opening Qatar GP. Only when he received version six at Assen did he really start to race. Until then he had struggled so much to control his bike that he kept running into rivals.

"The Kalex guys could open the gas and carry corner speed," he explained. "If I tried to carry corner speed I chattered my brains out, so I couldn't ride amongst the other guys. At the beginning of the year I looked like an idiot because I was riding into everybody."

Two weeks after Red Bull Ring the championship changed again. Márquez was ahead at Silverstone when he slid off, allowing Fernandez through for his second win, ahead of the ever-improving Jorge Navarro (Beta Tools Speed Up) and Binder.

That loss of 25 points unnerved Márquez and he shifted into points-protection mode, while Binder won again at Aragon and finished second in Thailand to Luca Marini (SKY Racing Team VR46 Kalex), who was also getting into the groove for the first time with Triumph power. Four races to go and Binder had moved into third overall, 44 points behind Márquez and four behind Fernandez. The championship was on.

Two weeks after Buriram the situation changed yet again. Binder started well at Motegi – second fastest on Friday – but rear tyre issues hampered him in qualifying and again in the race, when he slumped home 12th. Márquez only managed sixth, but Binder's late-season had stalled. For the moment, at least.

The next Sunday at Phillip Island Binder won again, while Márquez struggled to eighth. Just two races to go and Márquez had 33 points over Binder and 28 over Luthi, who was also enjoying a late renaissance after major set-up changes to his Kalex. But both the leader's challengers were fast running out of time.

Márquez finally made the title his own at Sepang, with an ice-cool ride to second place in suffocating tropical heat, just behind Binder and just ahead of Luthi. The 2014 Moto3 champ had buckled at earlier races, but was rock solid when it mattered most. He also made history: the first rider to win both the Moto2 and Moto3 crowns.

The hopes of Binder and Luthi had been hurt by machine issues. Luthi's strong start to 2019 – second in Qatar and first at COTA – fizzled out when his team struggled to find a good set-up with Dunlop's bigger rear tyre. It wasn't until the post-Austrian GP tests at Red Bull Ring that he came good again.

Moto2's other stand-out riders of 2019 were Fernandez and Navarro, who inherited Fabio Quartararo's Speed Up ride. The top rookies were Navarro's team-mate Fabio Di Giannantonio (Beta Tools Speed Up), 2018 Moto3 champ Jorge Martin (Red Bull KTM Ajo) and Enea Bastianini (Italtrans Racing Team Kalex).

But really the rookie of the year was Triumph Motorcycles. The British marque provided a larger-capacity Moto2 engine with extra torque that the riders loved and which allowed them to use different cornering lines. The 765 triple made 130 horsepower and propelled riders beyond 301kmh/187mph at Phillip Island.

The 765 had a 14,000rpm rev-limiter on upshifts, but many riders exceeded 15,000 on downshifts.

"Some of the guys are quite harsh with the engine," said Triumph's Steve Sargent, with a hint of understatement. "They are flat-out with the throttle down the straight and they're banging it down two gears while they've still got the throttle open!"

And yet Moto2 riders covered about 300,000km/186,000 miles in 2019 with no real engine issues. This was a remarkable performance from a forward-looking company that's very new to the white heat of Grand Prix racing.

Moto2™ WORLD CHAMPIONSHIP STANDING

	RIDER	NAT	MANUFACTURER	POINTS
1	Alex Márquez	SPA	KALEX	262
2	Brad Binder	RSA	KTM	259
3	Thomas Luthi	SWI	KALEX	250
4	Jorge Navarro	SPA	SPEED UP	226
5	Augusto Fernandez	SPA	KALEX	207
6	Luca Marini	ITA	KALEX	190
7	Lorenzo Baldassarri	ITA	KALEX	171
8	Marcel Schrotter	GER	KALEX	137
9	Fabio di Giannantonio	ITA	SPEED UP	108
10	Enea Bastianini	ITA	KALEX	97
11	Jorge Martin	SPA	KTM	94
12	Iker Lecuona	SPA	KTM	90
13	Xavi Vierge	SPA	KALEX	81
14	Tetsuta Nagashima	JPN	KALEX	78
15	Remy Gardner	AUS	KALEX	77
16	Sam Lowes	GBR	KALEX	66
17	Nicolo Bulega	ITA	KALEX	48
18	Andrea Locatelli	ITA	KALEX	46
19	Stefano Manzi	ITA	MV AGUSTA	39
20	Mattia Pasini	ITA	KALEX	35
21	Somkiat Chantra	THA	KALEX	23
22	Dominique Aegerter	SWI	MV AGUSTA	19
23	Marco Bezzecchi	ITA	KTM	17
24	Simone Corsi	ITA	NTS	10
25	Jake Dixon	GBR	KTM	7
26	Bo Bendsneyder	NED	NTS	7
27	Jesko Raffin	SWI	NTS	6
28	Joe Roberts	USA	KTM	4
29	Lukas Tulovic	GER	KTM	3
30	Khairul Idham Pawi	MAL	KALEX	3
31	Steven Odendaal	RSA	NTS	
32	Jonas Folger	GER	KALEX	
33	Philipp Oettl	GER	KTM	
34	Dimas Ekky Pratama	INA	KALEX	
35	Xavi Cardelus	AND	KTM	
36	Gabriele Ruiu	ITA	KALEX	
37	Adam Norrodin	MAL	KALEX	
38	Andi Farid Izdihar	INA	KALEX	
39	Teppei Nagoe	JPN	KALEX	
40	Tommaso Marcon	ITA	NTS	
41	Gerry Salim	INA	KALEX	
42	Sean Dylan Kelly	USA		

***LEFT TO RIGHT** | After Marc's eight-ball came Álex's bullseye; the eventual champion leads the early championship leader.*

TEAR UP THE RULE BOOK.
NEW
REDEFINING HYPERSPORT PERFORMANCE, EVEN IN THE WET.
The new SportSmart Mk3 hypersport tire has raised the bar in every aspect, changing the way you ride. With improved grip in the wet, increased mileage and enhanced all round performance. You can now go further, in more weather conditions, than ever before. Rules? What rules?
Find out more: dunlop.eu
SPORTSMART mk3
DUNLOP

DALLA PORTA: KING OF THE YOUNG GUNS

The action in Moto3 was as chaotic as ever – it took a man with a cool head and a lot of talent to come out on top

MotoGP's junior class was closer than ever in 2019. Only two of the 19 races were won by more than one second and half were won by a tenth of a second or less.

The racing was never less than edge-of-the-seat stuff: gangs of young guns, fighting millimetres apart and sometimes closer. The proximity of the competition demanded a tricky mix of perfection, aggression and strategy from riders. And yet, more often than not, carefully thought-out strategies came to nothing on last laps, when the race to the chequered flag became the petrol-head's equivalent of a bare-knuckle fight.

Moto3 can be cruel: the rider who crosses the finish line in tenth place, a second behind the winner, has ridden a race 99.8 percent as fast as the winner, but goes home with six points, instead of 25. And the difference between the two might have been one tiny slide exiting the final corner.

This harsh environment breeds riders of great mental strength, which is just as well for those heading to Moto2 and MotoGP.

Moto3's main men of 2019 were Lorenzo Dalla Porta and Aron Canet. But the racing was so tight that the 22-year-old Italian and 20-year-old Spaniard won fewer than half the races between them. Indeed there were no fewer than 12 different winners during the season: Dalla Porta won four races, Canet three, Toni Arbolino two and there were nine other riders who

CLOSKWISE, FROM TOP LEFT | *It was this close all year: Ramirez edges out Canet and Vietti at Barcelona. And it was this frantic all year: Foggia makes good use of the asphalt runoff; Dalla Porta got stronger and stronger; Honda celebrated its 60th anniversary of GP racing at Assen with this 1960s livery. With Toba and Ogura are Honda's Soichi Yamana, 1960s GP winner Kunimitsu Takahashi and team manager and 2009 250cc world champion Hiroshi Aoyama; Masia's first win in Argentina; Arbolino wins at Mugello; Dalla Porta's NSF250RW gets an engine change; Canet fought hard all year; poetry in motion in Argentina.*

took one victory each: Niccolo Antonelli, Albert Arenas, Romano Fenati, Sergio Garcia, Jaume Masia, John McPhee, Marcos Ramirez, Tatsuki Suzuki and Kaito Toba.

Thus the aim of the clever Moto3 rider was not to risk so much to win during the final stages of a race that he might make a mistake and slip from the front to the back of the lead pack, but instead to make sure he kept finishing on the podium.

Dalla Porta (Leopard Racing Honda) didn't win his first race of 2019 until July's German GP, but he made sure he finished on the podium at more than half the races.

"The strategy is always complicated in Moto3, because you never know what will happen or what the other riders will do," he said. "Of course, every race you prepare your strategy, but all you can do on the last lap is try your best. For example, during the race at the Sachsenring I understood I could win. I thought a lot and prepared my strategy to have just one rider in front of me before the brake point for the last-but-one corner at the bottom of the hill. But when I was about to overtake the rider in front of me another rider out-braked me, so then your strategy is gone and you just fight."

Canet (Sterilgarda Max Racing KTM) had the upper hand during the first half of the championship, but only just. He got a helping hand at June's Catalan GP when Dalla Porta crawled into the pits with an electronics fault. He responded with that fine victory in Germany, which moved him past Canet and into the championship lead with nine of 19 races done. The pair had their best duel of the season next time out at Brno, where Canet bettered Dalla Porta by 0.159 seconds to retake the series lead by three points.

Canet was the only rider who managed to make a proper break from the pack all year. At September's Aragon GP he left everyone wondering which way he'd gone, winning by more than four seconds.

"My strategy was always to push in the first two laps to try and leave the group, but it was so difficult to make that happen," he said. "Aragon was the only time it worked. At every other race it was always a big fight. In that case you need to try to stay in the top five and keep calm. You don't want to lead too much because then you use up your tyres. You wait until the last two or three laps and then you push to your maximum and sometimes a little more, because you want to overtake and you don't want to get overtaken."

Machinery was an important part of the title duel. Dalla Porta rode Honda's latest NSF250RW, while Canet rode KTM's 2019 RC250GP. Moto3's super-tight technical regulations ensure no manufacturer can gain a big advantage over its rival but once again the Honda was the better bike. The NSF250RW more than doubled KTM's victory tally and won the constructors' title for the third consecutive year.

CLOCKWISE FROM TOP LEFT | *Ramirez showed a lot of commitment; Paolo Simoncelli celebrates with Antonelli and Suzuki at Jerez; Arbolino got the Italian GP off to a good start; Toba started with a win, then struggled; Canet had the speed to win the title but too often didn't have the luck; Sky VR46 riders Foggia and Vietti; Sasaki and Migno have a misunderstanding; KTM's RC250GP improved for 2019 but was still out-performed by Honda's NSF250RW; Dalla Porta celebrates the title at Phillip Island.*

'THE STRATEGY IS ALWAYS COMPLICATED IN Moto3'
LORENZO DALLA PORTA

"But for sure the Honda and KTM were closer than they were in 2018," added Dalla Porta. "Last season the KTM riders had a difficult time at many races. This year KTM improved their chassis, so the bike was strong from corner entry to corner apex. At the same time Honda improved its engine, so we had an advantage at the faster tracks.

"The Honda chassis is very neutral, so my team found a good setting at the third race. After that we didn't touch the geometry or anything; we just worked with the springs. It's good when you have a bike that stays the same, because then you can adapt yourself to the situation."

Canet, who had previously ridden Hondas, found he had to transform his technique to make the KTM work. "My riding had to become completely different," he said. "When you ride the Honda you can use very open, flowing lines through the corners, but with the KTM you must stop the bike more, do the apex and then open the throttle early. It was always difficult fighting the Hondas because they had more speed on the straights and sometimes it wasn't easy even to draft them."

There are no factory specials in Moto3. All riders are equipped with the same spec engines and chassis from each manufacturer, with no updates allowed during the season.

Dalla Porta gained the upper hand as the year went on. And as he got up to full speed, Canet's season fell apart. At September's San Marino GP it was his turn to withdraw from a race with an electrical fault, which made it one DNF each and put Dalla Porta 22 points into the lead.

Canet came back fighting with his runaway Aragon success, which put him just two points behind his great rival. But after that things went from bad to worse when the paddock left Europe for the four flyaway races in Asia and Australia. At Buriram he was in the thick of a huge victory dogfight with Dalla Porta and the rest when he got taken out by Darryn Binder, younger brother of Moto2 contender Brad.

"I could not escape the group," explained Canet. "I braked very late, trying to overtake McPhee, when Binder attacked. He touched me and I crashed. The same thing happened at Silverstone, where I was fighting for the 25 points when another rider touched me and pushed me out of the points. I finished that race in 13th, so I got three points instead of 23."

Canet went into the Japanese GP needing a miracle. He did everything he could but it wasn't enough. He slid out of sixth place, while Dalla Porta won his first race since July to put one hand on the championship, now 47 points in front. The following Sunday in Australia Canet crashed again and Dalla Porta won again to take the title.

At Phillip Island he led home a Leopard one-two, beating team-mate Marcos Ramirez by a fraction. This was the 21-year-old Spaniard's breakthrough season. He won his first race at Barcelona, where he edged out Canet by 0.019 seconds, and his second at Silverstone where he beat Tony Arbolino by two tenths.

Arbolino (VNE Snipers Honda) also won his first Grand Prix in 2019. The 19-year-old Italian sent the Mugello crowd crazy by winning a brawl of a race, just 0.029 seconds in front of Dalla Porta. Four weeks later he won again at Assen, where this time he beat Dalla Porta by 0.045 seconds!

Rookie of the year was 18-year-old VR46 Academy rider Celestino Vietti, who impressed with his fast and free riding style, honed between each race by a day or two spent thrashing around Valentino Rossi's dirt-track ranch in Tavullia. The Sky VR46 KTM youngster took just four races to climb the podium, at Jerez, and he made several other visits during the year.

Ai Ogura (Honda Team Asia) was also remarkable. A graduate from the Red Bull MotoGP Rookies Cup and the FIM CEV Moto3 Junior Championships, the 18-year-old Japanese rider took his first front row at Le Mans and his first podium at Aragon.

At the opposite end of the Moto3 experience scale was John McPhee, one of only two riders on the grid who could remember racing 125cc two-strokes at Grand Prix events. The 25-year-old Briton – an old man by Moto3 standards! – joined the Petronas Sprinta Honda outfit and proved his maturity with consistent points-scoring rides, topped by a brilliant last-gasp victory at May's French GP.

Niccolo Antonelli won his first Moto3 race at Brno in 2015, but drifted into the doldrums for the next few seasons. Finally the 23-year-old Italian found his missing speed in 2019, taking his first victory in almost four years at Jerez, where he beat Sic58 Squadra Corse Honda team-mate Tatsuki Suzuki by two tenths. Sadly his season turned bad at Misano where he broke a wrist and collarbone.

Four months after Jerez, Suzuki made Paolo Simoncelli an even happier man by winning his first Grand Prix at the Misano World Circuit Marco Simoncelli. Undoubtedly the most emotional moment of the Moto3 season.

Moto3™ WORLD CHAMPIONSHIP STANDING

	RIDER	NAT	MANUFACTURER	POINTS
1	Lorenzo Dalla Porta	ITA	HONDA	279
2	Aron Canet	SPA	KTM	200
3	Marcos Ramirez	SPA	HONDA	183
4	Tony Arbolino	ITA	HONDA	175
5	John McPhee	GBR	HONDA	156
6	Celestino Vietti	ITA	KTM	135
7	Niccolò Antonelli	ITA	HONDA	128
8	Tatsuki Suzuki	JPN	HONDA	124
9	Jaume Masia	SPA	KTM	121
10	Ai Ogura	JPN	HONDA	109
11	Albert Arenas	SPA	KTM	108
12	Dennis Foggia	ITA	KTM	97
13	Andrea Migno	ITA	KTM	78
14	Jakub Kornfeil	CZE	KTM	78
15	Sergio Garcia	SPA	HONDA	76
16	Romano Fenati	ITA	HONDA	76
17	Alonso Lopez	SPA	HONDA	71
18	Gabriel Rodrigo	ARG	HONDA	67
19	Kaito Toba	JPN	HONDA	63
20	Ayumu Sasaki	JPN	HONDA	62
21	Raul Fernandez	SPA	KTM	60
22	Darryn Binder	RSA	KTM	54
23	Filip Salac	CZE	KTM	32
24	Makar Yurchenko	KAZ	KTM	29
25	Stefano Nepa	ITA	KTM	24
26	Xavier Artigas	SPA	HONDA	16
27	Kazuki Masaki	JPN	KTM	14
28	Tom Booth-Amos	GBR	KTM	10
29	Ryusei Yamanaka	JPN	HONDA	8
30	Carlos Tatay	SPA	KTM	8
31	Can Oncu	KTM	TUR	8
32	Riccardo Rossi	ITA	HONDA	8
33	Jeremy Alcoba	SPA	HONDA	2
34	Elia Bartolini	RSM	KTM	1
35	Deniz Oncu	TUR	KTM	
36	Davide Pizzoli	ITA	KTM	
37	Gerry Salim	INA	HONDA	
38	Vicente Perez	SPA	KTM	
39	Kevin Zannoni	ITA	HONDA	
40	Rogan Chandler	NZE	KALEX KTM	
41	Gerard Riu Male	SPA	KTM	
42	Aleix Viu	SPA	KTM	
43	Maximilian Kofler	AUT	KTM	
44	Julian Jose Garcia	SPA	HONDA	
45	Ryan van de Lagemaat	NED	KTM	
46	Meikon Kawakami	BRA	KTM	
47	Dirk Geiger	GER	KTM	
48	Brandon Paasch	USA	KTM	

LEFT TO RIGHT | *The Leopard squad won the riders' and teams' championships; There was hardly a dry eye in the house when Tatsuki Suzuki won at Misano World Circuit Marco Simoncelli.*

THE THIRD MotoGP eSport WORLD CHAMPIONSHIP BRINGS DRAMA AND A NEW WORLD CHAMPION!

The Circuit Ricardo Tormo in Valencia, Spain played host to a star-studded final round, which featured appearances from three MotoGP riders, a roster of glitzy prizes and edge-of-the-seat racing to crown the 2019 MotoGP eSports World Champion.

The three title contenders delivered the drama in a thrilling finale that went all the way to the final corner of the final race, from which ultimately Ducati Team's AndrewZh emerged victorious to claim his first crown. In the end, just five points covered the first three riders in the Championship after three action-packed rounds in the Global Series.

A tearful AndrewZh accepted the brilliant first prize of a rapid BMW M135i xDrive before Dorna CEO Carmelo Ezpeleta handed out the silverware in the final podium ceremony. While disappointed on missing the chance to win his third successive eSports title, Monster Energy Yamaha MotoGP's trastevere73 picked up a new Yamaha YZF-R3 for finishing second overall. Team Suzuki Ecstar's Cristianmm17 received a Lenovo Legion™ Y730 high-speed computer as reward for third.

MotoGP™19 brings an irresistible challenge: a chance to compete in the MotoGP™ eSport Championship. Now available on Sony PlayStation4, Xbox One and PC, it is the unique opportunity to race against the best players out there and compete in the Global Series.

The Global Series gathers the 12 best players from all around the world who have been selected through the Online Challenges and ProDraft.

esport.motogp.com

ELECTRIC FERRARI!

De Angelis leads the charge at Misano

The battle for the FIM Enel MotoE World Cup was hugely entertaining and went down to the wire at Valencia

MotoGP made history during its 70th birthday year with Grand Prix racing's first electrically powered championship. After two-strokes and four-strokes the FIM Enel MotoE World Cup brought a new power source into the paddock. And with more and more electric cars and bikes on the streets, this new kind of racing is only going to grow.

The first EV Grand Prix championship brought together a huge mix of riders, from MotoGP veterans Sete Gibernau and Randy de Puniet to Aprilia test rider Bradley Smith and from 125cc world champions Mike Di Meglio and Nico Terol to former Moto3 rider Matteo Ferrari, former Moto2 man Niki Tuuli and former Moto2 and Moto3 rider Eric Granado.

The races were short and sweet, cramming plenty of action into 12-minute dashes. And instead of the deafening roar of petroleum explosions the grid of Energica Ego Corsa machines sounded like a squadron of TIE fighters from Star Wars, peeling off for a dogfight with a group of Rebel X-wing fighters. In its own way, MotoE made an impressive noise.

Tuuli won the historic first round at Sachsenring, run on a still-drying track following early morning rain. The battle at the front quickly turned into four-way fight between the 23-year-old Finn, Smith, Di Meglio and former Tech 3 Moto2 man Hector Garzo. Tuuli, who had started from pole position, was surprised by the aggression of his rivals who quickly pushed him down to third. Smith (One Energy Racing) and Di Meglio (EG 0,0 Marc VDS) disputed first place over the next few laps, but Tuuli (Ajo MotoE) had other plans.

"We found a really good set-up during practice but today's weather convinced us to go softer with the settings," he said. "The first time we hit the brakes going into Turn One the forks bottomed, so I had to change the way I was riding. The other guys were riding aggressively, so I decided I had to push too."

On lap four Tuuli retook the lead from Smith and was pushing hard to open a gap when the red flags came out. Lorenzo Savadori (TRENTINO Gresini MotoE) had crashed at the high-speed Turn Eight, his bike puncturing the air-fence.

Smith finished second, four tenths down, just ahead of Di Meglio and was delighted to be at the front again. "It's nice to lead a race – it's been a very, very, very long time," said the Briton, who scored his last win in the 2015 Suzuka Eight Hours.

Tuuli's best lap was 13kmh/8mph slower than Marc Marquez's MotoGP best, which wasn't bad for a first attempt from an entirely new kind of motorcycle racing.

After MotoGP's mid-season holiday the E-Paddock reconvened at Red Bull Ring, where riders got to race their EV machines for the first time in the rain. Di Meglio was the winner after Granado

CLOCKWISE, FROM TOP LEFT | *History-maker Ferrari; Garzo leads at Sachsenring; the Gresini team celebrates the title; MotoGP star Smith led races but didn't win any*

crashed out of the lead and then Garzo fell on the last lap while trying to attack the Frenchman.

"I knew Garzo was coming but I didn't know he had crashed, so I braked as late as possible to the end," said the 21-year-old Frenchman after moving into the championship lead.

Former MotoGP rider Xavier Simeon (Avintia Esponsorama Racing) was delighted to get second in his first EV ride with rain tyres, and Smith took his second consecutive podium in third place to stay second overall.

Five weeks later MotoE had its first double-header event at September's San Marino Grand Prix, with one race on Saturday afternoon and the second on Sunday morning. And this was the turning point of the championship.

Ferrari (TRENTINO Gresini MotoE) won both races to take the points lead, while Tuuli and Smith crashed and Di Meglio retired with a technical issue. The 22-year-old Italian had arrived at Misano holding sixth place in the title chase and went home in the lead, 19 points in front of Garzo, who rode strongly in both races, taking two second places.

The multiple crash that claimed Tuuli, Smith and Mattia Casadei left Tuuli with a broken left wrist and left femur that ended his championship aspirations and did no good to Smith's hopes.

The E-paddock had to wait two months before the second double-header weekend that would decide motorcycling's first-ever EV world crown. Ferrari went into the Valencia finale knowing that the title was his if he handled the pressure and took home a reasonable points score in both races.

Saturday's penultimate race was a real thriller, with three riders fighting for victory: 23-year-old Brazilian Granado, 21-year-old Spaniard Garzo and 28-year-old Briton Smith.

The final laps were frantic, with Granado taking the lead from Smith, who struggled to counter-attack because he was busy defending second place from Garzo. Granado made it to the chequered flag half a second in front, while Garzo won a big battle with Smith that had the pair swapping places six times on the final lap.

"Finally, my first MotoE victory after a lot of mistakes from me in the first races," said Granado, who more than doubled his points score from the season's first four races. "I didn't get the best start but I told myself to stay calm, went step by step and passed Bradley as quick as I could because these races are so short. I knew Garzo was coming at the end, so I pushed my 100 percent. Victory is awesome!"

Granado's win was also the first by a Brazilian at a Grand Prix since Alex Barros won the 2005 Estoril MotoGP race aboard a Honda RC211V.

HJC
MICHELIN
OCTO
PRAMAC
MISSION WINNOW
PRETTL
Beta
TRENTINO
GS ASTRA
enel x
Allianz
TRENTINO
GRESINI RACING
enel x
DHL
falper.
MICHELIN
ENERGICA
Icel

MOTUL

MICHELIN
MICHELIN
MICHELIN
HJC
enel x
enel x
enel x

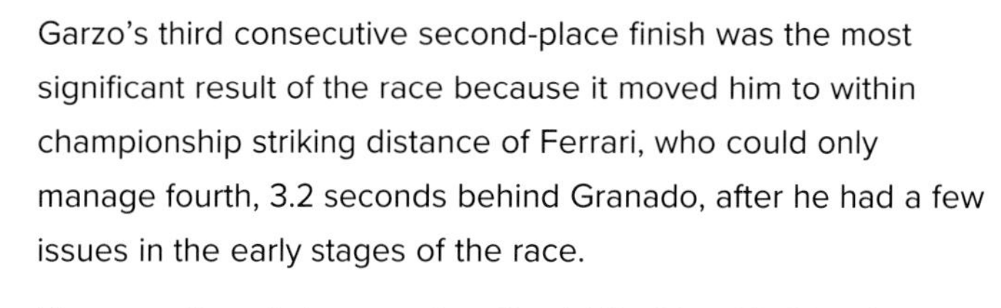

Garzo's third consecutive second-place finish was the most significant result of the race because it moved him to within championship striking distance of Ferrari, who could only manage fourth, 3.2 seconds behind Granado, after he had a few issues in the early stages of the race.

However, Garzo's joy was short-lived. Like MotoGP, Moto2 and Moto3, all MotoE bikes are equipped with TPMS (tyre pressure monitoring system) units in their wheel rims, to ensure that teams keep tyre pressures within sensible limits. Garzo's rear wheel registered a reading below the minimum pressure advised by MotoE tyre supplier Michelin. He was therefore disqualified from the race, which also dropped him out of the title fight.

Ferrari had finished the penultimate outing expecting to go into the Sunday finale with a 12-point lead over Garzo. Instead he went into the race holding a 20-point advantage over Smith, who knew he had to win the seven-lap sprint to stand any chance of taking the title.

Smith led from the start and pulled out a small advantage, but Granado was flying once again. The last lap was a battle royal, the pair passing each other four times and colliding at Turn 11, Granado coming out ahead. Smith made a last-corner lunge for victory but ran wide, giving the double win to Granado.

Ferrari took the flag in fifth to make history as the first-ever winner of the FIM Enel MotoE World Cup. "What an incredible sensation!" he said. "To be the first champion of a completely new kind of racing is a very special feeling."

Next year's Energica machines will undergo numerous subtle improvements: more low-end torque, revised fork damping and improved Michelin slicks. All races will be a lap longer, thanks to top-up chargers used on the grid after the sighting lap.

MotoE™ WORLD CHAMPIONSHIP STANDING

	RIDER	NAT	MANUFACTURER	POINTS
1	Matteo Ferrari	ITA	Energica	99
2	Bradley Smith	GBR	Energica	88
3	Eric Granado	BRA	Energica	71
4	Hector Garzo	SPA	Energica	69
5	Mike Di Meglio	FRA	Energica	63
6	Xavier Simeon	BEL	Energica	58
7	Alex de Angelis	RSM	Energica	47
8	Jesko Raffin	SWI	Energica	47
9	Niccolo Canepa	ITA	Energica	46
10	Mattia Casadei	ITA	Energica	39
11	Sete Gibernau	SPA	Energica	38
12	Nicolas Terol	SPA	Energica	33
13	Joshua Hook	AUS	Energica	28
14	Maria Herrera	SPA	Energica	27
15	Niki Tuuli	FIN	Energica	26
16	Lorenzo Savadori	ITA	Energica	24
17	Randy de Puniet	FRA	Energica	21
18	Kenny Foray	FRA	Energica	11

CLOCKWISE, FROM TOP LEFT | *Tuuli's bike centre stage after winning the Sachsenring opener; Pramac mechanics tend the Energica of De Angelis; Simeon in the E-Paddock; Granado fought hard to win both Valencia races; a new kind of racing power; Di Meglio cuts inside Smith; Tuuli, Smith and Di Meglio at Sachsenring; blast off at Red Bull Ring; Ferrari takes the title at Valencia.*

TATAY TRIUMPHS WITH PACE AND INTELLIGENCE

Spain has a new star. Carlos Tatay won the Cup and he won it every way: he won a race by ten seconds, he won by a tenth and he scored points every time he started, even when he jump started and had to suffer a ride through penalty.

No one came close; the 16-year-old Spaniard dominated the 2019 Red Bull MotoGP Rookies Cup season and clinched the title at Misano with two of the 12 races remaining. He was promptly given a wild card World Championship entry in Aragon, qualified third and raced to 12th in the Moto3 Grand Prix while his fellow Rookies battled through the last two Cup races.

That huge win in Mugello was the exception though; for the most part the thirteenth season of the Cup featured five, ten, even fifteen KTM RC250Rs battling through the race with passes at every turn and the result still in doubt as the pack charged the line.

Tatay did win four straight races but that was only part of it; in the first seven he wasn't off the podium. That is tough to beat and his opposition couldn't mount a constant challenge - they fell short either through experience, ability or poor fortune.

It was certainly bad luck that took Yuki Kunii out of the equation. The Japanese 16-year-old won the first race of the season and ran Tatay a close second in Race Two, so the pair left Jerez tied on points.

It had been a very exciting start to the year; two great races that also featured 15-year-old Belgian Barry Baltus who took a strong third in Race One, but crashed trying to do even better on Sunday.

Though the trio of second-year Rookies had broken away, the battle in the pack behind featuring first-year teens was just as intense and in Race Two it was French 15-year-old Lorenzo Fellon who was third across the line. Unfortunately, as he battled with Matteo Bertelle, Jason Dupasquier, Haruki Noguchi, David Salvador and the rest of the pack he exceeded track limits too often and received a three second post-race penalty.

So close was the finish that it dropped him to 11th and it was Italian 15-year-old Bertelle who actually climbed the podium steps.

Bertelle played an even bigger part in his home race at Mugello a few weeks later, but it was not the role he wanted. While Tatay won, Bertelle had a big last lap moment and precipitated a multi-bike fall that also took out Kunii, Billy van Eerde and Marcos Uriarte.

Only Kunii was injured but the joint Cup points leader needed an operation on broken bones in his right hand. It was the beginning of misfortune that would wreck his racing year, through no fault of his own.

Up ahead Pedro Acosta, the 15-year-old Spaniard, put in the perfect last lap to take second ahead of 17-year-old Japanese Noguchi. Acosta had missed the Jerez races after a practice fall. That was a great shame as he is one of those young riders, a first-year Rookie, who has natural ability and confidence - enough of both to take the battle to the more experienced and measured Tatay.

He did exactly that at the next race in Assen but it was still Tatay who came out ahead with a perfect triple: pole and two race victories.

Nothing like the distant win in Mugello though and it all came down to the chicane on the last lap, as Baltus dived for the lead only to have the front tuck and put him in the gravel. That gave Tatay the lead but Acosta had the better drive and almost stole the win.

"Just full throttle at the end," explained the exhausted and very sweaty Acosta. "It was a great race. I had a plan for the last lap, to get into the right position for the chicane. But then Barry passed me and I thought 'Oh $&%!' So I just had to be in a good place to see what happened. When I saw him crash I just turned and gave it full gas to the line and I almost got it."

Tatay's comment was not quite so colourful. "I tried to push and get away as I did in Mugello but when I realised that was not possible I accepted it and just raced with the other guys without pushing too hard and taking risks."

The podium mirrored Mugello with Noguchi taking third as the leader of the chasing pack. "I'm happy that in the end I got on the podium and I'm happy that it was a better race than at Jerez and Mugello. Earlier in the season I could not follow the fastest but this time I was in the front group and that is what I needed to do," explained Noguchi.

Race Two in the Netherlands indicated the Cup's destiny because while both Acosta and Noguchi fell, Tatay won again. Victories and consistency: a combination that can't be beaten. "My plan again was to try and break away but when I realised that I could not do that I told myself to be cool and clever. To slow my rhythm down a little bit and wait for the end of the race," said Tatay.

Second went to Salvador, on the podium for the first time and ahead of Saturday's faller Baltus, both fast and able to race with Tatay but unable to either finish ahead or match him for regularity.

Having just completed a run of four straight victories Tatay's closest Cup rival was still Kunii who, coming back from the Mugello injury, put in two heroic rides to finish seventh and sixth. The Japanese knew he would be fitter at the Sachsenring but had missed it in 2018 and would have to learn the track.

No problem - he grabbed pole and while Tatay was second fastest, Noguchi completed the front row. The first race was a thriller, unfortunately cut short by a red flag when Colombian 16-year-old Nicolás Hernández crashed. He would be OK but it looked nasty at the time.

That gave the win to Acosta ahead of Kunii and Tatay. Race Two ran the full distance and what a belter it was. The struggle for the win came down to a duel between Tatay and Kunii. The Spaniard seemed to have eked out an advantage by the second-to-last lap but Kunii was not done.

He closed... and closed, put in a brilliant last lap and made his move at the penultimate corner. Tatay tried to come back but couldn't. Kunii won and kept his title hopes alive having finished in front of Tatay in both German races. Britain's 16-year-old Max Cook took third in Race Two when van Eerde was penalised post-race for track limit infringements.

"I am so happy with that," smiled Kunii. "When Carlos got past me I made a mistake, got in the wrong gear and he got away. Then I pushed to catch him and in the end I managed it. Coming down the hill to the last two corners I don't think he realised how close I was and it was quite easy to go inside. My wrist was just starting to really hurt at the end but I concentrated and pushed it out of my mind."

It should have been all on between the two of them for the rest of the year but Kunii was the innocent party in a start line crash at Brno, when he had a Moto3 wild card ride in the Czech Grand Prix, and would miss the rest of the season with a re-injured hand.

Austria without Kunii still supplied plenty of drama. Tatay jumped the start in Race One but finished 14th, while Acosta scored a brilliant victory out of a race-long battle and last corner scramble. Van Eerde finally got his podium ahead of Noguchi.

Noguchi grabbed the Race Two win after another huge contest, outmanoeuvring Tatay at the final turns with van Eerde third.

Van Eerde was in excellent form but unfortunately not in the Cup chase having DNF'd the first four races of the season. Noguchi was scoring well but two crashes had put a big dent in his total. The same for Salvador and so Tatay headed for Misano with one hand already on the Cup.

Back in Italy Tatay might have played it easy but as a racer he wanted to win. He headed a huge pack all going for the podium and was still trying for victory into the last few turns as Salvador and Acosta elbowed past and relegated him to third. Acosta snatched his third win of the season.

Tatay had the title though - a very worthy champion.

So while the Cup winner jumped to the Grand Prix class, the remaining Rookies still had two fabulous races in Aragon. A huge lead pack in both races and victory decided at the last corner.

Van Eerde continued his superb end to the season with a win and a second. Salvador collided with Baltus in Race One but won on Sunday. Second in Race One belonged to Noguchi and the third places went to first-time-podium Spaniards Alex Escrig and Marcos Uriarte.

That was the end of the 13th Red Bull MotoGP Rookies Cup season; more riders headed for GP success like so many before them. Brad Binder scored the 100th GP victory for ex Rookies when he won the Moto2 race in Sepang. By then the Selection Event for the 2020 Rookies Cup was complete - 109 riders from 37 nations all looking to take that thrilling step into next season's Cup.

LEFT-RIGHT | *Tatay celebrates winning the Cup in Misano; Tatay leads Baltus and Kunii in Jerez; Acosta 2nd, Tatay 1st and Noguchi 3rd in the 2019 Cup.*

WHAT WE DO

For the last thirty years we have been working with the enormous goodwill of the motorcycle community to make sure healthcare reaches people in the poorest and most remote parts of Africa.

In many parts of Africa, where there is no reliable public or private transport, and with few surfaced roads, fuel stations or other infrastructure, getting care reliably to where it is needed is impossible. Vehicles break down, clinics don't get run, tests are delayed, women with complications give birth unaided. The consequences are deadly.

Operating in countries including Lesotho, Malawi, Nigeria and The Gambia, the programmes we support, run by Riders for Health, focus on transport for health professionals.

By providing maintenance, fuelling, monitoring and training, nurses, doctors, midwives and other health workers are able to get to communities day in, day out. With reliable transport it is possible to immunise newborns, diagnose disease, educate in childhood nutrition, provide preventative measures to combat disease and help women in dangerous labour.

WE SHOW THAT MOTORCYCLES REALLY CAN SAVE LIVES.

HOW WE DO IT

With the support of the MotoGP™ paddock, teams and riders Two Wheels for Life raises money for these vital programmes. We offer exclusive paddock experiences across Europe, fantastic auctions for team experiences and rider memorabilia, exclusive press conference access and paddock passes.

New for 2019, Dorna Sports, Enel and Energica teamed up in support of Two Wheels for Life for a new fundraising initiative. Ride for Life invites members of the public to bid on a once-in-a-lifetime opportunity to ride the highly anticipated Energica Ego electric motorcycle in front of the MotoGP™ race crowd. The experience that includes VIP Village hospitality and access to race grids has been incredibly popular with riders who have been blown away.

This year we celebrated 30 years of Day of Champions, our annual family fun day out, kick-starting the British Grand Prix. We raised a staggering £300,000, something we could not have done without the support of the MotoGP™ family and the racing fans.

FIND OUT MORE

To find out about the incredible experiences and events we offer to racing fans, or the life-saving work we support, visit our brand new website:

PLEASE CONSIDER DONATING A SMALL AMOUNT MONTHLY TO HELP US PROVIDE SUSTAINABLE SUPPORT FOR THESE LIVE SAVING PROGRAMMES.

TWOWHEELSFORLIFE.ORG

WHY BIKES ARE BEST FOR HEALTHCARE DELIVERY IN AFRICA

Two Wheels talked to Salifu Jabang, Head Technician at Riders for Health, The Gambia on Why Bikes are Best.

If you're reading this you're probably more than a bit keen on motorcycles. Do you love them because it feels so amazing to ride out on open roads, because you love the excitement of seeing them whizz around a race track, or simply because they look so damn good? Salifu Jabang would agree with any one of these.

But he has his own particular reasons for his love of the motorbike. Sal has been working with Riders for Health, whose programmes we support, since he was sixteen. Now head motorcycle technician at Riders for Health in the Gambia, and a motorcycle rider himself, he absolutely loves bikes because they're perfect for getting healthcare to people in his homeland.

At Riders' main workshop in Gambian capital Banjul, Sal talks about the challenges for health workers in the Gambia. "During the rainy season even if you have four wheel it's difficult. With a motorcycle you can just ride and go," says Sal. "Mud? Water? Doesn't matter." From June to October, it's impossible for most vehicles to leave the main roads and get down the dirt tracks to remote villages. Anyone living in these areas is often unable to visit a doctor or nurse, even in an emergency.

Motorcycles mean heath workers in the Gambia reach people with vital services – immunisations, checking pregnant and new mothers, their newborn babies and well as the under fives. And in urban areas, riders can nip (carefully!) through traffic jams. "Our roads are very tight," says Sal. "On a motorcycle, you can get to where you need to be."

Cost is another huge factor that makes motorcycles so useful in the Gambia and many other parts of Africa. They are cheaper to buy than four wheel vehicles and less costly to maintain. This makes a difference when money is tight and health services have to be delivered on a shoestring. Maintenance – Sal's area of expertise – is key to keeping costs low.

Sal's team make sure the bikes will never break down: mechanics service bikes regularly and health workers are taught to look after their own bikes so they can rely on them to last and last. This is what Riders calls 'zero breakdown' and it's something they are world experts in.

All of us love motorcycles, but Sal has turned his passion into something immensely valuable for the world around him. As he puts it, when talking about why he loves his job: "Using two wheels has changed everything for health workers here – it is essential. Nobody can buy a life, but by using motorcycles for health care we are saving lives every day".

Motorbikes make our lives better in all kinds of ways. By supporting Two Wheels for Life and the work of Sal and his team, we can use your love of motorbikes to improve the lives of people in The Gambia, and across Africa.

500cc

YEAR	RIDER	NAT	MANUFACTURER
1949	Leslie Graham	GBR	AJS
1950	Umberto Masetti	ITA	GILERA
1951	Geoff Duke	GBR	NORTON
1952	Umberto Masetti	ITA	GILERA
1953	Geoff Duke	GBR	GILERA
1954	Geoff Duke	GBR	GILERA
1955	Geoff Duke	GBR	GILERA
1956	John Surtees	GBR	MV AGUSTA
1957	Libero Liberati	ITA	GILERA
1958	John Surtees	GBR	MV AGUSTA
1959	John Surtees	GBR	MV AGUSTA
1960	John Surtees	GBR	MV AGUSTA
1961	Gary Hocking	CAF	MV AGUSTA
1962	Mike Hailwood	GBR	MV AGUSTA
1963	Mike Hailwood	GBR	MV AGUSTA
1964	Mike Hailwood	GBR	MV AGUSTA
1965	Mike Hailwood	GBR	MV AGUSTA
1966	Giacomo Agostini	ITA	MV AGUSTA
1967	Giacomo Agostini	ITA	MV AGUSTA
1968	Giacomo Agostini	ITA	MV AGUSTA
1969	Giacomo Agostini	ITA	MV AGUSTA
1970	Giacomo Agostini	ITA	MV AGUSTA
1971	Giacomo Agostini	ITA	MV AGUSTA
1972	Giacomo Agostini	ITA	MV AGUSTA
1973	Phil Read	GBR	MV AGUSTA
1974	Phil Read	GBR	MV AGUSTA
1975	Giacomo Agostini	ITA	YAMAHA
1976	Barry Sheene	GBR	SUZUKI
1977	Barry Sheene	GBR	SUZUKI
1978	Kenny Roberts	USA	YAMAHA
1979	Kenny Roberts	USA	YAMAHA
1980	Kenny Roberts	USA	YAMAHA
1981	Marco Lucchinelli	ITA	SUZUKI
1982	Franco Uncini	ITA	SUZUKI
1983	Freddie Spencer	USA	HONDA
1984	Eddie Lawson	USA	YAMAHA
1985	Freddie Spencer	USA	HONDA
1986	Eddie Lawson	USA	YAMAHA
1987	Wayne Gardner	AUS	HONDA
1988	Eddie Lawson	USA	YAMAHA
1989	Eddie Lawson	USA	HONDA
1990	Wayne Rainey	USA	YAMAHA
1991	Wayne Rainey	USA	YAMAHA
1992	Wayne Rainey	USA	YAMAHA
1993	Kevin Schwantz	USA	SUZUKI
1994	Mick Doohan	AUS	HONDA
1995	Mick Doohan	AUS	HONDA
1996	Mick Doohan	AUS	HONDA
1997	Mick Doohan	AUS	HONDA
1998	Mick Doohan	AUS	HONDA
1999	Àlex Crivillé	ESP	HONDA
2000	Kenny Roberts, Jr.	USA	SUZUKI
2001	Valentino Rossi	ITA	HONDA

MotoGP™

YEAR	RIDER	NAT	MANUFACTURER
2002	Valentino Rossi	ITA	HONDA
2003	Valentino Rossi	ITA	HONDA
2004	Valentino Rossi	ITA	YAMAHA
2005	Valentino Rossi	ITA	YAMAHA
2006	Nicky Hayden	USA	HONDA
2007	Casey Stoner	AUS	DUCATI
2008	Valentino Rossi	ITA	YAMAHA
2009	Valentino Rossi	ITA	YAMAHA

MotoGP™

YEAR	RIDER	NAT	MANUFACTURER
2010	Jorge Lorenzo	ESP	YAMAHA
2011	Casey Stoner	AUS	HONDA

MotoGP™

YEAR	RIDER	NAT	MANUFACTURER
2012	Jorge Lorenzo	ESP	YAMAHA
2013	Marc Márquez	ESP	HONDA
2014	Marc Márquez	ESP	HONDA
2015	Jorge Lorenzo	ESP	YAMAHA
2016	Marc Márquez	ESP	HONDA
2017	Marc Márquez	ESP	HONDA
2018	Marc Márquez	ESP	HONDA
2019	Marc Márquez	ESP	HONDA

250cc

YEAR	RIDER	NAT	MANUFACTURER
1949	Bruno Ruffo	ITA	MOTO GUZZI
1950	Dario Ambrosini	ITA	BENELLI
1951	Bruno Ruffo	ITA	MOTO GUZZI
1952	Enrico Lorenzetti	ITA	MOTO GUZZI
1953	Werner Haas	GER	NSU
1954	Werner Haas	GER	NSU
1955	Hermann Paul Müller	GER	NSU
1956	Carlo Ubbiali	ITA	MV AGUSTA
1957	Cecil Sandford	GBR	MONDIAL
1958	Tarquinio Provini	ITA	MV AGUSTA
1959	Carlo Ubbiali	ITA	MV AGUSTA
1960	Carlo Ubbiali	ITA	MV AGUSTA
1961	Mike Hailwood	GBR	HONDA
1962	Jim Redman	CAF	HONDA
1963	Jim Redman	CAF	HONDA
1964	Phil Read	GBR	YAMAHA
1965	Phil Read	GBR	YAMAHA
1966	Mike Hailwood	GBR	HONDA
1967	Mike Hailwood	GBR	HONDA
1968	Phil Read	GBR	YAMAHA
1969	Kel Carruthers	AUS	BENELLI
1970	Rodney Gould	GBR	YAMAHA
1971	Phil Read	GBR	YAMAHA
1972	Jarno Saarinen	FIN	YAMAHA
1973	Dieter Braun	GER	YAMAHA
1974	Walter Villa	ITA	HARLEY DAVIDSON
1975	Walter Villa	ITA	HARLEY DAVIDSON
1976	Walter Villa	ITA	HARLEY DAVIDSON
1977	Mario Lega	ITA	MORBIDELLI
1978	Kork Ballington	ZAF	Kawasaki
1979	Kork Ballington	ZAF	Kawasaki
1980	Anton Mang	GER	Kawasaki
1981	Anton Mang	GER	Kawasaki
1982	Jean-Louis Tournadre	FRA	YAMAHA
1983	Carlos Lavado	VEN	YAMAHA
1984	Christian Sarron	FRA	YAMAHA
1985	Freddie Spencer	USA	HONDA
1986	Carlos Lavado	VEN	YAMAHA
1987	Anton Mang	GER	HONDA
1988	Sito Pons	ESP	HONDA
1989	Sito Pons	ESP	HONDA
1990	John Kocinski	USA	YAMAHA
1991	Luca Cadalora	ITA	HONDA
1992	Luca Cadalora	ITA	HONDA
1993	Tetsuya Harada	JPN	YAMAHA
1994	Max Biaggi	ITA	APRILIA
1995	Max Biaggi	ITA	APRILIA
1996	Max Biaggi	ITA	APRILIA
1997	Max Biaggi	ITA	HONDA
1998	Loris Capirossi	ITA	APRILIA
1999	Valentino Rossi	ITA	APRILIA
2000	Olivier Jacque	FRA	YAMAHA
2001	Daijiro Kato	JPN	HONDA

250cc

YEAR	RIDER	NAT	MANUFACTURER
2002	Marco Melandri	ITA	APRILIA
2003	Manuel Poggiali	SMR	APRILIA
2004	Dani Pedrosa	ESP	HONDA
2005	Dani Pedrosa	ESP	HONDA
2006	Jorge Lorenzo	ESP	APRILIA
2007	Jorge Lorenzo	ESP	APRILIA
2008	Marco Simoncelli	ITA	GILERA
2009	Hiroshi Aoyama	JPN	HONDA

Moto2™

YEAR	RIDER	NAT	MANUFACTURER
2010	Toni Elías	ESP	MORIWAKI
2011	Stefan Bradl	GER	KALEX

Moto2™

YEAR	RIDER	NAT	MANUFACTURER
2012	Marc Márquez	ESP	SUTER
2013	Pol Espargaró	ESP	KALEX
2014	Tito Rabat	ESP	KALEX
2015	Johann Zarco	FRA	KALEX
2016	Johann Zarco	FRA	KALEX
2017	Franco Morbidelli	ITA	KALEX
2018	Francesco Bagnaia	ITA	KALEX
2019	Alex Márquez	ESP	KALEX

125cc

YEAR	RIDER	NAT	MANUFACTURER
1949	Nello Pagani	ITA	MONDIAL
1950	Bruno Ruffo	ITA	MONDIAL
1951	Carlo Ubbiali	ITA	MONDIAL
1952	Cecil Sandford	GBR	MV AGUSTA
1953	Werner Haas	GER	NSU
1954	Rupert Hollaus	AUT	NSU
1955	Carlo Ubbiali	ITA	MV AGUSTA
1956	Carlo Ubbiali	ITA	MV AGUSTA
1957	Tarquinio Provini	ITA	MONDIAL
1958	Carlo Ubbiali	ITA	MV AGUSTA
1959	Carlo Ubbiali	ITA	MV AGUSTA
1960	Carlo Ubbiali	ITA	MV AGUSTA
1961	Tom Phillis	AUS	HONDA
1962	Luigi Taveri	CHE	HONDA
1963	Hugh Anderson	AUS	SUZUKI
1964	Luigi Taveri	CHE	HONDA
1965	Hugh Anderson	AUS	SUZUKI
1966	Luigi Taveri	CHE	HONDA)
1967	Bill Ivy	GBR	YAMAHA
1968	Phil Read	GBR	YAMAHA
1969	Dave Simmonds	GBR	Kawasaki
1970	Dieter Braun	GER	SUZUKI
1971	Ángel Nieto	ESP	DERBI
1972	Ángel Nieto	ESP	DERBI
1973	Kent Andersson	SWE	YAMAHA
1974	Kent Andersson	SWE	YAMAHA
1975	Paolo Pileri	ITA	MORBIDELLI
1976	Pier Paolo Bianchi	ITA	MORBIDELLI
1977	Pier Paolo Bianchi	ITA	MORBIDELLI
1978	Eugenio Lazzarini	ITA	MBA
1979	Ángel Nieto	ESP	MINARELLI
1980	Pier Paolo Bianchi	ITA	MBA
1981	Ángel Nieto	ESP	MINARELLI
1982	Ángel Nieto	ESP	GARELLI
1983	Ángel Nieto	ESP	GARELLI
1984	Ángel Nieto	ESP	GARELLI
1985	Fausto Gresini	ITA	GARELLI
1986	Luca Cadalora	ITA	GARELLI
1987	Fausto Gresini	ITA	GARELLI
1988	Jorge Martínez	ESP	DERBI
1989	Àlex Crivillé	ESP	JJ COBAS
1990	Loris Capirossi	ITA	HONDA
1991	Loris Capirossi	ITA	HONDA
1992	Alessandro Gramigni	ITA	APRILIA
1993	Dirk Raudies	GER	HONDA
1994	Kazuto Sakata	JPN	APRILIA
1995	Haruchika Aoki	JPN	HONDA
1996	Haruchika Aoki	JPN	HONDA
1997	Valentino Rossi	ITA	APRILIA
1998	Kazuto Sakata	JPN	APRILIA
1999	Emilio Alzamora	ESP	HONDA
2000	Roberto Locatelli	ITA	APRILIA
2001	Manuel Poggiali	RSM	GILERA

125cc

YEAR	RIDER	NAT	MANUFACTURER
2002	Arnaud Vincent	FRA	APRILIA
2003	Dani Pedrosa	ESP	HONDA
2004	Andrea Dovizioso	ITA	HONDA
2005	Thomas Lüthi	CHE	HONDA
2006	Álvaro Bautista	ESP	APRILIA
2007	Gábor Talmácsi	HUN	APRILIA
2008	Mike di Meglio	FRA	DERBI
2009	Julián Simón	ESP	APRILIA

125cc

YEAR	RIDER	NAT	MANUFACTURER
2010	Marc Márquez	ESP	DERBI
2011	Nico Terol	ESP	APRILIA

Moto3™

YEAR	RIDER	NAT	MANUFACTURER
2012	Sandro Cortese	GER	KTM
2013	Maverick Viñales	ESP	KTM
2014	Alex Márquez	ESP	HONDA
2015	Danny Kent	GBR	HONDA
2016	Brad Binder	ZAF	KTM
2017	Joan Mir	SPA	HONDA
2018	Jorge Martin	SPA	HONDA
2019	Lorenzo Dalla Porta	ITA	HONDA